"*Reading the Prophets as Christian Scripture* takes a deep yet accessible dive into the prophetic literature. Covering a wide range of material, Tully guides readers through a thick interpretive forest for the sake of understanding one of the Bible's more challenging sections. The Prophets often intimidate readers. How can we understand unless someone teaches us? Tully's introduction takes its place as an answer to this question. Students and teachers alike will benefit from Tully's clear guidance and excellent teaching."

—**Mark S. Gignilliat**, Beeson Divinity School

"It is rare to find a volume on the prophetic books that merges the literary, canonical, and theological aspects of the Prophets in such a lucid way. The interpretive framework allows the reader to consider both the ancient and contemporary significance with ease and clarity. Tully serves visual learners especially well. Excellent data is compiled into tables and displayed graphically in figures, in sections entitled 'Thinking Visually,' and these illumine the facts and make hard concepts accessible to the serious student. I will use this as a textbook in the classes I teach on the Prophets."

—**Donna Petter**, Gordon-Conwell Theological Seminary

"*Reading the Prophets as Christian Scripture* invites readers to encounter the prophetic books of the Old Testament afresh. Like the prophets of old, Tully is highly visual as well as creative, with the goal of making the Prophets accessible to contemporary readers without ignoring recent debates and challenging issues. This volume provides a helpful interpretive framework for understanding the prophets as people and books before introducing the prophetic texts from Isaiah to Malachi. A superb primer for those who have always wanted to understand the Prophets."

—**Mark J. Boda**, McMaster Divinity College

"This book beautifully fulfills its stated purpose. It is a clear and concise but also thorough introduction to the Prophets. It opens up their world, describing their historical context and the theological conflicts that swirled around them. It also explores their rhetoric and the question of how oral messages, in which the prophetic word came in the form of sermons and spoken oracles, transitioned into becoming a set of canonical, written texts. Tully also includes a careful introduction to each prophetic book. The whole discussion is framed for the Christian reader and aims to show that the Prophets speak to the church. Finally, the book is beautifully laid out and easy to read, which adds considerably to its value."

—**Duane A. Garrett**, The Southern Baptist Theological Seminary

READING *the* PROPHETS *as* CHRISTIAN SCRIPTURE

• READING •
CHRISTIAN
SCRIPTURE

VOLUMES AVAILABLE

———

Reading the Prophets as Christian Scripture
Eric J. Tully

———

Reading the New Testament as Christian Scripture
Constantine R. Campbell and Jonathan T. Pennington

———

READING *the* PROPHETS *as* CHRISTIAN SCRIPTURE

A LITERARY, CANONICAL, AND THEOLOGICAL INTRODUCTION

ERIC J. TULLY

Baker Academic

a division of Baker Publishing Group

Grand Rapids, Michigan

Published by Baker Academic
a division of Baker Publishing Group
PO Box 6287, Grand Rapids, MI 49516-6287
www.bakeracademic.com

Printed in the United States of America

Library of Congress Cataloging-in-Publication Data
Names: Tully, Eric J., author.
Title: Reading the prophets as Christian scripture : a literary, canonical, and
    theological introduction / Eric J. Tully.
Description: Grand Rapids, MI : Baker Academic, a division of Baker
    Publishing Group, [2022] | Series: Reading Christian scripture | Includes
    bibliographical references and index.
Identifiers: LCCN 2021031057 | ISBN 9780801099731 (cloth) | ISBN
    9781493435104 (ebook) | ISBN 9781493435111 (pdf)
Subjects: LCSH: Bible. Prophets—Criticism, interpretation, etc.
Classification: LCC BS1505.52 .T85 2022 | DDC 224/.06—dc23
LC record available at https://lccn.loc.gov/2021031057

Baker Publishing Group publications use paper produced from sustainable forestry practices and post-consumer waste whenever possible.

22   23   24   25   26   27   28   7   6   5   4   3   2   1

Contents

Acknowledgments

I would like to express my appreciation to those who assisted me with this volume in significant ways. I am grateful to the faculty and administration of Trinity Evangelical Divinity School for granting me a sabbatical in the spring semester of 2019, during which I wrote the first eight chapters. I have enjoyed working through some of the material in this book in the classroom with several sections of my MDiv course Interpreting the Latter Prophets over the last several years. Our students at Trinity are bright, dedicated, creative, and passionate about the gospel and the church. It is a joy to learn alongside them as we all continue to grow in our knowledge of God's Word.

I cannot overstate how much I have been helped by my TA, Stephanie Juliot, who edited the entire manuscript and made insightful suggestions as to content. Her careful eye has improved every aspect of this work.

My thanks go to my wife, Traci, and our two daughters, Lauren and Kate, for their ongoing encouragement. They are God's greatest gifts to me. It has been especially enjoyable to work on this book while in COVID quarantine together as a family and doing online school together.

Finally, I am so appreciative to Jim Kinney, Dave Nelson, James Korsmo, and Brandy Scritchfield at Baker Academic. I am honored to participate in this wonderful series and to work with such an impressive team.

Visit www.bakeracademic.com/professors
to access study aids
and instructor materials for this textbook.

Abbreviations

Old Testament

Gen.	Genesis	Eccles.	Ecclesiastes
Exod.	Exodus	Song	Song of Songs
Lev.	Leviticus	Isa.	Isaiah
Num.	Numbers	Jer.	Jeremiah
Deut.	Deuteronomy	Lam.	Lamentations
Josh.	Joshua	Ezek.	Ezekiel
Judg.	Judges	Dan.	Daniel
Ruth	Ruth	Hosea	Hosea
1 Sam.	1 Samuel	Joel	Joel
2 Sam.	2 Samuel	Amos	Amos
1 Kings	1 Kings	Obad.	Obadiah
2 Kings	2 Kings	Jon.	Jonah
1 Chron.	1 Chronicles	Mic.	Micah
2 Chron.	2 Chronicles	Nah.	Nahum
Ezra	Ezra	Hab.	Habakkuk
Neh.	Nehemiah	Zeph.	Zephaniah
Esther	Esther	Hag.	Haggai
Job	Job	Zech.	Zechariah
Ps(s).	Psalm(s)	Mal.	Malachi
Prov.	Proverbs		

New Testament

Matt.	Matthew	1 Cor.	1 Corinthians
Mark	Mark	2 Cor.	2 Corinthians
Luke	Luke	Gal.	Galatians
John	John	Eph.	Ephesians
Acts	Acts	Phil.	Philippians
Rom.	Romans	Col.	Colossians

1 Thess.	1 Thessalonians	1 Pet.	1 Peter
2 Thess.	2 Thessalonians	2 Pet.	2 Peter
1 Tim.	1 Timothy	1 John	1 John
2 Tim.	2 Timothy	2 John	2 John
Titus	Titus	3 John	3 John
Philem.	Philemon	Jude	Jude
Heb.	Hebrews	Rev.	Revelation
James	James		

General

ANE	ancient Near East
AT	author's translation
ca.	circa
e.g.	for example
ESV	English Standard Version
LXX	Septuagint
NIV	New International Version

ISRAEL

KING	DATES OF REIGN	REFERENCES	KEY FEATURES OF REIGN
Jeroboam	930–909	1 Kings 12:20	Took throne in the last year of Solomon (1 Kings 14:20)
Nadab	909–908	1 Kings 15:25	Assassinated by Baasha in 908 (1 Kings 15:27)
Baasha	908–886	1 Kings 15:33	Killed all the house of Jeroboam (1 Kings 15:29)
Elah	886–885	1 Kings 16:8	Assassinated by Zimri while drunk (1 Kings 16:8–14)
Zimri	885	1 Kings 16:15	Attacked by Omri, then suicide by fire (1 Kings 16:17–18)
Tibni	885–880	1 Kings 16:21	Civil war with Omri (1 Kings 16:21–22)
Omri	885–874	1 Kings 16:23	War with Tibni for first five years; became sole ruler in 880
Ahab	874–853	1 Kings 16:29	Died in battle (1 Kings 22:33–37)
Ahaziah	853–852	1 Kings 22:51	Died childless (2 Kings 1:2, 17)
Joram/Jehoram	852–841	2 Kings 3:1	Killed by Jehu (2 Kings 9:24)
Jehu	841–814	2 Kings 9:13	Killed Joram in chariot and executed Jezebel (2 Kings 9:24, 33)
Jehoahaz	814–798	2 Kings 13:1	
Jehoash	798–782	2 Kings 13:10	

Elijah 860–852

Elisha 855–796

JUDAH

KING	DATES OF REIGN	REFERENCES	KEY FEATURES OF REIGN
Rehoboam	930–913	1 Kings 14:21	
Abijah	913–910	1 Kings 15:1–2	
Asa	910–869	1 Kings 15:9–10	
Jehoshaphat	872–848	1 Kings 22:41–42	Coregent with Asa, 872–869
Jehoram	853–841	2 Kings 8:16–17	Coregent with Jehoshaphat, 853–848; married to Athaliah
Ahaziah	841	2 Kings 8:25–26	Killed by Jehu in Israel (2 Kings 9:27–28)
Athaliah	841–835	2 Kings 11:3	Ahaziah's mother (2 Kings 11:1)
Joash	835–796	2 Kings 12:1–2	Began reigning at age 7 (2 Kings 11:21)
Amaziah	796–767	2 Kings 14:1–2	Assassinated at Lachish (2 Kings 14:19)

ISRAEL

KING	DATES OF REIGN	REFERENCES	KEY FEATURES OF REIGN
Jeroboam II	793–753	2 Kings 14:23	Coregent with Jehoash, 793–782
Zechariah	753–752	2 Kings 15:8	Assassinated by Shallum (2 Kings 15:10)
Shallum	752	2 Kings 15:13	Assassinated by Menahem (2 Kings 15:14)
Menahem	752–742	2 Kings 15:17	Made an alliance with Pul, king of Assyria (2 Kings 15:19–20)
Pekahiah	742–740	2 Kings 15:23	Assassinated by Pekah (2 Kings 15:25)
Pekah	752–732	2 Kings 15:27	Reigned in Gilead, 752–740, overlapping with Menahem; reigned over united Israel, 740–732; assassinated by Hoshea (2 Kings 15:30)
Hoshea	732–722	2 Kings 15:30; 17:1	Appointed by Tiglath-pileser III

Prophets (Israel): Jonah 792–753; Amos 767–753; Hosea 755–725

JUDAH

KING	DATES OF REIGN	REFERENCES	KEY FEATURES OF REIGN
Uzziah/ Azariah	792–740	2 Kings 14:21; 2 Chron. 26:3	Coregent with his father, Amaziah, 792–767; began reigning at age 16 (2 Kings 14:21); struck with leprosy for offering incense in 750, then lived in a separate house while his son governed (2 Chron. 26:16–21)
Jotham	750–735	2 Kings 15:32–33	Coregent with Uzziah, 750–740; removed from the throne in 735
Ahaz	735–715	2 Kings 16:1–2	16 years counted from death of Jotham in 732 (2 Kings 15:38)
Hezekiah	729–686	2 Kings 18:1–2	Coregent with father, Ahaz, 729–715; Sennacherib attacked Judah in 701 BC (2 Kings 18:13)

Prophets (Judah): Isaiah 740–695; Micah 742–686

JUDAH

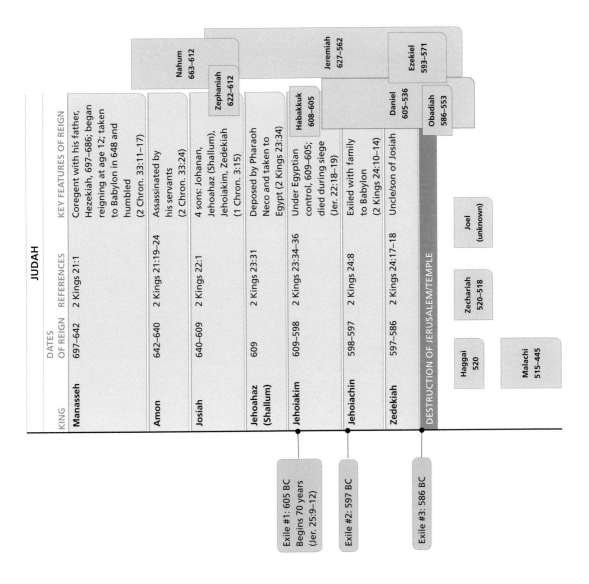

KING	DATES OF REIGN	REFERENCES	KEY FEATURES OF REIGN			
Manasseh	697–642	2 Kings 21:1	Coregent with his father, Hezekiah, 697–686; began reigning at age 12; taken to Babylon in 648 and humbled (2 Chron. 33:11–17)		Nahum 663–612	
Amon	642–640	2 Kings 21:19–24	Assassinated by his servants (2 Chron. 33:24)		Zephaniah 622–612	
Josiah	640–609	2 Kings 22:1	4 sons: Johanan, Jehoahaz (Shallum), Jehoiakim, Zedekiah (1 Chron. 3:15)			Jeremiah 627–562
Jehoahaz (Shallum)	609	2 Kings 23:31	Deposed by Pharaoh Neco and taken to Egypt (2 Kings 23:34)	Habakkuk 608–605		
Jehoiakim	609–598	2 Kings 23:34–36	Under Egyptian control, 609–605; died during siege (Jer. 22:18–19)			Daniel 605–536
Jehoiachin	598–597	2 Kings 24:8	Exiled with family to Babylon (2 Kings 24:10–14)		Obadiah 586–553	Ezekiel 593–571
Zedekiah	597–586	2 Kings 24:17–18	Uncle/son of Josiah			

DESTRUCTION OF JERUSALEM/TEMPLE

Haggai 520   Zechariah 520–518   Joel (unknown)

Malachi 515–445

Exile #1: 605 BC Begins 70 years (Jer. 25:9–12)

Exile #2: 597 BC

Exile #3: 586 BC

CHAPTER ONE

Introduction

But Paul said, ". . . King Agrippa, do you believe the prophets? I know that you believe." And Agrippa said to Paul, "In a short time would you persuade me to be a Christian?"

Acts 26:25–28

When we think of Scripture that explains the essence of the Christian faith, or what might persuade someone to be a Christian, our minds probably go first to books in the New Testament like John or Romans. But for the apostle Paul, whose Bible contained only the Hebrew Scriptures, the essence of the Christian faith was taught in the Old Testament prophetic books. King Agrippa also recognized that the Prophets speak about God's redemption in Christ—that is why, in the passage quoted above, he becomes defensive in response to Paul's question. Both Paul and Agrippa believed that the Prophets of the Old Testament were not just Jewish Scripture; they were *Christian* Scripture.

This book is an introduction to "The Prophets" of the Old Testament as Christian Scripture (as the series title indicates). These books include Isaiah, Jeremiah, Ezekiel, Daniel, Hosea, Joel, Amos, Obadiah, Jonah, Micah, Nahum, Habakkuk, Zephaniah, Haggai, Zechariah, and Malachi. They are complex books that present the conversations, actions, preaching, and predictions of the classical prophets, who spoke for God in particular historical circumstances.

Reading the Old Testament as Christian Scripture

I have given a lot of thought to the word "as" in the title of this book. Perhaps it gives the impression that these prophetic books are not inherently

Christian Scripture, but it is possible to read them "as" Christian Scripture. Far from it! The Old Testament does not *become* Christian Scripture through our reading it with a certain technique or according to a certain set of rules, nor does it become something else if read in a different way. The prophetic books of the Old Testament *are* Christian Scripture. They may not use the name "Jesus" or contain the word "church" or "baptism," but they speak of God's great plan of salvation, which stretches from God's creation of the world and the sin of Adam and Eve to God's eternal kingdom at the end of time. And they speak of God's Messiah—from the family of David, born in Bethlehem, suffering for the sins of his people, rising again in victory, and ruling as king in peace and justice.

In the New Testament, Paul writes to a young pastor named Timothy, "All Scripture is breathed out by God and profitable for teaching, for reproof, for correction, and for training in righteousness, that the man [or woman] of God may be complete, equipped for every good work" (2 Tim. 3:16–17). At the time when Paul wrote this, the books of the New Testament were still in the process of being written, identified, and collected, so Paul is referring to the *Old* Testament, including the prophetic books. They are God's Word, intended for us to strengthen our faith, teach us about God, and equip us to serve him.

We do not read the prophetic books in a special way to make them Christian Scripture; but recognizing that they are Christian Scripture does have some important ramifications for the way that we read them. First, the prophetic books of the Old Testament are part of the Christian canon of Scripture, including both the Old Testament and the New Testament. The word "canon" refers to what is official, what counts. It refers not only to what is included as Scripture but also to what is excluded. Consider this nerdy example: some people talk about the "Star Wars canon" and which movies and books really count for the *real* Star Wars story and universe. I could sit down and write a story about Luke Skywalker, but it would not be canon, and no one would be required to take it seriously. But perhaps you are a longtime fan and do not like one of the new Star Wars movies: too bad! If it is one of the official movies, it counts. It is canon, and the story is authoritatively part of the larger universe long, long ago whether we like it or not. Similarly, each of the prophetic books in our Bible is part of the biblical canon. That means that they are recognized as being official—the Word of God—and just as authoritative as Genesis or 1 Corinthians.

In the quote above from 2 Timothy 3:16, Paul writes that "all Scripture is breathed out by God." This is what we call "inspiration." The human authors of the prophetic books wrote in a particular language (Hebrew or Aramaic), in a particular time, in a particular place and circumstance, to a particular audience. For that reason, they are all quite different from each other, with different personalities addressing different concerns. However, because they are all "breathed out by God" and part of the biblical canon, there is one ultimate, divine author (God) who is speaking in them. They represent many prophetic voices, but these voices are all speaking for one living God who does not change. Therefore, the prophetic books do not contradict each other. They may give different perspectives or look at an event from different angles, but they do not offer *conflicting* perspectives. They do not have opposing understandings of what God is like or what he has done in history.

Second, because the Old Testament prophetic books are inspired, canonical, Christian Scripture, we approach them as readers under their authority. There are different ways that we *can* read a text. When I find a piece of "junk mail" in my mailbox, I read it with suspicion, assuming that I am wasting my time. When I read a news report about something happening in the government, I am open to learning, but still cautious because I know that every reporter has an agenda. When I read the instructions on my income tax forms, I seek only to understand and obey. Income tax forms are authoritative—it does not matter if I agree with them or not. We adopt a particular stance when we read anything: a sweet note from a parent or spouse, instructions from a supervisor at work, or someone's ramblings on social media.

Because the Old Testament Prophets are Christian Scripture, we approach the text not to critique it or find fault with it but to hear God's Word and know him. In addition, as Christians we read the Old Testament Prophets as *insiders*. If we are disciples of Jesus Christ and members of his church, then we are part of the true people of God and can anticipate, not dread, what God has in store for those who love him. Whatever the prophets demand, we will obey. Whatever they critique, we will purge from our lives. Whatever they assert about God, we will incorporate into our theology and take seriously.

Perhaps this sounds naive. Will we not read critically? Yes, we will be critical in the sense that we will try to be detailed and analytical. And we will attempt to take the text on its own terms, not foisting our own preconceptions on it. Sometimes this will mean rejecting common ideas and interpretations that we have heard all of our lives.

The Old Testament Prophets Are Difficult

The Old Testament is important for the church, but it is not always easy to understand. In its pages we read violent stories, laws that seem strange, lists of kings or geographical districts, and wild visions and symbols. For many modern Christians, the Prophets are particularly difficult to comprehend, and it is challenging to see their relevance for today. It will be helpful to identify some of the reasons that the Prophets are difficult, since these are the very issues that we will seek to address in this book.

First, the Old Testament Prophets are often difficult for us because they assume that the reader is well acquainted with all that came before in God's dealings with Israel and his revealed word. The prophetic books assume that we understand this *theological* context. The ethics of the Prophets are based on the law given to Moses in Exodus, Leviticus, and Deuteronomy. God had made specific demands of his people that they (typically) rejected and failed to obey. Nevertheless, these laws reflect God's values, and he holds his people accountable to them. Much of the prophetic message is related in some way to the covenants that God had made in Genesis, Exodus, and 2 Samuel. The more we understand the rest of the Old Testament, the more these theological references will be obvious and make sense. The Prophets are just one part of a grand theological vision given to us in Scripture. They do not start at the beginning and catch us up. When we enter a prophetic book, we are stepping into the middle of a discussion already in progress.

Second, the Old Testament Prophets are difficult because they are often so closely tied to a particular *historical* context. They speak against specific sins that characterize ancient society. They refer to religious movements and the actions of priests and false prophets. They urge their listeners to trust God in the face of actual invading armies on their way to steal, rape, murder, and oppress. They speak against the evil of neighboring nations that have victimized the poor and built wealth by exploiting others. In the pages of the prophetic books, we hear about the persecution that a prophet suffers at the hands of the king or those in political power. In many cases, the message of the prophet is anchored in these specific events. And yet they do not provide us with the background that we need to understand—they assume it. Therefore, in order to read the prophetic books well, we must make extra effort to study the historical background and situation.

A third reason that the prophetic books are difficult is that they are complex literature. They are not straightforward narratives (like 2 Samuel), nor are they short poems (like many Psalms). They are a mix of narrative and poetry, sermon and prophetic oracle. They are often emotionally raw and intense: identifying terrible sins, lamenting over total destruction, and trying to grasp the glory and holiness of God.

Fourth, a prophetic book does not have a table of contents. I remember attempting to read a book like Isaiah when I was in high school, and it seemed like its contents had been put into a blender and scattered around the sixty-six chapters. I could not discern how one prophetic oracle or story related to the next one. To be sure, biblical scholars have also struggled to discern the structure of prophetic books. One scholar says that the book of Amos is "arranged with almost no regard for content or chronological order."[1] Another scholar writes that one would be correct in thinking that the prophetic books are "a hopeless hodgepodge thrown together without any discernible principle of arrangement at all."[2] We will need to discuss this question of structure as we investigate each prophetic book. (Spoiler alert: each prophetic book *is* arranged in a meaningful way!)

The prophetic books are difficult for these four reasons and others as well. All of these features have to do with the "genre" of these works. Genre is crucial for interpretation of any text. If I say to you, "A clown, a priest, and a duck walked into a bar," you interpret my statement as a joke. Then, you decide whether my next statement (the punch line) is humorous. Or if I say to you, "In witness whereof the parties hereunto have set their hands to these presents as a deed on the day, month, and year herein before mentioned," you interpret it as part of a legal document. In this case, you look for the place to enter the date below your signature.[3] As we negotiate a variety of types of texts in society, we are constantly evaluating not only what they mean, but how they create meaning and how we should read them in that light. In the same way, we must understand what Old Testament prophecy is, how it works, how prophets communicate, and so on if we are to read them competently, faithfully, and on their own terms.

The Structure of This Book

Because the Old Testament prophetic books have such a distinct genre (or genres) and because they are difficult for the modern reader to understand, the next seven chapters will deal with these issues in more depth. Chapters 2 and 3 deal with the *context* of the prophetic books. Chapter 2 addresses the theological context, situating the prophetic books within biblical theology and the story line of God's plan of salvation. Chapter 3 surveys the historical context, providing an overview of major events in the history of Israel and how the Prophets relate to each other chronologically.

Chapters 4–8 deal with the phenomenon of prophecy. In chapter 4, we explore the essential "job description" of an Old Testament prophet. This examination of the prophetic task continues, from the opposite perspective, in chapter 5, where we examine false prophets in Israel and in the surrounding nations. The true prophets of God were often in conflict with false prophets and distinguished themselves from them. In chapter 6, we will survey some of the key messages that come to us in the Prophets. In chapter 7, we look at the particular strategies used by Old Testament prophets to communicate (often) unpopular messages to an audience that is (often) hostile. Finally, in chapter 8 we will discuss the origins of prophetic books themselves, how they were formed into biblical books, and the implications for interpretation.

In chapters 9–24, we will spend one chapter on each of the prophetic books of the Old Testament. As you might imagine, the chapters on the long or complex books (such as Isaiah or Ezekiel) are longer, while other chapters are much shorter. Each chapter has a similar structure: We begin with "Orientation," in which we consider the identity of the prophet and his particular situation. Next, in "Exploration" we examine the literary structure of the book and then discuss its contents, section by section. Finally, in "Implementation" we summarize some of the key theological points in the book and consider their particular significance within the whole Christian Bible and our faith. Each chapter ends with some discussion questions for further consideration.

A Worthy Journey

It is my hope that this book will be a helpful guide as you read the Prophets for yourself. But it is just that—a guide. The real value comes from reading the text of Scripture. It is God's holy Word, living and active, and able to make us "complete, equipped for every good work" (2 Tim. 3:16). As I have read the Prophets in the preparation of this book, my faith in God and his redemption in Jesus Christ has been encouraged and built up. It is my hope and prayer that your faith will be bolstered as well as you work through these books of the Bible. The prophets lived long ago, but the Word of God does not pass away, and their message is crucial for the church today as we seek to love God with all our heart, soul, strength, and mind.

Christian Reading Questions

1. In your own words, describe what it means to read the Prophets as Christian Scripture. Other than Acts 26:25–28 and 2 Timothy 3:16–17, which texts inform your answer?
2. With what stance have you previously read the Prophets? How might that stance need to change as you approach them moving forward?
3. What have you found most intimidating or difficult about reading the Prophets? Which topics do you hope to learn more about, or what skills do you hope to acquire as you engage with this material?

PART 1

The Context
of the Prophets

CHAPTER TWO

The Theological Context of the Prophets

And [Jesus] said to them, "O foolish ones, and slow of heart to believe all that the *prophets* have spoken! Was it not necessary that the Christ should suffer these things and enter into his glory?" And beginning with Moses and all the *Prophets*, he interpreted to them in all the Scriptures the things concerning himself.

Luke 24:25–27[1]

I magine that you are at a party and you walk up to several friends in the middle of their conversation.

". . . and that's why Kate quit her job on Thursday."

"Are you serious? I thought she was trying to get the Hamilton account!"

"I know! But I think she's been hoping to go to Tokyo next year."

We have all had this kind of experience. Your ability to catch up and follow the conversation depends on two things. First, you need to know some specific details. Who is Kate? Where was she working? What is the "Hamilton account"? Second, for a full understanding, it would really help to know the bigger picture of Kate's life: her personality, values, and dreams. Did she like her job? Is she usually an impulsive person, or is it likely that she had a good reason to quit? What has it cost her to lose the Hamilton account? Why does she want to go to Tokyo?

When we pick up a prophetic book in the Old Testament, it is similar to walking in on the middle of a conversation. Without a theological context, some statements seem odd at best! For example, the prophet Jeremiah lived about four hundred years after King David, but he says that in the *future*, the Israelites will "serve the LORD their God and David their king" (30:9).

Comments like this may seem strange in isolation, but they make key contributions to the overall "conversation"—the grand narrative of God's plan of salvation that starts in Genesis, builds throughout the Old Testament, comes to a climax in the redemptive work of Jesus Christ, and concludes in the book of Revelation. The Prophets make a unique and significant contribution to the great theological story of the Bible, but they do not stop to introduce concepts or review what has already taken place. Therefore, if we want to understand the Prophets, we need to be acquainted with where we are in the conversation: what has come before and what the Prophets are building toward.

In Luke 24:25–27, quoted at the beginning of this chapter, Jesus says several important things. First, he mentions the Prophets as a distinct collection. There is a part of Scripture called "the Prophets," and they have something specific to contribute to theology and faith. Second, the Prophets contribute to the message of "all the Scriptures." In other words, there is a unified message to all of Scripture. Of course, there are many different messages in the Bible's different books, but they all interconnect to form one great message. Third, the Prophets ultimately speak of God's great plan of salvation, which culminates in Jesus himself. Therefore, Jesus says, failing to "believe all that the prophets have spoken" leads to misunderstanding his ministry and missing his offer of salvation.

In this chapter, we will undertake a basic survey of the great theological story in the Old Testament. There are many lengthy and complex books that deal with Old Testament theology, each from a different angle or approach. Each one has a different idea of what constitutes the "center" of Old Testament theology, a theme around which everything else revolves. For one it might be the theme of land, for another it might be kingship, Messiah, promise, God's glory, covenant, or some combination of these. We will consider the story of the Old Testament by focusing on the last of these: covenant. This is because the Prophets are particularly focused on God's covenants with Israel as major turning points in redemptive history, including what God will accomplish in the future.

Covenant

The word "covenant" (Hebrew: *berit*) occurs 287 times in the Old Testament. It is sometimes translated "treaty" or "agreement." The following is a working definition: "A [covenant] is an enduring agreement which establishes a defined relationship between two parties involving a solemn, binding obligation to specified stipulations on the part of at least one of the parties toward the other, which is taken by oath under threat of divine curse, and ratified by a visual ritual."[2] There are some key points in this definition. First, a covenant is "enduring" and does not have a sunset clause indicating when it will no longer be valid. Second, a covenant defines a relationship with specific expectations and benefits for the two parties. This is different from a contract, which does not necessarily have a relational component. I can sign a wireless contract for my phone with no personal relationship to the company. I'm obligated to pay them for a certain amount of time, but that does not mean that if I switch carriers later, I have been unfaithful! But in a covenant, it is the relationship that is the basis for the obligations. Third, because of this relational element, covenants are taken very seriously: breaking the covenant results in the breaking of a relationship, animosity between the parties, and consequences. Therefore, the covenant is made in a special ceremony with built-in reminders for the parties so that they might avoid consequences for unfaithfulness.

We might say simply that a covenant is a formal agreement that establishes a new relationship between two parties, with obligations for at least one of them. In the ancient Near East, there were political or military covenants between a great king (a "suzerain") and the lesser kings who ruled over territories within his domain ("vassals") (more on this below). Another example of a political covenant is the agreement that King Zedekiah makes with the people of Jerusalem that they will set free all of their slaves (Jer. 34:8–10). In Genesis 14:13, the word "covenant" refers to a military treaty between Abram/Abraham and some Amorite brothers; there it is often translated as "allies" in English versions. Covenants can also be personal agreements, such as the one in which Laban insists that his son-in-law, Jacob, treat his daughters well (31:44). Marriage is also called a "covenant" in Malachi 2:14. It is not just a contract with legal language that will hold up in court—it establishes a relationship that begins a new reality for the man and the woman.

Because covenants were a regular part of political and daily life in the ancient world, God uses them as models for establishing and defining his relationship with his people. People knew the concepts and components of covenants, so they would be better equipped to understand the significance of living in relationship with God, including the expectations for each side of the relationship. There are five major theological covenants in the Old Testament (see table 2.1).[3]

These covenants are the critical junctures at which God carries along his plan of redemption. They form a framework and trajectory for the combination of God's promises and action in which he uses his people to bring about a Savior for the sake of all people, for deliverance of the world from

Table 2.1. Major Theological Covenants

Covenant	Key Passages
Covenant with Noah	Genesis 6:18; 9:1–17
Covenant with Abraham	Genesis 12:1–3; 15:1–21; 17:1–21
Covenant with Israel	Exodus 19:3b–8; 20:1–24:18
Covenant with David	2 Samuel 7:4–17
New covenant	Jeremiah 31:31–34

sin, and for his glory. For each covenant we will discuss the *reference(s)* where it is found, the *participants*, the central *promise(s)* that God makes in the covenant, the *obligation* that God imposes on the participants, and the formal *sign* of the covenant that God designates as a solemn assurance of his fidelity.

It is noteworthy that the story of God's salvation does not begin with God's creation of Israel in the wilderness but with God's creation of the world in the book of Genesis. The relationship between God and his people, told and regulated in the Bible, is set within God's larger purposes for all of the created order.[4] In the beginning—of Genesis—we are told that there is only one God. He has created everything and he rules everything. He has created humans to know him and to be in relationship with him. Humans are to rule over creation as God's representatives. They find their purpose in serving God, and they relate properly to each other as they are properly related to God. All the world is properly ordered. In the garden there is peace and freedom.

However, Adam and Eve refuse to submit to God's instructions and to rule over creation as representatives of God. When they sin by disobeying God, there are catastrophic and wide-ranging consequences that affect all of creation. But unlike a giant conventional bomb, which does great damage one time and then ceases in its destructive power, the sin of humanity is like a nuclear weapon, which wreaks havoc when it detonates and then continues to destroy, kill, and cause suffering year after year through its deadly radiation.

We can point to four fundamental consequences that come to humanity because of the fall into sin. First, sin leads to death. Although the first sin might seem relatively insignificant (eating the fruit), it causes the undoing of creation; and while Adam and Eve do not die immediately, death is unavoidable (Gen. 2:17; 3:19). This is not what God intended for them: death is not a natural part of the created order but an unnatural consequence. Second, relationships are broken. The most fundamental relationship broken is between humanity and God. This is illustrated when God comes to the garden to meet with Adam and Eve, and they hide themselves because of their shame (3:8–10). Later, it becomes clear that horizontal relationships between people are also deeply damaged. In Genesis 4:1–16, Cain kills his brother, Abel, also breaking his relationship with his parents. A third consequence is that their rule over creation is damaged. Rather than being subdued and ruled by humans as God had intended (1:26), now creation will work against them and make life difficult (3:16–19). A fourth consequence is that this new state of suspicion, animosity toward God, and disordered relationships is now intrinsic to their makeup as human beings. They not only sin, but they have a propensity to sin. And even worse, this new nature is passed to their offspring, and then to their offspring. God's conclusion is not only that "the wickedness of man was great in the earth" but also that "every intention of the thoughts of his heart was only evil continually" (6:5).

Creation/Sin

Every living creature

Figure 2.1 represents the scope of God's creation and the universal reality of sin. It is a very simple diagram because it is all-inclusive at this point in redemptive history: there is one world that is dying, hostile toward God, and failing to fulfill the purposes he has for it.

God's Covenant with Noah

The first of the major covenants is God's covenant with Noah. When we get to Genesis 6, God has two responses to the universal wickedness that he sees on the earth. First, he determines to destroy all living things in a great flood as an act of judgment. At the same time, he also determines to save one man and his family. When the flood subsides and the danger is past, God makes a covenant with Noah, indicating that saving Noah's family from the flood is not only pragmatic (to preserve the human race), it is also revelatory (see table 2.2). God's actions in history, combined with this covenant relationship, are the first step in revealing the nature of his ultimate salvation.

Table 2.2. Covenant with Noah

References	Genesis 6:18; 9:1–17
Participants	God and all creatures on earth (9:10, 12, 15, 16, 17)
Promise	Negative: Will never again destroy all life with a flood Positive: Will create positive conditions for life
Obligation	Respect for life (cf. 9:4–6)
Sign	A "bow"

The Scope of the Covenant with Noah

Figure 2.2

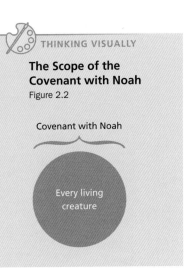

Covenant with Noah

Every living creature

God first mentions this covenant to Noah in Genesis 6:18 in connection with his instructions on building the ark, the means of his salvation. The primary discussion of the covenant is in 9:1–17. We often refer to this as God's covenant with Noah, but it is really a covenant between God and all living things on the earth. Note the repetition in the passage: God has killed almost "every living creature" (8:21) and saved some of "every living creature" on the ark (9:10), and now he will make his covenant with Noah, his family, and "every living creature" (see 9:12, 15, 16). God says that the covenant is established between himself and "all flesh that is on the earth" (9:17). Therefore, our diagram of this covenant is as seen in figure 2.2. The diagram looks very similar to figure 2.1 because, in terms of scope, the covenant relates to all of creation. It reflects God's desires for the whole world that he has made, in spite of the sin that has done so much damage.

The central promise of the covenant has negative (what God will not do) and positive (what God will do) aspects. The negative promise comes in Genesis 9:11: "I establish my covenant with you, that never again shall all flesh be cut off by the waters of the flood, and never again shall there be a flood to destroy the earth." Positively, God intends for there to be life on the earth, not death. This is not explicitly stated, but it becomes clear in his instructions to humanity. First, they are to be fruitful and multiply (9:1, 7). This is an echo of God's original intention in the garden (see 1:22, 28). Second, life is so important to God that, paradoxically, the only appropriate punishment for murder is the death penalty. God says:

> Whoever sheds the blood of man,
>   by man shall his blood be shed,
> for God made man in his own image. (9:6)

In a sense, this respect for life is also the obligation that is required by the covenant. Just as God cares deeply about life, he expects people to respect and preserve life as well. The sign of this covenant is the rainbow in the sky. It is not miraculous, since it occurs naturally when light hits water particles in the air, but God designates it as an enduring reminder that he will never again destroy all life with a flood (9:15, 17).

The covenant with Noah (and all creatures on the earth) reveals that in spite of humanity's wickedness, it is God's preference and intention to bring life rather than death. We cannot take this mercy for granted! It is, in fact, a great surprise in Genesis that God would respond to rebellion by seeking life for humanity rather than death. Sin's just consequence is worldwide destruction, but God is unwilling to let that be the last word. His covenant with Noah and all life on earth indicates that he is a God of grace. Of course, this covenant is very restricted in what it reveals. There is no hint here of how God will deal with the problem of sin, and there is no hint of a Messiah or of what God's plans entail. Yet, it is enough to know at this point in the progress of revelation that he is planning to bring grace rather than judgment.

Unfortunately, soon after this, Noah plants a vineyard and ends up drunk, naked, and in a shameful situation with his sons (Gen. 9:20–25). This is evidence that although God has saved Noah's life and the lives of his sons, their hearts have not been cured. One scholar writes, "The sin of Noah sheds light on the human plight. At one time or another, most people become disgusted with what is going on in the world—the intractable problems among people: hatred, prejudice, and greed that lead to cruelty and war. . . . In response, the idealistic ones among us ask: 'What if we started over? What if we expunged history and wiped the slate clean?' The account of Noah puts the lie to that solution."[5] It is significant that this story of salvation from judgment concludes with a sordid episode. We are being warned that physical deliverance will not be enough to fix the ultimate problem that lies in our hearts.

God's Covenant with Abraham

God's covenant with Abraham is the second of the major covenants in the Old Testament. The first eleven chapters of Genesis have a worldwide scope, dealing with universal issues such as the creation of the world, the fall into sin, the flood, and the creation of languages at the Tower of Babel (Gen. 11:1–9). However, in Genesis 12, the discussion shifts dramatically to center our attention on one man, Abraham, and his descendants (fig. 2.3). This structure of Genesis suggests that God's particular dealings with Abraham (chaps. 12–25) are the beginning of his answer to the universal problems put forward in chapters 1–11. Whatever God is doing with Abraham and his family line is intended to benefit everyone else. This becomes explicit when God states in Genesis 12:1–7 that he will make Abraham into a great nation and that he will be a blessing to all of the other families of the earth. Mysteriously, the people of the earth will need to be properly oriented toward ("bless") Abraham in order to receive blessing from God.

A second important conversation between God and Abraham comes in Genesis 15:1–21. God repeats and amplifies his promises to give Abraham

Abraham within the Structure of Genesis
Figure 2.3

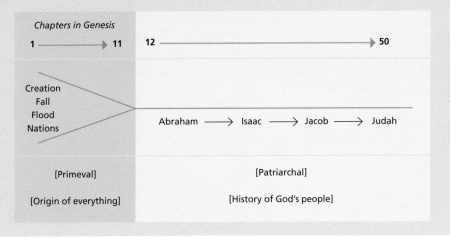

offspring and a land to possess. To seal the promises, God instructs Abraham to divide animal carcasses. After sundown, God passes through the halves as a symbolic way of binding himself to his word (15:7–11, 17).

The formal covenant comes in Genesis 17:1–21 (see table 2.3). God makes several promises to Abraham, some of which were anticipated in 12:1–3 and 15:1–21. First, he will give Abraham offspring that will grow into nations, although as we saw above, one of those nations in particular (Israel) will be the focus of God's attention (17:5–6). Abraham's offspring are the result of this covenant, but they are also participants in the covenant. God says in 17:7a, "And I will establish my covenant between me and you and your offspring after you throughout their generations for an everlasting covenant." Therefore, we can illustrate the scope of this covenant with figure 2.4 (which is obviously not to scale!). Whereas the covenant with Noah was between God and all life on earth, the covenant with Abraham and his offspring has a very limited scope: it is between God and one man and his descendants. However, the text is explicit that the covenant is still

Table 2.3. Covenant with Abraham

References	Genesis 17:1–21 (cf. 12:1–7; 15:1–21)
Participants	God and Abraham and his descendants
Promise	Offspring → nation (17:5–8) Relationship with God (17:7) Land (17:8)
Obligation	Faith in God's promise (17:1)
Sign	Circumcision (17:10–14)

ultimately intended to bring blessing to all the families of the earth. In the illustration, Abraham and his family line are represented by the small white dot, and the arrows indicate the implications of the covenant. Abraham and his descendants will somehow be a source of blessing for everyone else.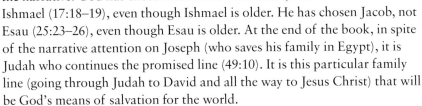

The book of Genesis has already shown a great interest in tracing a particular genealogical line from the very beginning. We learn that the godly line continues through not Cain but Seth (4:25). Seth's descendant is Noah (5:6–29). Noah singles out his son Shem, not Ham or Japheth (9:26). Shem's descendant is Abraham (11:10–26). Now, with the covenant to Abraham, the particular lineage through which God is working becomes a focal point of the narrative. God has chosen Abraham's son Isaac, not Ishmael (17:18–19), even though Ishmael is older. He has chosen Jacob, not Esau (25:23–26), even though Esau is older. At the end of the book, in spite of the narrative attention on Joseph (who saves his family in Egypt), it is Judah who continues the promised line (49:10). It is this particular family line (going through Judah to David and all the way to Jesus Christ) that will be God's means of salvation for the world.

A second promise is that Abraham and his offspring will have a special relationship with God. He states in Genesis 17:7b that he is establishing this everlasting covenant "to be God to you and to your offspring after you." Further, he says at the end of 17:8, "I will be their God." A third promise is to give Abraham's offspring a land. A nation cannot exist without a place to live. God promises Abraham, "I will give to you and to your offspring after you the land of your sojournings, all the land of Canaan, for an everlasting possession" (17:8).

The obligation of this covenant is that Abraham must have faith in God and his promises. At the beginning of Genesis 17, God says, "I am God Almighty; walk before me, and be blameless, that I may make my covenant between me and you" (17:1–2). Abraham had already demonstrated this faith in 15:6, where the narrator says that Abraham "believed the LORD, and he counted it to him as righteousness." This faith is a crucial component of taking part in the blessings of the covenant. And, because the covenant is not ultimately intended to bless only Abraham but to bring blessing to all the peoples of the earth, faith is required for *anyone* who wants to be the recipient of that blessing. Reflecting on this, Paul writes in Galatians 3:8–9, "And the Scripture, foreseeing that God would justify the Gentiles by faith, preached the gospel beforehand to Abraham, saying, 'In you shall

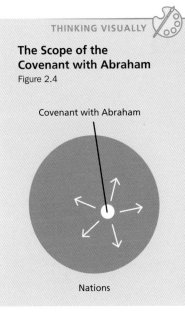

The Scope of the Covenant with Abraham
Figure 2.4

Covenant with Abraham

Nations

all the nations be blessed.' So then, those who are of faith are blessed along with Abraham, the man of faith."

Finally, the sign of the covenant with Abraham is circumcision (Gen. 17:11). We have seen that this covenant is primarily concerned with Abraham's offspring. Thus, it is appropriate that the sign of the covenant be related to reproduction. God states that every male of Abraham's line should be circumcised throughout the generations, even those who have been brought into the household from outside (17:12). Like the rainbow, which signifies the covenant with Noah and all life, this sign has nothing miraculous about it either. In fact, circumcision was a fairly common practice in the ancient world. But it is now commanded of Abraham as a permanent reminder of God's promises and Abraham's new status as the source of God's blessing to all the families of the earth.

God's Covenant with Israel

As God promised, Abraham did have many offspring. His son Isaac had Jacob. Jacob, later named "Israel," had sons and grandsons who became the fathers of the twelve tribes of Israel. The end of Genesis relates how Jacob's sons and their families moved to Egypt in a time of famine because of Joseph's influence and protection. When we open the book of Exodus, four hundred years have passed, and there are two new realities. First, Abraham's offspring have exploded into a great nation. Exodus 1:7 tells us that "the people of Israel were fruitful and increased greatly; they multiplied and grew exceedingly strong, so that the land was filled with them." The Hebrew word translated "increased greatly" is often used for *swarming* insects. This is a vivid way of describing the vast number of Israelites. However, there is a second new reality. The political and social situation has changed in Egypt, and the descendants of Jacob have gone from being favored subjects under Joseph to being mistreated slaves under a new king who did not know Joseph (1:8).

We are told that God has compassion on the people in their suffering because of his prior covenant with Abraham *and his offspring*. These are already God's chosen people—he is already in relationship with them—because that covenant is still in effect. The following verses illustrate this connection:

> And God heard their groaning, and God remembered his covenant with Abraham, with Isaac, and with Jacob. (Exod. 2:24)

And he said, "I am the God of your father, the God of Abraham, the God of Isaac, and the God of Jacob." (3:6)

God also said to Moses, "Say to the people of Israel: 'The LORD, the God of your fathers, the God of Abraham, the God of Isaac, and the God of Jacob, has sent me to you.'" (3:15)

God also alludes to his prior covenant with Abraham in Exodus 4:5; 6:3, 8; 32:13; and 33:1.

With great power and wonders, God brings his people out of Egypt and into the wilderness. There he makes a covenant with them at Mount Sinai. God indicates the primary purpose and promise of this covenant in Exodus 19:5–6 when he says, "Now therefore, if you will indeed obey my voice and keep my covenant, you shall be my treasured possession among all peoples, for all the earth is mine; and you shall be to me a kingdom of priests and a holy nation." There are two key elements in this statement. First, the primary promise of the covenant is that God will have a special relationship with Israel. They will be his "treasured possession" and a "holy nation," which means that they will be set apart for a special purpose. Second, they will be a "kingdom of priests." The task of a priest is to mediate between God and people. A priest does not come before God primarily for himself, but for the sake of others. This foreshadows the role that Israel has in God's future plans of salvation, which also goes back to the covenant with Abraham—that God would use Abraham's offspring to bless the nations.

Because this covenant is central to the life and governance of the nation of Israel, it is not restricted to a few passages as we saw in the covenants with Noah and Abraham. Rather, it dominates the books of Exodus, Numbers, and Deuteronomy. Furthermore, it lies in the background of the historical books (Joshua–Kings), and it is the basis for much of the messages of the prophets. Key passages include Exodus 20:1–23:19, which present the initial covenant obligations; Exodus 24:3–8 and 25:16, which describe the ratification and deposit of the covenant; and Leviticus 26 and Deuteronomy 28, which set forth the blessings and curses for obedience or disobedience. See table 2.4.

Table 2.4. Covenant with Israel

References	Exodus 19:5; 20:1–23:19; 24:3–8; 25:16; Leviticus 26; Deuteronomy 28
Participants	God and the nation of Israel
Promise	Relationship with God Priests for the nations
Obligation	Obedience to the law of Moses, including total and exclusive loyalty to God
Sign	Sabbath (Exod. 31:13, 16–17)

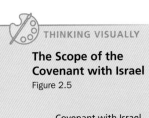
The Scope of the Covenant with Israel
Figure 2.5

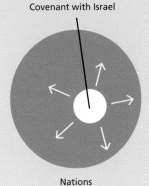

Covenant with Israel

Nations

As noted above, the participants of the covenant are God and the nation of Israel. The following diagram illustrates the scope of the covenant (fig. 2.5). The larger white circle (in comparison to fig. 2.4 on the covenant with Abraham) represents Abraham's offspring that have now become a nation. Just as the previous covenant was with Abraham and his offspring, this covenant is also with Abraham's offspring. The arrows continue to indicate that the purpose of the covenant is ultimately for the benefit of the rest of the world. The covenant is between God and the nation of Israel, but it quickly becomes clear that not everyone who belongs to ethnic/national Israel is faithful to God. Some of the members of the covenant community are included by birth rather than by faith. In other words, the community is *mixed*: composed of those who walk in Abraham's footsteps, righteous as a result of their faith in God, as well as those who reject obedience to God. One indication that the community is mixed is the distinction between typical sins and those that are done defiantly. The following is an example: "And the priest shall make atonement before the LORD for the person who makes a mistake, when he sins . . . , to make atonement for him, and he shall be forgiven. . . . *But the person who does anything with a high hand*, whether he is native or a sojourner, reviles the LORD, and *that person shall be cut off from among his people*. Because he has despised the word of the LORD and has broken his commandment, *that person shall be utterly cut off*; his iniquity shall be on him" (Num. 15:28, 30–31). To sin with a high hand does not mean "deliberate" (for as we all know, most of our sins are deliberate), but rather "unrepentant."[6] This passage recognizes that some in the covenant community of Israel do not want to submit to God and do not care about his commands; the consequence for a defiant, unrepentant sin is removal from the community. 🎨

We also see the mixed nature of the covenant membership in narrative passages. In Numbers 16:1–35, a group of Israelites rebels against Moses and Aaron, whom God has placed in authority. As a result, God kills the leaders of the group (16:31–33), and then fire from heaven kills another 250 men (16:35). These are members of the covenant with Israel, but they are under judgment.

One of the most pronounced examples comes from the book of Joshua. God instructs Israel to destroy utterly the city of Jericho and all of its inhabitants. This will be judgment for the great evil of the Canaanites in the land. In Joshua 2, Joshua sends spies to scout out the city before the attack, and they meet a woman named Rahab. If there is anyone who meets the

Members of the Covenant with Israel
Figure 2.6

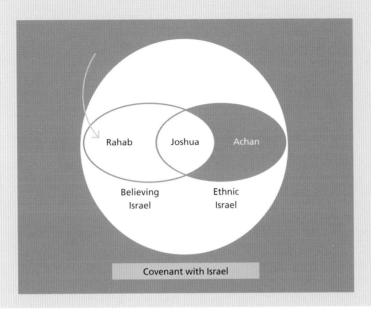

criteria for judgment among the enemy population, it is Rahab: a Canaanite prostitute in Jericho! And yet, because she fears YHWH and wishes to
join his people, she is saved (Josh. 6:17) and lives as a member of the covenant community in Israel "to this day" (6:23–25). In sharp contrast, an
Israelite man named Achan disobeys God after the battle of Jericho (7:1).
If there is anyone who meets the criteria for membership in God's covenant
community, it is Achan from the tribe of Judah, the foremost tribe in Israel
and the one that will produce King David and eventually the Messiah! And
yet, because of his faithlessness, Achan and his family are utterly destroyed
(the same fate that God intended for the Canaanites) (7:24–26). This is a
significant episode, because it illustrates that *ethnic* Israel and *believing*
Israel are not the same thing. This can be illustrated by a Venn diagram (see
fig. 2.6). In this diagram, the dark area around Israel represents the surrounding nations, which are not followers of YHWH. Achan is a member
of ethnic Israel, but he is not a follower of YHWH, and so he is judged
like the surrounding nations. Joshua is both an ethnic Israelite and a follower of YHWH. Rahab is from the nations, but because she believes, she
is included in Israel as well. The point here is that because God has made
the covenant with the entire nation of Israel, the membership includes both
those faithful and those unfaithful to God. They live together in the community, enjoying the blessings of the covenant and (later) experiencing the
consequences of breaking the covenant as well. This concept is foundational for discussions in some of the Prophets.

The covenant with Israel is modeled after common political covenants from the ancient Near East (ANE).[7] Table 2.5 is a simplified comparison between a Bronze Age ancient Near Eastern covenant and the covenant with Israel as presented in Exodus 20–25. Looking at the center column, we see that a typical covenant might begin with the great king identifying himself and announcing a covenant relationship. He then reviews what he has already done to benefit his subordinate or lesser king (vassal) within his territory. Perhaps he came to the aid of the subordinate king and helped defend him from attacking enemies. This historical event was the foundation for the covenant, which now requires obligations on the part of the vassal. These obligations would be clearly stated: for example, the vassal might be required to provide military or financial support on a regular basis. The king might also have ongoing obligations to the subordinate king. Once the covenant was ratified, it would be deposited in a sacred place or inscribed in a public location, where it was an ongoing witness to the necessity of obedience and faithfulness on the part of the subordinate. The covenant giver would invoke his deities as witnesses to the covenant who would ensure either blessings on the recipient (for faithfulness) or curses and consequences (for unfaithfulness).

Table 2.5. Ancient Covenants and the Covenant with Israel

	ANE Covenant	Covenant with Israel
Identification of the covenant giver	The king bestows a gracious relationship on a subordinate.	God identifies himself as the covenant maker, who saved Israel from slavery in Egypt (Exod. 20:2).
Historical prologue	The past is the foundation for present obligation; the king had already benefited the subordinate, who must now respond.	
Obligations	The subordinate has obligations to the king.	The "Ten Commandments" (Exod. 20:3–17, expanded in 20:22–23:19) are Israel's obligations to God.
Ratification ceremony	The king and his subordinate put the covenant into effect.	The people agree to the covenant (Exod. 24:3) and perform a ritual act (24:5–8).
Deposit and periodic public reading	The covenant was also binding on the vassal's subjects.	Moses is to deposit the Ten Commandments in the ark of the covenant (Exod. 25:16).
List of witnesses	The king calls on the gods to witness the covenant and hold the subordinate accountable.	The witnesses to the covenant are nature (Deut. 30:19; 31:28), a song (31:19), and the people themselves (Josh. 24:22).
Blessings and curses	The king makes threats and promises to the subordinate, depending on obedience.	God promises blessings for obedience and curses for disobedience (Lev. 26; Deut. 28).

We see this same pattern in God's covenant with Israel. In Exodus 20:2, God begins by identifying himself and announcing that the historical basis of the covenant is something that he has already done when he rescued Israel from slavery in Egypt. Note that the obligations come next, as a *response* to a relationship that is already established. Israel does not create the relationship with God if they obey. Because God has already benefited them, they must reflect God's character and live in a community that corresponds to his values. The Ten Commandments in 20:3–17 are a summary of the covenant obligations, expanded on in 20:22–23:19. These involve everything from the regulation of worship (20:25; 22:29) to servants in the household (21:1–6) to cursing one's father or mother (21:17) to prohibition of magic and sorcery (22:18) to sexual ethics (22:19) to social justice and care for the poor (23:6–8).

The people of Israel ratify the covenant first by verbal assent (Exod. 24:3) and then by a ritual act involving the blood of a sacrificed animal (24:5–8). The people say, "All that the LORD has spoken we will do, and we will be obedient." Moses then takes blood from the animals; half he throws on the altar, and the other half he throws on the people. The Levites deposit the stone tablets containing the Ten Commandments (symbolic of the entire covenant) into the ark of the covenant as an enduring reminder of Israel's responsibility before God (Exod. 25:16; 40:20). In an ancient Near Eastern situation, a king can call on the gods to be witnesses to the covenant. But this covenant is between God (the only God!) and Israel, so who shall serve as witnesses? In Deuteronomy, God calls on heaven and earth as symbolic witnesses because they will last from generation to generation (30:19; 31:28). Moses also teaches the people a song as a witness to remind them of the commitment they have made (31:19). Later, in the book of Joshua, the people renew the covenant, and Joshua states that the people themselves are witnesses (Josh. 24:22).

The last component of the covenant is the blessings and curses. God first announces the blessings for obedience (Lev. 26:3–13; Deut. 28:1–14) and then the curses for disobedience (Lev. 26:14–39; Deut. 28:15–68). Table 2.6 presents a comparison of the passages. They contain distinctive blessings and curses, but there is also substantial overlap. Note the proportions: there is a total of twenty-five verses given to blessings, but sixty-eight verses (more than twice as many) given to detailed and troubling curses. Unfortunately, Israel will eventually break this covenant and experience all these curses, including land that does not produce food, defeat by enemies, cannibalism of their own children, and exile in foreign lands.

There is an awareness within Deuteronomy that the people will not successfully keep the covenant. The problem is that their hearts are inherently

Table 2.6. Covenant Blessings and Curses

Leviticus	Blessings		Deuteronomy
26:4	Fruitful agriculture	Blessed womb and agriculture	28:3–6, 11
26:5	Long harvests		
26:6	Peace in the land		
26:7–8	Victory over enemies	Victory over enemies	28:7, 10
26:10	Plentiful food		
26:11–13	God's presence with them	Holiness before God	28:9
		Economic prosperity and power	28:12–13

Leviticus	Curses		Deuteronomy
26:16a	Panic and diseases	Pestilence and diseases	28:21–22, 27, 35
		Madness, blindness, confusion	28:28–29
26:16b	Vain agricultural efforts		
26:17	Defeat by enemies	Defeat by enemies	28:25–26
26:19–20	Unproductive land	Unproductive land	28:16–19, 23–24
		Curses and confusion until death	28:20
26:22	Wild beasts		
26:25–26	Sword, plague, and famine		
		Abducted wives, children, animals	28:30–33
26:29	Cannibalism of their own children	Cannibalism of their own children	28:53–57
		Unproductive land	28:38–40
26:30	Religious sites destroyed		
26:31–33	Ruined cities and exile	Exiled children	28:41
26:34–35	Desolate land	Desolate land	28:42
26:36–39	Fear before enemies	Submission to foreigners	28:43–44
		Defeat by enemies	28:48–52
		Diseases that kill	28:58–63
		Exile to foreign lands	28:64–68

faulty. What is needed is a change of heart, an internal transformation that will enable them to obey. Note the following verses:

> But to this day the LORD has not given you a heart to understand or eyes to see or ears to hear. (29:4)

> This people will rise and whore after the foreign gods among them in the land that they are entering, and they will forsake me and break my covenant that I have made with them. (31:16)

Circumcise therefore the foreskin of your heart, and be no longer stubborn. (10:16)

And the LORD your God will circumcise your heart and the heart of your offspring, so that you will love the LORD your God with all your heart and with all your soul, that you may live. (30:6)

The ominous prediction of Israel's unfaithfulness makes clear that it will not be a question of the nation figuring out a way to be better; they will need a substantial transformation of their hearts. In the meantime, they will fail and break this covenant. However, there is hope if they "return to the LORD" (30:2). Leviticus 26:41–42 says: "If then their uncircumcised heart is humbled and they make amends for their iniquity, then I will remember my covenant with Jacob, and I will remember my covenant with Isaac and my covenant with Abraham, and I will remember the land." We will see in the course of our study of the Prophets that this is one of their fundamental messages to Israel. Their only hope in the midst of bitter consequences and death is repentance and wholehearted return to God. And yet they will need God's intervention to do even that.

The sign of God's covenant with Israel is the Sabbath. When God introduces the covenant with the Ten Commandments, he instructs Israel to keep the Sabbath day as holy. Of the ten commands in this list, the command to keep the Sabbath is accompanied by the most extensive elaboration: "Six days you shall labor, and do all your work, but the seventh day is a Sabbath to the LORD your God. On it you shall not do any work. . . . For in six days the LORD made heaven and earth, the sea, and all that is in them, and rested on the seventh day. Therefore the LORD blessed the Sabbath day and made it holy" (Exod. 20:9–11). Later in the book of Exodus, God states that the Sabbath is the sign of this covenant with Israel: "Above all you shall keep my Sabbaths, for this is a sign between me and you throughout your generations" (31:13). He continues, "The people of Israel shall keep the Sabbath, observing the Sabbath throughout their generations, as a covenant forever" (31:16). This is such an important command that it is mentioned forty-two times from Exodus to Deuteronomy. Once again, it is not a miraculous sign. Rather, a period of time is designated by God as an enduring reminder that the people belong to God. The use of Sabbath as a sign and representation of the entire covenant helps explain why some of the prophets focus such attention on Sabbath as a marker of who is truly a follower of YHWH (see, e.g., Isa. 56:2–6 or Ezek. 20:12).

God's Covenant with David

From the beginning of Israel's existence as a nation in the wilderness, there was an expectation that they would eventually be ruled by a king (see Deut. 17:14–20). God instructed that the king would write for himself a copy of God's law, read it all the days of his life, and learn to fear YHWH by obeying it (17:18–19). The king was to lead his people continually toward faithfulness to God. He was to model and execute justice in the land and care for the poor, setting an example of faithfulness to the covenant that God had made with Israel.

And at the end of the period of Judges, the people ask for a king. They specifically request a king "like all the nations" (1 Sam. 8:5). Even after Samuel warns them that this kind of king will exploit them and build his own power and legacy at their expense, they reply that they want to be "like all the nations" with a king who will fight their battles (8:20). Samuel is discouraged, but God states that this is not a rejection of Samuel's leadership; it is a rejection of God's rule as king over Israel. Thus, there are two competing agendas. God desires to be the ultimate king and leader of Israel himself, with a human king serving on his behalf, enacting his covenant with Israel by teaching the people the law, modeling faithfulness, and executing justice. But the people are not interested in being God's distinctive people; they prefer to be like every other nation with a human king who will lead them into battle. The people get their wish: Saul, who turns out to be a king just like those of all the nations. He is selfish, disobedient, and interested only in his own success. Because of his disobedience God takes the kingship from him, and he is killed on the battlefield.

His successor is David. This time, it is God's agenda that prevails, as he chooses a man who may not look like much but who has a submissive heart toward God (1 Sam. 16:7). While David commits serious sins that do great damage to his own family and to the people of Israel, he models and implements God's covenant with Israel because he remains tenaciously loyal to God alone and turns from his sin.

Because of David's commitment to God, he hopes to build a "house" (a temple) for God, since until this point God's dwelling among the people has been the tabernacle (a tent) (2 Sam. 7:2). At first, the prophet Nathan confirms David's desire the build a temple. However, that same night God instructs Nathan that David is not to build the temple. Instead, God will establish a covenant with David. In the primary passage describing the covenant, 2 Samuel 7:8–16, God does not use the word "covenant." But in David's last words, he calls it a covenant when he says, "For [God] has made with me an everlasting covenant" (23:5). Psalm 89:3–4 also refers to God's covenant with David:

> You have said, "I have made a covenant with my chosen one;
> I have sworn to David my servant:
> 'I will establish your offspring forever,
> And build your throne for all generations.'"

 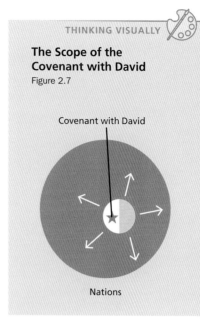

The Scope of the Covenant with David
Figure 2.7

Covenant with David

Nations

The immediate participants of this covenant are God and David, although the purpose of the covenant is to establish God's eternal kingdom for his people. See table 2.7.

In figure 2.7, the star represents David, who is a member (and leader) of Israel, which is represented by the white circle. In light of the discussion above, the white circle is divided into two halves by a vertical line in order to portray the mixed nature of Israel as a covenant community. Some are faithful believers while others are members only by birth. As in the figures illustrating the covenants with Abraham and Israel, the arrows indicate that, ultimately, the covenant is intended to bring blessing to all the peoples of the earth (the larger shaded circle). One thing that these diagrams illustrate is that God continues to make covenants with smaller entities as the means by which he will bless the rest of the world: Abraham and his offspring, then Israel as the nation that comes from Abraham's offspring, then David as the ruler of Abraham's offspring.

The promises of the covenant are divided into two parts. The first part (2 Sam. 7:8–11) describes promises that God makes directly to David for his own lifetime. He promises that he will make David's name great (7:9), secure the land for Israel (7:10), and give David rest from his enemies all

Table 2.7. Covenant with David

References	2 Samuel 7:8–16; 23:5; Psalm 89:3–4
Participants	God and David (with implications for the nation)
Promises	During David's lifetime (2 Sam. 7:8–11): • Great name • Place for Israel • Rest from enemies After David's lifetime (2 Sam. 7:12–16): • Eternal offspring • Eternal kingdom
Obligation	Loyalty to God's covenant with Israel
Sign	None

around (7:11a). These concrete, immediate promises are then extended to greater promises for the future in 2 Samuel 7:12–16. God uses a play on words: David had intended to build God a "house" (a temple), but instead God will make David a "house" (a dynasty) (7:11b). God will give David offspring who will rule over his kingdom forever (7:12–13).

Therefore, the promised line that began in Genesis continues. God chose Abraham, Isaac, Jacob, and Judah. Judah's son Perez was the ancestor of Boaz. With Ruth, Boaz fathered Obed, who was the father of Jesse, the father of David (Ruth 4:18–22; 1 Chron. 2:4–15). When the nation divides in a civil war, David's offspring will be kings of Judah. Some of them will be wicked and will require discipline (2 Sam. 7:14–15), but God's promise will not fail. David's offspring will ultimately rule over an eternal kingdom and an eternal throne (7:16). How is that possible? How can God give David an eternal "house"? There are only two ways. One possibility is that the dynasty will be perpetual and unbroken forever. The facts of history rule out this possibility. A second possibility is that there will eventually be an heir to the throne who will never die.[8]

There are no explicit obligations in the covenant with David. However, since this covenant is built on the foundation of God's covenant with Israel, the expectation is that David and his offspring will be true to those obligations. God does not designate a sign for this covenant.

The New Covenant

In spite of God's gracious initiative in delivering Israel from Egypt and calling them into relationship with himself, they are unwilling or unable (or both) to be faithful to him. Although they have seen countless miracles on their behalf, they grumble in the wilderness. When they enter the promised land, they break God's commands. They adopt the gods and religions of the surrounding peoples and put their confidence in their own military or their ability to forge alliances with other nations. They fail to reflect the character of God, their covenant partner. They abuse and exploit the vulnerable in society, steal, murder, and commit degenerate sexual acts. The kings that come from David's line also follow their fellow Israelites' pattern of faith and failure. Because Israel breaks the covenant obligations, God announces through the prophets that he is bringing the covenant curses on them.

The failure of Israel is intensified by statements that success in their relationship with God will not come from trying again and perhaps giving it more effort next time. As we mentioned above, the book of Deuteronomy

Table 2.8. New Covenant

Reference	Jeremiah 31:31–34
Participants	God and Israel/Judah (faithful followers)
Promises	1. Internal law, written on the heart (v. 33b) 2. Relationship with God (v. 33c) 3. Believing members (v. 34a) 4. Forgiveness (v. 34b)
Obligation	Obedience to God's law (implicit)
Sign	None

anticipates this failure. They are fundamentally defective and unable to do what God asks. Later, in the final years before God brings the ultimate covenant curse—exile from the land—the prophet Jeremiah echoes the words of Deuteronomy:

> Circumcise yourselves to the LORD; remove the foreskin of your hearts . . . ; lest my wrath go forth like fire, and burn with none to quench it, because of the evil of your deeds. (Jer. 4:4)

> I will punish all those who are circumcised merely in the flesh— . . . for all these nations are uncircumcised, and all the house of Israel are uncircumcised in heart. (9:25–26)

> Can the Ethiopian change his skin or the leopard his spots? Then also you can do good who are accustomed to do evil. (13:23)

Like Deuteronomy, Jeremiah states that, because there is a fundamental problem with their hearts, they will never be faithful covenant partners if left to themselves. However, there is good news. The prophets announce that God is going to establish a new covenant that will have several key differences from the original covenant with Israel.

A number of passages in the Prophets speak of a covenant distinct from the previous covenant with Israel. Isaiah speaks of a future covenant that will be accomplished by God's "servant." He states that the servant will himself "be" a covenant for the people (42:6). Note that he does not say that the servant will initiate or establish or mediate the covenant—he will *be* the covenant. Isaiah 54:1–10 anticipates a "covenant of peace." Similarly, Ezekiel states that God will "remove the heart of stone from their flesh and give them a heart of flesh, that they may walk in my statutes and keep my rules and obey them" (11:19–20). He will set over them "one shepherd, my servant David, and he shall feed them," and he will "make with them a covenant of peace" (34:23, 25). This will lead to a new heart, a new spirit,

New Covenant

Nations

and a living relationship with God (36:25–26). In several passages, God speaks of an "everlasting covenant" (see Isa. 55:1–5 and Jer. 50:5). However, the key passage for the new covenant—and the one that gives it its name—is Jeremiah 31:31–34.

In Jeremiah 31:31–32, God states that he will make a new covenant with his people that is not like the covenant that he made with their fathers when he brought them out of Egypt. This is a reference to the covenant with Israel, which they broke, even though he was their husband (31:32). God had been good and caring and had given them no reason to break the relationship, and yet they did.

Then in Jeremiah 31:33–34, God gives them four promises in this new covenant (see table 2.8). First, in 31:33b, he states, "I will put my law within them, and I will write it on their hearts." This is a direct echo and reversal of previous passages stating that Israel's hard and uncircumcised hearts kept them from being faithful. In this new covenant, God will inwardly transform their hearts. Rather than law-keeping being something foreign and external (and therefore unpleasant), the law will come naturally from their new nature.

Second, in Jeremiah 31:33c, he states that in this new covenant, he will finally accomplish what he had intended all along: to be in relationship with his people. He will belong to them, and they will belong to him. In this way, the intimacy and freedom they shared in the garden, before there was sin, will be restored.

Third, he announces the end of the mixed community in 31:34a: "And no longer shall each one teach his neighbor and each his brother, saying, 'Know the LORD,' for they shall all know me, from the least of them to the greatest." As we noted above, the membership of the previous covenant with Israel was composed of believers and unbelievers—of those who sought after God and were faithful to him and those who rebelled against him. Therefore, there was a need, *within the covenant community*, for one person to urge another to follow God and commit themselves to him. But in this new covenant, that will no longer be the case because "they shall all know me." In other words, the membership of this new covenant will be fundamentally different: it will be composed only of those who know and are faithful to God. Therefore, there will be no need for "evangelism" within the community. The covenant is made with "the house of Israel and the house of Judah" (Jer. 31:31, 33), but it includes only the believing portion (see fig. 2.8).

Paul plays on the word "Israel" similarly in Romans 9:6 when he says, "For not all who are descended from Israel belong to Israel." His first use of "Israel" must refer to national, ethnic Israel because he speaks of those who are physically descended from Jacob's sons. But his second use of "Israel" refers to the believing people of God: "and not all are children of Abraham [i.e., of faith] because they are his offspring" (9:7). A few verses later, he quotes Isaiah 10:22: "Though the number of the sons of Israel be as the sand of the sea, only a remnant of them will be saved" (Rom. 9:27). Note that the arrows in figure 2.8 point inward. In the previous covenants, the outward-pointing arrows indicate that each covenant is ultimately intended to bless the nations. In the new covenant, this blessing is clarified: it consists of inviting the nations to come *into* this new community of faith that God creates. This explains why the prophets speak of the nations streaming to Jerusalem (the center of God's kingdom) and experiencing salvation.

The fourth promise of the new covenant is found in Jeremiah 31:34b. God says, "I will forgive their iniquity, and I will remember their sin no more." Jeremiah does not explain how this forgiveness will come about, only that it will be the basis of the people's relationship with God. The New Testament will explain how this is accomplished in Christ.

No explicit obligations are given for the new covenant in Jeremiah 31:31–34, but it is clear from this and other passages in the Prophets that new covenant members will now be able (and expected) to obey God's commands. This is the point of having a law "within them" and "on their hearts" (31:33). God has given his law that reveals his character and the specific ways that his people are to relate to him and to each other. Members of the new covenant community—transformed and forgiven—will now behave as the true people of God.

The Covenants and Christ

The five major covenants in the Old Testament are revealed progressively, over a long period of time. This might give the impression that one covenant ends when the next begins. Rather, each covenant continues to remain in place, and the covenants build on each other. We might use the illustration of an app update on your phone. Just as the essential app continues, while some features are added and others become obsolete, in God's plan of salvation there is continuity and continuation from covenant to covenant, but some features may become obsolete.[9] What we see is not total replacement but *addition* and adjustment. Some passages in the Prophets mention all of the covenants together, because they are all still active.

The Interrelationship of the Covenants
Figure 2.9

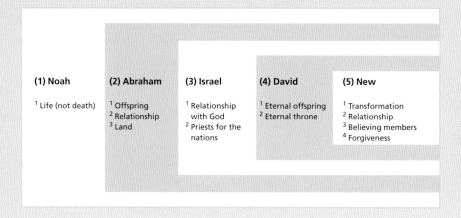

(1) Noah	(2) Abraham	(3) Israel	(4) David	(5) New
[1] Life (not death)	[1] Offspring [2] Relationship [3] Land	[1] Relationship with God [2] Priests for the nations	[1] Eternal offspring [2] Eternal throne	[1] Transformation [2] Relationship [3] Believing members [4] Forgiveness

For example, consider Ezekiel 37:24–26 (with the individual covenants in *italics*):

> My servant *David* shall be king over them, and they shall all have one shepherd. They shall walk in my rules and be careful to obey my statutes [*Israel*]. They shall dwell in the land that I gave to my servant Jacob, where your fathers lived [*Abraham*]. They and their children and their children's children shall dwell there forever, and *David* my servant shall be their prince forever. I will make a covenant of peace with them. It shall be an everlasting covenant with them [*new covenant*]. And I will set them in their land and multiply them, and will set my sanctuary in their midst forevermore [*Israel*].

Jeremiah 33:14–26 is another prophetic passage that speaks of God's Davidic king fulfilling the various covenants. Figure 2.9 illustrates this progression and continuation. Each covenant enacts the promises in previous covenants. One (oversimplified) way to see this is to read figure 2.9 backward, from right to left. The *new* covenant (internal, permanent transformation and forgiveness) is the means by which the *Davidic* king will rule over God's redeemed kingdom in order to fulfill the covenant with *Israel* by bringing YHWH into relationship with his people, so that *Abraham* might be a blessing to all nations, because God desires that all of humanity would flourish and live rather than perish (the covenant with *Noah*).

It is only when we place this framework in the context of the entire biblical canon that we see the full picture. From the time of humanity's fall into sin in the garden, God has preserved a particular offspring that is traced throughout the Old Testament (Seth → Noah → Abraham → Isaac → Jacob → Judah → Boaz → David → Kings of Judah → Zerubbabel) and all the way to Jesus Christ (Matt. 1:1–17; Luke 3:23–38). Along the way, God chose representatives of humanity to create a trajectory toward, and represent, his means of salvation for everyone else. God chose Abraham and his offspring, the nation of Israel, and then he chose David out of Israel as the source of his king and *Messiah*. Jesus Christ redeems Israel and invites all of humanity to come into his people by faith, as they wait for him to repair the broken cosmos and usher in a new heaven and earth (fig. 2.10).

In this way, Jesus Christ fulfills each of the five covenants. First, he fulfills the covenant with Noah and all life on earth because he brings life rather than judgment and offers salvation out of worldwide cataclysm for those who believe. Second, he is the culmination and goal of Abraham's offspring, who brings blessing to the nations. When Peter speaks to the Jews in Jerusalem in Acts 3:25–26, he says, "You are the sons of the prophets and of the covenant that God made with your fathers, saying to Abraham, 'And in your offspring shall all the families of the earth be blessed.' God, having raised up his servant [Jesus], sent him to you first, to bless you by turning every one of you from your wickedness." Third, Jesus fulfills the covenant at Sinai because he "tabernacled" (i.e., lived) among his people (John 1:14) and made a way for them to be in permanent relationship with him through his once-for-all sacrifice. The author of Hebrews writes in 9:13–14, "For if the blood of goats and bulls, and the sprinkling of defiled persons with the ashes of a heifer, sanctify for the purification of the flesh, how much more will the blood of Christ, who through the eternal Spirit offered himself without blemish to God, purify our conscience from dead works to serve

Jesus Christ and the Covenants
Figure 2.10

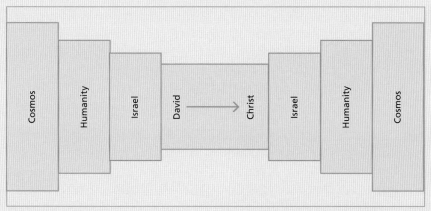

See Stephen G. Dempster, *Dominion and Dynasty: A Theology of the Hebrew Bible* (Downers Grove, IL: IVP Academic, 2003), 231–34.

the living God." Fourth, Jesus is the anointed, Davidic king who perfectly executes God's plan and manifests God's character. In his kingdom, he rules with justice and righteousness (Matt. 6:33). Finally, the new covenant is realized in the death and resurrection of Jesus (Matt. 26:28; 1 Cor. 11:25). By faith in his work on the cross, people from every nation and tribe and language are incorporated into the promises of God—united with Christ, adopted into his family, gifted with his Spirit, and completely forgiven for their sins (Acts 2:5; Eph. 2:13–22; Rev. 7:9).

Conclusion

The theological narrative discussed in this chapter is crucial context for understanding the message and ministry of the Old Testament prophets. Although the prophets receive distinctive messages from God for particular times and circumstances, their words build on this already-firm foundation. They are preachers who *apply* the previous covenants to their listeners or readers, as well as *reveal* the new covenant that God will accomplish in the future.

These covenants form the theological backbone of the Prophets. Because God is the creator of the entire world, all humans are valuable to him. God loves his people, Israel, but he also cares deeply for all other nations. God's status as creator also means that all humans are accountable to him. This is the foundation of the prophets' condemnation of the evil of the nations and announcement of judgment on those who harm Israel and each other. However, because of God's love, he has set a redemptive plan in motion that will be accomplished through the offspring of Abraham. Abraham's offspring grew into the nation of Israel, and God made a special covenant with them; but they failed him, falling far short of his expectations and showing themselves to be fundamentally flawed. In the short term, the covenant curses are coming on them, even as restoration and hope are promised for the future. The prophets look for this hope in the dynasty of David and his city, Jerusalem. Israel is stubborn and determined to rebel, but God is even more determined to restore them to himself. In the end, his people will live in peace, wholeness, and prosperity in a good world of safety and justice, ruled by their king in a new heavens and earth. The curse of sin will be undone and all will be well.

1. Define "covenant" in your own words. What are the similarities and differences between a covenant and a contract?

2. Is there a difference between covenant "obligations" and "conditions"? Do covenant obligations and their corresponding signs invariably lead to legalism?

3. What does it mean that the covenant community in the Old Testament was "mixed"? What are the implications of the mixed nature of covenant membership for how we read the Prophets and the Old Testament as a whole?

4. Can you identify a goal that underlies all the covenants? What does this goal suggest about God's overall purpose for human history?

5. Explain how Jesus fulfills each covenant. Reference key biblical texts in your answer.

CHAPTER THREE

The Historical Context of the Prophets

And all the prophets who have spoken, from Samuel and those who came after him, also proclaimed these days. You are the sons of the prophets and of the covenant that God made with your fathers, saying to Abraham, "And in your offspring shall all the families of the earth be blessed."

Acts 3:24–25

Long ago, at many times and in many ways, God spoke to our fathers by the prophets, but in these last days he has spoken to us by his Son, whom he appointed the heir of all things, through whom also he created the world.

Hebrews 1:1–2

Imagine that someone who lives a thousand years in the future, in a very different culture from ours, decides to read the messages of Martin Luther King Jr. However, this person does not know about the history of slavery in the United States, segregation, the Montgomery bus boycott, or the Vietnam War. These are very complex topics involving dates, names, and events that are ancient and foreign to this reader. But this future reader could not say, "I won't worry about those things. I'll just read what King had to say that still rings true today." This would be impossible, for while King's message will always be relevant, it is so inextricably rooted in those historical events that it cannot be properly understood in isolation. In fact, reading Dr. King's work without knowing his world will lead not only to *confusion* about his message but also to *distortion* of it. This reader would have to put in the hard work and study necessary to understand how twentieth-century America is similar and dissimilar to their own situation.

Like Dr. King, the prophets were not isolated philosophers meditating in a mountain shrine. Their messages are rooted in and related to specific events and social experiences. Further, their books do not appear in the biblical canon in chronological order, so it is often difficult to open up Ezekiel or Hosea and have a sense of where we are in the history of Israel. Their messages allude to what has happened in the past, they address specifically what is happening in the present, and they proclaim what God will do in the future. Therefore, we must get our historical "bearings."

In the previous chapter, we examined the theological context of the prophets to understand what voices they are echoing from the past and what voices they are contributing as God's program moves forward. In this chapter, we will examine the broad historical context of the prophets to understand how their situation shaped their message. In order to do this, we will locate the prophets in seven periods in Israel's history: (1) Israel in the wilderness and the land, (2) tenth century, (3) ninth century, (4) eighth century, (5) seventh century, (6) the exile, and (7) the postexilic period. As in chapter 2, our overview will be oversimplified and highly selective. The goal is not to give a full-blown history of Israel but to situate the prophets in historical relation to each other and to key events in their times.

Israel in the Wilderness and in the Land

Since the nineteenth century, critical biblical scholars have maintained that most of the Pentateuch (Genesis–Deuteronomy) comes from late in Israel's history. In fact, they argue that some of the legal portions of the Pentateuch are among the latest books in the Old Testament, produced after Israel's exile in Babylon. If so, this would mean that much of the Pentateuch was a later development in Israelite religion. However, according to the Bible there was a historical Moses, it was to him that God revealed the covenant, including the law, on Mount Sinai, and it was he who is responsible for the majority of Genesis–Deuteronomy in the wilderness period. Although there are a few references to prophets before Moses,[1] he is the *beginning* and *foundation* of the institution of prophecy in Israel. Moses is the first prophet in the Old Testament to receive a message from God, write it down, and then teach it to his contemporaries. For this reason, he has been called the "fountainhead" of Old Testament prophecy.[2]

Moses is not just the first spokesman for God; he is also the greatest Old Testament prophet. When Miriam and Aaron (Moses's sister and brother) speak against Moses and wonder whether he is really so special, God defends him in Numbers 12:6–8, "Hear my words: if there is a prophet among you, I the LORD make myself known to him in a vision; I speak with him in a dream. Not so with my servant Moses. He is faithful in all my house. With him I speak mouth to mouth, clearly, and not in riddles, and he beholds the form of the LORD. Why then were you not afraid to speak against my servant Moses?" According to this passage, Moses was not only the first of the prophets, but he was also unique in the degree of access that he had to God. Though he had his faults, Moses established and modeled what a prophet of God was to do. Interestingly, Moses, the *peak* of Old Testament prophecy, came at the very beginning.

After Moses died, Israel entered the promised land and lived there, governed by a number of regional judges. The prophet Samuel was the next significant step in the development of the prophetic institution. He was the last of the judges who governed Israel and the first prophet to be God's representative before an Israelite king (Saul).

Samuel's role as a prophet began when he was just a boy. According to 1 Samuel 3, he was serving in the tabernacle under the guidance of the priest Eli. When the story begins, the narrator tells us that "the word of the LORD was rare in those days; there was no frequent vision" (1 Sam. 3:1). During the night, when Samuel and Eli were both lying down, God called to Samuel. Samuel thought it was Eli, so he ran to answer him, but Eli told him that he did not call. This occurred two more times because "Samuel did not yet know the LORD, and the word of the LORD had not yet been revealed to him" (3:7). Finally, Eli told Samuel, "Go, lie down, and if he calls you, you shall say, 'Speak, LORD, for your servant hears'" (3:9). When God eventually spoke to Samuel, he had bad news for Eli and his family. Samuel was understandably reluctant to repeat the word of God, but in the morning, Eli demanded that Samuel tell him everything: "What was it that he told you? Do not hide it from me. May God do so to you and more also if you hide anything from me of all that he told you" (3:17).

This is a significant story for the way that it lays out the essential task of the prophet with Samuel as the role model.[3] First, Samuel passively received the word of God. He did not ignore it, get it from others (such as Eli the priest), or create anything out of his own mind. Second, he repeated it fully. He delivered exactly the message that God had for Eli even though it was incredibly difficult. He did not hide anything, understanding that the content of the message and the receptivity of the audience were irrelevant. It was his job to repeat it, come what may.

The second way that Samuel set the pattern for future prophets was by acting as God's spokesman to Israel's king. The king was intended to represent God's rule over the people, teaching them the covenant, modeling faithfulness, and executing justice. This was because Israel was a *theocracy*:

God was ultimately the king, while a human king served under his authority and enforced his will. The prophet stood before the king, conveying God's will or, more often, critiquing the king for disobeying God and failing to submit to him. The true prophet of YHWH was independent of the king's influence, ready and willing to denounce him or to tell him what he did not want to hear. Samuel modeled this prophetic role first. God informed him that Saul would be the first king (1 Sam. 9:16–17), and Samuel anointed Saul as king over God's people (10:1). When Saul disobeyed God, Samuel was there to rebuke him and then to announce that God had rejected Saul as king (15:23, 26). Later, the prophet Nathan also embodied this role. He delivered God's covenant to David (2 Sam. 7:4–5), confronted David over his sin with Bathsheba (12:1–15), and ensured that David's son Solomon became king at David's death (1 Kings 1:11–37).

Map 3.1. The divided kingdoms of Israel and Judah

Israel in the Tenth Century BC

Solomon's rule over a united Israel was marked by wisdom, wealth, and security. He built the temple, expanded Israel's territory, and made powerful political alliances with other nations, which brought in great wealth. However, he became increasingly syncretistic as his heart was drawn to the gods that his many foreign wives imported from their homelands. Because Solomon had not kept the covenant, God told him that he would tear the kingdom away from him. However, in order to keep his covenant promise to David, he would give one tribe (Judah) to Solomon's son (1 Kings 11:11–13). When Solomon died, his son Rehoboam came to the throne in Jerusalem. But due to Rehoboam's political missteps and God's sovereign plan, the ten northern tribes of Israel chose Jeroboam to be king over them instead. Thus the nation split in two and erupted into civil war. The southern state, called "Judah" throughout the Prophets, had Jerusalem as its capital;

the remaining ten tribes in the north were called "Israel" (or "Ephraim" after their southernmost representative), with their capital in Tirzah (see map 3.1).

King Jeroboam, in the Northern Kingdom, was concerned that if his citizens traveled to Jerusalem to worship in the temple, as YHWH had commanded, he would lose their allegiance. Therefore, he set up calf idols and worship sites with priests and altars in the extreme north at Dan, and in the extreme south of his nation at Bethel (see map 3.1). Jeroboam announced that the calf idols that he made represented the gods who had brought Israel up out of slavery in Egypt (1 Kings 12:28–33). For the prophets, these were not merely alternative locations for worshiping YHWH—they were false gods and represented a systemic sin in the Northern Kingdom. As long as the people worshiped at those sites, they were in violation of God's covenant and unfaithful to him. This explains the particular attention especially paid to Bethel in Amos and Hosea, who were prophets to the Northern Kingdom.

The "Time Line of the Prophets" in the front matter locates the prophets chronologically in relation to the kings and nations in which they served. It is recommended that you reference that time line in the following discussion. The Northern Kingdom is on the left, and the Southern Kingdom is on the right. The prophets are presented as shaded boxes. Some of the reigns of various kings overlap because, at times, a father and son reigned simultaneously as coregents. The chronology of the kings of Israel and Judah is complex, and there are certain problems that scholars have yet to work out conclusively.

Israel in the Ninth Century BC

In the first half of the ninth century, Assyria (the great military superpower in the east) was aggressively expanding its territory and putting pressure on Israel and the small nations that surrounded it. In response to the Assyrian threat, King Omri of Israel (885–874 BC) moved the capital city of the Northern Kingdom from Tirzah to Samaria—a key junction for trade between Arabia and the Mediterranean—to stabilize the nation's economy (1 Kings 16:24). He also created a political alliance with the kingdom of Tyre to the north, the great economic power in the region. The alliance was secured when Omri arranged a marriage between his son Ahab and Jezebel, the princess of Tyre. However, Jezebel brought more than trade to Israel—she introduced Baal, the Phoenician god of fertility. Her husband, King Ahab, built a temple for Baal in Samaria and erected other ritual objects for idolatry as well. Thus, the narrator of 1 Kings states that Ahab did more to provoke YHWH to anger "than all the kings of Israel who were before him" (16:32–33). Jezebel hunted and killed the faithful prophets of YHWH and financially supported her own prophets of Baal and the goddess Asherah. This explains the continual conflict in the Northern Kingdom between the faithful prophets of YHWH (Elijah, Elisha, Amos, and Hosea) and the kings who supported the worship of Baal.

Elijah represents the third major development of prophecy prior to the prophets for whom we have books. He was a "covenant prosecutor"[4] who charged God's people with breaking God's covenant with Israel by worshiping other gods and abusing the poor and vulnerable. Whereas Moses often functioned as an intercessor, requesting YHWH's mercy for the people, Elijah *accused* the king and people of infidelity to YHWH. Therefore, we can see the combination of the roles of Moses (the spokesman with access to God), Samuel (the spokesman to the king), and Elijah (a covenant prosecutor) in the writings of the prophets who follow them (Isaiah–Malachi). This will be explored more fully in chapter 4.

Israel in the Eighth Century BC

With the death of the Assyrian king Shalmaneser III (824 BC), Assyria went into a period of decline until 745 BC. While Assyria was relatively weak and concerned with its own affairs in the east, Israel flourished. This coincided with the stable and long reign of Jeroboam II (793–753 BC). It was during this time that **Jonah** (2 Kings 14:23–25) and **Amos** (1:1) prophesied in the Northern Kingdom; **Hosea**'s ministry began at the end of the reign of Jeroboam II. During the next thirty years, the Assyrians began to expand and conquer territories once again, threatening to overturn the stability that Israel and its neighbors had briefly enjoyed.

The kingship in Samaria was also very unstable. Following Jeroboam II, Zechariah became king, but he was assassinated by Shallum. Shallum was assassinated by Menahem. He was followed by Pekahiah, who was assassinated by Pekah, who was in turn assassinated by Hoshea. This constant revolving door of illegitimate kings may be the reason that despite Hosea's long prophetic ministry in the Northern Kingdom, he dates his ministry by the reigns of the kings of the Southern Kingdom (see Hosea 1:1).

In the meantime, **Micah** (1:1) and **Isaiah** (1:1) were prophesying in Judah. Isaiah's call to ministry came in the same year that Uzziah, king of Judah, died (Isa. 6:1). Uzziah's reign had been prosperous and stable because of the absence of the Assyrians. But when the Assyrian king, Tiglath-pileser III, began to expand his empire aggressively to the west, the local kings were forced to decide whether they would submit and pay tribute, or whether they would form alliances and try to fight. Ahaz, the new king of Judah, was in favor of submitting to Assyria. But Pekah, king of Israel, formed an alliance with Rezin, the king of Damascus, to fight Assyria, and they asked Ahaz and Judah to join them. When Ahaz refused, they attacked Judah in an attempt to remove him from the throne and replace him with a new king whom they could control. This is the backdrop for Isaiah's interactions with Ahaz in Isaiah 7–11.

When Pekah of Israel rebelled against the Assyrians, they came and conquered most of the Northern Kingdom, taking many captives into exile and appointing the last king, Hoshea, to the throne. Israel became an Assyrian province. Finally, Hoshea rebelled, and the Assyrians were out of patience. They besieged Samaria for three years, and the city fell in 722 BC, marking the end of the Northern Kingdom. Many people were sent into exile, where they were lost to history. Others from Israel, perhaps including the prophet Hosea, fled as refugees to Judah.

At this time, Hezekiah was on the throne in Jerusalem. He was faithful to YHWH and carried out religious reforms throughout Judah, destroying pagan idols and worship centers. Although his father, Ahaz, had submitted to Assyria, Hezekiah rebelled in 705 BC. Knowing that the Assyrians would respond with brutal force, he immediately began to prepare for the inevitable invasion by constructing a massive new wall (to fend off Assyrian battering rams) and an underground tunnel to bring fresh water from outside the city walls into Jerusalem, a necessity in time of siege. When Sennacherib, the new king of Assyria, arrived, he devastated the cities of Judah and besieged Jerusalem. However, at Isaiah's urging, Hezekiah trusted in YHWH rather than looking elsewhere for help. In response, YHWH destroyed the Assyrian army and had Sennacherib killed when he returned home (Isa. 37:36–38).

Israel in the Seventh Century BC

In the seventh century, the Northern Kingdom was already destroyed, and the Southern Kingdom remained alone. Judah and its neighbors Ammon, Moab, and Edom maintained some independence as vassals under the control of Assyria, but the nations to the west and north, including Israel, became provinces of Assyria (see map 3.2).

© Baker Publishing Group

Map 3.2. Judah remains alone

In 640 BC, Josiah became king of Judah at the age of eight when his father, Amon, was assassinated by his own servants. Unlike his father, Josiah followed the example of his ancestor David and remained faithful to God's covenant with Israel. When Josiah ordered repairs on the temple in Jerusalem, the high priest discovered a book of the law (possibly the book of Deuteronomy) and read it to the king (2 Kings 22:8–10). When Josiah heard it, he tore his clothes, realizing that Judah had not obeyed YHWH's covenant (22:11–13). As a result, he initiated a substantial religious reform in Judah and Jerusalem, destroying images, chopping down altars to Baal, and burning the bones of the idolatrous priests (2 Chron. 34:1–7). However, in spite of his efforts, the people and leadership of Judah quickly reverted to their unfaithfulness. It was during this time that the prophets **Zephaniah** (1:1) and **Jeremiah** (1:1) began their ministries. Josiah's attempts to revive obedience to the book of the law and the reform's impermanence set the scene for Jeremiah's proclamation that the people had broken the covenant and that only a "new covenant" would effectively restore them to the Lord.

In 612 BC, Nineveh, the capital city of Assyria, fell to the Neo-Babylonian Empire after a three-month siege.[5] This fulfilled the primary message of the prophet **Nahum**, who used the destruction of Nineveh and its king as an example of God's judgment against all who oppose him. As the Chaldeans (to the northeast of Israel) were ascending as the military superpower in the ancient Near East, Egypt was growing strong and asserting influence on the other side of Israel (to the southwest). After Josiah died, Egypt took control of Judah, removed the new king, Jehoahaz, from the throne in Jerusalem, and installed Jehoiakim in his place. Judah and its neighbors were caught in the middle of this power struggle. This situation and the constant anxiety it caused are reflected in the prophet **Habakkuk**, who was troubled by the violence and unfaithfulness that he saw in Judah (1:2–4). YHWH responded that he was raising up the Chaldeans, who would be his instrument of judgment against Judah (1:6). In the period of the Old Testament prophets, "Chaldeans" and "Babylonians" refer to the same group—the rising empire in the east.

Israel in Exile

In 605 BC, the Chaldeans came west and fought the great Battle of Carchemish against Egypt and what was left of the Assyrian forces. They defeated the pharaoh and pursued the Egyptian army all the way back to Egypt. On the way through Judah, King Nebuchadnezzar stopped in Jerusalem and received tribute (i.e., a "payoff") from Jehoiakim. Nebuchadnezzar also took a first group of captives into exile, including the prophet **Daniel** and his three friends (1:1–7). Daniel lived and prophesied in Babylon for almost twenty years before Jerusalem was finally destroyed in 586 BC. This destruction began the (approximately) seventy years of exile that Jeremiah had predicted (Jer. 25:11).

King Jehoiakim had paid tribute to Nebuchadnezzar for several years, but he was pro-Egypt since the pharaoh had originally placed him on the throne. When Nebuchadnezzar was occupied elsewhere, Jehoiakim rebelled against Babylon. It was not long before Nebuchadnezzar came to Judah with his army and besieged Jerusalem. During the siege, Jehoiakim died and his son Jehoiachin came to the throne, but only for three months. In early 597 BC, Nebuchadnezzar captured the city, set a new king on the throne (Zedekiah, Jehoiachin's uncle), and took Jehoiachin into captivity along with the prophet **Ezekiel** and many others. This was the second deportation. Ezekiel dates his call to prophetic ministry to the fifth year of King Jehoiachin's exile, which would be 593/592 BC (1:2). Like

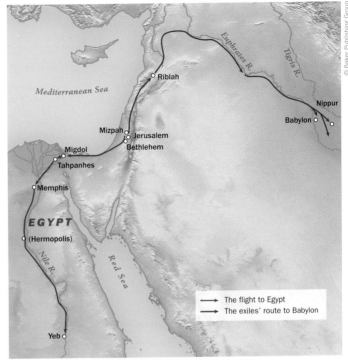

Map 3.3. The exile to Babylon and the flight to Egypt (586 BC)

Daniel, Ezekiel prophesied in Babylonia—in exile—while the prophet Jeremiah was still delivering God's messages back in Jerusalem.

Jeremiah continued to warn the people of Jerusalem and Judah that the end was near. In Jeremiah 19:3, he proclaims, "Thus says the LORD of hosts, the God of Israel: Behold, I am bringing such disaster on this place that the ears of everyone who hears of it will tingle." This deeply unpopular message was rejected by Zedekiah and his advisers, and they persecuted Jeremiah, but his word came to pass. King Zedekiah rebelled against Nebuchadnezzar (even though Nebuchadnezzar had placed him on the throne), triggering a final Babylonian invasion and siege of Jerusalem. The people inside the city starved and suffered to the point that they ate their own children (Lam. 4:10), a fulfillment of the covenant curse in Deuteronomy 28:53. In 586 BC, the city fell. The Babylonians tore down the temple, razed the city, and carried its inhabitants into exile. They killed Zedekiah's sons, blinded him, and then took him into captivity as well (2 Kings 25:7). Meanwhile, in Babylonia, a fugitive from Jerusalem arrived and told Ezekiel that the city had fallen (Ezek. 33:21).

During the Babylonian assault on Jerusalem, the Edomites cheered on the devastation of YHWH's people. The nation of Edom, Judah's neighbor to the southeast, was descended from Esau, Jacob's (Israel's) twin brother. In light of this, the prophet **Obadiah** proclaims a short but blistering condemnation of Edom's behavior, announces judgment on them, and uses them as an example of God's ultimate victory—realized by both the salvation of his people and the destruction of his enemies.

Some Judahites fled to Egypt and settled there, while many were taken to Babylonia (see map 3.3). Back in Jerusalem, Nebuchadnezzar chose an official of Judah named Gedaliah to be governor over the conquered territory. The same year that he was installed, however, a group of Judahites assassinated him. Knowing that the Babylonians would retaliate against them, they fled to Egypt and took the prophet Jeremiah with them, even though he told them this was not God's desire (Jer. 43:1–7).

We do not have much information about life in exile, but it seems that life was somewhat pleasant in Babylon for the people from Judah. There is evidence that the exiles were not mistreated; in fact, some rose to high positions in the government and the military. Nevertheless, they remained distinct and lived in their own communities (see Ps. 137 for the concern that they would assimilate into the culture). In what had been Judah, by contrast, Jerusalem and the other cities were in ruins, the economy was in shambles, the people were poor, and the temple had been destroyed.

Israel in the Postexilic Period

When King Nebuchadnezzar died in 562 BC, the Neo-Babylonian Empire began a slow decline through a series of weaker kings. Finally, Nabonidus came to the throne in 555 and ruled for seventeen years. He was unpopular with some in the empire because he promoted his own patron deity over the Babylonian god Marduk and refused to participate in Marduk's New Year's festival. He also spent at least ten years away from the capital city. Nabonidus's son Belshazzar ruled as coregent while he was away, but he was a weak and ineffective leader (see Dan. 5). Therefore, when King Cyrus of the Persians began to expand his territory, Babylon was vulnerable.

In 539 BC, Cyrus entered Babylon without a fight, perhaps aided from the inside by some of those who were unhappy with Nabonidus. This was a major turning point in the history of the ancient Near East. Just as Babylon had replaced Assyria as the major power at the end of the seventh century, now Persia had replaced Babylon. Persia gained control over what had been the entire Neo-Babylonian Empire, from the Tigris River in Mesopotamia to the Sinai Peninsula in Egypt (see map 3.4).

It was Cyrus's general policy to allow exiled peoples to return to their homes. No doubt this was a political calculation designed to secure the

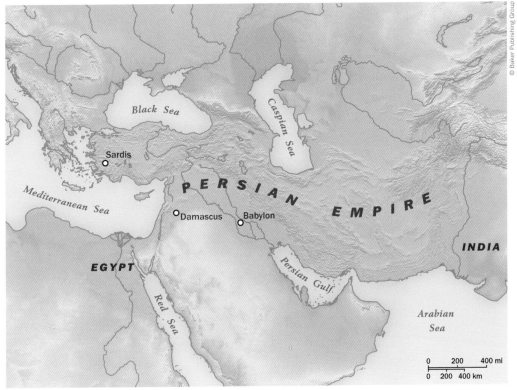

Map 3.4. The extent of the Persian Empire

loyalty of his diverse subjects. In the "Cyrus Cylinder," a famous text inscribed on a barrel-shaped cylinder of clay, Cyrus decrees that not only did he return the peoples to their places but he also reestablished their places of worship. Evidently, similar decrees were made to various people groups in the empire, including the exiles from Judah. A version is recorded in 2 Chronicles 36:23 (see also Ezra 1:2–3): "Thus says Cyrus king of Persia, 'The LORD, the God of heaven, has given me all the kingdoms of the earth, and he has charged me to build him a house at Jerusalem, which is in Judah. Whoever is among you of all his people, may the LORD his God be with him. Let him go up.'"

The Persian Empire was divided into twenty regions called satrapies, which were in turn divided into smaller provinces. The province around and including Jerusalem was called Yehud, which is where the word "Jew" comes from (see map 3.5). When given the choice, however, many exiles from Judah chose to stay in Babylonia/Persia rather than return to their homeland. They were comfortable and secure, and it was the only home that the younger generation had known. But a small group, motivated by loyalty to YHWH and faith in his purposes, chose to return to the land after Cyrus's decree. They returned to the land in several waves. The first

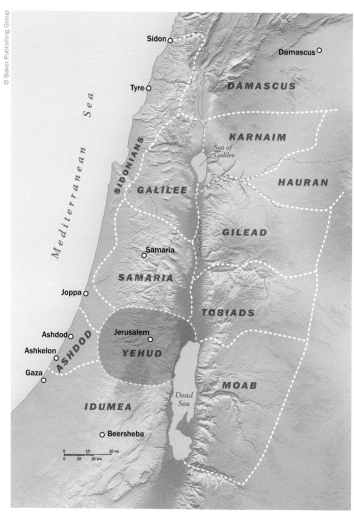

Map 3.5. Palestine in the Persian Empire

return in 538/537 BC, led by Sheshbazzar, comprised a small group (Ezra 1:8).

Another group of exiles returned to the land led by Joshua the priest and Zerubbabel. They built an altar to YHWH, initiated sacrifices, and in 536 BC laid the foundations of a new (second) temple. Then, for the next sixteen years, from 536 to 520 BC, the work stopped. This was partly due to conflicts with the surrounding peoples in the land who wanted to share in the building of the temple. When Zerubbabel and Joshua rejected their help, they intimidated the people of Judah and even wrote an accusation against them to the Persian authorities (Ezra 4:1–16). The king responded that the work must stop, as he did not want any more rebellions in the province (4:17–22). A second reason that the work on the temple stopped, according to the prophets **Haggai** and **Zechariah**, was that the people had misplaced priorities and did not care as much about building God's temple as about improving their own estates (see Hag. 1:4). The word of YHWH came to Haggai in the sixth month of 520 BC (1:1) and to Zechariah two months later (Zech. 1:1). As a result of the preaching of these two prophets (Ezra 5:1), the people were motivated to complete the temple in 515 BC, twenty years after the foundations were laid (Ezra 6:15).

The date of **Joel**'s ministry is uncertain, but it is likely that he proclaimed his messages around this time in the postexilic period (see chap. 14). The last prophet in the Old Testament is **Malachi**. The dates of his ministry are also uncertain, but a likely range is 515–445 BC. Around this

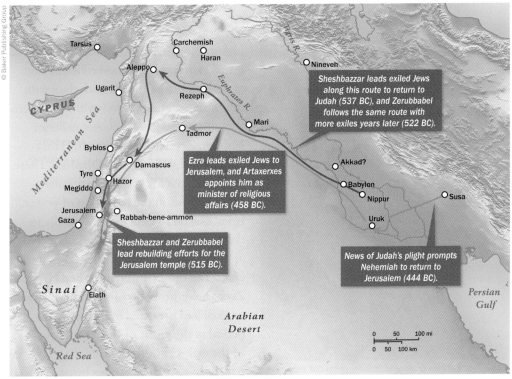

Map 3.6. The return of the exiles to Judah

time there were two more waves of exiles returning to the land. In 458 BC Ezra led one return to reform and reestablish worship and the public reading of the law of YHWH. Thirteen years later, Nehemiah, who was living in Persia, heard that the walls of Jerusalem were broken down, leaving the city defenseless. He secured permission and funding from the king and led another return to the land to rebuild the walls, arriving in 444 BC (see map 3.6).

Conclusion

Geographically, the prophets were scattered across the promised land, and their messages sounded forth from every corner. Jonah and Hosea were from the Northern Kingdom, Amos was from Judah but ministered in the Northern Kingdom, and the rest of the prophets lived and ministered in Judah (see map 3.7).

Chronologically, the prophets were just as scattered. Looking at the "Time Line of the Prophets" in the front matter, perhaps you notice that the majority of the prophets served as spokesmen for YHWH in three clusters that center on key transitions in Israel's history. The first cluster

PART 2

The Old Testament Prophet

CHAPTER FOUR

The Role of the Old Testament Prophet

> Do not think that I have come to abolish the Law or the Prophets; I have not come to abolish them but to fulfill them.
>
> Matthew 5:17

In his Sermon on the Mount, Jesus references the "Law or the Prophets" as two authoritative collections in God's Word that speak to the great plan of redemption that culminates in himself. The law was given in a relatively short time to Moses at Mount Sinai when God created Israel as a nation and made a covenant with them. By contrast, as we saw in chapter 3, the prophets consisted of diverse men and women, from different regions and times, speaking to different situations and challenges. And yet Jesus states that they all have a unified message and agenda. Whatever they are saying in their own particular contexts, they are all contributing in harmony to one great message about the God who created the world, judges sin, and mercifully provides a way out of judgment by his grace.

What accounts for this unified voice within such diversity? The answer is that the prophets of the Old Testament are not speaking for themselves; they are speaking for God. They are his spokespeople, passing on messages that they have received from him. Even though they present those messages with their own voices, in their own circumstances, with their own personalities, they are representing one God. And because they are all representing the same God, the message is unified. In this chapter we will define "prophecy" in the Old Testament, consider the prophet's job description according to Deuteronomy 18:15–19, and observe some important trends in the prophets of YHWH as a whole.

"Prophet" Defined

In the book of Exodus, YHWH presents himself to Moses in a burning bush and calls him to go to Pharaoh and demand the release of all Israelite slaves. At this time, Moses is a fugitive and a shepherd in the middle of nowhere, and he is understandably uncertain about this task. He does not feel qualified, is not sure how the people will respond, and complains that he is not eloquent and will not be a good spokesman for God before the mighty Pharaoh (4:10). At this point, YHWH becomes angry and says, "Is there not Aaron, your brother, the Levite? I know that he can speak well. . . . You shall speak to him and put the words in his mouth. . . . He shall speak for you to the people, and he shall be your mouth, and you shall be as God to him" (4:14–16). Moses is the leader, but Aaron will serve as his spokesman. Moses will tell Aaron what to say, and then Aaron will repeat it. Later, when Moses again expresses his sense of insecurity, YHWH says, "See, I have made you like God to Pharaoh, and your brother Aaron shall be your *prophet*. You shall speak all that I command you, and your brother Aaron shall tell Pharaoh to let the people of Israel go out of his land" (7:1–2). This use of the word "prophet" illustrates its basic sense, that of a spokesperson or representative for someone else. Aaron is Moses's prophet, not because he is doing miracles or performing signs, but simply because he is repeating Moses's words to someone else.

When we talk about the prophets of YHWH, therefore, we can define a prophet in this way: a *prophet was chosen by God to receive his message and then to proclaim it to an audience in a particular historical situation.* The prophet is chosen by God, at God's initiative. He or she does not create the message but receives it passively from God. The prophet then proclaims the message to a particular audience even as it has ongoing relevance for God's people once it is incorporated into Scripture. We will expand on this definition as we investigate the prophetic pattern established in Deuteronomy 18:15–19.

The Prophet's Job Description (Deut. 18:15–19): True Prophets

In a key passage for understanding the job description and task of a prophet, Deuteronomy 18:9–22, Moses is speaking to the people of Israel as they are about to enter the promised land. He describes true and false prophets and warns the people to discern carefully the difference between them. The passage begins (18:9–14) and ends (18:20–22) with warnings against false prophets, which we will consider in the next chapter. In the center of the passage, Moses describes the true prophet in 18:15–19 by listing three characteristics of those who will teach God's true word:

> The LORD your God will raise up for you a prophet like me *from among you, from your brothers*—it is to him you shall listen—just as you desired of the LORD your God at Horeb on the day of the assembly, when you said, "Let me not hear again the voice of the LORD my God or see this great fire any more, lest I die." And the LORD said to me, "They are right in what they have spoken. I will raise up for them a prophet like you from among their brothers. *And I will put my words in his mouth, and he shall speak to them all that I command him.* And whoever will not listen to my words that he shall speak in my name, I myself will require it of him."

1. Called by YHWH (Deut. 18:15)

The first characteristic of the true prophet is found in verse 15: "The LORD your God will raise up for you a prophet." In other words, a true prophet is only the one who is called by YHWH. Because a prophet's primary purpose is to repeat YHWH's message, a person can only serve in that role if YHWH has taken the initiative and made the decision to call that person to do so. If YHWH does not choose to reveal a message, then what would there be for the person to do? Someone might decide on his own to become a prophet, and yet if YHWH has not chosen him, there will be no message to give unless he makes it up in his own head (we will discuss this scenario in chap. 5). 📜

In a number of cases, true prophets of YHWH do not even *want* to be called, daunted by the enormity of the task, their sense of personal inadequacy, or the inevitability of persecution. Like Moses, the prophet Isaiah understands his fundamental inadequacy. When YHWH reveals his glory and calls Isaiah to be a prophet, Isaiah responds, "Woe is me! For I am lost" (Isa. 6:5). Jeremiah's call narrative also sounds very similar to that of Moses. When YHWH says that he has appointed him as

Is Moses Predicting Jesus the Prophet?

Moses says, "The LORD your God will raise up for you a prophet *like me*" (Deut. 18:15). Because this is quoted in Acts 3:22 and 7:37, it is sometimes assumed to be a messianic prophecy. In this view, Moses has one particular prophet in mind—a prophet like him—who is Jesus. However, the context of each of these passages in Acts indicates that the quotation of Deuteronomy 18:15 refers to all the true prophets of YHWH. They are "like Moses" because he serves as the model for the prophetic role. First, in Acts 3:21, Peter is speaking to the crowd about the redemptive work of Jesus Christ, which is the climax of "all the things about which God spoke by the mouth of his holy prophets long ago." Then Peter quotes Deuteronomy 18:15, which says that Moses said YHWH would raise up a prophet like him. Peter continues, "And all the prophets who have spoken, from Samuel and those who came after him, also proclaimed these days" (Acts 3:24). Peter is talking throughout the passage about *all* the prophets of the Old Testament who have spoken about Jesus. Similarly, in Acts 7:37, Stephen quotes from Deuteronomy 18:15 in his attempt to show the crowd that they have rejected God's plan of salvation. He says in Acts 7:39 that the fathers refused to obey Moses, and a moment later he says the crowd is just like their fathers (7:51). In this case, Stephen is referring to Moses's prophetic authority as the prophetic model. If the fathers rejected Moses, then they rejected the prophets who came after him as well.

a prophet to the nations, Jeremiah responds, "Ah, Lord GOD! Behold, I do not know how to speak, for I am only a youth" (Jer. 1:6). YHWH responds that Jeremiah must not be afraid, for he will be with him (1:8). Ezekiel must have reacted similarly to his call, since YHWH tells him not to be afraid (Ezek. 2:6).

An instructive illustration is the prophet Amos's conversation with Amaziah, the high priest at Bethel, and the reference to his own calling. Amaziah tells Amos to stop prophesying against the idolatrous worship center at Bethel because "it is the king's sanctuary, and it is a temple of the kingdom" (Amos 7:12–13). In other words, Amos is on the king's turf, and the king does not want to hear what he has to say anymore. See how Amos responds in 7:14–16: "Then Amos answered and said to Amaziah, 'I was no prophet, nor a prophet's son, but I was a herdsman and a dresser of sycamore figs. But the LORD took me from following the flock, and the LORD said to me, "Go, prophesy to my people Israel." Now therefore hear the word of the LORD.'" Amos's point is that he did not call himself to ministry and therefore he is not the one Amaziah should blame for the bad news. He is only a messenger for YHWH! Amos is saying, "I'm not special! I was only a farmer, and YHWH called me to be a prophet and he told me what to say!" Then Amos repeats the message of judgment again. The point is that his lack of any professional background or qualifications to be a prophet actually serves to underscore his authority, because what he speaks has come from YHWH.

Because the prophets speak the words of YHWH, they are often deeply unpopular with their audiences. However, they are compelled to speak because their orders come directly from YHWH. In Jeremiah 20:7–9, the prophet laments over his prophetic ministry and admits that he is speaking against his will, but he is compelled to give the message that God has given to him.

> O LORD, you have deceived me,
>   and I was deceived;
> you are stronger than I,
>   and you have prevailed.
> I have become a laughingstock all the day;
>   everyone mocks me.
> For whenever I speak, I cry out,
>   I shout, "Violence and destruction!"
> For the word of the LORD has become for me
>   a reproach and derision all day long.
> If I say, "I will not mention him,
>   or speak any more in his name,"

there is in my heart as it were a burning fire
     shut up in my bones,
and I am weary with holding it in,
     and I cannot.

Jeremiah wishes that he did not have to say these things, and he is tired of being mocked and persecuted. But if he should attempt to refuse to speak, the word is like a burning fire inside, and he cannot hold it in.

The consequence of true prophetic calling is prophetic *authority*. These examples from Moses, Isaiah, Jeremiah, Ezekiel, and Amos demonstrate that the words given, no matter how unpopular, come from YHWH and therefore must be taken seriously and obeyed. The prophets are telling us, "I'm only the messenger! This is a word that comes directly from God. If you don't believe me, I am not the one you are rejecting, for I'm proclaiming it against my will."

2. A Member of the Lord's Covenant Community (Deut. 18:15)

The second characteristic of the true prophet is that he or she will be called "from among you, from your brothers." This means that a true prophet will be a member of YHWH's covenant community, a faithful follower. Of course, YHWH has the ability to speak through anyone or even anything. In Numbers 22:28–30, he uses a donkey to speak to Balaam. In 1 Samuel 28:12–19, he allows a medium to speak to Samuel (who is dead) in order to deliver a message to King Saul. In 1 Kings 13:20–22, a false prophet lies to a true prophet of YHWH and persuades him to come home with him. During the meal, YHWH really does speak through the false prophet and delivers a message. Nevertheless, although YHWH can speak in any way he desires, true prophets as a rule are those who come from within the covenant community.

3. Speaks a Message That YHWH Commands (Deut. 18:18)

The third characteristic of a true prophet is found in Deuteronomy 18:18: "I will put my words in his mouth, and he shall speak to them all that I command him." This means, as we have already mentioned above, that the true prophet speaks a message from God. The message does not come from his own observations, intuition, insight, judgment, or conclusions. It is not his own message; it is a message that came to him from God, and now he is simply passing it on.

A helpful analogy for the role of a prophet is that of a messenger, which can be illustrated by common ways of referring to messengers in the biblical text. Consider the following examples in table 4.1. The two columns on the left refer to standard, everyday situations in which someone asks someone to deliver a message. In the two columns on the right, two prophets deliver messages from God using the same pattern and even wording.

Table 4.1. The Speech Forms of Messengers and Prophets

	Genesis 32:3–5 *Messenger*	2 Kings 18:28–29 *Messenger*	1 Kings 21:17–19 *Prophet*	Amos 7:16–17 *Prophet*
1. Report of sending	Jacob sent messengers . . . to Esau his brother in the land of Seir . . .		Then the word of the LORD came to Elijah the Tishbite, saying,	
2. Commissioning of the messenger	"Thus you shall say to my lord Esau:		"Arise, go down to meet Ahab	
3. Summons to hear		"Hear the word of the great king, the king of Assyria!		Now therefore hear the word of the LORD. "You say, 'Do not prophesy. . . .'
5. Messenger formula	Thus says your servant Jacob,	Thus says the king:	'Thus says the LORD,	Therefore thus says the LORD:
6. Message	'I have sojourned with Laban.'"	'Do not let Hezekiah deceive you.'"	"Have you killed and also taken possession?"'"	'Your wife shall be a prostitute in the city.'"

Note: These examples come from Claus Westermann, *Basic Forms of Prophetic Speech* (Philadelphia: Westminster John Knox, 1967), 130–49.

This raises the question of inspiration, or how the prophets received the messages from God. When we talk about inspiration, we don't mean that the prophets were inspired in the way that a painter is inspired by a beautiful sunset or enters into some kind of highly creative state. In that case, the source of the inspiration is not always clear, and the artist does not always even know the meaning; it may be more of an emotion.[1] But a true prophet undergoes a different kind of inspiration. He or she knows that the word is from God, and the meaning of the words is understandable (though perhaps the prophet does not know the full implications). In the case of the artist, inspiration means that the content comes from within; in the case of the prophet, it means that the content comes from God.

The prophet is not the one who decides when the word of God will come; it is God who decides that. For example, in 2 Kings 4:27, a woman comes to Elisha in great distress, and Elisha does not know why. He says,

"She is in bitter distress, and the Lord has hidden it from me and has not told me." But later, the servant of the king of Syria complains that "Elisha, the prophet who is in Israel, tells the king of Israel the words that you speak in your bedroom" (6:12). Sometimes Elisha is privy to secret information (because God informs him), and sometimes he is not. At other times, God ceases to reveal his word because the people are sinful, as in the following examples.

> With their flocks and herds they shall go
>   to seek the Lord,
> but they will not find him;
>   he has withdrawn from them. (Hosea 5:6)

> Then they will cry to the Lord,
>   but he will not answer them;
> he will hide his face from them at that time,
>   because they have made their deeds evil. (Mic. 3:4)

> "Behold, the days are coming," declares the Lord God,
>   "when I will send a famine on the land—
> not a famine of bread, nor a thirst for water,
>   but of hearing the words of the Lord." (Amos 8:11)

God's means for inspiring the prophets are as diverse as the prophecies themselves. Sometimes prophetic inspiration is associated with music. Miriam (the female prophet) is known for singing a victory song with a tambourine and dancing (Exod. 15:20). In 1 Samuel 10:5, Samuel tells Saul that he will "meet a group of prophets coming down from the high place with harp, tambourine, flute, and lyre before them, prophesying." In this case, the "prophesying" might refer to some kind of ecstatic behavior rather than proclaiming a message from God, but there is a connection to music. Later, men in the time of David "prophesied with lyres, with harps, and with cymbals" (1 Chron. 25:1). The clearest example of music as a mechanism for inspiration is when the king of Israel asks Elisha for a word from YHWH. Elisha responds, "But now, bring me a musician." When the musician plays, "the hand of the Lord [comes] upon him" (2 Kings 3:15).

A second possible mechanism for inspiration is dreams. The Bible records a number of occurrences when God speaks to people in dreams (Gen. 20:3; 31:10, 24; 37:5; 1 Kings 3:5, 15). However, in many cases, dreams are *distinguished* from true prophecy. For example, when Saul inquires of YHWH, "the Lord [does] not answer him, either by dreams, or by Urim, or by prophets" (1 Sam. 28:6). Note that "dreams" and "prophets" are two separate sources of knowledge. Furthermore, in the Prophets, dreams are often associated with false prophecy. The following examples from Jeremiah illustrate this.

> The prophets . . . prophesy lies in my name, saying, "I have dreamed, I have dreamed!" (23:25)

> Let the prophet who has a dream tell the dream, but let him who has my word speak my word faithfully. (23:28)

> Behold, I am against those who prophesy lying dreams. (23:32)

> For thus says the LORD of hosts, the God of Israel: Do not let your prophets and your diviners who are among you deceive you, and do not listen to the dreams that they dream. (29:8)

Visions were often a means of inspiration. The entire books of Isaiah (1:1), Obadiah (1), and Nahum (1:1) are considered to be visions of the prophet. When God reveals his plans to Habakkuk, he refers to the revelation as a "vision" (2:3). Ezekiel has several key visions, including the presence of God in exile (1:1), a visit to Jerusalem (8:3), and his description of the new temple (40:2). God reveals mysteries to Daniel in visions as well (see 2:19; 8:1; 10:7). However, false prophets claimed to have received visions as well. God warns the people, "Do not listen to the words of the prophets who prophesy to you, filling you with vain hopes. They speak visions of their own minds, not from the mouth of the LORD" (Jer. 23:16; see also Ezek. 13:6).

In many cases, we are not told the mechanism of the inspiration. The text simply states that YHWH "says" something through the prophet. Furthermore, because the prophet is speaking on behalf of God, there is no sense of a two-step process in which the prophet first receives and then proclaims a message. Sometimes it is very difficult to tell the difference between the voice of the prophet and the voice of YHWH. For example, in the announcement of coming destruction on Judah in Jeremiah 4:19, is the speaker God or the prophet Jeremiah?

> My anguish, my anguish! I writhe in pain!
> Oh the walls of my heart!
> My heart is beating wildly;
> I cannot keep silent,
> for I hear the sound of the trumpet,
> the alarm of war.

The reference to strong emotions, a wildly beating heart, and the inability to keep silent would suggest that this is the voice of Jeremiah. However, previously in 4:6, he says, "I bring disaster from the north," which certainly must be God. And later, in 4:22, he says, "For my people are foolish; they know me not," which again sounds like it must be God speaking. One scholar uses the analogy of a symphony to describe this ambiguity.[2] The voice of God and the voice of the individual prophet meld together. As in music, one part may be in the foreground while the other recedes for a time. Yet together the two parts produce a work of power. In prophecy, the word of God is spoken through a person with emotional reactions, personal struggles, and distinct points of view.

As a symphony is cohesive, the prophetic word is a unified whole. If there are many prophetic voices but one divine voice behind them all, then we should rightly expect the diverse prophets each to contribute to a coherent and noncontradictory revelation of God's character and purposes. The divine origin of the prophetic word means that it is a unity.

If the true prophet's word comes from God, it must also be a word with authority. Moses concludes Deuteronomy 18:15–19 with this stark warning from YHWH: "Whoever will not listen to my words that [the prophet] shall speak in my name, I myself will require it of him." Jesus says something similar in Luke 11:49–51: "Therefore also the Wisdom of God said, 'I will send them prophets and apostles, some of whom they will kill and persecute,' so that the blood of all the prophets, shed from the foundation of the world, may be charged against this generation, from the blood of Abel to the blood of Zechariah, who perished between the altar and the sanctuary. Yes, I tell you, it will be required of this generation." Because the prophets proclaim the very word of God, that word is authoritative and binding. All who reject it will be held strictly accountable. Peter states the divine authority of the prophetic word explicitly in 2 Peter 1:21, "For no prophecy was ever produced by the will of man, but men spoke from God as they were carried along by the Holy Spirit."

Finally, the divine origin of prophecy means that the accountability goes both ways: just as the people are accountable to God for their response to true prophecy, the prophet is accountable to God for speaking or for failing to speak. This is most explicitly stated in God's instructions to Ezekiel (3:16–21). God uses the analogy of a watchman, whose job it is to warn a city of impending danger. If God announces to the wicked that they are under judgment but Ezekiel says nothing, then he will be held accountable in their place (3:18). However, if Ezekiel passes on the warning and the people reject it, then they are held responsible (3:19). Similarly, if Ezekiel fails to warn the righteous person to avoid evil and the righteous person does wrong, then Ezekiel will be held responsible (3:20). But if Ezekiel warns the righteous person and they sin, they are accountable for rejecting the message (3:21). In other words, the only thing that matters is *faithfulness*. The prophet is not held responsible for how the message is received, only for stating it accurately and faithfully. This is an important word to God's representatives today, especially pastors and teachers. We too have God's word, intended for the people under our care. And we too are responsible to proclaim the whole counsel of God, whether it is culturally acceptable and will make us popular or not.

True Prophets of YHWH in the Old Testament

Table 4.2 presents in general chronological order all prophets of YHWH who are specifically mentioned in the Old Testament. (A list of false or foreign prophets is provided in chap. 5.) The prophets from whom we have books are shaded.

Table 4.2. True Prophets in the Old Testament

Prophet	Special Note	Audience/Context	Reference
Abraham			Genesis 20:7
Miriam	*female prophet*	Israel	Exodus 15:20
Moses		Israel	Deuteronomy 18:15; 34:10
Deborah	*female prophet*	Israel	Judges 4:4
(no name)		Israel	Judges 6:8
Samuel	"prophet"/"seer"	Israel	1 Samuel 3:20–4:1; 9:19
(no names)	*group*	near Gibeath-elohim	1 Samuel 10:5
Saul		people of Gibeah	1 Samuel 10:10–13
(no names)	*group*	near Naioth in Ramah	1 Samuel 19:20–24
Gad	"seer"	David	1 Samuel 22:5; 2 Samuel 24:11
Nathan		David	2 Samuel 7:2; 1 Kings 1:11–37
David		Israel	Acts 2:30
Zadok	"seer"	David	2 Samuel 15:27
Heman	"seer"	David	1 Chronicles 25:5
Asaph	"seer"	David	2 Chronicles 29:30
Jeduthun	"seer"	David	2 Chronicles 35:15
Ahijah		Jeroboam	1 Kings 11:29; 14:1–16
Iddo	"seer"	Jeroboam	2 Chronicles 9:29
(no name)	"man of God"	Jeroboam	1 Kings 13:1

Prophet	Special Note	Audience/Context	Reference
(no name)		"man of God"	1 Kings 13:11, 20
Shemaiah		Rehoboam	2 Chronicles 12:5
Hanani	"seer"	Asa	2 Chronicles 16:7
Jehu the son of Hanani		Baasha	1 Kings 16:1–7
Elijah		Ahab	1 Kings 17:1
Elisha		Ahab	1 Kings 19:16
(no name)		Ahab	1 Kings 20:13
(no name)		Ahab	1 Kings 20:35
Micaiah		Ahab, Jehoshaphat	1 Kings 22:7–8
Jehu the son of Hanani		Jehoshaphat	2 Chronicles 19:2
Eliezer		Jehoshaphat	2 Chronicles 20:37
"sons of the prophets"	*group*	Elijah and Elisha	2 Kings 2:3, 5, 7, 15
Zechariah the son of Jehoiada		Joash	2 Chronicles 24:20
(no name)		Amaziah	2 Chronicles 25:15
Jonah		Jeroboam II	2 Kings 14:25
Amos	"prophet"/"seer"	Uzziah, Jeroboam II	Amos
Hosea		Uzziah–Hezekiah	Hosea
Micah		Jotham–Hezekiah	Micah
Oded		Ahaz	2 Chronicles 28:9
Isaiah		Uzziah–Hezekiah	2 Kings 19:1–2; Isaiah
(no name)	*female prophet*	wife of Isaiah	Isaiah 8:3
(no names)	*group/"seer"*	Manasseh	2 Kings 21:10–15; 2 Chronicles 33:18
Nahum		Nineveh	Nahum
Huldah	*female prophet*	Judah	2 Kings 22:14; 2 Chronicles 34:22
Zephaniah		Josiah	Zephaniah
Jeremiah		Josiah–Zedekiah	2 Chronicles 36:12; Jeremiah
Uriah		Jehoiakim	Jeremiah 26:20–23
Habakkuk		Judah	Habakkuk
Daniel		Babylon	Daniel
Ezekiel		Babylon	Ezekiel
Obadiah		Edom	Obadiah
Haggai		Yehud/Judah	Haggai
Zechariah		Yehud/Judah	Zechariah
Malachi		Yehud/Judah	Malachi
Joel		Israel; uncertain	Joel

Several important observations can be made in light of this data. First, prophecy is not an isolated or rare phenomenon, particularly in the Old Testament. In the previous chapter we located the sixteen prophetic books in relation to the major turning points in Israel's history. However, this table reveals that there were many more prophets who spoke for YHWH when called on.

Second, note that in a number of cases, we are not given the prophet's name. Beyond that, if we examine the individual passages where these prophets appear, we find that many of them are not introduced at all, or, when they are introduced, we are given very little background about them. They appear in the narrative, speak or act, and then are not mentioned again. The text frequently keeps the focus on the *word of God*, rather than the one who gives it. We are told a good deal of information about Jeremiah, Ezekiel, Daniel, Hosea, and Jonah, but we know almost nothing about Joel, Obadiah, or Nahum.

Third, we mentioned above in chapter 3 that, beginning with Samuel, a true prophet often served as YHWH's spokesman to the king of Israel or Judah. For example, there are six prophets associated with King David and five prophets who served during the reign of King Ahab, though two are not named. Elijah was in continual conflict with King Ahab. The most extreme example of this is in 1 Kings when Elijah kills the prophets of Baal (18:40), and Ahab's wife Jezebel responds by making a solemn vow that she will kill Elijah by that time the next day (19:1). Elijah flees into the wilderness, despondent and feeling as though he is the only person left who is faithful to YHWH (19:10). YHWH responds, "Yet I will leave seven thousand in Israel, all the knees that have not bowed to Baal, and every mouth that has not kissed him" (19:18). We will see in the next chapter that the false prophets had a very different relationship with the king. They served *him* and sought to maintain his power and position rather than holding him accountable to God.

Fourth, we see in table 4.2 that female prophets play an important but relatively limited role in the Bible. Miriam leads the congregation in a song of victory after the escape from the Egyptians and later is mentioned with Aaron and Moses as a leader of the people (Exod. 15:20; Mic. 6:4). Deborah, who was a judge in Israel, is identified as a female prophet (Judg. 4:4), as is Isaiah's wife (Isa. 8:3). Finally, the female prophet Huldah lived during the time of King Josiah in Judah (2 Kings 22:14). Out of these four, only Huldah is presented as giving a prophetic word from YHWH (2 Kings 22:15–20). This is not to say that the other women did not give prophetic messages, but the text is silent on this. There is an additional reference to female prophets in Joel 2:28, but this is a prediction about the future "latter days" (see chap. 6). The New Testament makes two references to female prophets: Anna, the elderly woman who greets the infant Jesus in the temple (Luke 2:36), and the four daughters of Philip (Acts 21:8–9). There are female false prophets in the Bible as well, but we will consider them in the next chapter. We do not know why there were so few female prophets and can only observe that the biblical authors reference them, like Huldah, without any additional explanation or apparent surprise.

Fifth, in addition to individual prophets called by YHWH, some prophets apparently lived and worked in groups. In the text, these are referred to as a "company of prophets" or the "sons of the prophets." The first of these groups occurs during the time of King Saul (1 Sam. 10:5; 19:20–24). It is not clear that they gave prophetic messages, since they are only presented as engaging in distinctive behavior (prophetic trances?) accompanied by musical instruments. The text also mentions multiple prophets who spoke God's word to King Manasseh (2 Kings 21:10–11). Most references to the "sons of the prophets" occur during the time of Elijah and Elisha. A number of passages suggest they were organized in groups of fifty (1 Kings 18:4; 2 Kings 2:7, 16). They seem to have lived together, since they mention taking meals together (2 Kings 4:38–41) and sharing quarters (2 Kings 6:1–7). But one of these prophets was married and had children (2 Kings 4:1). There is one passage in which one of these "sons of the prophets" gives his own prophetic message (1 Kings 20:35), but it seems that in other cases they may have served as assistants for the prophets rather than functioning in a prophetic role themselves. For example, in 2 Kings 9:1–4, Elisha sends one of the sons of the prophets to deliver his prophetic message to Jehu, the commander of the army. The young man is referred to as "the servant of the prophet" (9:4).

Finally, table 4.2 indicates that several different words are used to refer to prophets in the Old Testament. The most common is the Hebrew word *nabi'* (prophet), which occurs 317 times. This is the standard word for "prophet" and is not marked in the left-hand column ("Special note"). It may be derived or borrowed from the Akkadian word *nabū*, meaning "to call." A second word is *ro'eh* (seer), from the Hebrew verb meaning "to see." It occurs twelve times in the Old Testament and apparently refers to a person who sees what is hidden. The word may be an older term in the language. First Samuel 9:9 says, "Formerly in Israel, when a man went to inquire of God, he said, 'Come, let us go to the seer,' for today's 'prophet' was formerly called a seer." Samuel is called both a "prophet" and a "seer," so the words must have a substantial overlap in meaning. A third word, *hozeh*, is also translated "seer" in English. Like *ro'eh*, it is usually used of prophets who have direct interaction with a king. Other words are used to refer to prophets in the Old Testament as well, including "watchman" (Isa. 21:11; Hosea 9:8), "man of God" (Deut. 33:1; 1 Sam. 9:6), and "servant" (2 Kings 21:10; 24:2). Each of these words highlights an important function of prophets—to see what is hidden, to represent God before the king, and to speak to the people on God's behalf.

This thirty-thousand-foot view of the life of Old Testament prophets reveals that (1) prophecy was a significant part of the faith life of Israel; (2) the biblical emphasis falls on the inspired *words* of the prophet rather than his or her personal *identity*; (3) kings were often the intended audience of prophetic messages; (4) female prophets were uncommon but not unheard-of; (5) many prophets worked in groups; and (6) different names for the prophetic role highlight its different facets.

Conclusion

In the ancient world, gods were often believed to be mysterious and unpredictable, striking out at their people capriciously. Their will was unknown, so it was impossible to please them. In this context, it was not a given that God should create people with the capacity to know him or that he would reveal himself to his creatures. Nevertheless, when prophets within Israel's covenant community responded to God's call and acted according to the biblical pattern—boldly proclaiming God's message without human manipulation or regard for the personal cost—the invisible God of Israel stooped down to speak directly into Israel's circumstances. Through his true prophets, God told his people who he is, what he desires, how they can live and flourish, what will bring them harm, and how he will rescue them when they choose to rebel against him. We must not take for granted that God "reveals his thoughts to man" (Amos 4:13 CSB). It is a great gift that God raised up prophets to be his spokespeople.

Like so many gifts of God, the prophetic role is subject to distortion at the hands of the self-interested. It is to this distortion we now turn, examining the false prophets of the Old Testament, as well as prophecy among the nations around Israel. This will enable us to get a fuller picture of prophecy in the ancient world and throw into relief the uniqueness of YHWH's true spokespeople.

Christian Reading Questions

1. Read Hebrews 1:1–4. In what ways is Jesus's ministry consistent with the ministries of Old Testament prophets, and in what ways does he surpass them?
2. Which features of the prophetic job description are shared by all believers today? Which New Testament texts inform your answer?
3. Read Ezekiel 3:16–21. How does this analogy shape how you view your calling as God's representative?

CHAPTER FIVE

False Prophets and the Prophets of the Nations

Woe to you, when all people speak well of you, for so their fathers did to the false prophets.

Luke 6:26

I n the Gospels, Jesus tells his disciples that following him will require self-denial and even suffering in the present, but the future will be one of joy and ultimate satisfaction. In Luke 6:26 (quoted above) he warns that one aspect of this self-denial is that our faith will bring rejection from others. God's truth and his salvation in Christ are disruptive to the present order and are often unpopular and divisive. This may seem counterintuitive for the Christian who wants to be winsome and to represent a faith that is appealing to others. Do we not want people to think and speak well of us? There is always a temptation to soften the message and to omit the "unpleasant" parts rather than proclaiming the whole truth. In the short term, that may take off the sharp edges and make us more likable, but in doing so we put ourselves in dangerous company—the false prophets of the Old Testament. They said what their listeners wanted to hear for the sake of their own status, but they became enemies of God.

In the previous chapter, we focused our attention on the positive qualifications of true prophets of YHWH. In this chapter, we will continue to develop an understanding of the phenomenon of prophecy in the Old Testament by examining counterfeit prophets both inside and outside Israel. We will begin by discussing the remaining portions of Deuteronomy 18:9–22, which describes what true prophets are *not*. Following that, we will consider the characteristics of prophecy and divination in the nations surrounding Israel.

The Prophet's Job Description (Deut. 18:9–14, 20–22): False Prophets

As we noted previously, Deuteronomy 18:9–22 is a foundational passage for understanding Old Testament prophecy. As the people of Israel prepare to take possession of the promised land, Moses sets expectations for future prophets who will deliver God's word to them. In the center of the passage, verses 15–19, he states positively that the true prophet will (1) be called by YHWH, (2) be a member of YHWH's covenant community, and (3) speak a message from God rather than one that originated from within himself. If a prophet speaks for God, then he must be obeyed and followed. If he only *pretends* to speak for God, then his words must be rejected completely since he is a liar and a fraud. Therefore, it is crucial that the people know how to distinguish the true prophet from the false one.

The beginning and end of Deuteronomy 18:9–22 provide criteria for identifying a true prophet by describing a false prophet. Verses 9–14 prohibit (1) popular religious practices, like magic and divination. In the context of the following verses, there is a suggestion that false prophets are associated with such things. Verses 20–22 go on to state that the false prophet will (2) speak something that God has not commanded, (3) speak in the name of another god, and (4) speak a word that does not come true. Furthermore, the one who does these things (5) must receive the death penalty. Let us look at each of these characteristics in more detail.

1. Tempted to Practice Popular Religion (Deut. 18:9–14)

Moses introduces the passage on prophets by warning that Israel must have no part in pagan religious practices.

> When you come into the land that the LORD your God is giving you, you shall not learn to follow the abominable practices of those nations. There shall not be found among you anyone who burns his son or his daughter as an offering, anyone who practices divination or tells fortunes or interprets omens, or a sorcerer or a charmer or a medium or a necromancer or one who inquires of the dead, for whoever does these things is an abomination to the LORD. And because of these abominations the LORD your God is driving them out before you. You shall be blameless before the LORD your God, for these nations,

which you are about to dispossess, listen to fortune-tellers and to diviners. But as for you, the LORD your God has not allowed you to do this.

Moses states *seven times* in Deuteronomy 18:9–14 that true prophecy is completely distinct from these practices, and the prophet must not participate in them. He says, "You shall not learn to follow [them]"; they are "abominable"; "There shall not be found among you"; "Whoever does these things is an abomination"; the Canaanites are being punished "because of these abominations"; "You shall be blameless"; and "Your God has not allowed you to do this." It is impossible to mistake his meaning with such repetition. These practices are deeply offensive to God. Why is that?

While many of the practices were inherently sinful, such as child sacrifice, many were abominable because of their intended effect—manipulation of God. Following the reference to child sacrifice in verse 10, every practice that Moses mentions—divination, fortunes, omens, sorcery, charmers, mediums, necromancers (vv. 10–11), fortune-tellers and diviners (v. 14)—is a kind of divination. Whereas magic is the attempted *control* of the divine world, divination is concerned with obtaining *information* from the divine world. Both of these categories are connected to a society's view of the origins and composition of the world. They are rooted in the belief that there are various gods or powers in control of nature that can themselves be controlled and manipulated by people who know which strings to pull. These deities may have their own jurisdiction over various areas of the natural world or society or the actions of other people. If a person can find the right ritual or other motivation, the power of the deities can be used for one's own benefit.

If there are deities or powers that have secret information, that would be incredibly useful for anyone who had to make an important decision. Kings would consult omens and inquire of diviners before going to war, constructing a major public building, arranging a marriage, or making a treaty.[1] For example, Ezekiel 21:21–22 speaks of the king of Babylon using divination to decide where he will attack next: "For the king of Babylon stands at the parting of the way, at the head of the two ways, to use divination. He shakes the arrows; he consults the teraphim; he looks at the liver. Into his right hand comes the divination for Jerusalem, to set battering rams, to open the mouth with murder, to lift up the voice with shouting, to set battering rams against the gates, to cast up mounds, to build siege towers." This passage mentions three divinatory actions that the king takes to discern what he should do: shaking arrows, consulting teraphim (images or idols), and looking at a liver. These rituals indicate that he should go to Jerusalem, so he decides to attack there.

There were a number of different techniques for divination in the ancient Near East. The passage above refers to the king looking at a liver, a practice called *extispicy*. This was a complex and sophisticated system that involved "reading" the entrails of a slaughtered animal. The elaborate ritual began at the end of a day. During the night, divinatory specialists would recite prayers, asking a deity a specific question and requesting that he or she write the answer to it on the entrails of an animal that was to be sacrificed—usually a ram or a lamb. At sunrise, the animal was slaughtered and its lungs, intestines, heart, kidney, bladder, pancreas, spleen, and (especially) the liver were removed.[2] The expert would examine these organs, looking for deviations from what was normal. Was the organ in its usual location? Was it of normal size? Did it have unusual color or texture, parasites, holes, or protrusions? In this way, the deity revealed a message to the one who knew what to look for. Archaeologists have discovered clay models of sheep's livers in the cities of Megiddo and Hazor in Israel. Perhaps these were used for training purposes.[3]

Another technique of divination was *astrology*. Specialists would observe the sky, looking at the courses of the stars, the phases of the moon, and various eclipses. This may have been connected to astral religion, which was widespread in the ancient Near East. There are several references in the prophets to the worship of the sun, moon, and stars (Jer. 8:2; 19:13; Ezek. 8:16). Jeremiah 7:17–18 refers to the people making a fire and kneading dough to prepare offering cakes for the "Queen of Heaven."

Hydromancy was divination with water. It is uncertain how this was done, but in Genesis 44:5, the Egyptian steward tells Joseph's brothers that he uses his cup for divination (see also 44:15). *Necromancy* involved consulting the dead. Isaiah 19:3 says that the Egyptians "will inquire of the idols and the sorcerers, and the mediums and the necromancers." King Manasseh of Judah also practiced these things (2 Kings 21:6). *Rabdomancy* was divination with trees or wood. Specialists would listen for the rustling of leaves, look for shadows on trees, or observe unusual budding on twigs.[4] This also involved throwing sticks or wooden arrows to see how they landed (see the actions of the king of Babylon in Ezek. 21 quoted above).

Contemporary scholars tend to classify prophecy as a subcategory of divination, which then refers to any practice by which humans gain secret knowledge from the divine world.[5] Perhaps that is true in the nations surrounding Israel. However, the biblical claim is that true prophecy, in which an individual represents YHWH, is completely incompatible with divination. This is first because divination is rooted in polytheism. Second, divination is done at the initiative of humans to pry information from the gods, perhaps against their will. It is not a god communicating with a human; it is a human who is "wringing a secret from the gods."[6] Sometimes it was thought that a god might even punish a seer for finding out something that the deity wanted to keep hidden.[7] By contrast, the true prophet waits for YHWH to reveal a message. He serves YHWH, proclaiming what YHWH tells him to speak, when YHWH tells him to speak it. A prophet seeks to elicit human response to YHWH's commands, but a diviner demands the deity's response to human questions. It is a question of control, and who serves whom.

2. Speaks Something That God Has Not Commanded (Deut. 18:20)

The last three verses of Deuteronomy 18, verses 20–22, tell the people of Israel how to recognize a false prophet:

> "But *the prophet who presumes to speak a word in my name that I have not commanded him to speak*, or who *speaks in the name of other gods*, that same prophet shall die." And if you say in your heart, "How may we know the word that the LORD has not spoken?"—when a prophet speaks in the name of the LORD, *if the word does not come to pass or come true*, that is a word that the LORD has not spoken; the prophet has spoken it presumptuously. You need not be afraid of him.

Recall that one of the characteristics of the true prophet is that "he shall speak to them all that I [God] command him" (Deut. 18:18). By contrast, the false prophet speaks something that YHWH has not commanded (18:20). This may mean that the false prophet speaks the opposite of what YHWH has said, or it may mean that the false prophet speaks a message that YHWH never gave to him. In either case, he is claiming to represent YHWH authoritatively, but the message did not originate with YHWH. One might say that this is the definition of false prophecy. Let us look briefly at two narratives from the biblical text.

A fascinating (though somewhat complicated) story in 1 Kings 13 illustrates the difficulty—but the necessity—of knowing what YHWH has actually said. A "man of God" (a prophet) travels from Judah to the Northern Kingdom to deliver a message to the king (13:1–3). Afterward, the king invites him home for refreshment, but the man of God refuses: "I will not eat bread or drink water in this place, for so was it commanded me by the word of the LORD, saying,

THEOLOGICAL ISSUES

What about the Urim and Thummim?

Divination, as practiced by the surrounding nations, is strictly prohibited in Scripture (see Lev. 19:26, 31; 20:6, 27). However, when YHWH established the priesthood as a part of the covenant with Israel, he gave instructions for the Urim and Thummim to be placed in the breastplate of the high priest (Exod. 28:30; Lev. 8:8). It is uncertain what these were exactly or how they functioned. The mechanism was an invitation for the civil ruler to inquire of YHWH when he needed guidance.[a] However, YHWH did not always answer (see 1 Sam. 14:37), and sometimes the answer was more than a basic yes or no (see 1 Sam. 10:22). There is no evidence that the Urim and Thummim were used after the time of David. Unlike divination generally, they were instituted by YHWH through the priesthood, and he chose whether or not to speak.

'You shall neither eat bread nor drink water nor return by the way that you came'" (13:8–9). Apparently, YHWH had given him strict instructions not to eat or drink while on his mission. But later an old prophet, who lives in Bethel, finds the man of God sitting under a tree by the side of the road and invites him to come home to eat. Again, the man of God refuses because of his instructions from YHWH. The old prophet responds with a lie, that YHWH told *him* (through an angel) to invite the man of God back to his home for a meal (13:18). Now there is a conflict: who is speaking the true word of YHWH? On the one hand, the man of God knows what YHWH told him; on the other hand, the old prophet is making a claim that sounds authoritative (and the man of God is hungry). The man of God goes with the old man, and they sit down to the meal (13:19). However, during the meal, YHWH speaks again to the man of God, this time through the old prophet who moments before had lied (13:20–22). YHWH says that the man of God will not return home alive because he has been disobedient. The man of God saddles his donkey and starts on the way, but a lion meets him on the road and kills him. Interestingly, in the course of this narrative, the old prophet comes to realize the seriousness and authenticity of God's true word (13:32). The word of YHWH is not always easy to discern, but it is crucial that we do so, for it must be obeyed without exception.

A second illustration of false prophecy comes from 2 Chronicles 18. The king of Israel and the king of Judah meet in Samaria and agree that they will go up to fight against a city called Ramoth-gilead, their common enemy. However, the king of Judah first wants to inquire of YHWH to see if this is wise.

The king of Israel assembles four hundred prophets and asks them what the kings should do. They all respond confidently, "Go up, for God will give it into the hand of the king" (18:5). The great number, combined with their unanimity and solidarity, certainly makes them sound authoritative. However, as is often the case with false prophets, they are telling the king what they think he wants to hear.

For some reason, in spite of this overwhelming agreement, the king of Judah is not convinced. He

William Blake's *The Marriage of Heaven and Hell*

William Blake, a British poet and painter who lived from 1757 to 1827, believed that the Old Testament prophets were merely guessing at the mysteries that lie in humanity and in the universe and were simply conveying their own thoughts on these subjects. In his work *The Marriage of Heaven and Hell* he imagines having dinner with Isaiah and Ezekiel:

The Prophets Isaiah and Ezekiel dined with me, and I asked them how they dared so roundly to assert that God spoke to them; and whether they did not think at the time that they would be misunderstood, and so be the cause of imposition.

Isaiah answered: "**I saw no God, nor heard any,** in a finite organical perception, but my senses discovered the infinite in everything, and as I was then persuaded, and remain confirmed, that the voice of honest indignation is the voice of God, I cared not for the consequences, but wrote."[c]

In other words, the prophets' firm conviction, nothing more, is the basis for what they say. However, this is a better description of false prophets in the Old Testament. The consistent biblical claim is that the true prophets of YHWH speak only what has first been revealed to them.

wonders if there is another prophet they might ask. It sounds ridiculous to suggest that it is prophet number 401 who will tell the truth but, ironically, this is actually the case. However, the king of Israel has had negative experiences with this prophet: "And the king of Israel said to Jehoshaphat, 'There is yet one man by whom we may inquire of the LORD, Micaiah the son of Imlah; but I hate him, for he never prophesies good concerning me, but always evil'" (18:7). Note that, in this statement, the king reveals the pressure on prophets to be "yes-men" who will ingratiate themselves and support the king's power. Nevertheless, the kings send a messenger to summon Micaiah.

The two kings are sitting on thrones at the entrance of the city gate, and the four hundred prophets are prophesying before them, proclaiming that there will be a victory in battle (18:11). As Micaiah approaches, the messenger tells him, "Behold, the words of the prophets with one accord are favorable to the king. Let your word be like the word of one of them, and speak favorably" (18:12). The pressure on Micaiah increases; now, behind the scenes, he is being told what to say so as not to anger the kings. But Micaiah responds, "As the LORD lives, what my God says, that I will speak" (18:13). That is the task of a true prophet.

Jeremiah speaks about false prophets who say only what reinforces the status quo, a message that God has not commanded. "They say continually to those who despise the word of the LORD, 'It shall be well with you'; and to everyone who stubbornly follows his own heart, they say, 'No disaster shall come upon you'" (23:17). And "I did not send the prophets, yet they ran; I did not speak to them, yet they prophesied" (23:21). Similarly, Ezekiel prophesies against the prophets of Israel who "prophesy from their own hearts" and "who follow their own spirit, and have seen nothing!" (13:2–3). "They say, 'Declares the LORD,' when the LORD has not sent them, and yet they expect him to fulfill their word" (13:6).

3. *Speaks in the Name of Another God (Deut. 18:20)*

A second characteristic of the false prophet in Deuteronomy 18:20 is that, no matter how sincere or convincing he is, if a prophet speaks on behalf of a deity other than YHWH, he must be rejected. True prophets were frequently in conflict with the prophets and followers of other deities. The most famous example is the contest between Elijah and the prophets of Baal on Mount Carmel (1 Kings 18:17–40). Isaiah makes passionate arguments against idol worship (e.g., 40:19–20; 44:9–20). Hosea speaks against fertility religion (2:13), and Ezekiel critiques the followers of the god Tammuz (8:14).

Deuteronomy 13:1–3 warns that no matter how compelling a prophet is, even to the point of doing impressive miracles, if he represents other deities or encourages the worship of them, he is to be rejected. "If a prophet or a dreamer of dreams arises among you and gives you a sign or a wonder, and the sign or wonder that he tells you comes to pass, and if he says, 'Let us go after other gods,' which you have not known, 'and let us serve them,' you shall not listen to the words of that prophet or that dreamer of dreams." In other words, the most significant criterion for discerning between true and false prophets is not even miracles, but faithfulness to YHWH. This idea continues in the New Testament in 1 John 4:1–3: "For many false prophets have gone out into the world. By this you know the Spirit of God: every spirit that confesses that Jesus Christ has come in the flesh is from God, and every spirit that does not confess Jesus is not from God."

4. Speaks a Word That Does Not Come True (Deut. 18:22)

A true prophet speaks for YHWH—a God who is trustworthy, knows the future, and declares his thoughts to people (Amos 4:13). The true prophet speaks the very words of God, and he speaks only those words that God commands (Deut. 18:18). Therefore, when that prophet proclaims a message concerning something that will happen in the future, his audience can be assured that it will come true. If a prophet is speaking for YHWH, then he is just as capable of speaking accurately about the future (even the distant future) as about the past or present.

This capability is presented in Deuteronomy 18:22 as a test to discover a false prophet: "When a prophet speaks in the name of the LORD, if the word does not come to pass or come true, that is a word that the LORD has not spoken." The prophet's message is falsifiable. This does not refer to vague predictions like those found in a horoscope—"You will meet your goal today" or "A trusted friend will disappoint you"—which can never be verified. Rather, if the prophet states that something specific will happen in the future but it does not come true, then it will be obvious that the word did not come from God. And since the true prophet does not speak words that do not come from God (Deut. 18:20), the prophet whose word does not come true must be a false prophet. The following passages recognize the connection between fulfilled prophecy and authentic prophecy:

> And Samuel grew, and the LORD was with him and let none of his words fall to the ground. And all Israel from Dan to Beersheba knew that Samuel was established as a prophet of the LORD. (1 Sam. 3:19–20)

> As for the prophet who prophesies peace, when the word of that prophet comes to pass, then it will be known that the LORD has truly sent the prophet. (Jer. 28:9)

> When this comes—and come it will!—then they will know that a prophet has been among them. (Ezek. 33:33)

We must mention a few limitations to this test. First, note that the test is presented in the negative and only applies if the prophet makes a short-term prediction that *can* be verified. A prophet may not make a prediction at all. Or, he may make distant predictions that cannot be verified by his present audience because they will not happen for hundreds or even thousands of years. In these cases, the audience will have to wait and see, listening carefully and discerning. For this reason, it is common for prophets to mix short-term and long-term predictions together. This is not only an effective communicative strategy, it also allows the audience (or reader) to confirm the short-term prediction, thereby bolstering their confidence in the long-term prediction (for more on this, see chap. 7 below).

A second caveat is the possibility that a prophet's prediction is conditional—that is, that the outcome will depend on the response of the audience. For example, a prophet may call his audience to repent and announce coming judgment. However, if they repent, then that predicted judgment will not come to pass because YHWH shows mercy. Conditional prophecies are sometimes not explicitly announced as provisional. However, because YHWH always prefers to show mercy, he is usually willing to forgo the judgment. For example, Jonah tells the people of Nineveh, "Yet forty days, and Nineveh shall be overthrown!" (3:4). The people of Nineveh respond with great demonstrations of sorrow and repentance, and YHWH changes his mind.[8] An additional example comes from Isaiah 38:1, when Isaiah tells King Hezekiah, "Thus says the LORD: Set your house in order, for you shall die, you shall not recover." However, when Hezekiah prays to YHWH and weeps bitterly, YHWH sends Isaiah with a new message that he will give the king fifteen more years. In this case, Isaiah is not a false prophet. The prophecy was conditional, even though that was not explicitly stated at the outset.

Because false prophets were not actually hearing from YHWH, the most that they could hope to do was give vague messages or future predictions that seemed likely to occur. In Daniel 2, King Nebuchadnezzar insists that his magicians and sorcerers not only interpret his dream but tell him the contents of the dream first! The magicians are aghast, saying, "The thing that the king asks is difficult, and no one can show it to the king except the gods, whose dwelling is not with flesh" (2:11). The king, recognizing that they are frauds, orders their execution (2:12). Later Daniel tells the king that "there is a God in heaven who reveals mysteries, and he has made known to King Nebuchadnezzar what will be in the latter days" (2:28). Whereas the false prophet makes his best attempt at explaining something or giving advice, the true prophet speaks actual revelation.

Given that this test of true prophecy is so bold and unflinching, and given that the stakes are so high that failure incurs the death penalty (see below on Deut. 18:20), the biblical text is making the unambiguous claim that not only *can* true prophets predict the future, we should *expect* them to do so. Yet it is common among some biblical scholars to explain future predictions in the text as only *appearing* to be predictive. One common assertion is the false dichotomy that prophets are "forthtellers," not "foretellers." That is, prophets speak to their own contemporaries about their own contemporary situations, but they do not really speak about the future. While it is true that forthtelling is an important part of the prophetic task and message, this is a false dichotomy and reductionistic. Old Testament prophets clearly foretell the future; in fact, they mix together recitals of past history, commentary on present realities, and statements about the future. We will discuss this prophetic interplay of past, present, and future further in chapter 7.

A second common view is that prophets were able to predict accurately, in the short term, events that appeared likely. One scholar states that the prophets announced events that were "already on the point of coming to pass."[9] We have experience with this in our present day; pundits predict that a country will undergo regime change, or they use polling data to forecast the outcome of a presidential election. In other words, any insightful person in ancient Israel, with careful observation, might be able to anticipate the rise of a military power or the defeat of a wicked king. Perhaps someone paying attention would have been able to foresee that the Babylonians were on the rise and would eventually conquer Jerusalem. However, this possibility is undercut by the *absolute* nature of the criterion in Deuteronomy 18:22. It does not say that a prophet's predictions will come true most of the time. It says if they *ever* fail, then the prophet did not receive that message from God and therefore cannot be trusted at all. This is because the true prophets were not making educated guesses. The only way to get it right every single time is to speak the word of God, who knows the end from the beginning.

Third, some future predictions are explained by some scholars as actually having been made after the fact. If prophetic books are dated after the events that they describe, then what may sound like a future prediction is really a reference to the past. This is called *ex eventu* prophecy. For example, many scholars date the book of Daniel to the second century BC. Therefore, Daniel's predictions regarding the coming Persian and Greek empires would have actually already happened. Dating prophetic books is sometimes quite challenging, and the chronology has to be established on a case-by-case basis. However, it is important to recognize that books like Daniel *claim* to be making future predictions and are received as such by later New Testament authors.

Complicating matters further are the arguments that prophetic books went through a complex process of *redaction*. Redaction criticism is the scholarly attempt to identify later literary additions in the text. Perhaps a prophet gave oracles to his contemporaries and wrote them down in his own context, forming the core of a prophetic book. Later, an editor came along and added material here and there. More editors followed, adding material throughout the text in order to give it a new emphasis or to make theological clarifications until the book reached its final form. The idea here is that if what looks like a future prediction is actually located in a later literary layer, then it is not a prediction at all, because it did not come from the original prophet. As an illustration, let's say that I start a letter to my aunt, predicting that I will win my football game on Friday night. I write, "I'm sure that we will win!" but I do not send it. On Saturday morning, now that the game is complete, I add ". . . we will win 21–10!" My aunt is amazed that I was able to predict the score with such accuracy. However, while most of the letter was written before the game, that detail was added later. One scholar, for example, argues that the prophet Amos made a general prediction. Later, an editor came along and added historical facts that occurred after the prophet's lifetime. Because the editor does not identify himself in the text, the facts look original and predictive, but they are not.[10]

These three approaches are only some of the ways that scholars frequently explain predictive prophecy. They are serious attempts to wrestle with the text and arise from sophisticated and careful reasoning. However, it should be recognized that they go against the claims of the text. Furthermore, they allege behavior in the canonical Old Testament prophets that Deuteronomy 18 ascribes to false prophets. They insist that the prophets were not actually able to predict the future but did their best and sometimes presented their work as predictive when it was not.

5. Deserves the Death Penalty (Deut. 18:20)

Moses states in Deuteronomy 18 that the stakes in prophecy are extremely high, for someone is purporting to speak on behalf of YHWH, the God of heaven and earth. In 18:19, YHWH states that whoever will not listen to the true prophet, "I myself will require it of him." God expects his word to be obeyed, and those who hear that word from the prophets will be held accountable for it. In the case of a false prophet who claims to speak a word in God's name, it is the prophet who will be accountable. The text says simply, "That same prophet shall die" (18:20). He is a liar who will damage the faith and fidelity of the community. If his word were really from YHWH, it would have to be obeyed without question; but it is fraudulent, proclaimed for the prophet's own benefit. Not only must the prophet die, but his word is to be rejected (18:22).

Table 5.1 is a list of the false or foreign prophets specifically mentioned in the Old Testament. While the list is not long, there are many more general references to false prophets in the Old Testament. It is easy to understand why someone would be motivated to be a false prophet. There is a desire for power. It is a weighty thing to stand before people and say "Thus says the LORD" while they attend to one's every word. False prophets were also motivated by personal gain. Micah connects false prophecy with financial support, even implying that prophets would be in opposition to those who did not feed them.

> Thus says the LORD concerning the prophets
> > who lead my people astray,
> who cry "Peace"
> > when they have something to eat,

Table 5.1. False Prophets in the Old Testament

	Special Note	Audience/Context	Reference
(no names)	*group*	Ahab/Jezebel	1 Kings 18:19–40
(no names)	*group*	Ahab, Jehoshaphat	1 Kings 22:6
Zedekiah		Ahab, Jehoshaphat	1 Kings 22:11
(no names)	*group*	Jehu	2 Kings 10:18–19
Hananiah		Zedekiah	Jeremiah 28:1
Ahab and Zedekiah		Exiles in Babylon	Jeremiah 29:21
Shemaiah		Exiles in Babylon	Jeremiah 29:31–32
(no names)	*group; female prophets*	Exiles in Babylon	Ezekiel 13:17
Noadiah	*female prophet*	Nehemiah	Nehemiah 6:14
(no names)	*group*	Nehemiah	Nehemiah 6:14

Table 5.2. Prophets in Israel and the Ancient Near East

	Old Babylonian	Neo-Assyrian	Israelite (canonical)
Dates	1800–1700 BC	700–600 BC	1000–400 BC
Titles	*apilum/apiltum* (answerer) *muhhum* (ecstatic) *asinnum* (cult singer) *nabu* (ones called)	*raggimu* (proclaimer) *mahhu* (crazy, frenzy) *shelutu* (worshiper)	*hozeh* (seer) *ro'eh* (seer) *nabi* (called)
Deities	Speak for many gods and goddesses (e.g., Addu, Dagan, Marduk, Nergal, Shamash)	Speak primarily for goddesses (Ishtar, Mullissu)	Speak for YHWH alone
Mechanics of inspiration	Little information; mention of dreams, ecstasy	Ecstatic experiences; inability to prophesy if in right mind	YHWH speaks to the prophet; dreams, ecstasy very limited
Coherence of messages	Conflicting advice	Conflicting advice	Any conflicts indicate that one prophet is false
Gender	Equal numbers male and female	Majority female (speaking for goddess)	Vast majority are male
Message	Primary theme: support for the king Secondary theme: support for the temples and worship	Requests for attention to the priesthood and temple; focus on reassurance to the king	Application of covenant: focus on faithfulness, justice, and righteousness; message addressed to whole people or to king as representative
Relationship to divination	Divination is the preferred means of communication; prophecy is verified by divination	Little indication of verification (unless the message is unfavorable)	Divination is strictly prohibited; prophecy is verified independently
Relationship to king	Reassurance, warning of dangers, some complaints about king's neglect of a temple; financial support from the king	Primary concern is whether the word is favorable for the king, not whether it is true or false	Independent; anoint and depose kings; critique kings for covenant unfaithfulness

not done more for a particular deity or shrine.[19] In the Bible, true prophets of YHWH may be strongly associated with certain kings and interact with them in fundamental ways, but it is a relationship of accountability to a higher authority. The prophet is supportive of the king if the king is obedient to YHWH. If he is not obedient, then the prophet is a fierce critic because his ultimate loyalty is to YHWH.

Conclusion

We have seen in Deuteronomy 18:9–22 and throughout the Old Testament that false prophets, motivated by their own interests, support those who can benefit them (i.e., the king) and give messages that will bring them success. We see similar behavior among the prophets of the nations, who speak in the names of other gods (18:20). In doing so, these "prophets" are not simply giving an alternative viewpoint. They are perverting the true word of YHWH with counterfeit messages, or they are advocating faith in other deities.

The New Testament warns Christians that false prophets of various kinds continue to be a threat to the community of faith. An eyewitness to the truthfulness of Jesus, Israel's greatest prophet, the apostle Peter highlights the ongoing danger of false prophecy: "But false prophets also arose among the people, just as there will be false teachers among you, who will secretly bring in destructive heresies, even denying the Master who bought them, bringing on themselves swift destruction. And many will follow their sensuality, and because of them the way of truth will be blasphemed. And in their greed they will exploit you with false words. Their condemnation from long ago is not idle, and their destruction is not asleep" (2 Pet. 2:1–3). The stakes are high, the cost of deception is great, and prophecies don't weigh themselves. For this reason, Paul urges believers to "test everything; hold fast what is good" (1 Thess. 5:21). There will always be a need to distinguish between a faithful representation of God's word and the self-serving imitation designed to deceive. It is to the patterns of this true word of God that we turn in the next chapter, examining key themes in the messages delivered in the Prophets.

Christian Reading Questions

1. The "abominable practices" of the nations were offensive to God in part because they sought to manipulate him. In what ways do Christians today—whether purposefully or inadvertently—seek to manipulate God?

2. How were God's people to tell the difference between true and false prophecy? Which of these principles of discernment can be appropriated by believers today in weighing teaching?

3. Deuteronomy 18 identifies the death penalty as the appropriate punishment for false prophets. Why does false prophecy warrant such harsh punishment?

4. Read 1 Timothy 6:3–14; Titus 1:10–16; and Jude 10–23. What do these New Testament passages add to the biblical characterization of false prophets and teachers? How do they instruct believers to respond to false teaching?

CHAPTER SIX

The Message of the Prophets

And taking the twelve, he said to them, "See, we are going up to Jerusalem, and everything that is written about the Son of Man by the prophets will be accomplished."

Luke 18:31

In the New Testament passage quoted above, Jesus reflects on the message of the Old Testament Prophets and the common response to it. He suggests that, in spite of the diverse times, places, and circumstances in which they lived, the prophets spoke a unified message that includes his own actions and ministry. Furthermore, the prophets spoke about him hundreds of years prior, and yet "everything" will come to pass.

Having discussed the role of the prophet in chapter 4 and counterfeit prophets in chapter 5, we now turn to the message of the Old Testament prophets. Our objective is to consider five basic elements of the prophetic message and create some categories to which we can relate the various ideas that we will encounter in the chapters that follow. The goal is not to oversimplify the prophets or to be reductionistic. Of course, each prophet has a complex, distinctive message and unique audience. However, by recognizing some recurring patterns in what the prophets have to say, we will have something of a basic road map before we begin exploring individual prophetic books.

The Prophetic Message: Five Phases

It is commonly assumed that because the prophets are delivering a message from God, they are always predicting the distant future or revealing a new phase in God's plan of redemption. To be sure, these are important aspects of the prophetic message. However, a significant proportion of the prophets' attention is on the past and present. They are continually looking backward to what God has already done in the world and in Israel and describing how people in the past have responded to those acts. In addition, they are interested in the present: whether God's people are currently obeying the covenant and putting their faith in him.

In this section, we will examine various aspects of the message of the Old Testament prophets as they relate to five time periods relative to the prophet. First, the prophets function as covenant prosecutors and accuse the people of having failed to honor the obligations of YHWH's covenant with Israel in the past. Second, they announce YHWH's wrath on those who do evil and coming consequences in the near future. Third, they call the people to repent of their sin and to return to YHWH so that he will restore them from the covenant curses in the near future. Fourth, the prophets proclaim a greater restoration and transformation of the world in the distant future. They explain that this great transformation and renewal will come in the reign of a new Davidic king (a reference to the covenant with David). Through this new David, God will rule over all of his creation. Fifth, the prophets warn that there is a final eschatological judgment in store for the enemies of God.

Not all of the prophets address all five of these categories, and sometimes the prophets address other issues. But these five phases help us organize a good portion of what the prophets, as a group, have to say to their respective audiences. As we read through the Prophets, we will see these ideas arise again and again.

1. Accusation of Covenant Unfaithfulness (Past)

In a court of law, the prosecuting attorney represents the government. He or she brings charges against the defendant and produces evidence that a specific crime has been committed. Similarly, the prophets function as "covenant prosecutors," representing YHWH and producing specific evidence that the people have violated their covenant relationship with the God of Israel. Therefore, they rely heavily on God's prior revelation to Israel in the wilderness as they were headed toward the promised land.

Since the prophets depend on this wilderness revelation for their own messages, the historical relationship between the Pentateuch and the Prophets is important. The view among many biblical scholars is that the Pentateuch was not written by Moses, but by various individuals or groups over a period of hundreds of years. Beyond this basic assertion, there is no one explanation of the development of the text. Instead, there are many different complex and even conflicting views as to how many literary sources there were and how they were all put together into the "Five Books of Moses" that we now have. Furthermore, as we noted above, many scholars also assert that most of the prophetic books underwent later editing and development over a period of many years. They claim that while the original prophet is responsible for some of the material in the book, later writers added more material, changed the structure, and completed various editions of a book until it became the final version we have now.

These views can have a significant impact on the ways we understand the relationship between the Law and the Prophets. For example, the critical consensus states that King Josiah and his supporters did not "find" the book of the law (probably Deuteronomy) in the temple (2 Kings 22:8); rather, they *wrote* an early edition of Deuteronomy to support their religious and political agenda and then claimed that it was ancient and authoritative. In this reconstruction, Josiah's reforms are self-serving and deceptive rather than faithful to the covenant. This example highlights the critical perspective that, sometimes, when prophetic books refer to key ideas in Deuteronomy, either (1) they are participating in the *creation* of those Deuteronomic ideas, or (2) these prophetic references reflect additions to the prophetic book much later, after the Pentateuch was finally finished.

By contrast, the traditional evangelical view is that the Pentateuch was authored by Moses in the wilderness period after the Israelites came out of Egypt. This is based on the claims made in Scripture (e.g., Exod. 24:4; Num. 33:2; Deut. 31:9; Mark 12:19; John 1:45) and the overall narrative and progression of the biblical text. In this understanding, notwithstanding some necessary updating (such as replacing ancient city names with their contemporary versions and adding passages like the account of Moses's death in Deut. 34), Moses wrote the Pentateuch under God's inspiration in order to serve as the foundational charter of the nation at the beginning of Israel's history. It sets forth the covenant that YHWH made with Israel and the accompanying obligations to which God would hold Israel responsible as they settled in the promised land. Deuteronomy was discovered by Josiah's supporters, as the text states in 2 Kings 22:8, thereby triggering a *reform* rather than a *development* in Israel's religion. The prophets, beginning with those in the eighth century BC, are looking back and reflecting on the entirety of the law given to Moses, including the priestly material in Numbers and Leviticus and the ordinances in Deuteronomy. As they do so, it is clear that the people have consistently broken the covenant and have been unfaithful to YHWH as his particular people.

The essence of the covenant, and therefore the law, is summarized in Deuteronomy 6:5: "You shall love the LORD your God with all your heart and with all your soul and with all your might." Indeed, Jesus considered this to be the first great commandment (Matt. 22:37). Deuteronomy goes on to say that there is an inherent connection between loving God and obeying him: "And now, Israel, what does the LORD your God require of you, but to fear the LORD your God, to walk in all his ways, to love him, to serve the LORD your God with all your heart and with all your soul" (10:12; see also 11:1, 13, 22; 19:9; 30:16). However, the prophets are clear that Israel loves other things more than God. They love bribes (Isa. 1:23), foreign gods (Jer. 2:23–25), lies (5:31), and evil (Mic. 3:2).[1] The problem is partially due to Israel's willful ignorance: even birds know when it is time to migrate, but God's people do not know the law (Jer. 8:7). This is poignant in a context in which Josiah's workers had discovered the long-lost book of the law lying neglected in the temple.

Just as the people are to love God (resulting in obedience), a second general entailment of the covenant is that they are to love each other (resulting in ethical treatment and justice). It is difficult to find a more blunt command—and warning—than Exodus 22:22–24: "You shall not mistreat any widow or fatherless child. If you do mistreat them, and they cry out to me, I will surely hear their cry, and my wrath will burn, and I will kill you with the sword, and your wives shall become widows and your children fatherless." The requirement was justice: ensuring that each person received treatment without bias. The Israelites were not allowed to be partial in lawsuits, even to the poor (Exod. 23:3). They were to help feed the poor (Lev. 23:22) and were not to look for "loopholes" in the law (Deut. 15:7–11). They were not to oppress hired workers (24:14) or pervert justice for foreigners or widows or the vulnerable (24:17). Justice is not just a value that arises from social consensus—it is a divine concern that is rooted in God's character and expressed in his covenant. However, the prophets consistently accuse Israel and Judah of failing to reflect the values of God. They crush the poor (Isa. 3:14–15) and make prey of widows and orphans (10:2). The blood of the poor, whom they have oppressed and trampled, stains their clothing (Jer. 2:34; Ezek. 22:29; Amos 2:7).

Not only do the prophets accuse the people of breaking the covenant's general standards of love and justice; they also mention specific covenant obligations that have been violated. Table 6.1 lists the Ten Commandments in Exodus 20 and corresponding accusations in the Prophets.

The prophets also indict the people for more general violations of their covenant relationship with YHWH. One example of this is the prophetic accusation that the people have put their confidence in human power rather

Table 6.1. The Ten Commandments in the Old Testament Prophets

	Decalogue (Exodus)	Example References in the Prophets
1	Do not have other gods (20:3)	"Their land is filled with idols" (Isa. 2:8)
2	Do not make carved images, idols* (20:4–6)	"They . . . trust in carved idols" (Isa. 42:17) They provoke God to anger with carved images (Jer. 8:19) They serve other gods (Jer. 44:3) "With their silver and gold they made idols" (Hosea 8:4) "Its maker trusts in his own creation" (Hab. 2:18)
3	Do not take the name of YHWH in vain (20:7)	"There is swearing" (Hosea 4:2)
4	Keep the Sabbath (20:8–11)	One who keeps the Sabbath is faithful (Isa. 56:2, 4, 6; 58:13) Do not work on the Sabbath (Jer. 17:21, 24, 27) "I gave them . . . Sabbaths"; they rejected my laws "and profaned my Sabbaths" (Ezek. 20:12, 16, 24)
5	Honor parents (20:12)	"Father and mother are treated with contempt" (Ezek. 22:7) "The son treats the father with contempt, the daughter rises up against her mother" (Mic. 7:6)
6	Do not murder (20:13)	They "steal, murder, commit adultery, swear falsely" (Jer. 7:9)
7	Do not commit adultery (20:14)	"There is swearing, lying, murder, stealing, and committing adultery" (Hosea 4:2)
8	Do not steal (20:15)	They have false balances (Hosea 12:7)
9	Do not lie / give false witness (20:16)	"Woe to him who heaps up what is not his own" (Hab. 2:6)
10	Do not covet (20:17)	"They covet fields and seize them, and houses, and take them away" (Mic. 2:2)

*Other texts are connected to idolatry through the use of the same Hebrew word (ḥmd): Isa. 1:29 ("They shall be ashamed of the oaks [idol trees] that you *desired*"); 44:9 ("All who fashion idols are nothing, and the things they *delight* in do not profit").

than trusting in YHWH, who promised to fight for them (cf. Deut. 20:1–4). They have placed their trust in political alliances with powerful nations and in military strength. Isaiah 31:1 mentions both of these:

> Woe to those who go down to Egypt for help
>   and rely on horses,
> who trust in chariots because they are many
>   and in horsemen because they are very strong,
> but do not look to the Holy One of Israel
>   or consult the LORD!

In the book of Hosea, this trust in alternative sources of salvation is characterized as a kind of idolatry. The prophet says, "When Ephraim saw his sickness, and Judah his wound, then Ephraim went to Assyria, and sent to the great king. But he is not able to cure you or heal your wound" (5:13). In this case, Assyria was the greatest potential existential threat to Israel, and it was Assyria who eventually destroyed the Northern Kingdom! And yet the prophet laments that Assyria's power is so impressive that the kings of Israel still look to it for help in time of need. The prophets accuse Israel and Judah of trusting in their own resources and their own attempts to secure safety and prosperity. This lack of trust in YHWH was a covenant violation, for he had promised these things if they would only serve him faithfully (Deut. 28:7–8). However, they had chosen their own strength as a substitute god (Hab. 1:11).

A second problem is empty religious practice. YHWH explicitly requires sacrifice and pilgrimage and holy days in the covenant obligations. What is curious, however, is that the people are fastidious and even extreme in continuing to practice these things, even as they murder, steal, practice sexual deviancy, treat each other unjustly, and make idols. What accounts for the simultaneous swell in ritualism and downward spiral of morality? The answer is that they want to have it both ways. They are seeking to manipulate YHWH by giving him what they think he wants (sacrifices and pilgrimages) in order to gain his favor, while at the same time they do whatever their own desires dictate. However, the prophets proclaim that this is offensive to YHWH and will not work. The following passage in Isaiah is a good example:

> What to me is the multitude of your sacrifices?
>   says the Lord;
> I have had enough of burnt offerings of rams
>   and the fat of well-fed beasts;
> I do not delight in the blood of bulls,
>   or of lambs, or of goats.
>
> When you come to appear before me,
>   who has required of you
>   this trampling of my courts?
> . . . .
> When you spread out your hands,
>   I will hide my eyes from you;
> even though you make many prayers,
>   I will not listen;
>   your hands are full of blood. (1:11–12, 15)

It is remarkable that YHWH says "Who has required [this] of you?" The obvious answer is, he himself did, in explicit commands in the law! But that is not what he means. The reason for his rejection comes at the end of verse 15: "Your hands are full of blood." Why would he appreciate their outward worship if their wicked hearts are manifested in murder? This is an area where the prophets have much to teach the Christian church, for the propensity to focus on outward worship rather than obedience and true faith is common to all of us.

Finally, the prophets also bring charges against the nations surrounding Israel. Though they are not directly responsible to a national covenant like Israel, they are responsible to their consciences and to YHWH as the creator and one true God. Most of the accusations against the nations relate to either sinful pride or violence toward the poor and vulnerable. Regarding the former, Isaiah says, "I will punish the world for its evil, and the wicked for their iniquity; I will put an end to the pomp of the arrogant, and lay low the pompous pride of the ruthless" (13:11). Pride is a universal crime against God, charged against Philistia (Zech. 9:6), Moab (Isa. 16:6; Jer. 48:29), Edom (Jer. 49:16; Obad. 3), Tyre (Isa. 23:9), Assyria (Zech. 10:11), Babylon (Isa. 14:13–14), and Egypt (Ezek. 32:12). Likewise, the nations—no doubt because of their pride—mistreat those who cannot defend themselves. The best example of this is Amos 1:3–13, in which the prophet accuses nation after nation for their crimes: Syria, which "threshed" the people of Gilead with farm implements; Philistia, which sent a whole people into exile; Tyre, which delivered a whole people to Edom; Edom, who pursued his brother with a sword; and Ammon, which ripped open pregnant women. Thus, not only Israel but all the nations have fallen short of the standard that God set for them (cf. Rom. 3:23).

2. Warning of God's Judgment (Near Future)

Having produced evidence that the people have broken the covenant, the prophets announce that God's response is wrath. Unlike the wrath of the gods of the nations, God's wrath is never presented as unpredictable, irrational, or disproportionate.[2] However, his reaction to the disobedience of his people is characterized as emotional and affecting. It is a righteous anger, rooted in his established character and intensified by his love for the victims of sin, including the perpetrators themselves.

The prophets describe God's wrath as terrible and frightening. Jeremiah says, "At his wrath the earth quakes, and the nations cannot endure his indignation" (10:10). Similarly, Nahum asks, "Who can stand before his indignation? Who can endure the heat of his anger? His wrath is poured out like fire, and the rocks are broken into pieces by him" (1:6). Apart from repentance and submission, which is almost always offered and mercifully accepted, nothing can stop God's anger. Consider the following:

> Behold, the storm of the LORD!
>   Wrath has gone forth,

a whirling tempest;
    it will burst upon the head of the wicked.
The anger of the Lord will not turn back
    until he has executed and accomplished
    the intents of his heart.
In the latter days you will understand it clearly. (Jer. 23:19–20)

Our attitude toward the wrath of God depends on our theology and worldview. If we do not understand sin to be a very serious problem, then God's wrath becomes the problem. We might simplistically assume that if God is love, he can never be truly angry. However, this is a misunderstanding of both the gravity of evil and the holiness of God. One scholar writes, "Those of us to whom the crimes of the world are mere incidents, and the agony of the poor is one of the many facts of life, may be inclined to describe the God of the prophets as stern, arbitrary, inscrutable, even unaccountable. But the thought of God and indifference to other people's suffering are mutually exclusive."[3] When one considers the damage that sin does to the person who commits it, to the victim, to those nearby, and to society at large, then it is good news that God reacts with righteous anger toward those who have broken his law and rebelled against him. God is not indifferent to evil. He alone knows the full weight of sin and its destructive nature, so his wrath follows from his love.

In chapter 2, we saw that YHWH not only required specific obligations in his covenant with Israel; he also promised detailed blessings for obedience and curses for disobedience (see table 2.6). There were to be no surprises: Israel knew exactly what was expected. They knew what would happen if they maintained exclusive loyalty to YHWH, or if they did not. Among the various blessings that YHWH offered, one of the most important to an ancient society was fruitful agriculture. For example, Deuteronomy 28:11–12 declares the results of obedience: "The Lord will make you abound in prosperity, in the fruit of your womb and in the fruit of your livestock and in the fruit of your ground, within the land that the Lord swore to your fathers to give you. The Lord will open to you his good treasury, the heavens, to give the rain to your land in its season and to bless all the work of your hands." All of these—children, livestock, and agriculture—lead to security and wealth. However, if the people disobey, it is not just that they will fail to experience these good blessings. Rather, God will actively work against them and ensure that they fail and suffer. Deuteronomy 28:16–19 states, "Cursed shall you be in the city, and cursed shall you be in the field. Cursed shall be your basket and your kneading bowl. Cursed shall be the fruit of your womb and the fruit of your ground, the increase of your herds and the young of your flock. Cursed shall you be when you come in, and cursed shall you be when you go out." Even worse, YHWH will take away the good gifts that he has given previously:

> You shall betroth a wife, but another man shall ravish her. . . . You shall plant a vineyard, but you shall not enjoy its fruit. Your ox shall be slaughtered before your eyes, but you shall not eat any of it. Your donkey shall be seized before your face, but shall not be restored to you. Your sheep shall be given to your enemies, but there shall be no one to help you. Your sons and your daughters shall be given to another people, while your eyes look on and fail with longing for them all day long, but you shall be helpless. (Deut. 28:30–32)

The prophets not only serve as prosecutors to establish guilt; they also function as spokespeople for the judge (God) and announce the sentence for the crime. They announce that, just as Moses said in Deuteronomy 28:15, all these curses are coming on the people because they have not obeyed. For example, YHWH says in Hosea 2:9, "Therefore I will take back my grain in its time, and my wine in its season, and I will take away my wool and my flax." Likewise, Joel declares the consequences of the people's disobedience: "The fields are destroyed, the ground mourns, because the grain is destroyed, the wine dries up, the oil languishes" (1:10). In Amos 4:7–11, God notes that even though he has withheld rain and brought mildew on their gardens and vineyards, they still have not submitted and returned to him. Even in the postexilic period, God says that because they have not prioritized the temple, he has called for a drought on everything that the land brings forth (Hag. 1:11).

Many curses are mentioned in Leviticus 26 and Deuteronomy 28, but the ultimate consequence for disobedience is that YHWH will remove the people from the promised land that he had given them in fulfillment of the covenant with Abraham. He will allow them to be conquered by their enemies and exiled to foreign lands, as Moses says in Deuteronomy 28:64–65: "And the LORD will scatter you among all peoples, from one end of the earth to the other. . . . And among these nations you shall find no respite, and there shall be no resting place for the sole of your foot, but the LORD will give you there a trembling heart and failing eyes and a languishing soul."

The preexilic prophets announce that this covenant curse is coming to pass. Hosea, a preexilic prophet in the Northern Kingdom, states in 8:13,

> As for my sacrificial offerings,
>   they sacrifice meat and eat it,
>   but the LORD does not accept them.

> Now he will remember their iniquity
>> and punish their sins;
>> they shall return to Egypt.

Here Hosea uses Egypt as representative of exile, bringing out the irony that YHWH saved Israel from captivity in a foreign land, and now he is sending them back to captivity once again. Amos is more blunt and visceral in his description of exile in 7:17:

> Therefore thus says the LORD:

>> "Your wife shall be a prostitute in the city,
>>> and your sons and your daughters shall fall by the sword,
>>> and your land shall be divided up with a measuring line;
>> you yourself shall die in an unclean land,
>>> and Israel shall surely go into exile away from its land."

Exile was common in the ancient world. Many nations conquered and exiled each other in their grasping for power and influence (e.g., see Amos 1:6). However, according to the prophets, Israel and Judah were not exiled to foreign lands because they were simply in the path of another nation's military campaign or because they were random victims of conquest. It was God who orchestrated the tragedy, using the mighty empires of Assyria and Babylon as his tools to judge Israel for covenant unfaithfulness.

3. Call to Repent and Prediction of Restoration (Near Future)

Even as the prophets make the case for Israel's guilt and announce the consequences, they assure their audiences that God is ready and willing to forgive if they will turn to him in repentance. The theological basis for this confidence comes from YHWH's self-revelation in Exodus 34:6–7, when he passes before Moses and proclaims, "The LORD, the LORD, a God merciful and gracious, slow to anger, and abounding in steadfast love and faithfulness, keeping steadfast love for thousands, forgiving iniquity and transgression and sin, but who will by no means clear the guilty." In other words, confession and repentance will surely lead to forgiveness, but there is no other way to be cleared of guilt.

Several of the prophets quote this "grace formula" directly. Joel urges his listeners to repent, saying, "Return to the LORD your God, for he is gracious and merciful, slow to anger, and abounding in steadfast love; and he relents over disaster" (2:13). Joel uses his confidence in God's grace as a motivation for repentance. It is as though he is saying, "If you know that

God will forgive you, then why not come to him?" The prophet Jonah also knows God's reputation for grace. After he announces doom on Nineveh, without even giving them any hope of a positive response from God, the people enthusiastically repent. Of course, this is what he was afraid of! He hates the Ninevites and was looking forward to their destruction. He angrily complains to God that he *knew* this would happen, since God is "slow to anger and abounding in steadfast love, and relenting from disaster" (4:2). Ironically this becomes powerful evidence that repentance is effective and that God loves to forgive. God says so himself in Ezekiel 18:21–23: "But if a wicked person turns away from all his sins that he has committed and keeps all my statutes and does what is just and right, he shall surely live; he shall not die. None of the transgressions that he has committed shall be remembered against him; for the righteousness that he has done he shall live. Have I any pleasure in the death of the wicked, declares the Lord God, and not rather that he should turn from his way and live?"

It is important to note two qualifications to God's eager grace. First, repentance requires more than lip service; it requires a change in behavior to demonstrate that there has been a change in heart. The prophets insist that if the people return to God, they must put away the sin that he hates. Isaiah 1:16–17 says,

> Wash yourselves; make yourselves clean;
> > remove the evil of your deeds from before my eyes;
> cease to do evil,
> > learn to do good;
> seek justice,
> > correct oppression;
> bring justice to the fatherless,
> > plead the widow's cause.

While Isaiah urges a turning from sins against others in the community, Ezekiel emphasizes the removal of false gods, saying, "Repent and turn away from your idols, and turn away your faces from all your abominations" (14:6). A second qualification is that there will come a time when it is too late to repent. For example, Isaiah 55:6 says, "Seek the Lord while he may be found; call upon him while he is near." God is incredibly patient, "not wishing that any should perish, but that all should reach repentance" (2 Pet. 3:9). However, God cannot be manipulated or taken for granted. His offer of mercy is generous, but at some point it will be rescinded. Therefore, the prophets are characterized by a palpable intensity in their messages. The stakes could not be higher, and time will eventually run out.

As we have seen, the prophets are confident that if the people truly repent, God abounds in mercy and will show favor to them. This will result in restoration and a reversal of the covenant curses, including the climactic consequence of exile in foreign lands. Jeremiah predicts that just as God brought Israel out of captivity in Egypt in the past, he will bring them back from the land of their exile: "Therefore, behold, the days are coming, declares the LORD, when it shall no longer be said, 'As the LORD lives who brought up the people of Israel out of the land of Egypt,' but 'As the LORD lives who brought up the people of Israel out of the north country and out of all the countries where he had driven them.' For I will bring them back to their own land that I gave to their fathers" (16:14–15). The prophets look forward to a time when the people are resettled and they rebuild the ruined cities. Amos 9:14 says,

> I will restore the fortunes of my people Israel,
>   and they shall rebuild the ruined cities and inhabit them;
> they shall plant vineyards and drink their wine,
>   and they shall make gardens and eat their fruit.

Most importantly, the temple will be rebuilt, symbolizing YHWH's presence and ongoing relationship with his people. Isaiah looks forward to the decree of the Persian emperor Cyrus, who, as we discussed above in chapter 3, made the decree to let the people return and even gave them the resources to restore the temple in Jerusalem. In the words of Isaiah, God says that Cyrus will fulfill all of his purpose, "saying of Jerusalem, 'She shall be built,' and of the temple, 'Your foundation shall be laid'" (Isa. 44:28).

Jeremiah announces that the exile will last seventy years, after which YHWH will return his people to their land (25:11; 29:10). It is uncertain whether these seventy years (rounded up) mark the time between the first deportation (605 BC) and the first return (539) or whether the seventy years are counted from the destruction of the temple (586) to the year that it was rebuilt and dedicated (515).

One aspect of true restoration is justice. What about Assyria and Babylon, those fierce nations who devastated and exiled God's people? Will they ever answer for what they have done? This raises something of a theological paradox. On the one hand, the murder, rape, starvation, and other suffering that Assyria and Babylon inflicted on God's people call for a reckoning. On the other hand, the prophets insist that the destruction and exile was the work of God, who used these nations as tools to bring judgment on his people. How then is it right for them to be punished when God used their evil for his own good purposes? The prophets do not resolve this paradox; rather, they state both that God used the nations and that they will be punished for what they have done. Isaiah says that when YHWH has finished his work (of judgment) in Jerusalem and on the temple, he will punish the king of Assyria for his pride. Lest Assyria think it has been successful against Israel because of its own strength, God says, "Shall the axe boast over him who hews with it, or the saw magnify itself against him who wields it? . . . Therefore the Lord GOD of hosts will send wasting sickness among his stout warriors" (Isa. 10:12, 15–16). This is shocking: Here God considers, for the moment, the Assyrian soldiers to be his warriors against his people. They are the axe in his hand. However, he will punish them for their pride. Jeremiah also states that God will punish the king of Babylon and that nation for their iniquity (25:12).

All of this is good news for God's people. After a time of exile, God will return the people to their land, they will rebuild, and their enemies will be destroyed. However, just as the historical exodus from Egypt anticipated a historical return from exile in the near future, that return from exile anticipates an even greater restoration in the more distant future.

4. Announcement of Restoration (Eschatological Future)

Alongside references to God's restoration in the near future, the prophets also make long-range predictions about God's ultimate renovation of the world and reclamation of those who truly belong to him. We call this final, future time the "eschaton" or the "eschatological future." From the perspective of human history, it is the end of all things. But in reality, it is the beginning of eternity.

One challenge in the Prophets is to distinguish the near future from the eschatological future. Imagine that the prophet is standing on the top of a ridge, looking out over mountains. He sees one range of mountains immediately in front of him and then, some distance away, a second range that extends as far as he can see (see fig. 6.1). The two ranges are distinct, and yet they are similar and related. From his vantage point, it is not clear how broad the valleys are, how much distance separates the two ranges. In the same way, as God reveals the future to the prophets, they look forward across the years. They see events in the near future (such as the return from exile) and also more distant events. Because God works in patterns, the near future and distant future events resemble each other in certain ways, just like the mountain ranges. But from their vantage point, it is difficult to discern how much time separates the first horizon from the second horizon.

When the prophets speak about God's actions or a state of affairs in the eschatological future, they signal this with specific terminology related

Figure 6.1. A mountain vista (Zugspitze Mountain Range, Germany)

Stephen Cullum / shutterstock.com

to a "day" or "days." This language is most clearly and accurately seen in the original Hebrew, but table 6.2 summarizes the various terms in English translation.

Table 6.2. Old Testament Phrases Referring to the Eschatological Future

Terminology	Occurrences in the Prophets
"the day of the LORD"	16
"a day belonging to the LORD"	2
"a day of the anger of the LORD"	2
"on that day"	109
"in those days"	16
"a day is coming"	6
"days are coming"	18
"the latter days"	9

The first three phrases, the "day of the LORD" and its derivatives, are usually used in the context of judgment; it is not a twenty-four-hour period but a time when God breaks into human history and disrupts the status quo. Amos states that some in Israel are looking forward to the day of YHWH, thinking it will mean their vindication, when in reality they should be dreading it since they have broken the covenant. When God comes, he will be against them. "Woe to you who desire the day of the LORD! Why would you have the day of the LORD? It is darkness, and not light, as if a man fled from a lion, and a bear met him" (5:18–19). Other expressions such as "on that day" or "a day is coming" (and their plural forms) refer to a time in the indeterminate future when there will be a new state of affairs. Figure 6.2 illustrates a simplified time line of future events from the prophet's perspective. The shaded arrow represents those events that are referred to as "that day" or "the latter days." It gradually darkens as it goes further down the time line (to the right), illustrating that while these phrases are sometimes used of events in the prophet's near future and sometimes of events in the time of Christ's incarnation and the New Testament, they most often refer to the *eschaton*, when history comes to a completion with the return of Christ and the new heavens and new earth.

However, while "the day" often refers to one of these specific phases in redemptive history, it can sometimes encompass several periods of time or even one long period that stretches from the prophet's immediate future all the way to the end of time. For example, in Daniel 2, King Nebuchadnezzar dreams of a statue with a head of gold, chest and arms of silver, thighs of bronze, legs of iron, and feet partly of iron and partly of clay. Then a stone comes and breaks the statue and fills the whole earth. Daniel says that God "has made known to King Nebuchadnezzar what will be in *the latter days*" (2:28). And yet, when Daniel interprets the dream, the head of gold is Nebuchadnezzar himself (in Daniel's own time period), the other parts of the statue are subsequent earthly kingdoms leading up to the time of the New Testament, and the stone that becomes a mountain is God's eternal kingdom, which "shall break in pieces all these kingdoms and bring them to an end, and it shall stand forever" (2:44). In other words, the time that Daniel refers to as "the latter days" stretches from his own time (in the sixth century BC) all the way to the end of time, when God rules over his kingdom forever.

The point here is that this terminology is very specific in that it refers to the indeterminate future when God creates a new state of affairs, usually in the eschaton. But it is also quite elastic since, from the prophet's perspective, the various "mountain ranges" of time all seem to run together. Just

THINKING VISUALLY

The Prophet's View of the Future
Figure 6.2

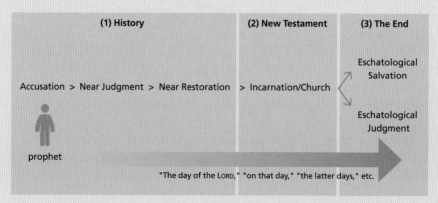

as a mountain climber does not always have clear depth perception when she looks out over a vast range of mountains, a prophet cannot or does not always distinguish between near, further, and furthest periods of time in the future. For the messenger, they are just "that day" or "those days" when God will act and bring about something new. As we will see in chapter 7, this is sometimes a deliberate rhetorical strategy to consider future events in relation to each other when God's acts occur in patterns.

The prophets predict a glorious, final restoration for God's people in the eschatological future. The land will be transformed so that it is fruitful and productive, and there will never again be famine (Ezek. 36:29–30). Because God will be reconciled with his people, he will give them the covenant blessings of flourishing agriculture, abundant food, and wealth that he had intended for them from the start. Hosea looks forward to a time when God will say,

> I will heal their apostasy;
>   I will love them freely,
>   for my anger has turned from them.
> . . . .
> They shall return and dwell beneath my shadow;
>   they shall flourish like the grain;
> they shall blossom like the vine;
>   their fame shall be like the wine of Lebanon. (14:4, 7)

"In that day," the mountains shall drip sweet wine, and the hills shall flow with milk (Joel 3:18; cf. Amos 9:13). Zechariah says that "the vine shall give its fruit, and the ground shall give its produce, and the heavens shall give their dew" (8:12). For an ancient subsistence farmer who depended on consistent rain and struggled to feed a family with meager crops, this is a picture of paradise.

Even more, the "latter days" will involve a transformation of the entire created order so that suffering and evil will be replaced by peace. Isaiah 11:6–9 tells of predator and prey lying down together and children playing freely near poisonous snakes. Everything will be made right because "they shall not hurt or destroy in all my holy mountain; for the earth shall be full of the knowledge of the LORD as the waters cover the sea." But then there is even better news. Isaiah goes on to say that YHWH will "swallow up death forever; and the Lord GOD will wipe away tears from all faces, and the reproach of his people he will take away from all the earth" (25:8).

However, the renewal in the end of time will not be confined to the world around us—it will involve internal transformation as well. God will give his people a new heart that will enable them to relate to him as they should. Throughout Israel's history, they had consistently fallen short of God's expectations and failed to demonstrate exclusive loyalty to him. It became clear over time that they were *incapable* of doing so. In the end, however, God will take the initiative to change them. As we saw in chapter 2, Jeremiah says that "the days are coming" when God will make a new covenant (31:31). "For this is the covenant that I will make with the house of Israel *after those days*, declares the LORD: I will put my law within them" (31:33). Hosea says that though the people of Israel are like a prostitute who runs again and again to her lovers, in the end they will be reconciled to God, they will have a new nature, and they will seek after him. "*Afterward* the children of Israel shall return and seek the LORD their God, and David their king, and they shall come in fear to the LORD and to his goodness *in the latter days*" (3:5).

The prophets' claims of the transformation of nature, the death of death, and the renewal of the human heart are radical and would require supernatural intervention. This begs the question, By what means will God accomplish these things? The answer is that there will be a new king, in the line of David, who will bring salvation and victory from Jerusalem. Following his description of the new covenant, YHWH says through Jeremiah that his covenant with David will never be broken. His statement alludes to the other covenants (indicated in brackets):

> Thus says the LORD: If you can break my covenant with the day and my covenant with the night, so that day and night will not come at their appointed time, then also my covenant with David my servant may be broken [David], so that he shall not have a son to reign on his throne, and my covenant with the Levitical priests my ministers [Israel]. As the host of heaven cannot be numbered and the sands of the sea cannot be measured [Abraham], so I will multiply the offspring of David my servant [David], and the Levitical priests who minister to me [Israel]. (Jer. 33:20–22)

It is this offspring of David that will culminate in a king who will reign over God's people on the transformed earth forever (Isa. 9:7). This king, sitting in the "tent of David," will rule with justice and righteousness (16:5). Ezekiel looks forward to a time when "my servant David shall be king over them." In that time, God's people will finally successfully conform to God's standards: "They shall walk in my rules and be careful to obey my statutes" (37:24).

The prophets locate this new Davidic king's rule in Jerusalem; it is the epicenter of God's salvation and of victory for the rest of the world. In the end, all those among the nations who have turned to God in repentance will look to Jerusalem as the seat of his authority and will come there to worship him.

> It shall come to pass *in the latter days*
>   that the mountain of the house of the LORD
> shall be established as the highest of the mountains,
>   and shall be lifted up above the hills;
> and all the nations shall flow to it,
> and many peoples shall come, and say:
> "Come, let us go up to the mountain of the LORD,
>   to the house of the God of Jacob,
> that he may teach us his ways
>   and that we may walk in his paths." (Isa. 2:2–3; cf. Mic. 4:1–2)

The prophet Joel identifies Jerusalem as the place of hope and safety when God's judgment comes. It is there that "everyone who calls on the name of the LORD shall be saved. For in Mount Zion and in Jerusalem there shall be those who escape" (2:32).

5. *Announcement of Final Judgment (Eschatological Future)*

The "day of the LORD" will mean permanent peace and prosperity for God's people, but it will also bring judgment for those that ultimately reject him. The nations that do not submit to God will be destroyed so that they cannot rise again. For example, Zephaniah speaks of a great cataclysm in which God upends nature along with the wicked:

> "I will sweep away man and beast;
>   I will sweep away the birds of the heavens
>   and the fish of the sea,
>   and the rubble with the wicked.
> I will cut off mankind
>   from the face of the earth," declares the LORD. (1:3)

Similarly, the book of Isaiah ends with an assurance that God's people will celebrate his victory over his enemies: "And they shall go out and look on the dead bodies of the men who have rebelled against me" (66:24).

When the prophets speak of ultimate, eschatological judgment, their focus is on the relief that it will bring to God's people. Throughout Israel's history and world history in general, the nations have oppressed the true people of God, persecuting and maligning them because they represent

God's truth and rule over the earth. Therefore, when God destroys *his* enemies in the day of YHWH, his people will enjoy peace and freedom from persecution for all time.

Conclusion

The prophets are a diverse group, speaking and writing in reference to Israel, Judah, and other nations across hundreds of years. However, they all contribute to a unified message. God's people have broken his covenant and been unfaithful in every way. After a long period of patience, God pours out his wrath and carries out the consequences that were entailed by the covenant—the climax of which is removal from the land and exile in foreign lands. However, he will show mercy if the people repent. He will bring them back from exile and restore their fortunes so that their abundance is even greater than before; he will give them a new heart so that their relationship with him will no longer be threatened, set a righteous and permanent Davidic king over them, and usher in an eternal reign of peace and prosperity. This restoration won't happen all at once, but the prophets proclaim its coming in the indeterminate future.

The book of Hosea closes with a call to *wisdom* in light of the preceding prophetic message, and we will close this chapter in the same way. Overall, the prophets advocate a worldview and theology that is fundamentally different from our normal tendencies in religious practice. It is the natural predisposition of the people of Israel, and all of us as well, to approach

Table 6.3. Two Approaches to Our Worship of God

Religion	Revelation
Manipulation—attempt to control destiny through special insight or by directing gods a certain way through ritual	**Submission**—submitting to God's plans and trusting his leadership and guidance; the creature exists for the creator
Divination and magic—gods are predictable; can be "used" to gain an advantage over each other; manipulation	**Divine guidance and protection**—God protects and guides on his own terms
Pragmatism—a technique that enhances life; end justifies the means	**Divine wisdom**—God knows what is best even if it seems counterintuitive
Relative values—popular; rewards all who support common ideals and punishes anyone who challenges them; politically "correct"	**Counterculture**—courage and loyalty to the creator rather than the masses

Source: Adapted from Willem A. VanGemeren, *Interpreting the Prophetic Word: An Introduction to the Prophetic Literature of the Old Testament* (Grand Rapids: Zondervan, 1996), 19–27.

faith in God as religious activity rather than a devoted relationship. Consider the comparison of the two approaches in table 6.3.

"Religion" refers to the ways in which we relate to God (or gods) socially or externally. It is predictable and unintrusive, supporting our desires for prosperity and security. We succeed at religion when we perform certain activities or adopt socially acceptable perspectives. It is an attempt for humanity to reach out to God and get from him what we desire. Whether or not the practices of religion have been required by God, they become the means to an end—an opportunity to maintain good standing with God. Religion usually accepts the status quo in society and supports popular values and ideals. In ancient Israel, the people were religious; they thought that they could murder and act unjustly as long as they remembered to make sacrifices and fulfill other ritual obligations. God would be appeased. They thought that they could combine the worship of YHWH with worship of other Canaanite deities and use divination to extract information from the divine world at will. The priests and the false prophets supported the king in power, looked for ways to gain wealth, and told the people what they wanted to hear. In our own day, our religious institutions face similar temptations to bow to certain political parties, adopt progressive sexual ethics, overlook injustice, and pander to those with social standing. There is enormous pressure to take things into our own hands in an attempt to control even God, manipulating him to bend to our will. The creature has the agenda, and religion is a tool to achieve it.

By contrast, much of what the prophets teach—accusation of covenant breaking, the call to repentance, the call to trust in YHWH for deliverance, and the confidence that God will remake his people with a new heart in a new world—is a call to forgo socially acceptable *religion* and to submit to God's *revelation*. It is a call to godly wisdom, which involves recalibrating one's worldview to be aligned with the great creator to whom we must all give an account. The faith required by the prophets demands that we submit to God in whatever he requires and repent when we inevitably fall short. It rejects empty ritual and declares our control an illusion, trusting that only God can provide what we seek—whether peace, security, or wholeness. And because this faith is countercultural, it is often deeply unpopular. The challenges that this presents to the prophet are the subject of the next chapter.

1. How does the prophetic message encompass past, present, and future? Is this a different conception of the Old Testament prophetic books than you had previously?

2. Why is the Pentateuch so foundational to the message of the Prophets? Identify key passages from the Pentateuch on which the Prophets seem to draw most frequently.

3. In the covenant with Israel, God commands the nation to offer sacrifices and observe certain religious festivals. How can the tension be resolved between this expectation and passages such as Isaiah 1:11–13 and Amos 5:21–22?

4. In a few sentences, describe how the Prophets foresee the "day of the LORD" or the eschatological future when God sets all things right. How would you summarize the Prophets' teaching about this end of time?

CHAPTER SEVEN

The Persuasive Strategies of the Prophets

Blessed are you when others revile you and persecute you and utter all kinds of evil against you falsely on my account. Rejoice and be glad, for your reward is great in heaven, for so they persecuted the prophets who were before you.

Matthew 5:11–12

The prophets faced two significant challenges in proclaiming the word of YHWH to the people of Israel and Judah. First, as we saw in the previous chapter, the prophetic message was often unpopular. It challenged what was "sacred" in society: power structures, wealth, habitual behaviors and sins, and beliefs that were deeply embedded in culture. The prophets were not abstract philosophers who dealt in esoteric subjects far from the realities of everyday life. They called on people to reject popular religion, to act justly, and to put their confidence in God rather than their social networks and resources. Unfortunately, an unpopular message often leads to an unpopular messenger. In Matthew 5:11–12, quoted above, Jesus states that the prophets were reviled, persecuted, and spoken against because they were loyal to God above culture and power. Jesus's followers should expect the same treatment today because their message is just as offensive. God's will and message are often at odds with his people because of the conflict between God's holy wisdom and humanity's tendency to rebel. Therefore, those who proclaim that message will be mistreated.

There are many examples in the Old Testament of prophets under pressure. King Ahab calls Elijah a "troubler of Israel" (1 Kings 18:17) and his "enemy" (21:20). We noted above in chapter 5 that King Ahab says of Micaiah, "There is yet one man by whom we may inquire of the Lord, Micaiah the son of Imlah, but I hate him" (22:8). In 2 Chronicles 25:16, a prophet attempts to give a word of YHWH to King Amaziah, who responds with a threat, "Stop! Why should you be struck down?" Isaiah tells of people who say to the prophets, "Do not prophesy to us what is right; speak to us smooth things, prophesy illusions, . . . let us hear no more about the Holy One of Israel" (Isa. 30:10–11). The mistreatment Jeremiah faced is the most detailed in Scripture: he was ignored (Jer. 7:27), was beaten (20:1–2), was given a death sentence (26:11), had his written scroll burned by the king (36:22–23), was left to die in a muddy cistern (38:6), and was called a liar (43:2). It is no wonder Jesus says, "O Jerusalem, Jerusalem, the city that kills the prophets and stones those who are sent to it!" (Matt. 23:37), and Stephen asks the hostile crowd, "Which of the prophets did your fathers not persecute?" right before they stone him (Acts 7:52).

Not only were the prophets' messages often unpopular—a second challenge was that they required a response of faith. The prophet asks his audience to change loyalties: from what can be seen and what has always been done to a living but invisible God. The prophet asks his audience to care more about what God has done and will do (both presently intangible) than about here-and-now concerns such as the movement of physical armies, the threat of drought, and the possibility of alliances with neighboring governments. The prophets frequently faced audiences that were numb and unable to see their own need for a word from YHWH, whose condition was worse than they thought or more dangerous than they realized. These challenges not only confronted the prophets when they were communicating to their original audiences, they continue to be an issue for those of us who read their writings in Scripture. We also are a "tough crowd," not always liking what we hear from the prophets and finding their words from YHWH to be difficult and uncomfortable.

The stakes are high, and prophets are contending for the soul of people in a hostile environment. When they present their messages, they communicate the words of YHWH so powerfully and persuasively that the people have no excuse for dull ears and unresponsive hearts. In order to communicate clearly and effectively, they use a number of rhetorical, or persuasive, strategies. Prophets are not dispassionate orators who speak in a monotone and recite dry facts. They appeal to the emotions and the senses; they confront, surprise, and use clever language. Their messages are interactive and attention grabbing. Some of their techniques are so extreme that they seem strange or even insane. And yet their actions and words are carefully chosen for maximum impact, to break through resistance. The goal of prophecy is to change attitudes and behaviors—to wake people up from a stupor of "what is" to what God calls them to be.

If we want to read the Prophets well, then we want to be sensitive not only to *what* they are saying but also to *how* they are saying it. This will explain some aspects of the prophetic writings that seem foreign to us, and it will give us a framework of expectations that we can bring to the text in order to understand the full message that God has given in his Word.

In this chapter, we will consider fourteen common persuasive strategies used by the prophets. The first two strategies, location and sign-acts, involve the *delivery* of their messages. The next ten strategies involve the actual *content* of their messages and how they are packaged for maximum effect. The final two strategies, poetry and vision reports, might pertain primarily to the *written*, canonized, prophetic text that we now have in Scripture. It is difficult to know to what extent the prophets used poetic features and forms in their oral communication. Also, while some vision reports could easily have been given directly to an oral audience, others were apparently composed for the prophetic book (see for example Ezek. 1:1, which refers to Ezekiel's audience in the third person). Therefore, we will consider these final two strategies separately.

Persuasive Strategies in Delivery

1. The Location of Delivery

Although news reports on television are shot and edited earlier in the day, reporters prefer to deliver those reports "on location" during the newscast. This creates interest, bolsters the authority of the reporter, and visually indicates the relevance of the story. Before the reporter has said anything, the audience knows that the story pertains to the courthouse or the music festival or the intersection of Thirty-Fourth Avenue and Main Street. Similarly, the prophets often deliver their word from YHWH in a purposeful location.

In Isaiah 7:3, Isaiah goes to meet Ahaz at a specific place: the conduit of the upper pool on the highway to the Washer's Field. This is important for at least two reasons. First, Ahaz was likely checking out the city's defenses against a coming attack, and Isaiah's message was that the attack would fail. Second, in Isaiah 36:2, the emissary from Assyria stands in the same location when he makes demands of King Hezekiah. This invites us to consider the two events in relation to each other.

Jeremiah delivers his oracles in a number of significant locations. He stands at the gate of the temple to deliver the "Temple Sermon" (7:2), he stands at the People's Gate to deliver a message on the Sabbath (17:19), and he makes a declaration of judgment in the temple (19:14–15). In Jeremiah 26:1–9, Jeremiah stands in the temple and warns that it will be destroyed. The people are angry, asking, "Why have you prophesied that *this* house will be desolate?" Both prophet and people are right there, looking at the very stones and mortar that are under threat of doom. This makes the message more vivid and immediate. The threat of judgment is concrete and even tangible: the very temple in which they are standing will be torn down.

2. Sign-Acts

Anyone who teaches children or youth knows the importance of object lessons and role-playing alongside oral communication. Even adults benefit from the ways these strategies engage us and activate different learning styles. Likewise, the prophets used "sign-acts" or visible object lessons to accompany their preaching. Sometimes these were simply pointing to a nearby visual, and at other times they involved complex role-playing, complete with props. Table 7.1 presents a list of these prophetic sign-acts in the Old Testament.

Table 7.1. Prophetic Sign-Acts in the Old Testament

	Prophet	Sign-Act	Message	Reference
1	Samuel	Saul grabs Samuel's robe and tears it	YHWH has torn the kingdom of Israel away from Saul	1 Samuel 15:27–28
2	Ahijah	Tears his cloak into twelve pieces and gives ten to Jeroboam	YHWH will tear the kingdom from Solomon, give ten tribes to Jeroboam, and establish the Northern Kingdom	1 Kings 11:29–34
3	"man of God"	Preaches to the altar at Bethel	Josiah, a future king of Judah, will sacrifice idolatrous priests on that altar	1 Kings 13:1–2
4	"a certain man"	Asks a man to strike him so that he is wounded; pretends to have released a prisoner of war	Ahab has released his prisoner of war: Ben-Hadad the king of Syria	1 Kings 20:35–43
5	Zedekiah (false prophet)	Makes horns of iron	With these, Ahab and Jehoshaphat shall destroy the Syrians	1 Kings 22:11; 2 Chronicles 18:10
6	Elisha	Instructs Jehoash (king of Israel) to shoot an arrow out of the window and then to strike the ground with arrows, which he does three times	YHWH will give Israel victory over Syria, but only three times, and it will not be permanent	2 Kings 13:15–19

	Prophet	Sign-Act	Message	Reference
7	Isaiah	Writes a child's name ("Quick to plunder, speedy to prey") on a tablet; begets a child and gives him that name	Before the boy is old enough to talk, Damascus and Samaria will be spoil and prey for the king of Assyria	Isaiah 8:1–4
8		Takes off his sackcloth and sandals and walks naked and barefoot for three years	The king of Assyria will lead away Egyptian and Ethiopian captives naked; do not trust in them for help	Isaiah 20:1–6
9		Wears a linen belt, then hides it in a damp place until it becomes rotten	Judah also will go away into exile until it is "ruined" and useless; God will "ruin" their pride	Jeremiah 13:1–11
10		Forbidden by YHWH from marrying or having children	Parents and children will die of diseases, sword, and famine and will not be buried	Jeremiah 16:1–4
11		Observes potter working and reshaping clay pots	YHWH has the ability to reshape his plans, depending on repentance or rebellion	Jeremiah 18:1–11
12		Buys a pottery flask, preaches in the Valley of Hinnom, and then breaks the flask	YHWH will "break" the people and the city of Jerusalem	Jeremiah 19:1–13
13	Jeremiah	Makes yoke bars and straps and puts them on his neck	Every nation must submit to the "yoke" of Nebuchadnezzar, king of Babylon	Jeremiah 27:1–12
14		Purchases a plot of land outside Jerusalem, even though the city is about to fall	YHWH will bring his people back to the land	Jeremiah 32:1–15
15		Offers wine to the Rechabites; they refuse as their father had instructed them	The Rechabites have obeyed their father, but YHWH's people have not obeyed him	Jeremiah 35:1–19
16		Hides stones in the mortar at Pharaoh's palace	The stones will be a foundation for Nebuchadnezzar's throne when he destroys Egypt	Jeremiah 43:8–13
17		Instructs Seraiah to tie a stone to the book of Jeremiah's words and throw it in the Euphrates River after he gets to Babylon and reads it	Babylon will sink and will not rise again, because of the disaster that YHWH is bringing on her	Jeremiah 51:60–64
18	Hananiah (false prophet)	Breaks yoke bars from Jeremiah's neck (cf. Jer. 27:1–12)	YHWH will break the yoke of Nebuchadnezzar within two years	Jeremiah 28:10–11
19	Ezekiel	Shuts himself in his house and is bound with ropes so that he cannot go out to the people	The people also must be silent and take responsibility for their sin and rebellion	Ezekiel 3:24–27

could say, "Lauren doesn't eat very much." But if I use a metaphor and say, "Lauren eats like a bird," I have mapped the concept of *bird* onto *Lauren*. We all know how birds eat, and more importantly, we can picture them in our mind. We can visualize a girl picking at her food and only eating a few crumbs. Metaphors are powerful for the same reason that "a picture is worth a thousand words." They are vivid and memorable, and they allow a speaker to draw instantly on common knowledge that he or she shares with the audience in order to convey information or emotions about something else.

The prophets use metaphor and figurative language pervasively; Isaiah is an exemplar. In Isaiah 1:2–3, he quotes YHWH:

> Children have I reared and brought up,
>   but they have rebelled against me.
> The ox knows its owner,
>   and the donkey its master's crib,
> but Israel does not know,
>   my people do not understand.

God begins with a few metaphors we might not even initially notice.[4] First, he calls Israel his "children," using a metaphor to evoke a loving, family relationship. Second, he says he "brought [them] up," which is a metaphor that pictures guiding a child to adulthood as raising them up higher. (My use of "guiding" is also a metaphor: providing leadership is guiding through unknown territory.) However, the central metaphor in these verses is that Israel is like domestic farm animals. An ox and a donkey may not have a reputation for being the most intelligent creatures on the earth, but at least they know to whom they belong and who provides for them! Israel, on the other hand, does not even know that they belong to God or how to get "home" to him (another metaphor).

Later, Isaiah tells King Ahaz of Judah not to worry about the impending attack by Syria and the Northern Kingdom of Israel. He says that these two kings are merely "smoldering stumps of firebrands" (7:4). They may look fierce and produce a lot of smoke, but the fire and danger have gone out. Isaiah tells King Ahaz that Assyria is a "razor" that will shave Judah with its destructive power (7:20). He also compares Assyria to a great, overflowing river that will bring a destructive flood on Judah (8:6–8).

The prophets use certain subtypes of metaphors as well. *Personification* is a metaphor in which an inanimate object is represented as a person. For example, Isaiah says, "The mountains and the hills before you shall break forth into singing, and all the trees of the field shall clap their hands" (55:12). *Anthropopathy* is a type of metaphor in which human emotions are ascribed to divinity. In the book of Jonah, for example, YHWH compares his compassion for Nineveh to the compassion that Jonah has for a plant (4:10–11). *Anthropomorphism* is a type of metaphor in which a human body is ascribed to God. It is shocking when Isaiah asks God, "Why is your apparel red, and your garments like his who treads in a winepress?" (63:2). In other words, "Why do your clothes look like you've been stomping grapes?" YHWH answers, "I trod [peoples] in my anger and trampled them in my wrath; their [blood] spattered on my garments and stained all my apparel" (63:3). Here we see God pictured with human emotion (anger) and a human body.

4. Parable and Allegory

Parables or allegories are metaphors extended into a short story in which one or more features of the story relate to another concept. They are effective because, on the surface, they are simply interesting narratives that capture an audience's attention. It is only upon further thought that the underlying meaning is discerned. Thus, they can overcome an audience's resistance by allowing them to draw conclusions without putting up their defenses. When the prophet Nathan confronts King David for his adultery with Uriah's wife, Bathsheba, he tells David a story of a rich man who took a poor man's only, precious lamb. David is incensed at the injustice and the calloused attitude of the rich man, prompting Nathan to reply, "You are the man!" (2 Sam. 12:7).

The prophets likewise use extended parables to confront Israel for sin or to announce judgment. Isaiah tells of YHWH building a vineyard for himself (Israel), only to have it produce wild grapes, despite his attention and care (5:1–7). Ezekiel uses a graphic parable of Jerusalem as a whoring wife who took the good gifts that her husband (YHWH) had given to her and gave them to her lovers as payment for sexual favors (chap. 16). Later, he uses more graphic sexual imagery to describe Samaria and Jerusalem as sex-crazed sisters who lust after the nations (chap. 23).

5. Wordplay

Wordplay is the witty or clever use of language that draws attention to the words themselves. Effective speakers and writers use wordplay to create irony, highlight a surprise relationship between two concepts, or simply for amusement. For example, in Oscar Wilde's play *The Importance of Being Earnest*, the lead character's name is "Earnest" even though he creates fictional personae to escape various social obligations.

Because the prophets spoke and wrote originally in Hebrew, their plays on words are not usually observable in English translations. Nevertheless, a few examples will help us to get a sense for this rhetorical technique. In Jeremiah 1:11–12, YHWH says to Jeremiah, "What do you see?" Jeremiah answers that he sees an almond branch (Hebrew: *shaqed*). YHWH then says, "You have seen well, for I am watching [Hebrew: *shoqed*] over my word to perform it." Because the almond tree is one of the first to blossom in the spring, it serves as a sign of changing times. This image is reinforced by the wordplay between the noun "almond branch" and the verbal participle "watching."

In Jeremiah 34:17, YHWH mixes sarcasm and wordplay: "You have not obeyed me by proclaiming liberty [Hebrew: *deror*], every one to his brother and to his neighbor; behold, I proclaim to you liberty [Hebrew: *deror*] to the sword, to pestilence, and to famine." YHWH is saying that because they have not obeyed the covenant by setting servants free after six years, he will set them free to be killed and suffer in famine! The wordplay not only creates interest and captures the listener's or reader's attention, it also spotlights the close relationship between their unjust actions and the consequences that YHWH will send.

6. Historical Review and Allusion

Like all good preachers, the prophets needed illustrations to help their audiences understand their message and clearly see its relevance and application. The history of Israel was a source of effective illustrations because it was well known to the people; the prophets could make subtle or clever allusions that their audiences would recognize. It was also effective because of the strong sense of continuity from generation to generation. As we saw in chapter 2, YHWH had chosen Abraham's offspring to be a nation through which he would bless all other nations of the earth. The progression from generation to generation was a motivation for YHWH's mercy: he promises in Leviticus 26:42, following the description of covenant curses, that when the people repent, he will remember his covenant with the patriarchs so that he does not destroy his people utterly. However, subsequent generations of Israelites also found themselves falling into the same sinful patterns as their ancestors. The prophets use this cohesion between the generations as a kind of mirror, held up to the present people so that they will see their own actions and situation more clearly.

An example of this is found in Ezekiel 20:1–44.[5] In this passage, YHWH tells the prophet to speak to the people about "the abominations of their fathers" (20:4). He does this by surveying three successive generations in

Israel: the generation that came out of Egypt at the time of the exodus (20:5–10); the generation that lived in the wilderness (20:11–15); and their children, who entered the promised land (20:18–23). Although each generation was blessed and called to be exclusively loyal to YHWH, they rebelled against him. The exodus generation was unwilling to get rid of the idols of Egypt, and the wilderness generation broke the covenant and profaned the Sabbath, as did the third generation. In each case, YHWH brought limited judgment, but he was unwilling to destroy them completely. The pattern continued when Israel came into the promised land (20:27–29), and even in Ezekiel's time, the people chase after pagan religion, even going so far as to sacrifice their children. In spite of this grievous offense, however, YHWH's response will not be total annihilation. Just as he showed mercy to previous generations, he will show mercy to this one. He will bring them back from exile in a new "exodus," and all Israel will serve him as they should.

In this example, the prophet's survey of Israel's history accomplishes several things. It creates interest with a narrative about the people's ancestors. It establishes that the people's rebellion is nothing new but has always been a problem in Israel. This creates, on the one hand, a sense of hopelessness that they will ever do what is right. But the historical allusion also subtly hints that just as the people are in a repeating pattern of sin, YHWH is in a repeating pattern of patience and mercy. The surprise twist, that YHWH will restore and transform them through his own power, is not actually that much of a surprise after all.

7. Concrete Details

At the beginning of this chapter we saw that a prophet will sometimes speak in a particular location in order to give the message a sense of immediacy and make it tangible. For the same reason, the prophets use concrete, vivid examples. This is particularly the case when they are accusing their audiences of specific sins. Rather than saying that Israel is cruel or unjust generally, Amos says that they sell "the needy for a pair of sandals" (2:6). It is bad enough to sell someone into slavery, but to do it in return for something as mundane as shoes shows a callous attitude and a disregard for the inherent worth of a person. Rather than saying generally that wealthy individuals in Israel live in obscene luxury that they have gained at the expense of the poor, Amos provides a picture of fat women ordering their husbands to bring them another drink (4:1). They "lie on beds of ivory and stretch themselves out on their couches, and eat lambs from the flock . . . , who sing idle songs . . . , who drink wine in bowls and anoint themselves with the finest oils," but they are not concerned about the ruin of their land

(6:4–6). These vivid examples are memorable and force the audience to confront the vulgarity of what Amos sees in the Northern Kingdom.

8. Empathy with the Audience

As we noted previously, the role of the prophet is to mediate between God and his people. The vast majority of the time, a prophet takes the side of God. He accuses the people of unfaithfulness to God, calls them to repent and turn to God, and provides God's perspective on the current situation. He reveals a word from God that the people did not previously know and announces a new phase in God's redemptive program. The people in turn treat the prophet as God's representative, rejecting and persecuting him for telling them what they do not want to hear.

Sometimes, however, a prophet will adopt a different stance for rhetorical effect. Rather than positioning himself as God's spokesman, he presents himself as placed among the people or perhaps as an independent third party. For example, when the prophet Ezekiel describes his vision of the valley of dry bones in Ezekiel 37, he presents the scene as something that is unfolding before him. He is just a spectator, as surprised at what he sees as we are.[6] He sees a valley of many dry bones, and YHWH asks, "Son of man, can these bones live?" Ezekiel replies that God knows (37:3). Later, when he is told to prophesy to the bones, they begin to fit together piece by piece and become corpses. Ezekiel relates what he sees, in effect saying, "Here is what I saw. I too was surprised! Believe it or not."[7] This gives an impression of objectivity, encouraging the audience to take the prophecy seriously and act on it.

In another example, Hosea temporarily steps out of the role of YHWH's prosecuting attorney in chapter 6 and becomes just one of the people. Following an indictment of the people's sin, he says to them, "Come, let us return to the Lord; for he has torn us, that he may heal us; he has struck us down, and he will bind us up" (6:1). He uses the first-person plural forms ("us") to include himself among them, saying something like, "Look, I am one of you. I think it would be a good idea to turn to YHWH because the same God who judges also heals. Let's give it a try."

9. Time Displacement

One of the creative techniques that the prophets use is to speak as though they are addressing an audience that is in either the past or the future relative to their own time. In other words, although the prophet is actually speaking to his contemporaries, he portrays himself as speaking to people in the past or in the future. This allows the people present to "listen in" and learn from those outside of their own time.

An example of this comes from the prophet Obadiah, who accuses the nation of Edom. In the past, Edom rejoiced when the Babylonians conquered and entered Jerusalem. Even worse, they participated in the destruction and gloated over God's people. Yet, even though those events happened in the past, Obadiah speaks to the Edomites with present-tense commands: "Do not enter the gate of my people in the day of their calamity; do not gloat over his disaster in the day of his calamity; do not loot his wealth in the day of his calamity" (Obad. 13). Perhaps a (silly) analogy would be a person watching a suspenseful movie in a theater who suddenly yells at the screen, "No! Don't go in that room! There is someone hiding in there!" The only people who can actually hear the words are those sitting nearby; it certainly doesn't help the on-screen character. But the words do effectively raise the suspense level and communicate the person's thoughts on the situation. In the same way, Obadiah's speech to people in the past heightens their guilt. They have committed their evil long before, but he says to them, "No! Don't do it!"

10. Question and Answer, or Disputation

At times, the prophets present God's word to his people as a short dialogue or a disputation. This involves characterizing the attitude or perspective of the people as speech and then putting them in conversation with God. It is probably not the record of an actual conversation. Rather, by putting words in the people's mouth the prophet allows either himself or God to respond to them.

In Micah 6, the prophet announces God's case against Israel (6:1–2). God asks, "O my people, what have I done to you? How have I wearied you? Answer me!" (6:3). God is suggesting that there is no good reason for their rebellion against him because he has been a good leader (6:4–5). But an unspoken "everyman" responds, "With what shall I come before the LORD . . . ? Shall I come . . . with burnt offerings, with calves a year old? Will the LORD be pleased with thousands of rams, with ten thousand rivers of oil?" (6:6–7). In other words, it is God who asks too much! How could the questioner possibly satisfy his conscience? Does God want thousands of sacrifices? The prophet responds in 6:8, "He has told you, O man, what is good; and what does the LORD require of you but to do justice, and to love kindness, and to walk humbly with your God?" This short dialogue expresses the false perspective of the people in a sophisticated way. When they "speak for themselves," their attitude is self-evidently problematic. When their perspective is articulated, God and the prophet respond to it.

The book of Malachi is structured in six disputations in which God and Israel question each other, providing an opportunity for God to critique their behavior or perspective (1:2–5; 1:6–2:9; 2:10–16; 2:17–3:5; 3:6–12; 3:13–4:3). For more on this, see chapter 24.

11. Surprise Twist or Trap

In the preceding discussion of parable and allegory, we mentioned that the prophet Nathan used a parable to confront King David for his adultery with Bathsheba. The story was powerful not only because it was a parable but because David did not see the trap coming and incriminated himself. He was livid that a rich man who had many sheep would steal the poor man's one precious animal. The trap was shut, and Nathan replied, "You are the man!" (2 Sam. 12:7). There was nothing left for David to do but to admit, "I have sinned against the LORD" (12:13).

Other prophets use similar rhetorical traps to ensnare their audiences. In Amos 1–2, the prophet condemns the wicked behavior of the nations surrounding Israel, the Northern Kingdom. At first glance, this appears to be a standard unit of oracles against the nations, such as we find in other prophetic books, as a *comfort* to the prophet's audience. First, Amos attacks Syria, then Philistia, then Tyre, Edom, Ammon, and Moab. He introduces the oracle against each nation with the standard statement "For three transgressions of [the nation], and for four, I will not revoke the punishment." Geographically, he moves around Israel, first to one side and then to another. One can imagine his Israelite listeners cheering and giving their approval for the just judgment that God is bringing on these enemies. In 2:4–5, Amos critiques the Southern Kingdom. Again, Judah and Israel were frequently at war, so this would have been good news for Israelites. However, at the end of the unit, in Amos 2:6, the prophet says, "For three transgressions of Israel, and for four, I will not revoke the punishment." In a surprise twist, *Israel* has been included in this list of condemnations against wicked nations! This is an effective strategy: the prophet gains approval for the crimes of others and then shows that Israel is just as guilty as they are.

Other examples of these kinds of self-incriminating traps include Ezekiel 16, in which the reader naturally blames the promiscuous wife and identifies with the jilted husband. It is difficult not to be shocked and outraged at her behavior, until one realizes that she represents *us* in the allegory, while the angry husband represents YHWH.

12. Historical Events and Entities as Analogies for Eschatological Realities

Thus far we have considered a number of strategies in which the prophets make their messages accessible and relatable by accompanying them with things from everyday life: they speak "on location" (#1), they use sign-acts and role-play (#2), they review and allude to Israel's history (#6), and their examples are concrete and specific (#7). We can now add another strategy to this list. The prophets frequently use historical events and entities as analogies for eschatological realities. To put it more simply, the prophets explain eschatological realities (those in the distant future) by means of things that have already happened or are happening in their own times.

In chapter 6, we discussed the prophets' announcement of judgment and restoration in the "latter days" or the "day of the LORD" or "on that day." Prophecies about God's actions in this future time are inherently difficult for several reasons. First, unlike the past or the present, the future is always something that we have not experienced—it is unknown territory. Second, God's actions in the future are typically described as grand and global in scale. It is difficult to imagine what it would be like if there was no more war, or if all the evil nations were destroyed and God's people were at peace, or what it would mean for God to place a special Davidic king on the throne forever. Third, because we do not know when these things will take place, it is easy for them to be "out of sight, out of mind" and for us to disregard them as mystical and mysterious. If they do not call for my immediate attention, why should I bother with them? The prophets recognize that these are difficult concepts to wrap our minds around, so they provide us with historical analogies that are observable and obviously relevant.

For example, in Amos 1:11–12, the prophet announces judgment on the historical nation of Edom in the near future. Israel had been in periodic conflict with Edom throughout its history, going all the way back to the conflict between Esau and Jacob, the nations' respective ancestors. God announces that he will send fire on them and destroy their strongholds. This is understandable and relevant; it is the kind of news one would gossip about at the butcher's shop or discuss at the city gate. At the end of the book, in Amos 9:11–12, Amos speaks about God's eschatological restoration. God will "raise up the booth of David" (the Davidic dynasty that will lead to the Messiah) in order that "they may possess the remnant of Edom and all the nations who are called by my name." This reference to "Edom" goes beyond the historical nation situated to the southeast of Judah. Amos speaks of "Edom and all the nations." Here, Edom is being used as a symbol for all those outside of God's redeemed people and to illustrate what it will mean for his Davidic king to possess them. This is something that Amos's audience can relate to. They may have trouble grasping the concept of God incorporating his enemies into his reign and rule, but they know Edom. The extension from the historical entity to the eschatological reality helps them grasp the meaning and the implications of the prediction.

This technique helps us understand the ongoing relevance of some of the Old Testament books today. We may look at Nahum's oracles against Assyria or Obadiah's oracles against Edom and wonder what those books could possibly still teach us. Why does the book of Joel spend the first chapter describing a plague of locusts? The short answer is that in Nahum, Assyria becomes a symbol for all nations who will be destroyed because they have set themselves against God. In Obadiah, the prophet lists the crimes of the historical Edom and then says, "For the day of the LORD is near *upon all nations*" (Obad. 15), again using Edom as a symbol. The book of Joel is structured so that the description of the historical locust plague in 1:1–20 becomes an analogy for the eschatological day of YHWH in 2:1–11. It is as though Joel is saying, "You have experienced a locust plague with devastation, starvation, and ruin, but that is nothing compared to the devastating army and the final catastrophe that is yet to come."

Figure 7.1 illustrates this strategy. Horizontally, the figure distinguishes between the present time (history and near future) and the "eschaton" when God breaks into history with his great salvation and brings this age to a close. The prophets use temporal judgment as an analogy for eschatological judgment and temporal restoration as an analogy for eschatological restoration. As we saw in chapter 6, the prophets do not always clearly

History as a Pattern for the Eschatological Future
Figure 7.1

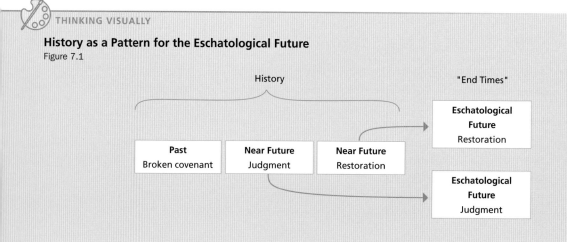

Merging Historical and Eschatological Eras
Figure 7.2

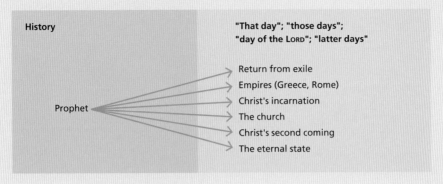

History

"That day"; "those days";
"day of the Lord"; "latter days"

Prophet

Return from exile
Empires (Greece, Rome)
Christ's incarnation
The church
Christ's second coming
The eternal state

distinguish between these two horizons. Sometimes "that day" or the "latter days" encompasses several periods of time, like mountain ranges that all seem to converge when one looks at them straight on. Sometimes this may be because a prophet cannot distinguish between them (1 Pet. 1:10–11). At other times, however, this merging of horizons becomes an additional, intentional rhetorical strategy (see fig. 7.2).

The prophets frequently speak about events in the near future (such as the return from exile) and those in the distant future (such as the transformation of earth) in the same paragraph, without indicating that they are addressing different time periods. It is as though they simply toss all these future realities into one "future" box. On the one hand, that can complicate things when we want to distinguish between different phases in redemptive history. We may ask, "Is that prediction related to the return from exile or the new heavens and new earth?" Or, "Is that comment related to the Messiah's first coming or second coming?" On the other hand, it is a clever strategy for helping us consider one event in the light of another.

For example, in Micah 4:6, YHWH says, "[I will gather] those who have been driven away and those whom I have afflicted." This at least alludes to the return from exile in history. But then he goes on to say, "and the lame I will make the remnant, and those who were cast off, a strong nation; and the LORD will reign over them in Mount Zion from this time forth and forevermore" (4:7). These two statements are in sequential verses, in the same paragraph. The prophet never says, "Now I am switching to the end of time," and does not provide us with a chronological key to his predictions. Yet this juxtaposition is important because it allows us to think of the *great* eschatological redemption in terms of the *historical* redemption.

Persuasive Strategies in the Written Text

13. Poetry

The final two strategies that we must consider are present in the canonical books of the Prophets, but it is difficult to know the extent to which they were used in the prophets' original oral speeches. As we will see in the next chapter, a prophetic book is not just a transcript of a prophet's ministry. The material has been edited, shaped, and augmented in order to become the books that we now have in our Bible. The first of these last two strategies is the pervasive use of poetry. While poetry may not be a *persuasive* strategy per se, it does increase the communicative power of the prophetic word.

Throughout the ancient world, poetry was the traditional means of expressing and transmitting religious experience.[8] About 35 percent of the Old Testament is composed of poetry.[9] It is found in Psalms and Wisdom literature as well as in the prophetic books. In addition, there are poetic texts embedded in narrative, such as Jacob's speech to his sons in Genesis 49, Moses and Miriam's song in Exodus 15, Deborah's song in Judges 5, and David's song in 2 Samuel 22. Interestingly, all of these are attributed to prophets or are prophetic in nature, including Jacob's speech, which is "what shall happen to you in days to come" (Gen. 49:1).

Poetry is an effective vehicle for communicating the word of God, the creator of heaven and earth, whose ways and thoughts are higher than ours (Isa. 55:8–9). Poetry is aesthetically pleasing and evokes emotion and wonder. It communicates more than the sum of its parts, relying on careful word choice and intentional structure. One scholar writes, "Since poetry is our best model of intricately rich communication, not only solemn, weighty, and forceful but also densely woven with intricate internal connections, meanings, and implications, it makes sense that divine speech should be represented as poetry."[10]

The form and elements of poetry are specific to different cultures and languages, but all poetry is marked by a particular register of language and word density. Language register refers to the variety of language that one uses in a particular social situation. For example, I speak differently when I am playing with my young daughters than when I am in a meeting with the president of my institution. A change in register can involve greater formality of language, a different lexical (vocabulary) set, different syntax, and so forth. Density refers to the amount of meaning that is present in a given amount of text. In narrative prose, it may take a paragraph to convey a particular point. In poetry, one phrase can communicate a poignant thought or powerful emotion because every word matters. Poetry is dense because it packs so much meaning into a small amount of "real estate." Because of this, poets choose words very carefully, often selecting words that are less common because they communicate just the right idea. Density also motivates poets to play with word order and syntactic relationships, to use a great deal of metaphorical language, and to use techniques such as repetition. All of this means that poetry challenges us as readers. It is more difficult than prose and must be pored over and meditated on. The language of the prophets is sometimes difficult to understand in English because it is difficult to understand in Hebrew. It requires careful thought and unpacking.

The primary characteristic of Hebrew poetry that we find in the Old Testament is *parallelism*. Parallelism refers to two or more poetic lines that contain corresponding elements. For example, Hosea 4:13 (my translation) says,

> Therefore, your **daughters** <u>fornicate</u>,
> And your **daughters-in-law** <u>commit adultery</u>.

In this example, "daughters" in the first line corresponds to "daughters-in-law" in the second. And "fornicate" corresponds to "commit adultery." It seems at first as though the prophet is saying the same thing twice. However, if we look again, there are differences. "Daughters" is a closer relation than "daughters-in-law." The combination of the two different words gives a sense that the scope of the sin is comprehensive: all the women of Israel are participating. Furthermore, the sexual sin is intensified as "fornicate" becomes "commit adultery," a sin that is more destructive to the fabric of society. This "intensification"[11] or "amplification"[12] from one line to the next is a common feature of parallelism. Hebrew poets use it to develop an idea in stages or to communicate it with greater sophistication. One scholar writes that it is like looking at a concept through a pair of binoculars; seeing a concept in two ways at once gives one greater depth perception.[13]

The study of Hebrew poetry, including poetry found in the Prophets, is a rich and complex field within biblical studies.[14] As you read prophetic books it is important to slow down, be sensitive to parallelism, look for larger structural units, be aware of figurative language, and think about not just what a prophet is saying but *how* he is saying it.

14. Vision Reports

Finally, the prophets provide vision reports. Rather than only telling us what they saw, the prophets tell us the circumstances of the vision, the mechanics of the revelation, and how they responded to it. By inviting us "behind the scenes," the prophets create a sense of intrigue and help us pay attention to the details. The reader gets to experience the vision along with the prophet, and thus this technique creates a sense of objectivity and neutrality. One scholar writes, "Such visions are powerful rhetorical tools, capturing the imagination of the audience through dramatic presentation and by creating an aura of intrigue and secrecy. The presentation of the vision allows for a gradual presentation of the scene, and the constant use of questions slows down the description and prompts the same questioning stance within the audience."[15]

These vision reports appear frequently in the Prophets. The book of Ezekiel begins with a dramatic vision of God's glory coming to the prophet in exile (1:4–3:15). Later Ezekiel is caught up and taken in a vision to Jerusalem, where he witnesses the abominations in the temple. He is then returned to the exiles, the vision comes to an end, and he reports what he has seen (8:1–11:25). The book ends with another significant vision, this time of a new, eschatological temple (40:1–48:35). The book of Daniel contains several visions of the future, including the four beasts (7:1–14); the ram, the goat, and the little horn (8:1–27); the seventy sevens (9:20–27); and the man clothed in linen (10:4–12:13). Zechariah has visions of horses patrolling the earth (1:7–17), four horns and four craftsmen (1:18–21), a man with a measuring line (2:1–5), a woman in a basket (5:5–11), and four chariots (6:1–8), among others.

Many of these visions are composed of elements taken from everyday life that are then given symbolic value.[16] Often, the symbols are present because the prophet has no other way to describe what he has seen; he is grasping for a way to communicate, since the vision cannot really be expressed in words.[17] One way to approach these visions is as we would approach an impressionist painting. They are designed not only to teach but to make us feel something: wonder, awe, or worship. Because the symbols are drawn from the literary context of the book or the historical and social context of the prophet, we often must do additional research to understand the sense of the symbol and what role it has in the book or had in that society.

Conclusion

Each literary genre in the Old Testament requires a different set of expectations and a different reading approach. The prophetic books are a challenging group of texts not only because they are rooted in a foreign time and place but because of their distinctive communication strategies. In this chapter, we have introduced and surveyed fourteen persuasive strategies that the prophets use to gain our attention, to make us feel the importance of the message, to influence us, and to help us retain the message. The goal of examining these strategies is to train us to be better readers of the Prophets, anticipating what they will do and considering not only *what* they say but *how* they say it.

We have established that the prophets were persuasive, powerful orators. However, faithful Israelites recognized that it was not the impressive quality of the prophets' speech that lent authority to their messages, but the divine voice discerned therein. This recognition and confirmation of God's voice in the prophetic speech is the key to how oral proclamations and prophetic ministries became canonical books of the Bible. To this process of canonization we now turn.

Christian Reading Questions

1. Do you think modern readers are more or less disposed to accept the teaching of the Old Testament prophets than their original audiences? What potential objections or challenges do you, as a reader, pose for the authors of the prophetic books as they attempt to communicate with *you*?

2. Try to think of examples of persuasive strategies in modern speaking and communication. How are these techniques different from or the same as what we see in the Old Testament Prophets? What might account for the differences?

CHAPTER EIGHT

From Prophetic Word to Biblical Book

For whatever was written in former days was written for our instruction, that through endurance and through the encouragement of the Scriptures we might have hope.

Romans 15:4

In chapters 2–6, we discussed the theological and historical contexts of the prophets, true and false prophets, and key elements of the messages of the prophets. These are all related to the historical prophets who lived and served in ancient Israel. In chapter 7, our discussion of the prophets' communication strategies began to address the *written* prophetic text. We observed that alongside the prophets' oral proclamation, some of their nonverbal communication has been passed down to us as well. In some cases, the text tells us where the prophet was standing when he spoke a word from God, how he was dressed, how he dramatically acted out the message, and how he used specific, concrete, and common details from everyday life as object lessons. The written text—the subject of this chapter—is not a simple transcript of prophetic statements; it is a complex of narrative background, poetry, conversations, disputations, and more.

The people of God are not a group that exists only in one time period. They stretch through history, beginning with creation, continuing in Abraham and the patriarchs, located within the nation of Israel, and persisting through thousands of years from every nation and language until Christ returns. While only a tiny segment of God's people were eyewitnesses to his great acts in history and the "live" revelation of his word through the prophets, future generations would gain the same benefit *if* these things were passed down to them. It is the written text that extends the truth-revealing, faith-building acts and words of God into the future so that generation after generation can know him and live faithfully before him, now and for all eternity. This is why Paul says in Romans 15:4, quoted above, that whatever was written in former days (i.e., ancient Israel) was written *"for our instruction, that . . . we might have hope."* Paul does not say that we discovered ancient texts and found that we could learn from them as well. He does not say that if we read these texts as though they were written for us, we will find them to be beneficial. He says that they *were* written for us. How the prophetic books came to be written for us and how we should approach them since they are ancient are the focus of this chapter.

Nonwriting Prophets, Former Prophets, Latter Prophets

While all prophets share the same essential role, not all prophets use the same mode of communication. Some prophets give oracles but do not communicate in writing. An example in this category is Nathan, who met with David, confronted him over sin, and involved himself in the royal succession of Solomon. Elijah and Elisha also fall into this category. While we have one example of Elijah writing a letter to someone announcing judgment (2 Chron. 21:12–15), this was a matter of interpersonal communication. The letter was not preserved as canonical Scripture. Otherwise, these two prophets performed miraculous acts, confronted Israel for breaking covenant, and condemned evil kings, but they did not compile their messages for future generations. Within Scripture, the primary focus is on their actions.

By contrast, some prophets write but do not deliver messages in a public ministry. Examples of this category include the anonymous authors of Joshua, Judges, Samuel, and Kings. While it is common to refer to these as "historical books," the Hebrew tradition calls them the "Former Prophets." Their raw material is historical narrative, but they select, arrange, and present events to communicate a theological point. Their writing is history, but it is more than history. As prophetic authors, they are making claims about what God has done and providing us with an authoritative interpretation of his acts and the actions of his people. However, they make these theological statements anonymously, in written form only, and not in the context of a public ministry. The Former Prophets provide us with the history into which the Latter Prophets speak.[1]

The Latter Prophets comprises a third group of prophets who both give public oracles in specific historical and geographical contexts *and* write

Narrative Story Line and Poetic Commentary

Old Testament scholar Stephen Dempster shows how the Old and New Testaments each present a story line that is interrupted by commentary and then resumed.

	Old Testament	New Testament
Narrative story line	Torah (Genesis–Deuteronomy)	Gospels and Acts
	Former Prophets (Joshua–Kings)	
Commentary	Latter Prophets (Isaiah–Malachi)	Letters
	Writings (Psalms, Proverbs, Job, Ruth, Lamentations, Ecclesiastes)	
Narrative story line	Writings (Esther, Daniel, Ezra–Nehemiah, Chronicles)	Revelation

In the Old Testament, according to the canonical arrangement of the Hebrew Bible, the story line begins with creation (Genesis) and goes to the exile (2 Kings). It is then interrupted by poetic commentary in the Latter Prophets, Psalms, and Wisdom literature. The story line resumes in the exile (Esther and Daniel), continues with the return of the exiles to Judah (Ezra–Nehemiah), and then concludes with a summary of the entire history of Israel from creation to the exile (Chronicles).[a] Therefore, the Latter Prophets come alongside the events in the Former Prophets and provide theological commentary.[b]

them down for the future people of God. As we noted above, this combination of prophetic proclamation and preservation in written Scripture was centered on the great turning points in Israel's history: the eighth century BC and conquest of the Northern Kingdom, the conquest of the Southern Kingdom and exile, and the postexilic period after the completion of the second temple. The messages of the Latter Prophets were crucial for God's people living in those "end times" of Old Testament history, but they also have relevance for the future people of God who live in the "end times" of God's redemptive program. Evidently, the messages of the nonwriting prophets did not need to be preserved, only their actions. And the prophetic depiction of Israel's history in the Former Prophets needed to be preserved, but not the life and actions of the authors. However, in the case of the Latter Prophets, both their historical ministries and their prophetic messages are joined and preserved together for the future people of God.

From Prophetic Word to Prophetic Book

How did the actions of the prophets and their words from God become the biblical, canonical books that we have now? One way to tell this story is to describe seven stages of growth.[2] Nowhere in the Bible are we told the process, but these seven stages are abstracted and inferred from the biblical evidence. They are (1) the prophetic event, (2) the rhetorical event, (3) the transcriptional event, (4) the compilation event, (5) the narratorial event, (6) the editorial event, and (7) the nominal event.

Stage 1—The Prophetic Event

First, the prophet receives a word from God. As we have discussed previously, this might take the form of a vision or a dream. In many cases, we are not told the mechanics of the inspiration. God speaks to the prophet and gives him a message to pass on to the people.

Stage 2—The Rhetorical Event

This stage consists of the prophet's delivery of the message to his immediate audience. It includes oral proclamation, such as a conversation with a king, a speech or sermon in the temple, or a meeting with a group in exile. It also includes nonverbal communication, such as sign-acts. The prophet and the original audience share the same language and culture. They also share the same circumstances: both prophet and audience are threatened by the same enemy army, subjected to the same wicked king, and part of the same society that acts unjustly. When the prophet makes particular historical or cultural references, the audience understands and shares in those networks of associations.

Stage 3—The Transcriptional Event

In the third stage, the prophet's oracles are committed to writing. Sometimes the prophets use letters to communicate to people far away, thus committing their words to writing. We have already mentioned Elijah's letter to Jehoram in 2 Chronicles 21:12–15. Jeremiah also writes a letter to the exiles in Babylon (29:1–32).

In Jeremiah 51:60, writing is part of a sign-act. Jeremiah writes in a book all the disaster that will come on Babylon. He then instructs Seraiah to tie a stone to the book, throw it into the Euphrates River, and declare that, in the same way, Babylon will sink down and rise no more (51:63–64). There must have been a copy of this book, because we can read Jeremiah's oracles against Babylon in chapters 50–51 of the biblical book.

Another reason that a prophet was instructed to write down the words of God was so they would be preserved for future generations. In Isaiah 30:8, YHWH tells Isaiah,

> And now, go, write it before them on a tablet
> and inscribe it in a book,

> that it may be for the time to come
> as a witness forever.

YHWH is clear that the purpose of writing down his word to Isaiah is that it will be a witness *forever,* not just to the present generation. A few verses later, in Isaiah 30:10, the rebellious people say to the prophets, "Do not prophesy to us what is right; speak to us smooth things, prophesy illusions." Unfortunately for them, the prophecy is not only true, but it has been written down and testifies against them. In Ezekiel 24:2, YHWH instructs Ezekiel to record the date, because that is the day that Nebuchadnezzar has besieged Jerusalem. Future generations will be able to look back and connect Ezekiel's prophecies to the broader history of Israel before and after the exile. Habakkuk also is told, "Write the vision; make it plain on tablets. . . . For still the vision awaits its appointed time" (2:2–3). Habakkuk was comforted by YHWH's words, for he saw that Babylon would not permanently escape justice. By writing down the vision, he ensured that anyone who had suffered at the hands of the Babylonians could experience that comfort as well. A final example comes from Daniel 12:4, when Daniel is told to "shut up the words and seal the book, until the time of the end." Again, his vision of the future will serve as an enduring witness and comfort to future generations.

We have very little information about the actual writing process, except in the book of Jeremiah. In Jeremiah 36:2, YHWH tells Jeremiah, "Take a scroll and write on it all the words that I have spoken to you." Jeremiah then calls his scribe Baruch, "and Baruch wrote on a scroll *at the dictation of Jeremiah* all the words of the Lord that he had spoken to him" (36:4). It is clear in this passage that dictation to a scribe is equivalent to Jeremiah writing the words himself.

Stage 4—The Compilation Event

If prophetic speeches and messages were written down here and there throughout the prophet's ministry, then at some point they would need to be compiled and gathered into a collection. This is the fourth stage. Isaiah 8:16 says, "Bind up the testimony; seal the teaching among my disciples." The idea here is that Isaiah's words from many different circumstances over many years needed to be collected so that the future people of God could benefit from them.

Returning to Jeremiah 36, YHWH tells Jeremiah, "Take a scroll and write on it all the words that I have spoken to you against Israel and Judah and all the nations, *from the day I spoke to you, from the days of Josiah until today*" (36:2). YHWH's instructions are to collect all of Jeremiah's prophesies from the beginning of his ministry and to put them on a scroll. After Jeremiah dictates all of the words to Baruch, he instructs Baruch to read the scroll in the temple (Jeremiah himself is banned from going there). When Baruch reads the words of the scroll, the people are afraid, for they realize they are not complying with what YHWH had commanded. They say, "We must report all of these words to the king" (36:16). But when the scribe Jehudi reads the words to King Jehoiakim, who is sitting before a fire in his winter palace, he systematically cuts off columns of the scroll and burns them in the fire (36:23). This passage illustrates the authority of the collected prophetic word. The prophet is not there, but the scroll now has an authority of its own as it confronts the people and the king over their sin. The people take it seriously and fear God, but the king makes a demonstration of his rejection and orders that Jeremiah and Baruch be found and arrested (36:26).

Stage 5—The Narratorial Event

The fifth stage involves the production or collection of narrative material in addition to the collected prophetic messages. This includes the circumstances of the prophetic event, the occasion, the date that the word of YHWH came to the prophet, the participants who spoke to the prophet or heard from him, and more. For example, Isaiah 6:1–8 is a brief narrative about Isaiah's vision of YHWH on his throne and about Isaiah's call to prophetic ministry, which in turn is followed by a prophetic oracle in 6:9–13. Then in Isaiah 7:1–6 there is more narrative about Isaiah going to meet King Ahaz by the upper pool and his conversation with him there. The books of Jeremiah and Ezekiel contain even more narrative than Isaiah about the prophets and the circumstances of the delivery of God's word. Hosea has a few statements about the prophet and his family in chapters 1–3 but none in chapters 4–14. Some prophetic books have no narrative at all, such as Joel, Micah, and Nahum.

Whatever narrative material is in a book, it was necessary to compose and collect it. The process obviously involved a great deal of selectivity. For example, Isaiah's ministry was over fifty years long, and only certain key events are recorded and then placed at strategic locations in the book's structure.

Stage 6—The Editorial Event

In the sixth stage, collected oracles and narrative material are selected, arranged, and written into a book. This is intended for a second audience that goes beyond the first audience, who knew and listened to the prophet. The material is shaped *for* this new audience, for future generations.

Imagine that a pastor preaches eight sermons to his congregation about a biblical view of marriage. It is the early summer at his small church in downtown Chicago. As he sits in his office and prepares the sermons, he can imagine the faces in his congregation who will be his audience. He has counseled some of them, and he knows about painful and difficult situations in some marriages in the church. As he preaches the sermons, he uses multiple illustrations, including the Chicago Cubs, a show on television, and a quote from Jane Austen. But he also uses some illustrations from their church life together, including a humorous story about one of the deacons. The following year, he decides to turn that material into a book. This time, as he sits at his keyboard, he imagines a different audience, people who come from a great variety of diverse backgrounds. He is selective about his illustrations, choosing some and omitting others. Most importantly, he changes the structure of the series. The seventh sermon becomes the introduction to the book, while he concludes the book with the material from the first sermon. He adds material related to the experience of marriage in a small town, a topic that was not relevant to his congregation in the sermon series. In addition, he is now able to look back on the whole series and observe how it was received.

This illustration has its limitations, but it seeks to show how a prophetic book is a different communicative vehicle than speeches and actions in a prophetic ministry. The book has a diverse audience that spans different times, circumstances, and cultures from those of the prophet. Individual speeches and narrative material are arranged and constructed into a new argument with broader implications and a grander perspective. Themes can be developed across the material, and the structure of the book allows for speeches that were previously unrelated to be brought into conversation with one another. A prophetic book is not just a record of a prophet's ministry in chronological order—it is an argument with objectives and goals aimed to persuade the people of God who will read it after the prophet's lifetime.

One important implication that this has for interpretation is that we expect the structure of the book to be purposeful, not accidental. An example of this comes from the book of Isaiah. As might be expected, many prophetic books *begin* with a prophet's call to be a spokesman for God (see Jer. 1; Ezek. 1; Hosea 1). In the book of Isaiah, however, chapters 1–5 begin the book with an accusation that Israel has broken the covenant, a preview of God's judgment, and the parable of Israel as a failed vineyard. Isaiah's oracles continue in chapters 7–12. But between these units we find the account of Isaiah's call, when Isaiah sees a vision of God's glory filling the

Table 8.1. The First Twelve Chapters of Isaiah

Chapters 1–5	Chapter 6	Chapters 7–12
Oracles of accusation and judgment	Isaiah's call narrative	King Ahaz and Assyria

temple and heavenly beings saying, "Holy, holy, holy is the LORD of hosts" (6:3; see table 8.1). YHWH asks, "Whom shall I send, and who will go for us?" and Isaiah answers, "Here I am! Send me" (6:8).

Why does Isaiah's call narrative not come until chapter 6? We might suggest that Isaiah gave some prophetic messages before he was formally called as a prophet, but that does not make much sense. Alternatively, John Calvin proposed that chapter 6 is not Isaiah's call but a later experience.[3] These suggestions are unnecessary. It is much more likely that chapter 6 *is* the narrative of Isaiah's initial call, but it has been placed in that location as a part of the developing argument of the book. Chapters 1–5 contain Isaiah's words from later in his ministry, but they have been placed at the beginning of the book in order to serve as an introduction. The book begins, in the first five chapters, by building a case that Israel is not serving God. Then chapter 6 uses the narrative of Isaiah's call to ministry as an illustration of what needs to happen in Israel: they too need to be cleansed of sin, respond to God's call, and be sent on a mission to the nations.[4]

One briefer example comes from the book of Hosea, which contains narrative about the prophet and his family as well as oracles concerning the Northern Kingdom. The last verse directly addresses the *reader* of the book:

> Whoever is wise, let him understand these things;
>   whoever is discerning, let him know them;
> for the ways of the LORD are right,
>   and the upright walk in them,
>   but transgressors stumble in them. (14:9)

This statement is illuminating because it shows an awareness of the book as a whole. The verse uses common wisdom language to motivate the reader to take the overall composition seriously and to study it carefully. This verse comes not from the time of the prophet's ministry but from the process of editing the book together into the shape that we now have.

Stage 7—The Nominal Event

In this last stage, the editor of the prophetic book adds a statement attributing the book to the prophet and often providing additional details that date the book to a particular historical context:

The vision of Isaiah the son of Amoz, which he saw concerning Judah and Jerusalem in the days of Uzziah, Jotham, Ahaz, and Hezekiah, kings of Judah. (Isa. 1:1)

On the fifth day of the month (it was the fifth year of the exile of King Jehoiachin), the word of the LORD came to Ezekiel the priest, the son of Buzi, in the land of the Chaldeans by the Chebar canal, and the hand of the LORD was upon him there. (Ezek. 1:2–3)

Some superscriptions are quite short:

The word of the LORD that came to Joel, the son of Pethuel. (Joel 1:1)

Table 8.2 compares the opening statements of the Prophets. Given what we are told about Jeremiah's use of the scribes Baruch and Seraiah, it is possible that while the prophets received the word from YHWH (stage 1) and proclaimed it (stage 2), other scribes were responsible for transcribing it (stage 3), compiling it (stage 4), producing the narrative (stage 5), editing the book (stage 6), and adding the superscriptions (stage 7). However, we must qualify that statement in a few ways. First, the process is not outlined explicitly, and it is always possible that the prophet was more involved in the actual writing. Second, even if other scribes edited and published the book, the prophet remains the author in the sense that the material comes from him. We should take the authorship attributions seriously: they make explicit claims that these books present the words of the prophets in particular historical time periods. Thus, if the prophet claims to be looking into the future, we cannot ignore those claims without undercutting the prophet's authority and therefore the doctrine of inspiration. Third, the writing situation probably varied across different prophetic books.[5] The book of Jonah, for example, is essentially a short narrative and may have been written all at once without going through these stages of composition. (It also makes no authorship claims.) Obadiah contains only twenty-one verses of oracles, with no narrative and barely a superscription. Not all books required all seven stages in the compositional process.

Critical Approaches to the Prophets

It may be helpful to consider briefly some different ways that scholars have approached the relationship between the historical prophet and the prophetic book. First, in earlier critical scholarship of the nineteenth and twentieth centuries, there was an attempt to get behind the written text to

Table 8.2. A Comparison of the Superscriptions in the Prophetic Books

	Description of Prophetic Word	Prophet's Name	Prophet's Lineage	Place of Prophecy	Prophet's Biographical Info	Contemporaneous Kings	Historical Info
Isaiah	"a vision" (*hazon*)	X	X			X	
Jeremiah	"words of"	X	X	X	X	X	
Ezekiel	"visions" (*mar'ah*)	X	X		X	X	
Daniel	*Opens with narrative*						
Hosea	"word of"	X	X			X	
Joel	"word of"	X	X				
Amos	"words of"	X			X	X	X
Obadiah	"a vision" (*hazon*)	X					
Jonah	*Opens with narrative*						
Micah	"word of"	X		X		X	
Nahum	"an oracle" (*massa'*) "a vision" (*hazon*)	X		X			
Habakkuk	"an oracle" (*massa'*)	X					
Zephaniah	"word of"	X	X			X	
Haggai	"word of"	X				X	X
Zechariah	"word of"	X	X			X	
Malachi	"an oracle" (*massa'*) "word of"	X					

the "pure," "original" prophetic voice. In this view, the prophet's original oracles and ministry were obscured by the layers of later editing and additions to the text. Think of an archaeological site as an illustration. After an ancient city is destroyed, another group comes to settle there, and they build new buildings. When those are torn down, others come and build on top of that rubble, and so forth, until there is a mound made up of layers on layers. If an archaeologist wants to study the earliest layer (or "stratum") of the city, he or she must dig down through the layers of dirt and debris—the additions caused by later inhabitants—to the earliest layer. In the same way, the prophetic text is composite, produced by different people who have edited and added to the text over time. If we want to understand the history, sociology, and religion of the prophet in the earliest layer, we have to identify those early remnants that we can still see in the text.

This approach is helpful in that it encourages us to read prophetic literature in the light of its original context. The prophet was responding to circumstances and beliefs in a particular time, and we do not want to flatten the book and divorce it from its historical context. The context puts controls on our interpretation, and we need to read it as it would have been understood in the time that it was created. However, this view has some serious problems as well. It disregards the explicit claims in the text of authorship and dating. It also undermines the unity of the book, which has been constructed to function as a totality. Furthermore, when scholars look for historical sources in the text, they often overlook the *message* of the text and what it has to say as Scripture. It becomes mere data to be mined— a historical artifact—and no longer has the ability to make theological claims on its recipients, as Scripture does. Even if we were somehow to use a time machine to record a video of Isaiah making a speech in Jerusalem or Jonah walking around Nineveh, that would not be Scripture (fascinating though it would be!). Scripture is the *written* word, an inspired *text* rather than a spiritual *event*, produced under the guidance of the Spirit for future generations.

A second approach is that of more recent critical scholars. In this view, the text is the result of stages of literary growth (or "redactions"). Therefore, the focus of our interpretation should not be on identifying original authors in the text (if they even existed). Rather, our focus should be on the editors and how they rearranged the text and made additions in later periods and circumstances. Thus, a prophetic book does not have a historical context; it has *multiple* historical contexts, each pertaining to one of the editions in the book's evolutionary growth.

An example of this view is Aaron Schart's explanation of the development of the end of the book of Amos in chapter 9 (see fig. 8.1). In Schart's view, the earliest layer of the text (A) was what is now Amos 9:1–4. Then, 8:14 (B) was inserted at the beginning of the unit. A later editor came and created a new ending to the book of Amos with 9:7–10 (C). The next layer (D) inserts a fragment between verse 4 and verse 7. Next, an editor added 9:11–15 (E). Previously, the book had ended in 9:10, but now it ended in

THINKING VISUALLY

The Fifth Vision of Amos
Figure 8.1

Aaron Schart, "The Fifth Vision of Amos in Context," in *Thematic Threads in the Book of the Twelve*, ed. Paul L. Redditt and Aaron Schart, Beihefte Zur Zeitschrift Für Die Alttestamentliche Wissenschaft 325 (Berlin: de Gruyter, 2003), 46–71.

9:15. Last, an editor adjusted the ending by adding some eschatological elements in 9:12a–13 (F). The oldest layer only lasted a few years before editors began to add to it. Schart writes, "Many generations tried to find their own situation in the sparse wording and meager imagery of this vision report."[6] 📝

This general approach is helpful in that it pays close attention to the structure of the text and literary artistry. It is unwilling to overlook challenging features of the text and instead seeks to explain them. Also, in contrast to the previous view, it is very interested in the message of the text (albeit, according to multiple competing editors). However, this approach has problems as well. As with the previous view, the explicit claims within the biblical text are frequently disregarded. Scholars following this approach are often overconfident in their ability to identify various editorial layers and their origins accurately.

A third approach to the text is a reaction to these trends in critical scholarship. Members of communities of faith often sense that higher criticism and the secular academy only have the tools to dissect the text of the Bible like a dead corpse. Rather than proclaiming the living word of God, critical scholars perform autopsies, fragmenting the text by looking for this author or that editor and focusing only on how the text came to be in existence, not what it says. Dissatisfied with this approach, members of faith communities have wanted to read the biblical text "as Scripture." This involves focusing on the final form of the text and reading what has been received within the religious community rather than thinking about historical context and literary development.

This approach is helpful because it seeks to recover the theological intent of the text. Furthermore, it tries to recover the reading of Scripture within the community of faith rather than in the secular academy. However, while this approach is admirable, it has its own pitfalls to be avoided. One must be careful not to concede the conclusions of skeptical critical scholars. Some in the "theological interpretation" approach do not try to defend Scripture against conclusions that would undermine its historical claims; they just dismiss them as not relevant to their reading strategy. Sometimes, in an attempt to evade challenges to the historicity of the text, readers end up decontextualizing the text. While they read it in the theological context of the literary canon, they ignore the original historical and social context and are therefore at risk of obscuring its message.

A better approach to reading the prophetic books is to look at the text from all these angles simultaneously. First, we read the text in light of its historical and social context, with confidence in the text's claims of authorship and historicity. The historical context provides "guide rails" for our interpretation. Rules of linguistics, historical circumstances, norms of the ancient Near Eastern worldview, and awareness of polemical interaction with contemporary voices form the boundaries within which our interpretations must reside. A prophetic book is anchored in a particular time period and should be understood in that light. Reading ethically means we must follow those cues from the biblical authors.

Second, we must read the text as a literary work, since it is the written text that is the inspired Scripture handed down to us. This means paying careful attention to a passage's literary features, position in the text's structure, and contribution to the overall argument. Rather than imposing our views on the text, we should read it on its own terms to uncover the author's intended meaning.

Third, our goal is to discern the theological message of the text. While we have confidence that any claims made in the text regarding history, religious practices, politics, and social conventions are true (since the Holy Spirit does not deceive), they are only vehicles for the message. We ask: What does this text teach about God? Humanity? Society? What problems is it addressing? What solutions does it present? We then recontextualize the message of the text into our contemporary situation. This requires an awareness of the original historical and theological context of the book as well as an awareness of *our* location or point of standing in redemptive history. Some books anticipate the exile of Israel, others anticipate the exile of Judah, others look forward to the return from exile, and all look forward to the climax of God's redemptive program in the New Testament. We look back on all these events as history, but the heart issues are all the same. We are the people of God, in new contexts with new manifestations of those same heart issues. Therefore, the prophetic books continue to be relevant for us. We have not stumbled upon their writings and then illegitimately or artificially appropriated them. They were written for us—to communicate God's message for our lives today, for his glory.

Conclusion

In this chapter we discussed the relationship between the ministries of the prophets in history and the written texts that pass on their actions and teachings as canonical Scripture. First, we presented a possible sketch, based on internal evidence, of how prophetic books came into being. After a prophet received the word of YHWH and proclaimed it to his contemporaries, the oracles were written down and collected. They were then combined with the written narratives of the prophet's activities and edited into the finished book. Finally, the authorship attribution, date, and other circumstances were added in the form of a superscription. Realizing that the written book is not a transcript of the prophet's ministry but a new creative endeavor is important for interpretation. As readers, we must be aware that a book contains carefully selected materials structured in a new way to present a theological message for new generations of the people of God.

Second, we briefly discussed various reading strategies that have been used for Prophets, including a search for the original author, redaction criticism, and theological or canonical reading. While each approach has strengths and contributions, we must avoid losing either the historical circumstances behind the text or the claims made by the text. Rather, we want to read the text in its context and also discover its theological contribution for us today.

Christian Reading Questions

1. How is our interpretation of the Old Testament Prophets affected when we recognize the difference between the prophet's first audience (in his own time period) and subsequent readers of his book? What do these two audiences share in common?

2. This chapter describes seven stages of growth that an Old Testament prophetic book might have undergone, from the original prophetic event (stage 1) to the nominal event (stage 7), when it was finalized and titled. Using these categories, discuss how this process may have been similar or different for a book in the New Testament, such as the book of Romans or the Gospel of Matthew.

3. Compare and contrast the various critical approaches to the text described in this chapter (and reactions to them). How can these approaches help us think about the text in a fresh way? What dangers do they represent? How do we know what our proper focus as readers should be?

4. Proper reading of a prophetic passage involves (a) reading the text in light of its original context, (b) reading it as a literary work and understanding its claims, and (c) discerning the theological message of the text. How would this process look the same or different when we're reading Leviticus? Or Judges? Or Proverbs?

PART 3

The Prophetic Books

CHAPTER NINE

Isaiah

Orientation

The first of the prophet books, Isaiah has been called "the centerpiece of prophetic literature."[1] It is a literary masterpiece, complex and sophisticated, providing a great theological overview of God's plan of redemption from the preexilic period of the Old Testament to the consummation of history and the end of time. Along the way, it addresses the nature of God, the temptations to idolatry, the relationship between judgment and salvation, the makeup of the true people of God, the essence of real faith, and many other themes central to our faith. Some passages are very familiar to us, such as Isaiah's vision of the "holy, holy, holy" God in his throne room (6:3), his promise of a sign in which "the virgin shall conceive" (7:14), his announcement of a divine and royal baby ("For to us a child is born" [9:6]), and, of course, his description of the suffering servant as "a man of sorrows" (53:3). We frequently use these texts in church, especially at Christmas and Easter, but it is important for us to hear the entire book. The authors of the New Testament certainly viewed Isaiah as relevant for Christian faith and theology—they allude to it or quote from it more than six hundred times! It points so clearly to the ministry of Jesus Christ that it has traditionally been called "the fifth gospel."[2]

Isaiah 1:1 states that the book comes from a vision of Isaiah the son of Amoz. In Hebrew, the name Isaiah means "the salvation of YHWH," a fitting name in view of the focus of his message. Isaiah was a prophet to the Southern Kingdom. The first part of the book, chapters 1–39, includes some narrative portions describing events between 740 and 701 BC. This time frame

---

HISTORICAL MATTERS

"Fact Sheet"—Isaiah

Author: Isaiah, the son of Amoz

Date: 740–695 BC

Location: Jerusalem

Political and social context: Isaiah prophesied in preexilic Judah during the reigns of Kings Uzziah, Jotham, Ahaz, and Hezekiah. Judah faced military threats from neighboring countries as well as from Assyria, a military superpower.

begins in the year that King Uzziah died (6:1), includes the reigns of Jotham and Ahaz, and ends in the time of Hezekiah (see the time line of Isaiah). 🕐

King Uzziah's reign (792–740) had been long and stable partly because Assyria, the military superpower in the east, experienced a succession of weak rulers that temporarily relieved pressure on small kingdoms like Judah. When the Assyrian emperor Tiglath-pileser III came to power in 745 BC, he and subsequent emperors once again began to expand their territory. Kings of Judah faced a decision: Should they be pro-Assyria and submit, or should they be anti-Assyria and try to defend themselves? A question like this may seem foreign and irrelevant to us, but it was "life or death" for the people of ancient Judah, and it forced King Ahaz and King Hezekiah to decide where they would put their trust. At the end of this first section, chapter 39 describes envoys from the new rising power in the east: the Neo-Babylonian Empire. It was this empire that would conquer Judah and take the people into exile.

The second part of the book of Isaiah, chapters 40–55, does not mention particular historical events during Isaiah's time. Some passages speak from a vantage point following the conquest of Jerusalem, during the Babylonian exile. Chapter 40 begins by announcing comfort to a people who have *been* punished for their sins (40:1–2). Furthermore, Isaiah announces in this section that God will return his people from exile (which in Isaiah's time has not yet happened) by means of a ruler named Cyrus (44:28; 45:1). As we discussed above in chapter 3, in 539 BC Cyrus, the ruler of the Persian Empire, conquered Babylon and issued a decree that the exiles could return to their homeland.

The third part of the book, chapters 56–66, also does not mention specific historical events during Isaiah's time. It expresses interest in themes not emphasized earlier in the book, such as sacrifice and Sabbath. The unit describes a new community of faith, which has been gathered by God (see 56:8).

Beginning in the eighteenth century, critical scholars began to propose that the book of Isaiah was actually composed by several different authors in different times.[3] An example of this is the work of the German scholar Bernhard Duhm on the book of Isaiah.[4] Duhm argued that the book of Isaiah was actually written by three different prophets (see table 9.1). According to this view, the material now found in chapters 1–39 essentially comes from the prophet Isaiah. Chapters 40–55 were added later by an anonymous prophet living in Babylon. Since we do not know his name, we might as well call him "Second Isaiah." Finally, chapters 56–66 were added even later by another anonymous prophet living in Jerusalem after the exile ("Third Isaiah"). Therefore, this view sees the book as an anthology of three writings that was finalized in the late postexilic period. Duhm

ISRAEL

KING	DATES OF REIGN	REFERENCES	KEY FEATURES OF REIGN
Jeroboam II	793–753	2 Kings 14:23	Coregent with Jehoash, 793–782
Zechariah	753–752	2 Kings 15:8	Assassinated by Shallum (2 Kings 15:10)
Shallum	752	2 Kings 15:13	Assassinated by Menahem (2 Kings 15:14)
Menahem	752–742	2 Kings 15:17	Made an alliance with Pul, king of Assyria (2 Kings 15:19–20)
Pekahiah	742–740	2 Kings 15:23	Assassinated by Pekah (2 Kings 15:25)
Pekah	752–732	2 Kings 15:27	Reigned in Gilead, 752–740, overlapping with Menahem; reigned over united Israel, 740–732; assassinated by Hoshea (2 Kings 15:30)
Hoshea	732–722	2 Kings 15:30; 17:1	Appointed by Tiglath-pileser III

Jonah 792–753

Amos 767–753

Hosea 755–725

JUDAH

KING	DATES OF REIGN	REFERENCES	KEY FEATURES OF REIGN
Uzziah/ Azariah	792–740	2 Kings 14:21; 2 Chron. 26:3	Coregent with his father, Amaziah, 792–767; began reigning at age 16 (2 Kings 14:21); struck with leprosy for offering incense in 750, then lived in a separate house while his son governed (2 Chron. 26:16–21)
Jotham	750–735	2 Kings 15:32–33	Coregent with Uzziah, 750–740; removed from the throne in 735
Ahaz	735–715	2 Kings 16:1–2	16 years counted from death of Jotham in 732 (2 Kings 15:38)
Hezekiah	729–686	2 Kings 18:1–2	Coregent with father, Ahaz, 729–715; Sennacherib attacked Judah in 701 BC (2 Kings 18:13)

Isaiah 740–695

Micah 742–686

Table 9.1. The Three Books of Isaiah

Book 1: Chapters 1–39	Book 2: Chapters 40–55	Book 3: Chapters 56–66
Messages of Isaiah of Jerusalem	Unknown prophet in Babylon	Unknown prophet in Yehud
740–700 BC	546–538 BC	537–520 BC
Isaiah	"Second Isaiah"	"Third Isaiah"

Source: Adapted from John W. Miller, *Meet the Prophets: A Beginner's Guide to the Books of the Biblical Prophets—Their Meaning Then and Now* (New York: Paulist, 1987), 92.

also suggested that certain passages *within* chapters 1–39 are also from much later times. For example, chapters 24–27 are often characterized as apocalyptic, coming from the late postexilic period. Later scholars identified other late additions throughout chapters 1–39 including 2:2–5; 4:2–6; 11:10–16; 12:1–6; 13:1–14:23; 15:1–16:14; 19:16–25; 21:1–11; 23:5–11, 15–16; 28:5–6; 29:17–24; and 30:19–26. One scholar concludes, "Looked at more carefully, then, the book of Isaiah turns out to be a highly complex mosaic of prophetic words and reports, emanating from an *ongoing* tradition of prophetic activity and spanning a period of centuries."[5]

Recent critical scholars have moved beyond Duhm's foundation in order to explain better the literary unity of the book as a whole. Rather than three independent authors in different periods writing in isolation, they argue, the book grew over time as later authors added their own comments and writings to it. For example, one scholar writes that the historical Isaiah of Jerusalem did not write a text that existed independently. Instead, "Second Isaiah" was deeply influenced by Isaiah, collected his unpublished material (now found in chapters 1–39), and edited it together with his own writings to link together chapters 1–39 and 40–55.[6] In other words, the later part of the book was written primarily to preserve the earlier part of the book that he had inherited.[7] Another scholar argues that it was "Third Isaiah" who added his own material and edited the book as a whole.[8] In these views, the book's structure and unity are explained as the work of a single author or series of authors who carefully edited the book together into a sophisticated whole. However, these authors are at the *end* of the process. Because they are living long after the time of Isaiah, the near-term predictive prophecies in the book are not predictive at all.

In spite of the sophistication and careful thought that have gone into these critical approaches, for a number of reasons it is better to understand the book as coming from the historical prophet Isaiah of Jerusalem. First, this is the straightforward claim of the book. We have no statements either in the book or from ancient documents that the book ever originated in parts. This is not an argument from silence because the book says that it came from Isaiah in the late seventh century (1:1). Second, the inspired

Table 9.2. New Testament References to Isaiah

Isaiah	New Testament	Attribution
1:9	Romans 9:29	"as Isaiah predicted"
6:9–13	Matthew 13:14–15	"the prophecy of Isaiah is fulfilled"
	John 12:39–41	"again Isaiah said"; "Isaiah said these things"
	Acts 28:25–27	"the Holy Spirit was right in saying to your fathers through Isaiah the prophet"
9:1–2	Matthew 4:14–16	"spoken by the prophet Isaiah"
10:22	Romans 9:27	"Isaiah cries out concerning Israel"
11:10	Romans 15:12	"and again Isaiah says"
29:13	Matthew 15:7–9; Mark 7:6	"well did Isaiah prophesy of you"
40:3–5	Matthew 3:3	"spoken of by the prophet Isaiah"
	Mark 1:2–3	"written in Isaiah the prophet"
	Luke 3:4–6	"written in the book of the words of Isaiah the prophet"
	John 1:23	"as the prophet Isaiah said"
42:1–4	Matthew 12:17–21	"spoken by the prophet Isaiah"
53:1	John 12:38	"the word spoken by the prophet Isaiah"
	Romans 10:16	"for Isaiah says"
53:4	Matthew 8:17	"spoken by the prophet Isaiah"
53:7–8	Acts 8:28–33	"he was reading the prophet Isaiah"
61:1–2	Luke 4:17–19	"[in] the scroll of the prophet Isaiah"
65:1–2	Romans 10:20–21	"Isaiah is so bold as to say"

authors of the New Testament quote or allude to passages throughout the entire book of Isaiah and attribute it all to him (see table 9.2). Third, apart from the issue of predictive prophecy, the case is weak that the later chapters reflect a later time period or location. For example, chapters 40–55 supposedly were written by a prophet in Babylon. Yet the references to mountains, forests, sea, snow, and Lebanon (among other things) are reflective of the land of Palestine; they are not found in Babylon. Furthermore, chapters 40–66 do not contain historical or social images reflective of life in Babylon.[9] Fourth, specific, predictive prophecy is not only present in the book; it is a central part of the book's *argument*. As Isaiah builds the case for God's ability to save, he announces that only a God who can declare the things that are coming is worthy of our trust and faith (see 40:21; 41:4, 26; 44:6–8; 46:10–11; 48:3, 5–6). Therefore, it contradicts and undermines the explicit theological points that Isaiah is making to say that his prophecy only appears to make predictions. For these reasons and others, it is important to maintain the conviction that God's Word is true in all that it asserts, including the claim that Isaiah is responsible for the oracles in the book.[10]

Exploration

In chapter 6 and in the discussion of persuasive strategy 12 ("Historical Events and Entities as Analogies for Eschatological Realities") in chapter 7, we saw that the message of the prophets is generally concerned with five phases of God's dealings with Israel. Isaiah addresses all five of these phases (see fig. 9.1). The stick figure represents the prophet's chronological location as he looks to the past and future.

First, Isaiah indicts Judah for breaking God's covenant. The nation engages in all kinds of evil and refuses to serve God as he requires. Because of this, God will devastate their land in the near future by means of the Assyrian and Babylonian empires from the east. Following this historical judgment, God will bring his people back from exile and settle them in the land again. Throughout the book, Isaiah looks to the eschatological future, in which he predicts forgiveness and protection for those who belong to God and terrible, lasting judgment for those who rebel.

It is common for scholars to divide the book of Isaiah into two parts: chapters 1–39 and chapters 40–66. This makes some sense since the first half references events in Isaiah's time while the second half has a greater focus on God's redemption in the future. However, the book is a complex literary whole, with shared themes and vocabulary linking the parts

THINKING VISUALLY

The Five Phases: Isaiah
Figure 9.1

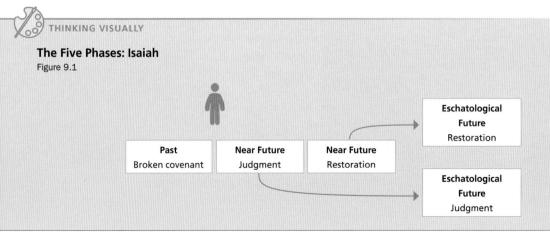

together. One example of this is the references to YHWH as the "Holy One of Israel," a phrase that occurs twenty-five times throughout the book[11] but only six times in the rest of the Old Testament.[12] Isaiah makes one cohesive argument, with earlier parts providing the background and basis for later parts. The overall structure of the book is as follows (see table 9.3).[13]

Table 9.3. The Structure of Isaiah

Superscription (1:1)	
The problem: Israel is not God's servant (chaps. 1–5)	A preview of the solution: Isaiah's call (chap. 6)

YHWH is the only deliverer (chaps. 7–39)
  • King Ahaz—an example of refusing to trust YHWH (chaps. 7–12)
    * Oracles against the nations (chaps. 13–23)
    * Oracles against the whole earth (chaps. 24–27)
    * Oracles against Israel and Judah (chaps. 28–35)
  • King Hezekiah—an example of trusting YHWH (chaps. 36–39)

Grace, deliverance, and transformation (chaps. 40–55)
  • YHWH's desire and ability to deliver (40:1–44:23)
  • The great deliverance: return from exile for Israel (44:24–48:22)
  • The greatest deliverance: atonement for the world (chaps. 49–53)
  • The invitation to deliverance (chaps. 54–55)

The new servants of YHWH (chaps. 56–66)
  • (A) A new people (56:1–8)
    * (B) Sin and obedience (56:9–59:15a)
      - (C) The warrior YHWH (59:15b–21)
        » (D) Salvation in Zion (chaps. 60–62)
      - (C′) The warrior YHWH (63:1–6)
    * (B′) Sin and obedience (63:7–66:17)
  • (A′) A new people (66:18–24)

Chapters 1–5 introduce the book as a whole by presenting the essential problem: Israel has been chosen by God and called to be his special people, but they will not submit to him and serve him. They break the covenant he made with them, worship idols, and refuse to respond to him even when he punishes them. In **chapter 6**, Isaiah's initial call to ministry functions as a pattern for what God will do with the nation. As with Isaiah, it is only when God's people acknowledge their sinfulness and trust completely in him that he will act on their behalf so that they can carry his message to their rebellious and captive world.[14] **Chapters 7–39** compose a lengthy unit in which Isaiah makes the case that only God is able to deliver Israel from sin and give them the restoration they long for. There are many potential "deliverers" around them, but they will all fail and come up short.

Having laid this foundation, Isaiah moves in **chapters 40–55** to state that God *wants* to deliver his people and is *able* to deliver them. In this section, Isaiah uses a prediction of the historical return from exile as a pattern for God's spiritual deliverance from guilt and for a transformation that he will bring about through the suffering of his faithful Servant. In this way, God will form a new people for himself, described in **chapters 56–66**. These will be chosen first out of Israel and then from every nation. God will accomplish what Israel could not do for themselves, but he expects obedience and allegiance to him through the covenant. Zion will be a magnet for the true people of God from every nation, and they will live in a new heavens and new earth in peace and prosperity.

A Snapshot of the Book

■ READ ISAIAH 1 ■

There is no table of contents in the book of Isaiah, but the first chapter is a preview of the most important themes in the book. God laments that he has chosen people for himself who have rebelled against him. They are wicked and corrupt, and even though God has brought judgment to bring them back to their senses, they are determined to rebel (1:5–9). Surprisingly, they are also incredibly religious! They make many sacrifices and burnt offerings, keep the holy festivals, and lift their hands in prayer (1:10–15). If they refuse to submit to God, why are they so enthusiastic in worshiping him? Either they think that these things will be sufficient, or they are trying to manipulate him. But what God really wants is righteousness (1:16–17). If they are willing to repent, he will forgive their sins (1:18–19), but if they refuse, he will destroy them (1:21–31). This is the central choice in the book as a whole.

God's Plans for Jerusalem versus Who She Is Now

■ READ ISAIAH 2–5 ■

In chapters 2–4, Isaiah contrasts God's future plans for Jerusalem with the actual Jerusalem that Isaiah can observe around him. Isaiah makes the contrast in an A-B-A structure. The opening, 2:2–4, describes Jerusalem as the epicenter of God's salvation, with his people from the nations flowing to it and his word coming out of it. The longer center section, 2:5–4:1, describes present Jerusalem as a place rejected by God. He will target Jerusalem with judgment, destroy its idols, bring famine and social unrest, take away their wealth, and kill them. Finally, 4:2–6 describes Jerusalem as a place full of holy, forgiven people, cleansed of bloodshed, dwelling with

God. The short beginning and end indicate God's plans for the city, while the longer center is a depressing picture of how far God's chosen people have fallen short of his expectations.

Isaiah 5 contains a brief parable to illustrate God's disappointment with his city. In it, the owner does everything he can to build a vineyard well. He rightly expects a good harvest, but in the end it only yields wild grapes. His determination to destroy the vineyard is a terrifying warning to "the house of Israel and Judah" (5:7) that it represents. Just as a farmer looks for good fruit, God has looked for justice and righteousness but has found only bloodshed. He will destroy them in his anger.

Isaiah's Call

▓ READ ISAIAH 6 ▓

As we noted in chapter 8, it is typical for a prophetic book to *begin* with God's call of the prophet (see Jer. 1; Ezek. 1; Hosea 1). This not only reflects actual chronology, it also establishes the authority of the prophet right from the outset. However, the book of Isaiah begins with five chapters introducing a problem—that Israel is not serving God. Chapter 6, the narrative of Isaiah's call to prophetic ministry, follows this introduction as a *preview* of what God is going to do for Israel.

In Isaiah's vision, the central idea he encounters is the holiness of God. Faced with this, Isaiah pronounces woe on himself because of his unclean lips and his membership in a community that is unclean. But God takes the initiative to cleanse Isaiah of his sin, restores him, and sends him on a mission to represent God to Judah. This is a picture of what God will do for Israel. When they recognize their need for purification, he will remove their sin (though he does not yet say how this will be accomplished), and then it will be their task to mediate his truth and salvation to all the nations of the earth (see table 9.4). Isaiah is dismayed to hear that the hearts of his audience will be hard and stubborn (6:9–13). This sets up the idea in the book that, as a whole, Israel will refuse to submit to God and will persist in rebellion. This is the tree that is felled (6:13a). But

CANONICAL CONNECTIONS

The Text of Isaiah 2:2–4

The text of Isaiah 2:2–4 is found with almost identical wording in Micah 4:1–3. Scholars are uncertain who actually wrote the text. It is possible that Micah borrowed it from Isaiah, or that Isaiah borrowed it from Micah. A third possibility is that it was a common saying in ancient Israel and both prophets used it in their books. Often, the Holy Spirit's inspiration of biblical authors involved guiding them as they used preexisting material. In Isaiah, the idea of God bringing people to Jerusalem appears again in Isaiah 56:6–8.

THEOLOGICAL ISSUES

"Woe to Those Who Call Evil Good"

Isaiah 5:20 pronounces "woe" (or doom) on those who call evil good and good evil. It is always a challenge for God's people when they are forced to choose between cultural values (which *seem* enlightened, thoughtful, and relevant) and Scripture (which *seems* old). Things like political beliefs or sexual behavior are so embedded in the running river of a society's beliefs that it can seem impossible to swim against the flow and call out evil for what it truly is. But, upstream of these cultural choices, the follower of God has a decision to make. The next verse, 5:21, says, "Woe to those who are wise in their own eyes." The choice is ultimately based on where we put our trust: our own wisdom or the wisdom of God.

Table 9.4. Isaiah as a Paradigm for Israel

	Isaiah	Israel
Problem	Unclean: "I am lost!"	Covenant unfaithfulness
Solution	Cleansing and redemption	Cleansing and redemption
Means	Burning coal → atonement	Painful exile → atonement
Goal	Faithfulness, service	Faithfulness, service
Mission	To Israel	To the world
Result	Israel will harden	The world will flock to Jerusalem

a *subgroup*—the true people of God—will be the holy seed that remains (6:13b). In other words, not all of ethnic Israel will be God's true people; there are other criteria for relationship with him.

An Example of Refusing to Trust YHWH

▓ READ ISAIAH 7–12 ▓

Isaiah's call to prophetic ministry ends with the difficult news that his audience will be hard-hearted. This is immediately realized in his conversation with King Ahaz in chapter 7. The Assyrian Empire is threatening the region, and two of Judah's neighbors, Syria and the Northern Kingdom, have decided to form an alliance to defend themselves (see the discussion above in chap. 3). Because Ahaz has chosen not to get involved, these neighbors are on their way to attack *him*. God tells Isaiah to meet King Ahaz "at the end of the conduit of the upper pool on the highway to the Washer's Field" (7:3). There, Isaiah tells Ahaz not to be afraid of these two kings because they are "two smoldering stumps of firebrands" (7:4), which may look impressive and frightening but are no danger at all (7:7–9). To bolster Ahaz's confidence in God's word, Isaiah invites him to request a sign from God, but Ahaz stubbornly refuses. Isaiah responds by announcing a sign anyway: "The virgin shall conceive and bear a son" (7:14). The focus of this sign is on *timing*. Before the child reaches a certain

Figure 9.2. Isaiah's lips cleansed by a burning coal (*Propheta Isaia* by Antonio Balestra)

age, Syria and Israel will be deserted (7:16). When Ahaz sees the child in the future, he will remember that God's word came true and that he should have listened. Because Ahaz has refused to trust in God and has instead trusted in an alliance with Assyria, God will bring Assyria against Judah in judgment (7:18–20).

In 8:1, Isaiah names his child Maher-shalal-hash-baz, which means in Hebrew, "Swift is the booty, speedy is the prey." This is an alarming prediction that Assyria will devastate Israel and Syria. But Judah is a target as well. Perhaps prompted by the conduit of the upper pool, Isaiah states that because Judah has rejected God (the gently flowing, consistent stream that gives life), they will get Assyria, a raging river that destroys like a flood (8:6–8). Assyria will be an instrument of judgment in God's hand (10:5–6). However, because of his sovereign power and justice, God will also hold Assyria accountable for what they have done (10:12–16). This should be a comfort to Judah.

Although this section announces the disastrous results of trusting in a nation like Assyria (powerful though it is), Isaiah simultaneously develops the theme that God will be his people's ultimate deliverer. In Isaiah 9:1–7, Isaiah proclaims hope through another child: a future messiah. He will be a light in the darkness (9:2) who will bring victory and peace (9:3–5). He will have divine and royal names (9:6) and will sit on the throne of David, "to uphold it with justice and with righteousness" forever (9:7). This individual is described further in chapter 11. He will come from the stump of Jesse (another reference to David) and will be empowered by the Spirit (11:1–2). His reign will bring justice (11:3–5) and a transformation of the world, centered on his "holy mountain" Jerusalem (11:6–9). Isaiah 7–12 concludes with a hymn, praising God for his grace, salvation, and comfort.

Oracles against the Nations

■ READ ISAIAH 13–23 ■

Chapters 13–23 contain Isaiah's oracles against the nations surrounding Judah. He announces judgment

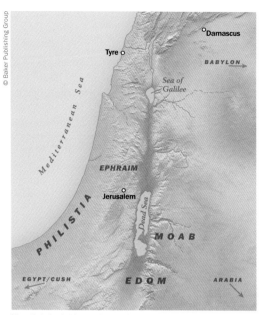

Map 9.1. Isaiah's oracles against the nations

against Babylon, Philistia, Moab, Damascus (Syria), Ephraim (Israel), Cush, Egypt, Edom, Arabia, Jerusalem (the "Valley of Vision"), and Tyre. The sections are arranged in a rough geographical pattern: first from east to west, then from north to south, then from west to east, then home to Jerusalem, and finally concluding in chapter 23 with Tyre, the economic powerhouse of the known world (see map 9.1).

It is not certain that foreign nations ever actually received these words. Today, when someone writes an open letter and distributes it widely, it is really intended for that broad audience, and it may not even matter whether the person to whom it is addressed receives it. In the same way, these messages in Isaiah are formally addressed to the nations but ultimately designed to persuade Judah. Isaiah's main point is this: "It would be foolish to put your trust in these nations to help you, when they are under judgment and about to be destroyed. They are all sinking ships; why would you expect them to deliver you?"[15]

Oracles against the Whole Earth

■ READ ISAIAH 24–27 ■

Isaiah extends his warning against trusting anyone or anything other than God. Whereas in the previous chapters he undermined trust in any of the surrounding nations, in this next unit he has in view the entire world. He begins by announcing its destruction: "The earth shall be utterly empty and utterly plundered, for the LORD has spoken this word" (24:3). Isaiah uses the image of two cities. The first city is a ruined city, representing the world as it stands against God. It is broken down (24:10), its gates are in shambles (24:12), and it will never be rebuilt (25:2). God humbles its inhabitants and throws it to the dust (26:5). Isaiah paints a terrifying picture of the earth's inhabitants feeling God's wrath but finding themselves unable to escape. But there is a second city, Jerusalem (24:23). There God will make a rich feast for his people (25:6), and he will swallow up death—their most-feared enemy—forever (25:8). The people of Judah will someday sing, "We have a strong city. . . . Open the gates, that the righteous nation that keeps faith may enter in" (26:1–2). In light of this hope, even with enemies closing in, Isaiah writes, "Trust in the Lord forever, for the Lord God is an everlasting rock" (26:4). ⚱

Oracles against Israel and Judah

▨ READ ISAIAH 28–35 ▨

Having subverted any confidence in the surrounding nations (chaps. 13–23) or the world as a whole (chaps. 24–27), Isaiah turns his attention back to Israel and Judah in chapters 28–35. This section is organized around six "woes" (sometimes translated "Ah"). In 28:1 he pronounces doom on drunkards who stagger and are full of filthy vomit (28:8). In 29:1–8, he attacks false religion and rebellious leaders. In 29:15, his target is leaders who conspire against God. In 30:1–2, he describes those who reject God and turn to Egypt for help. This is the subject of the fifth "woe" in 31:1 as well. They go down to Egypt and put their trust in horses, chariots, and horsemen (31:1–3). In the modern day, this would be like trusting in advanced weaponry and a superior air force. The last woe comes in 33:1, against Assyria. As Isaiah said previously in chapter 10, when Assyria has completed its work of judgment for God, it too will be judged because God is a righteous king (33:22). The theme that runs through this section is *trust*. God says through Isaiah that the people despise his word, trust in their own foolish plans, and seek security from those who will eventually oppress them (30:12). Instead, they should turn to him! "In returning and rest you shall be saved; in quietness and in trust shall be your strength" (30:15).

An Example of Trusting YHWH

▨ READ ISAIAH 36–39 ▨

When we come to Isaiah 36, King Hezekiah is ruling over Judah. He is the son of Ahaz, who refused to trust God in Isaiah 7. Whereas Ahaz was concerned about an attack by the local kingdoms of Israel and Syria, Hezekiah is facing a much greater threat: the Assyrian Empire. The Assyrian emperor Sennacherib has come to Judah to reestablish his power in the region.

When the Assyrians arrive, a high-ranking officer ("Rabshakeh") comes to stand by the "conduit of the upper pool on the highway to the Washer's Field" (36:2). This may sound like an insignificant detail, but it is the same location where Isaiah met King Ahaz in Isaiah 7, linking the two stories together. The Assyrians pose an existential threat, having already devastated Judah and besieged Israel's second-largest city, Lachish. But Hezekiah does

HISTORICAL MATTERS

"He Will Swallow Up Death"

The image of *swallowing* death is a clever reference to *Mot*, the Canaanite god of death. In ancient writings, *Mot* is pictured as a monster with a huge throat. One Canaanite text says, "Be careful, couriers of the gods: don't get near [Mot] . . . lest he take you as he would a lamb in his mouth, lest you be destroyed as a kid in his crushing jaws.[b] Another text speaks of descending into the throat of Mot, who boasts that he consumes heaps of things.[c] But God says that he will swallow the swallower. Paul quotes from this passage in 1 Corinthians 15:54 when he says that Christ will give his people victory over death forever by resurrecting us as he himself is resurrected.

not respond like his faithless father, Ahaz. Instead, "As soon as King Hezekiah heard it, he tore his clothes and covered himself with sackcloth and went into the house of the LORD" (37:1). God responds with overwhelming force: an angel strikes down the Assyrian army, and Sennacherib limps home, only to be assassinated by his sons (37:36–38). Isaiah also narrates the story of Hezekiah's trust in God when he became ill (chap. 38), and he introduces the Babylonians as the new power that will threaten Judah and eventually take them into exile (chap. 39).

A comparison of Ahaz (chaps. 7–12) and Hezekiah (chaps. 36–39) is instructive. Ahaz faces a relatively minor threat, and he is told by Isaiah not to worry. But he trusts in Assyria instead, and the result is catastrophic. By contrast, Hezekiah is up against a military superpower that has already devastated his land. But he trusts in God and is delivered. These two narratives serve as bookends around an entire unit (chaps. 7–39) that challenges our objects of trust and proclaims that only YHWH, the God of Israel, is a capable deliverer (see fig. 9.3).

It may seem like this concept is too simple to deserve twenty-three chapters of attention. But is it that simple? It is one thing to say we trust in God when the stakes seem relatively low. However, when our reputations or even our very lives are on the line, it is tempting to switch allegiances to that which is tangible and logical and somewhat under our control. Isaiah warns us that this is a false hope. Only God can accomplish what we really need.

The Lord's Desire and Ability to Deliver

■ READ ISAIAH 40:1–44:23 ■

At the end of Isaiah 39, the Babylonian envoys are showing interest in the treasures of Jerusalem, and Isaiah predicts that some of Hezekiah's

THINKING VISUALLY

Bookends in Isaiah 7–39
Figure 9.3

7–12	King Ahaz does not trust God ⟶ Judah destroyed	(historical)
13–23	Judgment on the nations (do not trust them!)	
24–27	Judgment on the earth (= trust God!)	(prophetic)
28–35	Judgment on Israel and Judah (do not trust in self)	
36–39	King Hezekiah does trust God ⟶ Judah saved	(historical)

sons will be taken into exile (39:7). Hezekiah responds that at least there will be peace in his days (39:8). In the next verse, we immediately sense that we are in a new major unit (40:1). Isaiah's message concerns a time years later. He is comforting his audience over the judgment of exile that has already taken place from his rhetorical standpoint. The book now turns its attention, primarily, to God's plan of salvation for his people and its repercussions.

Isaiah begins the new unit by assuring God's people that it is God's intention to deliver them. They could not take this for granted—the exile was a brutal outpouring of God's wrath. But Jerusalem has received from YHWH's hand their deserved punishment, and now he announces that he is coming to deliver them. Isaiah proclaims the good news: "Behold, the Lord GOD comes with might, and his arm rules for him; behold, his reward is with him" (40:10). God's power has been used to punish them, but now his mighty arm will heal and restore.

Having established the good news of God's grace, Isaiah begins to weave together two themes in this section. The first significant theme is that God is incomparable. Isaiah proves this by comparing God's power and superiority over everything with the futility and helplessness of idols made by human hands. Isaiah asks, Who else has measured the waters in his hand or weighed the mountains on scales (40:12)? He brings princes to nothing (40:23), and the whole earth trembles before him (41:5). Isaiah juxtaposes these attributes of God with the wood and metal from which idols are constructed—the craftsmen have to be careful that the idols do not rot or topple over (40:20)! In 44:9–17, Isaiah describes a man who cuts down wood, uses half of it to cook his dinner, and then makes the other half into an idol that he worships. Surely these created gods are nothing compared to the living God, who created all things! Furthermore, only God can know the future and announce it to his prophets in advance (41:22, 26). He challenges, "Who is like me? . . . Let them declare what is to come, and what will happen" (44:7).

Later in the book, Isaiah will make stunning claims about what God is planning to do. Not only will he return his people from exile in Babylon; he will *spiritually* redeem and transform them. And if that were not radical enough, he will accomplish the spiritual redemption of the entire world. God's incomparability and power are important theological groundwork for these claims. Someone may say to Isaiah, "No god I know could do these things!" to which Isaiah could respond, "Yes, but he is utterly unlike any god you've ever known."

A second theme that Isaiah begins to develop in chapters 40–44 and continues in chapters 45–53 is that of "servant." Most of the twenty occurrences of the word "servant" refer to Israel. They are intended to be his witnesses (43:10), but they are blind (42:19). However, there are four distinct poetic units that refer to a servant as a future, unnamed individual who will accomplish God's salvation *for* Israel. These four units have been called "Servant Songs."[16] The first of these is in 42:1–9, where the Servant is described as empowered by the Spirit (see the messianic, Davidic king in 11:2) and bringing justice to the nations. However, he will do this not with dominating, overpowering force but by being a "bruised reed" (see Matt. 12:18–20). Significantly, Isaiah does not say that this Servant will make a covenant with God's people—he will *be* a covenant. Through this individual, God is "doing a new thing" as he creates a people for himself who will declare his praise (43:19–21).

The Great Deliverance

■ READ ISAIAH 44:24–48:22 ■

In the previous section, Isaiah claimed multiple times that only God can predict the course of history and declare the end from the beginning. Now, in the present section, he demonstrates this by making a specific prediction. God will confirm the word of his prophets (44:26) and raise up Cyrus to fulfill his purposes (44:28). Again he says in 45:1, "Thus says the LORD to his anointed, to Cyrus, whose right hand I have grasped, to subdue nations before him." Throughout the subsequent chapter, Isaiah describes God's power as the creator of the earth and argues again that he is superior to idols because he can declare the future. At the end of the section, God announces that his purposes are to bring his people back from exile in Babylon. He says, "Go out from Babylon, flee from Chaldea, declare this with a shout of joy. . . . 'The LORD has redeemed his servant Jacob!'" (48:20). As Isaiah predicted, the Persian emperor Cyrus conquered Babylon and allowed the exiles to return home (Ezra 1:1–4). Isaiah uses God's physical, historical restoration from exile (in this section) as a pattern or token of spiritual restoration (in the next section). If Isaiah predicted the former and it came to pass, then the latter will come to pass as well.

The Greatest Deliverance

■ READ ISAIAH 49–53 ■

At Isaiah 49–53, we reach the literary and theological climax of the book. As we saw above, the first of the Servant Songs occurs in 42:1–9, in which Isaiah looks forward to an individual who will be the means of God's salvation for his people. This present section is organized around three more Servant Songs, in which the nature and task of the unnamed Servant become increasingly clear. The second Servant Song is found in 49:1–9. At first, it is confusing that God calls this individual "Israel" (49:3), since he is called to restore Israel (Jacob) a few verses later (49:5). Is the nation being described as an individual? No, just the opposite. The Servant is being called "Israel." This is because he is fulfilling Israel's role of mediating God's truth and salvation to the nations, a task that goes back to God's covenant with Abraham (Gen. 12:3). He will be fully "Israel" in a way that the nation could not because of its sin.[17] Isaiah makes this explicit claim in 49:6: "It is too light a thing that you should be my servant to raise up the tribes of Jacob and to bring back the preserved of Israel; I will make you as a light for the nations, that my salvation may reach to the end of the earth." In other words, in spite of Israel's history of rebellion, the Servant is *overqualified* to restore them! He will fulfill God's original plan to offer salvation to all the earth.

The third Servant Song is found in 50:4–9. With this song, it is becoming clear that the Servant is abused and mistreated. He says in 50:6, "I gave my back to those who strike, and my cheeks to those who pull out the beard; I hid not my face from disgrace and spitting." Even so, God will help the Servant to accomplish his task. In the next verse, Isaiah highlights the close alliance between God and the Servant by asking, "Who among you fears the LORD and obeys the voice of his servant?" (50:10).

The fourth and most well-known Servant Song is found in 52:13–53:12. The passage begins by announcing that the Servant will be successful in what he sets out to do ("My servant shall prosper," the ESV alternate reading in 52:13). As we continue in the poem and read about his wounds and humiliation, this introduction clarifies that it is not *in spite of* his suffering but *because of it* that he will succeed. This idea is developed further by the surprise that people experience when they see the Servant (52:14–53:1). Since chapter 40, Isaiah has spoken of God's mighty arm of salvation (40:10; 48:14; 51:5, 9). Now, when God finally bares his holy arm and unveils his means of salvation, it is . . . *this* person? He is like a young plant or a root in dry ground, with none of the outward qualities that one would expect of a great deliverer (53:2–3). Typically, our leaders are domineering, attractive, and obviously successful. But this Servant looks weak.

"About Whom Does the Prophet Say This?"

In Acts 8:27–40, Philip the apostle is told by an angel to meet an Ethiopian official on the road from Jerusalem. The Ethiopian is reading from Isaiah 53:7–8. When Philip asks him if he understands it, the Ethiopian responds, "About whom, I ask you, does the prophet say this, about himself or about someone else?" (8:34). Interestingly, this has been a question for other readers over the years. Many critical scholars identify the Servant as Isaiah, who suffers on behalf of Israel. But Philip tells the Ethiopian plainly that the Servant is Jesus and explains the good news about him from "this Scripture" (8:35). The Ethiopian believes and is immediately baptized, compelled by his new faith.

The reason comes in 53:4. The Servant suffers grief and repulsive wounds not because they belong to him but because he is carrying them *for us*. "He was pierced for our transgressions; he was crushed for our iniquities; . . . and with his wounds we are healed" (53:5). It was YHWH's will to crush him, for this is the way that God would deliver Israel and the nations. The Servant is a guilt offering, a sacrifice that makes atonement for sin (53:10). Because Israel failed as God's servant, a future individual will come to be the Servant. He will create a new people for God, from Israel and the nations, to be God's servants forever. Isaiah 52:13–53:12 is not just a simple prediction of Jesus's atoning death. It makes an important theological contribution within the book, exploring the contrast between the appearance of the Servant and his actual qualifications and ultimate success. There is a danger that one could stumble over his outward presentation and fail to recognize his power to redeem (see Paul's warning in 1 Cor. 1:23). This develops Isaiah's insistence earlier in the book that God is not only fully qualified as a deliverer; he is in fact the only possible savior.

The Invitation to Deliverance

■ READ ISAIAH 54–55 ■

Isaiah 54 begins this short section with a discussion of the implications of the Servant's atoning work. Because he makes "many to be accounted righteous, and he shall bear their iniquities" (53:11), the Servant is transforming a new people for God. Isaiah cries, "Sing, O barren one, who did not bear; break forth into singing and cry aloud, you who have not been in labor!" (54:1). Paul quotes this verse in Galatians 4:27, recognizing that the true people of God are those who are born in the new covenant and are members of the new Jerusalem. The work of the Servant is "the heritage of the servants of the LORD" (Isa. 54:17).

In chapter 55, Isaiah issues an invitation to the work of the Servant. He says, "Come, everyone who thirsts, come to the waters; and he who has no money, come, buy and eat! Come, buy wine and milk without money and without price" (55:1). Notice that he repeats the word "come" four times. This invitation is free, extended to those who have nothing—it is for those who are ready to give up trying to deliver themselves (55:2). When they come, God will make an everlasting covenant with them that is connected to his covenant with David (55:3). This is a reference to the new covenant, although Isaiah does not call it that. We have seen throughout the book that Isaiah has been promising a Davidic ruler who will bring hope to all people by suffering as God's Servant. Isaiah implores, "Seek the LORD while he may be found; . . . for he will abundantly pardon" (55:6–7).

A New People (A)

■ READ ISAIAH 56:1–8 ■

The last major division in Isaiah comprises chapters 56–66. As I indicate above in the outline of the whole book (table 9.3), these chapters are structured as a chiasm in which the first part (A) corresponds to the last part (A'), the second part (B) corresponds to the second to last part (B'), the third part (C) corresponds to the third part from the end (C'), and the middle part (D) forms the center and focus of the unit. In the following discussion, we will look at each part separately, in order, even though some of them are quite short. As a whole, the unit focuses on two main themes: a call for the people of God to be righteous and the good news that God's work will enable his people to meet this demand and live in relationship with him.

The Bible is consistent in its teaching that when God saves people, they will *necessarily* respond with obedience and good works (see James 2:14–17). In chapters 40–55, Isaiah announced that God would deliver his people from sin by the substitutionary work of the Servant. The people would not be delivered because they finally figured out how to obey and be faithful. Rather, they would be transformed as an act of God's grace, accomplished for them. Now, in 56:1–2, Isaiah calls them to the logical implication of that grace: "Keep justice, and do righteousness. . . . Blessed is the man who does this, and the son of man who holds it fast, who keeps the Sabbath, not profaning it, and keeps his hand from doing any evil." The Sabbath was the sign of God's covenant with Israel, and Isaiah uses it here as a token of allegiance and submission to God in covenant relationship.

Isaiah then gives two examples of those who would not normally be considered obvious candidates for membership in the people of God. First, the foreigner might think that he is "second class" because he is not ethnically Israelite (56:3a). But to the foreigners who have joined themselves to

Food and Drink

In Isaiah 55, the prophet uses food and drink as a metaphor for joining God's true people through the Servant. Jesus frequently used similar images in his teaching and preaching. In the Sermon on the Mount he says, "Blessed are those who hunger and thirst for righteousness" (Matt. 5:6). In the Gospel of John he says, "Do not work for the food that perishes, but for the food that endures to eternal life" (6:27); "I am the bread of life" (6:35); "Whoever feeds on my flesh and drinks my blood has eternal life, and I will raise him up on the last day" (6:54); "If anyone thirsts, let him come to me and drink" (7:37). The book of Revelation speaks of a "river of the water of life, . . . flowing from the throne of God" (22:1). In the last few verses of the biblical canon, the Spirit makes a final invitation based on Isaiah 55:1, "And let the one who is thirsty come; let the one who desires take the water of life without price" (Rev. 22:17).

YHWH, God says that he will bring them to his holy mountain and accept them (56:7). Second, the eunuch would also think that he would be left out and have no future (56:3b). This is especially so since under the covenant with Israel, eunuchs were banned from the assembly of YHWH (Lev. 21:20; Deut. 23:1). But God says that the eunuch who holds fast to his covenant will have a legacy better than sons and daughters (56:4–5). The point here is that membership in the true people of God depends on being covenant members who have joined with YHWH, not anything else. Ethnic Israelites who reject God's word will be excluded, while even foreigners and eunuchs will be accepted because of their faith that leads to obedience.

Sin and Obedience (B)

■ READ ISAIAH 56:9–59:15a ■

Obedience to God is the goal and expectation when he delivers by the Servant, but right now the people are still stuck in sin and rebellion. No one takes God seriously and practices righteousness. They worship fertility idols and "burn with lust among the oaks, under every green tree," even slaughtering their own children in the valleys as sacrifices (57:4–5).[18] They also show themselves to be unfaithful by trusting in political alliances with other nations (57:9). Isaiah lists a whole catalogue of sins including bloodshed, falsehood, and mistreatment of one another (59:1–15). However, in the midst of rehearsing all their failings, Isaiah assures them that God can and will heal them (57:14–21). What God prioritizes in worship is not heartless religious rituals but his people submitting themselves to him and doing justice. "Is not this the fast that I choose: to loose the bonds of wickedness, . . . to let the oppressed go free?" (58:6). As a whole, this section calls on God's people to obey, but it honestly states that they will not be able to do so without his help.

The Warrior YHWH (C)

■ READ ISAIAH 59:15b–21 ■

Israel's inability to do what God expects leads to the next section. When God looked and saw that there was no justice, "then his own arm brought him salvation, and his righteousness upheld him" (59:16). It is significant that the metaphor of God's mighty arm is identified as the Servant in 53:1. The people are unable to obey God. But his work through the Servant will not only allow for the forgiveness of their sins, it will also empower them to obey him and to be the people that he is calling them to be. God says to the Servant, "As for me [God], this is my covenant with them [Israel]. . . .

My Spirit that is upon you [Servant], and my words that I have put in your mouth, shall not depart out of your mouth . . . from this time forth and forevermore" (59:21). As we have seen previously, the Servant establishes a new covenant between God and his people. God will permanently bring them into relationship with him, enabled by the Spirit (see 11:2; 42:1).

Salvation in Zion (D)

■ READ ISAIAH 60–62 ■

In the center of the chiastic structure, Isaiah presents the good news of God's ultimate plans for his true people. There will be peace and prosperity. Not only will the nations no longer harm God's people; they will bring their wealth as gifts (60:5). To illustrate that there will be no more need for fear, Isaiah says that the gates of the city will never be shut (60:11). The people will not even need the sun any longer, since YHWH will be their everlasting light (60:19). Both of these statements are alluded to in Revelation 21:23–25 in a description of the new Jerusalem. Who will accomplish these things? In 61:1–3, Isaiah quotes an individual who uses language from chapters 9, 11, 42, and 49, all of which point to the Servant. The Servant says in 61:1, "The Spirit of the Lord GOD is upon me, because the LORD has anointed me to bring good news to the poor; he has sent me to bind up the brokenhearted, to proclaim liberty to the captives." In Luke 4:17–21, we read that Jesus sat down in the synagogue in Nazareth, asked for the scroll of Isaiah, read this passage, and said, "Today this Scripture has been fulfilled in your hearing" (v. 21). Jesus is the Servant who makes all things new. Is this too good to be true? No, God has demonstrated throughout Isaiah that he has the power to accomplish it by "his mighty arm" (62:8).

The Warrior YHWH (C')

■ READ ISAIAH 63:1–6 ■

Following the description of God's salvation for his people in Zion, we come to a second section depicting him as a warrior. The former section spoke of God's garments and armor as he comes to save his people (59:15b–21). The present, corresponding section also uses the image of God's garments. He comes from Edom (a frequent symbol for all nations who oppose him), and his garments are red. Isaiah asks, rhetorically, "Why is your apparel red, and your garments like his who treads in the winepress?" (63:2). The answer is that he has been trampling his enemies, and their blood has splashed on his clothing (63:3; cf. Rev. 19:13). Isaiah says that he looked, and there was no one to help YHWH accomplish salvation for his people, so YHWH says, "My own arm brought me salvation" (63:5). Once again we see a reference to his mighty arm. The same Servant who atones for sin also destroys his enemies. This is another aspect of his salvation. For those who are willing, God will obliterate the sin in their hearts. But when others continue to oppose him, his wrath is kindled and he will have no choice but to obliterate them as well.

Sin and Obedience (B')

■ READ ISAIAH 63:7–66:17 ■

This section corresponds to the previous call to obedience in 56:9–59:15a. Here, Isaiah begins with a lament. He recognizes that God's "glorious arm" worked saving miracles back in the days of Moses (63:12), but the question is, Will God come to save his people again now? (63:15). Israel's people have all become unclean, and even their righteous deeds are worthless. They say, "There is no one who calls upon your name, who rouses himself to take hold of you" (64:7). Once again we see Isaiah's theme that the people are called to be righteous, but they cannot get it right on their own. God is going to have to intervene. Those who call on him will receive help and power, but those who rebel will be destroyed. The central point in this section is that there are two groups within "Israel." God will give his true servants a dwelling place that is secure (65:8–9), but those who rebel are destined for death (65:11–12). In 65:13–16, God further describes the destiny of each group: his true servants will eat, drink, rejoice, and sing in gladness. But everyone else will be hungry, thirsty, and put to shame; cry out in pain; and be killed. God is creating a new heavens and new earth for his people where they will be free from all threats (65:17; see Rev. 21:1), and there will be no more fear or weeping (65:19; Rev. 21:4).

A New People (A')

■ READ ISAIAH 66:18–24 ■

The conclusion of the book is a glorious celebration of God's victory. Israel was not his servant (Isa. 1–5), but now he has made for himself a new people. It consists of faithful Israelites that he has regathered from among the nations. But he will also send those servants out as his witnesses to all nations, and they will bring in even more people to belong to him. They will be like an offering to him that he treasures in Jerusalem (66:20). Finally, in a great surprise, God states that some of these gentile believers will serve him as priests and Levites. This is radical! Not even every Israelite could be a priest, but only those from the tribe of Levi, from the sons of Aaron. But now, Isaiah is saying that those gentiles who are brought into the people of God will be full members, as he intended from the beginning. Isaiah ends the book with a final warning that God's true servants will go out and look with loathing on the dead bodies of those who rebelled against God (66:24). One scholar writes, "The purpose of visiting the cemetery is not to gloat, not even to pity . . . but to be repelled. To see and constantly refresh the memory that these are the consequences of rebellion, and so to turn in revulsion from such a thing and to be newly motivated to obedience by seeing that the wages of sin are indeed death."[19]

Implementation

Isaiah presents us with a grand theological vision and a sweeping overview of God's plan of salvation not only for Israel but for the nations of the world. Isaiah exhorted his contemporaries to trust God and then looked *forward* to a historical return from exile in Babylon, the coming of God's suffering servant, new people of God from the nations, the destruction of the wicked, and a glorious new heavens and new earth. However, Christians today have a different historical and theological point of standing. We look *back* to the historical time of the prophet, and the return from exile has already taken place. Likewise, the Servant has already come and suffered as an offering for guilt. Pentecost marked a new chapter in God's redemptive program, with people from every language and nation turning in faith to the true God of Israel and accepting his invitation to join a new covenant. But we are still waiting for the final salvation at Mount Zion. We are still waiting for a final transformation when, by God's power, our obedience matches our status as the people of God. And we are looking forward to a new heavens and new earth, when all is well and God's enemies have been put down. Although some of what Isaiah predicted has already occurred, this does not make his book less relevant for us . . . it makes it more trustworthy! What has already come to pass gives us new confidence that God really can tell the end from the beginning and that he is moving all of history toward its appointed end.

There are many themes in Isaiah that are crucial for Christian theology and are referenced and realized in the New Testament; let us consider just a few. First, Isaiah is clear that the natural state of humanity is opposed to God. In Isaiah 6:9–10, God tells Isaiah that the people will be blind and hard-hearted. In the New Testament, this is given as the reason that much of Jesus's teaching is in parables (Matt. 13:14–15; Luke 8:10). Because the teaching is not straightforward, those who are open to his teaching will understand, while others are further hardened. Paul quotes from Isaiah 6:9–10 to explain his mixed success: many Jews are unwilling to listen, but God's salvation has been sent to the gentiles as well (Acts 28:23–28). When we share the good news of salvation through Jesus Christ, we should not be surprised when our hearers reject us and our message. The hearers of Isaiah, Jesus, and the apostles did the same to them. According to Isaiah, our response should be not to question the truth of the message or to soften it, but to proclaim it faithfully, trusting that by God's power through the Spirit he will enable people to come to him.

A second theme is that *only* God can save and that he is more than qualified to do so. A large percentage of this long book (perhaps Isa. 12–47?) makes the argument that God is the only valid object of our trust. Why does Isaiah spend so much space making this point? It is because this is such a persistent struggle for all of us. In Isaiah's day, there were many nations, leaders, and gods offering their services in exchange for loyalty and trust. There are just as many voices today. We are tempted to put confidence in technology, education, political victories, armed forces, social connections, national allies, bank accounts—the list goes on. Isaiah calls us to forsake anything that interferes with total trust and allegiance to God. When my friend in college was discouraged by life, he would say, humorously, "Well, it's all going to burn some day." But that is only partially true—when all that thwarts him is destroyed, our victorious God will remain standing to take our sin, fix our hearts, and bring us home.

Third, Isaiah helps us to understand the Servant, Jesus Christ, and his salvation-securing work. Once I was teaching a course on Isaiah and I kept referring to "the Servant" in Isaiah. A student in the back raised his hand and asked, with some stress in his voice, "This is Jesus, right?! Why do you keep calling him the Servant? Why not just call him Jesus?" My response was that I wanted to make sure that we did not move too quickly to the New Testament, but that we allowed Isaiah to speak on his own terms, in a prospective way. In the same way here, I want Isaiah to be allowed to make his unique theological contribution within the argument of this book. Isaiah speaks of the Servant and a coming Davidic ruler with the same language: both are like a root (11:10; 53:2), both are equipped with the Spirit (11:2; 42:1), both care for the poor and needy (11:4; 42:7; 49:9; cf. 61:1), and there is a universal dimension to their work (9:6; 11:9–10; 42:4; 52:15). These statements refer to one person, who is later revealed to be Jesus Christ. Like the Servant, Jesus was not what people expected; they could not believe that this was God's "mighty arm" (53:1). In the New Testament, John quotes Isaiah 53:1 as an explanation for why, in spite of Jesus's many miracles, people still did not believe in him (John

12:37–38). However, appearances were deceiving. In spite of his under-whelming appearance, Jesus is *overqualified* to save only Israel (Isa. 49:6); he will be God's salvation for the ends of the earth. Jesus brings salvation not in spite of his suffering and death but through it. Isaiah anticipates substitutionary atonement more explicitly than any other Old Testament author when he proclaims that it is the *Servant's* suffering for *our* sin that brings about God's promised peace (53:4–6). Because of his innocence and obedience, the Servant would accomplish everything that God had called him to do.

Fourth, we have noted a number of times in the preceding discussion that God is establishing a new covenant (though Isaiah does not call it "new"). Isaiah says that the Servant *is* a covenant (42:6; 49:8). Similarly, Jesus says at the Last Supper that the cup "is the new covenant" in his blood (Luke 22:20; 1 Cor. 11:25). In Isaiah 55:3, God says that he will make an ev-erlasting covenant with his people, which expresses his "steadfast, sure love for David." David has been long dead, so what can he do? God is speaking of Jesus's heritage as a Davidic ruler—a new David who will form for him-self a new people whose membership is made up of those who hold fast to the covenant (56:4, 6; 59:21; 61:8). There is no other way to salvation. To those who join the covenant brought by Jesus, there will be peace and joy and security forever. To those who refuse, there will be suffering and eternal death. This is the sober choice that Isaiah puts before us.

Christian Reading Questions

1. The book of Isaiah has been called "the fifth Gospel." After reading this chapter, do you think that is an accurate label? How is it similar to a New Testament Gospel? What unique contribution does this book make (among other "Gospels") since it comes *before* Jesus's incarnation?

2. In Isaiah 5:20, the prophet pronounces doom on those who call evil good and good evil. What are some examples in your own culture in which biblical ethics have been turned upside down and good has been called evil? What does the Bible call evil that the culture calls good? Be specific.

3. Examine the specific imagery and poetic language in Isaiah 24–27. How does literary form enhance the prophet's message in this section of the book? What effect does it have on you?

4. Consider how Isaiah first describes the work of the suffering servant (chaps. 52–53) and then announces the necessary outcome of that work in chapter 56:1–2. Does order help illumine a passage like James 2:14–17?

5. Reread Isaiah 59:15–21 and 63:1–6. How does Isaiah's imagery of God as a divine warrior strengthen his argument in this section? How might this imagery be an encouragement in our personal walks of faith?

CHAPTER TEN

Jeremiah

Orientation

Some of the most popular songs, books, and movies in popular culture are intensely sad. A friend might recommend a movie and say, "Take along a box of tissues! I cried like a baby for two straight hours. It was *so* good—I'm going to see it again!" Why do we do this to ourselves? Why is it that time and again we pull up sad songs or reach for a novel that devastates us? Partly, it is because those are true reflections of what life is really like, and we find that comforting. Most of us find that there is plenty of sorrow amid the times of joy in life. One of the rich contributions of the Old Testament prophets is that they are so honest—they unflinchingly present the fear, grief, anger, lament, persecution, and frustration that often accompany living and speaking for God in a dark world. Jeremiah is the "weeping prophet," who speaks the truth, no matter how unpopular, sometimes against his own will. However, God is with him.

The book of Jeremiah is intense on multiple fronts. It is intense in the prophet's announcement of judgment: the end is here. The ultimate covenant curses of conquest and exile have come, and Jeremiah is an eyewitness to the devastation of Jerusalem and the destruction of the temple. The persecution that Jeremiah endures is also intense. Whereas other prophets are ignored or slandered, Jeremiah is beaten and imprisoned. But his good news is also intense. Out of all the prophets, he gives us the most explicit and detailed explanation of the "new covenant" and what it means to be a member of the transformed people that God is gathering for himself.

HISTORICAL MATTERS

"Fact Sheet"—Jeremiah

Author: Jeremiah, the son of Hilkiah, and Baruch, his scribe

Date: 627–562 BC

Location: Jerusalem

Political and social context: Jeremiah prophesied in preexilic Judah during the reigns of Kings Josiah, Jehoahaz, Jehoiakim, Jehoiachin, and Zedekiah. During his ministry, Judah was under siege and then conquered by the Chaldeans, the temple was destroyed, and Jeremiah was taken into exile in Egypt.

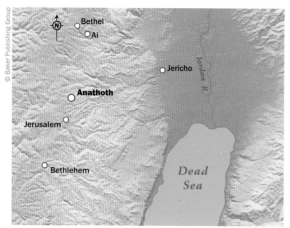

Map 10.1. The location of Anathoth

The superscription of the book (1:1–3) gives us some background. Jeremiah 1:1 states that the book contains the words of Jeremiah, the son of a priest who lived in Anathoth, which was a small village about two and a half miles northeast of Jerusalem (see map 10.1). The next two verses (1:2–3) give us the time frame of Jeremiah's ministry (refer to the time line of Jeremiah). It begins in the thirteenth year of Josiah (627 BC).

This was a period of Assyrian weakness, which removed some pressure from Judah. King Josiah begins a renovation of the temple, during which workers rediscover the book of law (2 Kings 22:8). This leads to a significant reform, in which Josiah attempts to destroy false religion in the land. But it does not work: the people are fundamentally unfaithful, and this problem will not be solved with a "reboot"—it is going to require divine intervention. This conclusion is a major theme in the book of Jeremiah. During the reign of Josiah, the Chaldeans conquered Nineveh (612 BC), the capital of Assyria, and emerged as the new superpower in the east.

The superscription skips Jehoahaz (Shallum), probably because he reigned only three months before going into exile in Egypt, where he died. The Egyptians, who were in control of Judah at that time, then set Jehoiakim on the throne (Jer. 1:3). After the Chaldeans took control of Judah, Jehoiakim rebelled against them (2 Kings 24:1). The Chaldeans responded by besieging Jerusalem in 597. During this time, Jehoiakim died, though it is unclear how. His son Jehoiachin (whom the superscription also skips) reigned for only three months before the Chaldeans took him, the prophet Ezekiel, and others into exile. The superscription also tells us that God's word came to Jeremiah until the eleventh year of Zedekiah (586 BC), which was also the year that Jerusalem was ultimately conquered by the Chaldeans. However, the narrative in Jeremiah continues past that point as Jeremiah is taken by exiles into Egypt, where he lives until he dies. 🕐

Unlike other prophetic books, the book of Jeremiah provides some internal description as to how it came to be written. The book is consistent in its claim that the prophetic words come from Jeremiah himself (e.g., 1:1; 7:1; 11:1; 14:1; 18:1). He then dictates those words to his scribe, Baruch (see 36:4, 6, 17–18). Chapter 36 narrates this process: Baruch writes Jeremiah's words on a scroll (36:4), which is then destroyed by King Jehoiakim. God instructs Jeremiah to produce a second scroll that contains the words of the first. Baruch writes a second scroll, again taking down Jeremiah's dictation, and also adds words (36:32). Perhaps, in addition to recording Jeremiah's words from God, Baruch also gathered other narrative material and assembled the book. In any case, the book strongly implies that it was composed during the ministry and lifetime of Jeremiah.[1]

The question of the text of Jeremiah and its transmission (or copying) is one of the most complex in the Old Testament. There are actually two different versions of the book: one represented by the Hebrew text and one represented in the Greek translation of the Old Testament, called the Septuagint. The Greek version is shorter by one-eighth, or twenty-seven hundred words, but it also has some words and phrases that do not appear in the Hebrew. In addition, the two versions have different structures.

TIME LINE

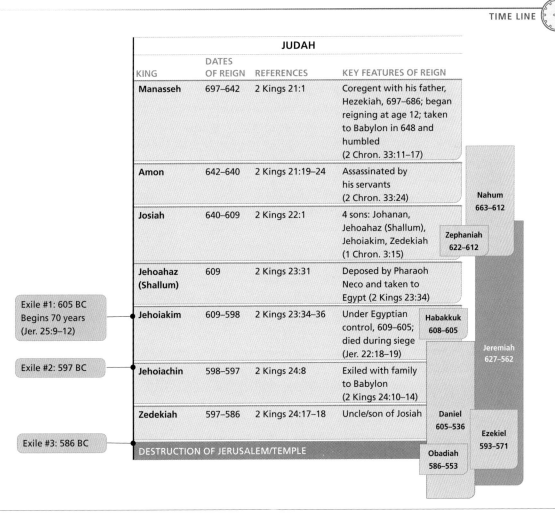

JUDAH

KING	DATES OF REIGN	REFERENCES	KEY FEATURES OF REIGN
Manasseh	697–642	2 Kings 21:1	Coregent with his father, Hezekiah, 697–686; began reigning at age 12; taken to Babylon in 648 and humbled (2 Chron. 33:11–17)
Amon	642–640	2 Kings 21:19–24	Assassinated by his servants (2 Chron. 33:24)
Josiah	640–609	2 Kings 22:1	4 sons: Johanan, Jehoahaz (Shallum), Jehoiakim, Zedekiah (1 Chron. 3:15)
Jehoahaz (Shallum)	609	2 Kings 23:31	Deposed by Pharaoh Neco and taken to Egypt (2 Kings 23:34)
Jehoiakim	609–598	2 Kings 23:34–36	Under Egyptian control, 609–605; died during siege (Jer. 22:18–19)
Jehoiachin	598–597	2 Kings 24:8	Exiled with family to Babylon (2 Kings 24:10–14)
Zedekiah	597–586	2 Kings 24:17–18	Uncle/son of Josiah

DESTRUCTION OF JERUSALEM/TEMPLE

Exile #1: 605 BC Begins 70 years (Jer. 25:9–12)

Exile #2: 597 BC

Exile #3: 586 BC

Nahum 663–612

Zephaniah 622–612

Habakkuk 608–605

Jeremiah 627–562

Daniel 605–536

Ezekiel 593–571

Obadiah 586–553

In the Greek version, Jeremiah's prophecies against the nations are found after 25:13, and the nations appear in a different order. In the Hebrew version, the prophecies against the nations are found at the end of the book, in chapters 46–51.

Table 10.1. The Two Versions of Jeremiah

	Greek Septuagint	Hebrew Masoretic Text
Length of text	Shorter by 1/8 2,700 fewer words	Longer
Relationship to other ancient versions	Represented in some Dead Sea Scroll texts	Represented by the Aramaic Targums, Syriac Peshitta, Latin Vulgate, and most Dead Sea Scroll texts
Sequence and position of chapters and verses	Prophecies against the nations are found after 25:13; nations occur in a different order	Prophecies against the nations are found at the end of the book (chaps. 46–51)

For many years, scholars thought that the Greek translator might have made these significant changes when he translated the book into Greek. However, when the Dead Sea Scrolls were discovered, both versions of Jeremiah were found on Hebrew fragments. This suggests that there were originally two different *Hebrew* versions, and the shorter one was translated into Greek. Scholars have a number of theories to explain how all of this occurred, but no certainty.[2] It may be that the shorter version was a draft of some kind, and the longer version is the finished book. The longer version is the standard text, reflected in other ancient versions such as the Aramaic Targums and the Latin Vulgate. It is also the basis of all the major English translations of the Bible.

Exploration

The book of Jeremiah addresses all five of the prophetic phases (see fig. 10.1). Especially in the early part of the book, the prophet accuses the people of Judah of breaking God's covenant with idolatry, false religion, and unbelief. Because of these sins, God is bringing destruction on Jerusalem—even on the temple. The people will be taken into exile. However, in seventy years, God will bring the people back to the land and resettle them in their homes once more. This restoration in the near future becomes a token or image of God's ultimate forgiveness and restoration in the eschatological future, which will come in the form of a new covenant. Jeremiah's oracles against the nations look forward to eschatological judgment for all those who refuse to submit to God.

over his people (33:15–17). This is as certain as the coming of day and night at their appointed times (33:19–20) and as secure as creation itself (33:22). God's interrelated covenants in the past will be fulfilled. The offspring of David (the covenant with David) will rule over the offspring of Abraham (the covenant with Abraham), for he will restore their fortunes (the new covenant) (33:26).

Faithless People, Faithless Kings

■ READ JEREMIAH 34–39 ■

Above we saw that Jeremiah's true message of God's judgment in chapters 2–25 was followed by his conflict with false prophets in chapters 26–29. Now, his true message of God's restoration in chapters 30–33 is followed by his conflict with faithless people and faithless kings, who oversee the fall of Jerusalem in chapters 34–45. Thus there is a great contrast between the creator of heaven and earth, who promises ultimate redemption, and rebellious kings who "go down with the ship."

The section begins with a proclamation that King Zedekiah will die in exile and with another illustration of the people's failure to keep the covenant (34:1–35:11). In chapter 36, we are taken back in time to King Jehoiakim. God tells Jeremiah to write on a scroll all the words that God has spoken to him thus far in his prophetic ministry and to read the scroll to the people in the hopes that they will repent (36:2–3). Jeremiah dictates the words to his scribe Baruch, who writes the scroll. However, because Jeremiah has been banned from entering the temple, Baruch goes in his place and reads the scroll to the people there. Initially, the people take it quite seriously. However, when Baruch reads it to Jehoiakim, the king systematically cuts off columns of the scroll and throws them in the fire until the entire scroll is burned up (36:23). The contrast between Jehoiakim and his father Josiah is stark. When Josiah read the scroll discovered in the temple, he tore his clothes, feared the wrath of God, and immediately sought to obey God (2 Kings 22:8–13).

Jehoiakim is not the only king who tries to silence the prophet rather than submit to God's word. In the time of Zedekiah, Jeremiah is accused of treason and thrown in prison (37:11–21). In 38:1–13, when Jeremiah tells Zedekiah that Jerusalem will fall to the Chaldeans, Zedekiah makes it known that he will not punish anyone who attacks Jeremiah. His men do not need to be told twice, and they throw Jeremiah into an empty water cistern, where he sinks down into the mud (38:6). It is only when an Ethiopian official tells the king that Jeremiah will die that the king orders him to be rescued.

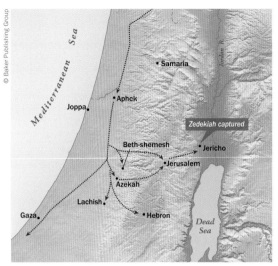

Map 10.2. The Chaldean conquest of Judah and Jerusalem

Finally, in 39:1–18 the ultimate covenant curse, threatened since the time of Moses, comes to pass as Jerusalem falls to the Chaldeans (see map 10.2). King Zedekiah tries to flee, but the enemy soldiers capture him by the Jordan River. They slaughter his sons, gouge out his eyes, and take him away to Babylon. Meanwhile, they break down the city walls, destroy the temple, and take many people into exile (39:8–9). Jeremiah is allowed to live among the people who remain in the land (39:14). God's word has proven true, and his prophet has been validated. The kings of Judah, despite their power and influence, have been shown to be helpless and bankrupt.

After the Fall of Jerusalem

■ READ JEREMIAH 40–45 ■

The second part of chapters 34–45 tells the story of what happens after the Chaldeans conquer Judah and Jerusalem in 586 BC. They appoint Gedaliah as governor, and the region begins to flourish once again (40:1–12). However, a band of men led by Ishmael, acting for the king of the nearby Ammonites, murders Gedaliah as well as other men of Judah and some Chaldean soldiers (41:1–3). A man named Johanan gathers his forces and defeats Ishmael (41:11–18). But the damage has been done. Johanan is afraid that the Chaldeans will retaliate because their governor has been killed, and he and his people decide to flee to Egypt. Jeremiah urges them to stay in the land, once again drawing on language from 1:10. If they remain, God says, "I will build you up and not pull you down; I will plant you, and not pluck you up" (42:10). On the other hand, if they decide to go to Egypt, they will die by the sword and by famine (42:22).

As has happened throughout Jeremiah's ministry, the people reject his word. They claim, "You are telling a lie. The LORD our God did not send you to say [that]" (43:2). They leave for Egypt, taking Jeremiah with them against his will (43:7) (see map 10.3). In Egypt the Judahites continue to reject Jeremiah's word, even though he has been proven correct. God announces more judgment on them, but they refuse to listen. Instead, they make offerings to the "queen of heaven"—an idol—just as they did back in the land (44:15–30). As the narrative portion of the book of Jeremiah comes to a close, we are left with the impression that nothing ever changes, and nothing will change, until God gives his people a new heart and enables them to obey.

Judgment against the Nations

■ READ JEREMIAH 46–51 ■

Prophecies against the nations are a common feature in prophetic books; we have already discussed Isaiah 13–23 previously. These words from God are addressed to other nations, like an open letter. Other than

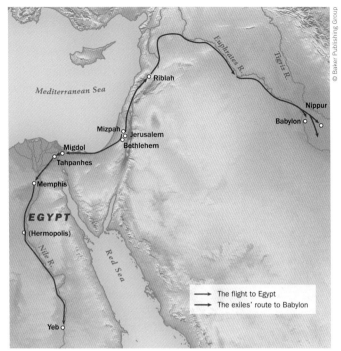

Map 10.3. The exile to Babylon and the flight to Egypt (586 BC)

Jeremiah's prophetic letter to Babylon (51:59–64), the intended audience of every prophecy is Judah and the reader of the book. Jeremiah announces judgment on Egypt (46:1–28), the Philistines (47:1–7), Moab (48:1–47), Ammon (49:1–6), Edom (49:7–22), the Arameans (49:23–27),[9] Kedar and Hazor (49:28–33),[10] Elam (49:34–39), and finally Babylon (50:1–51:64). Babylon has been God's tool of judgment, but they have *only* been a tool, and now they too will face judgment. No one besides God will ultimately be victorious, and he alone is worthy of allegiance and trust.

Postscript: The Ultimate Devastation and a Glimmer of Hope

■ READ JEREMIAH 52 ■

Although the fall of Jerusalem has already been described in chapter 39 in relation to Jeremiah, a postscript in chapter 52 recounts it again. The narrative is very similar to that found in 2 Kings 24:18–25:30. It is placed here to conclude the book with two key ideas. First, Jeremiah the persecuted prophet has been vindicated. The false prophets who said that all will be well

> **CANONICAL CONNECTIONS**
>
> **Babylon in the Book of Revelation**
>
> In the book of Revelation, Babylon is symbolic of all who rebel against God and persecute his people. Revelation 17:5 calls it the "mother of prostitutes and of earth's abominations." In 18:2, the angel celebrates the destruction of Babylon, saying, "She has become a dwelling place for demons, a haunt for every unclean spirit." God's people must stand firm against "Babylon," keep themselves from being enticed by it, and look forward to its ruin when God sets all things right.

have been proven wrong.[11] Second, there is still hope. God has promised that he will maintain the Davidic line in order to raise up a ruler. The book concludes with Jehoiachin, the furthest extent of the line of David (see fig. 10.3), released from prison and eating at the king's table (52:33–34). Salvation lies beyond judgment. In the midst of all of the destruction and failure, God's plan is still unfolding.

Implementation

The book of Jeremiah gives us the most revealing look at the life of a prophet. Jeremiah bears a message that confronts the people for their sin, and he represents God's perspective on the political and social situation in his time. For this, he is rejected, beaten, and imprisoned, and his life is threatened. He feels intensely alone. He wishes he could just live his life in peace, without speaking God's word, relieved of the weight that he carries. However, Jeremiah is compelled to speak for God. If it is wearisome to speak unpopular truth, it is even more exhausting to try to hold it in (20:9). So he clings to his faith in God and prays *honestly*, telling God about his fears and struggles and asking God to come to his aid, even if that means direct judgment on his enemies.

This is an important model for Christians who live a life of faithful witness in an evil society, especially for those who are called to speak God's word formally as pastors, teachers, campus missionaries, and those in other forms of full-time Christian service. It is hard to serve YHWH. Jeremiah

THINKING VISUALLY

The Line of David in the Last Kings of Judah
Figure 10.3

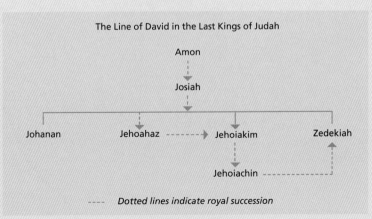

The Line of David in the Last Kings of Judah

Amon

Josiah

Johanan   Jehoahaz - - - - → Jehoiakim   Zedekiah

Jehoiachin - - - - - - - - - - - -

- - - - *Dotted lines indicate royal succession*

shows us what it means to speak what is true, even when it is unwanted. He complains about his message, but he never compromises or tries to soften it. Likewise, it is not enough for us to speak some truth; we must speak the *whole* truth—it is the only way that people can turn to God and be saved. Successful ministry is defined by being faithful to God, not by being well received by our listeners; that is a crucial distinction. But Jeremiah also shows us that we must turn to God when we are discouraged and need help. And God's reply to him, "I will be with you," is promised to us as well (Matt. 28:20). Furthermore, Jeremiah's word from God—though it was hated—was shown to be true. When we speak God's word in our culture, it may sound hopelessly out of date or even bigoted. And while we have a responsibility to reflect God's wisdom and mercy in our posture toward our audience, it is not our job to make the message palatable. Instead, we can only deliver it faithfully and wait on the Lord for vindication. He will always be proven true in the end.

It is difficult to overstate the significance of this book for Christian theology. We have seen throughout Jeremiah's messages that our fundamental problem as humans is not bad behavior but a bad *heart* that produces bad behavior. Jeremiah speaks of rebellious and "uncircumcised" hearts that lead to stubbornness (3:17; 4:4; 5:23; 9:26; 17:9). Furthermore, humans are unable to change their hearts any more than a person could change his or her skin color or a leopard could change its spots (13:23). Because of this, it is useless to call people to "do better" or to "try harder" when it comes to restoring their relationship with God. Asking people to do things like reject racism, be better spouses and parents, work hard, be honest, and so on is like fixing the paint job on a car with significant rust underneath. It may look better for a while, but before long that corrosion will come to the surface again. Jeremiah insists that the cure for the human heart is nothing less than total conversion, wrought by God in the new covenant (24:7; 31:33; 32:39–40). In the book of John, Jesus also talks about human inability to accept his words or to come to him (3:3, 5; 6:44, 63, 65; 12:39). Conversion requires a word of the Spirit to open a person's eyes and make them receptive to God's salvation.

Jeremiah also makes a significant contribution to our understanding of the new covenant as the climax of God's redemptive program. Other prophets, such as Isaiah, speak of an everlasting covenant through which God will bring people to himself, but it is the book of Jeremiah that most clearly sets out what this covenant entails. Members of the new covenant all know YHWH, have his law written on their hearts, and are forgiven of their sin. The covenant is permanent, and the invitation to join is open to all: "Come, let us join ourselves to the LORD in an everlasting covenant that will never be forgotten" (50:5).

In the New Testament, the book of Hebrews states that the new covenant, brought about through Jesus Christ, is better than the old covenant with Israel, "for if that first covenant had been faultless, there would have been no occasion to look for a second" (8:7). The fault of the old covenant, as we have said previously, is that it could not address the twisted human heart. It represented God's expectations and desire for relationship with his people, but it did not transform and empower them to obey. The priests offered the same sacrifices day after day, which temporarily covered the people's sins but did not forgive or remove them permanently (10:11). In the new covenant, however, "the blood of Christ . . . purif[ies] our conscience from dead works to serve the living God" (9:14). Christ's death was a single sacrifice to pay for all sins, "for all time" (10:12–14). The author of Hebrews concludes, "Where there is forgiveness of [sins and lawless deeds], there is no longer any offering for sin" (10:18).

As we read the book of Jeremiah today, the prophet's prediction of a new covenant has been fulfilled in the death and resurrection of Jesus Christ. When we commit ourselves to him and join his new covenant community by faith, our sins are forgiven, our hearts are transformed, and we have joined a permanent family of the true people of God, in relationship with him. However, the full realization of God's promises in Jeremiah—being fully built up and planted—lies yet in *our* future. In the new heavens and new earth, the devastation of conquest and exile will be gone, and we will live in our true home, in which YHWH is our God and we are his people forever.

Christian Reading Questions

1. Can you think of any other explanations of how there came to be two different versions of the book of Jeremiah, one represented in the Greek text and one in the Hebrew?
2. Explain in your own words how Jeremiah 1:10 functions as a thesis statement for the entire book.
3. Compare the oracles against the nations in Jeremiah 46–51 with those in Isaiah 13–23. What distinctive role do these chapters play in each book? (Hint: consider their location in the book's structure.)

4. Describe your own reaction to the complaining, sorrow, persecution, and bad news that pervade much of Jeremiah. How does this compare to the way that biblical faith is often presented in our churches? Do our churches need to adjust their perspective? In other words, is there room for serious faith that does not always feel happy? When?

CHAPTER ELEVEN

Ezekiel

Orientation

What is God really like? Ancient idols crafted out of wood, religious art on church ceilings, and even comedies like *Monty Python and the Holy Grail* all present images of God. And it is not just *other* people who have their own ideas of God. In 2018, researchers asked 511 American Christians to view three hundred sets of faces and select the pictures that captured how they view God. The combination of all the choices created a composite image. The resulting God of conservatives tended to look more masculine, older, more powerful, and wealthier. The God of liberals was more African American in appearance and looked more loving.[1] Our imaginations are unreliable, and we are always in danger of creating a god in our own image or as we would like him to be.

In the inspired book of Ezekiel God reveals himself as he truly is. He wants his people to know him as a fierce judge and as a powerful savior. In Ezekiel's strange visions, shocking allegories, and bizarre sign-acts, we are challenged to grapple with the mystery of God and to submit to him rather than attempt to "tame" him. Twice in the book, God tells Ezekiel that he must faithfully proclaim his message of warning and hope or he will be held accountable. And we too are accountable to read this book and allow it to shape our theology and our view of God.

The superscription to the book gives us the background of the prophet's message (1:1–3). It tells us that the book comes from the prophet Ezekiel, who was a priest living in the land of the Chaldeans among the exiles from Judah (1:3).[2] We learn later that he was married (24:16–18). His experiences and persona play an important role in this book, just as we saw with Jeremiah. Ezekiel and the other exiles were living along the Chebar Canal

(1:1), a sixty-mile waterway that joined two parts of the Euphrates River outside of Babylon (see map 11.1). They were living in enemy territory, among those who had captured them. Yet most of Ezekiel's messages focus not on Babylon but on the promised land they left behind, and later in the book he learns that Jerusalem has been conquered and the temple destroyed (33:21). Thus, the

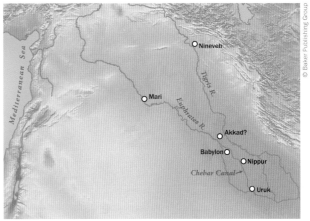

Map 11.1. The Chebar Canal

book comes from the perspective of those in captivity, away from home. We can identify, for we live in "exile" as well, among many enemies and away from our true home with God in heaven.

Life in exile was actually relatively comfortable. The Chaldeans kept exiled communities together and provided them with land in exchange for taxes and military service.[3] There is evidence that the exiles were well integrated into society, but Ezekiel's mention of the "elders" suggests that they had at least some form of self-rule (see 8:1; 14:1; 20:1). We do not know how many there were in the exilic community; scholarly estimates range from 10,000 to 250,000 people.[4]

In 1:1, we learn that Ezekiel's ministry began in "the thirtieth year," perhaps a reference to his age since that was when a man became a priest (see Num. 4:30; 8:24). But we also learn that it was the fifth year of the exile of King Jehoiachin (1:2), which means it was 593 BC, seven years before Jerusalem fell to the Chaldeans (see the time line of Ezekiel). King Zedekiah is currently on the throne in Jerusalem, but Ezekiel refers instead to *Jehoiachin*, who represented the furthest extent of David's royal line. Ezekiel begins as the book of Jeremiah ended: with a subtle statement of hope in God's promised redemption, even though Ezekiel is in captivity. Many of the messages in the book are specifically dated (see table 11.1). Therefore, the messages are arranged in the book in chronological order, except for 26:1 and 29:17 (because the oracles against the nations are grouped thematically).

HISTORICAL MATTERS

"Fact Sheet"—Ezekiel

Author: Ezekiel, the son of Buzi

Date: 593–571 BC

Location: In exile, by the Chebar Canal in Chaldea

Political and social context: Ezekiel prophesied during the last days of the Southern Kingdom, during the reign of Zedekiah, the fall of Jerusalem, and the years immediately afterward. Though separated from the land, the exiles lived in peace and security. There was a danger that they would assimilate and lose their identity as God's separate people.

Table 11.1. Dated Events and Oracles in the Book of Ezekiel

597 BC		Babylonians send an army to crush Judean rebellion Judah surrenders; notable individuals exiled to Babylon (including Ezekiel) Nebuchadnezzar sets Zedekiah on the throne in Jerusalem
593 BC	1:2	Beginning of Ezekiel's ministry
592 BC	8:1	God reveals that he will destroy Jerusalem Ezekiel sees the glory (*kabod*) leave the temple
591 BC	20:1	God tells Ezekiel to remind captives of their fathers' abominations
588 BC	24:1	Babylonians lay siege to Jerusalem
587 BC	29:1	Ezekiel is commanded to prophesy against Egypt
586 BC	26:1	Prophecy of Tyre's defeat because of her gloating over Judah's defeat
	30:20	Prophecy against Egypt
	31:1	Prophecies against Egypt
585 BC	33:21	**Survivor from Jerusalem arrives and announces the city has fallen** Turning point: with news of Jerusalem's fall Ezekiel turns to restoration
	32:1	Prophecy against Egypt
	32:17	Prophecy against Egypt
573 BC	40:1	Vision of the new temple
571 BC	29:17	Prophecy against Egypt: Babylon could not defeat Tyre, but YHWH will give Egypt as reward for work

TIME LINE

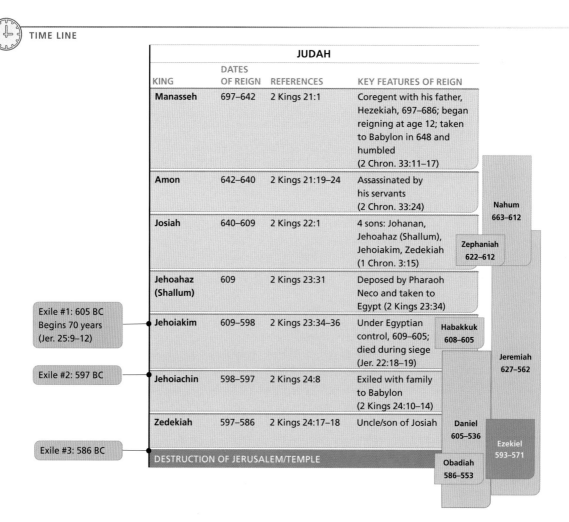

The Five Phases: Ezekiel
Figure 11.1

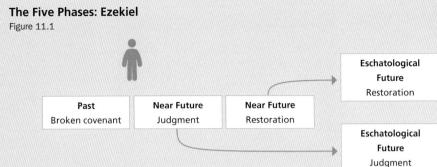

Exploration

The book of Ezekiel addresses all five of the prophetic phases (see fig. 11.1). With specific and graphic imagery, he calls Israel to account for its spiritual adultery against YHWH. Because of the abominations in Jerusalem, God will remove his glory from the temple and city and allow it to be destroyed by foreigners. However, he will eventually restore his people to their land. This judgment and restoration in history will be repeated in the eschatological future. God will transform his people and live with them in a glorious new land, while his enemies will be destroyed in a final judgment.

The book of Ezekiel has the structure indicated in table 11.2. In part 1, especially **chapters 4–24**, Ezekiel brings an indictment against Israel's pride and rebellion against God, which result in all kinds of abominations. Ezekiel presents a lengthy vision of God's glory leaving the temple and Jerusalem as a precursor to the coming destruction (chaps. 8–11). In chapter 24, he learns that Jerusalem is under siege by the king of Babylon. This foreshadowing of God's ultimate covenant curse (destruction and removal

Table 11.2. The Structure of Ezekiel

Superscription (1:1–3)	
Part 1: Messages of judgment for Judah and Israel (chaps. 1–24)	
chaps. 1–3	Ezekiel's call
chaps. 4–7	Sign-acts and prophecies against Jerusalem
chaps. 8–11	A vision of YHWH's glory leaving the temple
chaps. 12–24	A collection of judgment prophecies against Israel
Part 2: Messages of hope and restoration of Judah/Israel (chaps. 25–48)	
chaps. 25–32	Negative messages of hope for God's people
chap. 33	The end of an era: Jerusalem falls
chaps. 34–48	Positive messages of hope for God's people

Note: On the structure of Jeremiah I am heavily indebted to Block, *Book of Ezekiel: Chapters 1–24*; and Iain M. Duguid, *Ezekiel*, NIV Application Commentary (Grand Rapids: Zondervan, 1999).

from the land) ends the first part of the book, and Ezekiel pivots to messages of hope. Part 2 begins in **chapters 25–32** with the good news that God will hold the nations accountable for their evil and will avenge his people. In **chapter 33**, Ezekiel learns that the Chaldean siege is over and Jerusalem has fallen. He then turns his attention in **chapters 34–48** to the "last days," when God will make all things new and dwell with his people forever.

Ezekiel's Call to Prophetic Ministry

■ READ EZEKIEL 1–3 ■

Ezekiel's call narrative is longer and more complex than those in Isaiah and Jeremiah, comprising three chapters. As in other prophetic books, it is more than the story of how Ezekiel came to be a prophet; it also introduces key themes in the book. The call narrative in Ezekiel 1–3 begins with a strange vision of God's glory, continues with God's actual commissioning of Ezekiel to serve as his messenger, and concludes with a sharp warning that Ezekiel will be held responsible if he does not fully tell all that God has commanded.

In 1:4–28, Ezekiel has a vision of a kind of heavenly "vehicle." He first describes four living creatures, each having a human likeness but four faces: that of a human, a lion, an ox, and an eagle (1:4–14). He then describes four wheels within wheels (1:15–21), which are holding up a platform and moving it around (1:22–25). The text emphasizes that the creatures and the wheels move in different directions without turning and that they are all in sync because they are directed by the "spirit" (1:12, 20, 21). On top of the platform, there is a throne with a figure like a human and flashing brightness all around.

Ezekiel states that his vision of this strange vehicle and the four living creatures is a vision of "the likeness of the glory of the Lord" (1:28). But that raises an important question. Why is he seeing the glory of YHWH there in exile? It belongs back in Jerusalem, in the temple, above the ark of the covenant in the holy of holies. Although God is everywhere, this is where his glory took up residence after the completion of the tabernacle and the temple (Exod. 40:34; 1 Kings 8:27; 2 Chron. 7:1). He was physically

RECEPTION HISTORY

Rated "MA" for Mature Audiences Only

Ezekiel has a reputation for being difficult to understand, and it has also been viewed as potentially hazardous because Ezekiel recounts several visions of God's glory. Throughout history, stewards of Scripture have sought to shield immature audiences from Ezekiel 1 in order to uphold God's honor and otherworldliness, revealed in the striking vision of his throne.[a] In particular, the classical Jewish rabbis were concerned that great care should be taken in expounding Ezekiel 1 in the public synagogue. Tractate Hagigah 2:1 in the Mishnah states, "Forbidden sexual relations [i.e., Lev. 18; 20] may not be expounded to three, nor the work of creation [i.e., Gen. 1] to two, nor the Merkavah [i.e., Ezek. 1; 10] to an individual, unless he is wise [i.e., a scholar] and understands on his own." In other words, Ezekiel 1 is the most dangerous passage and should not even be taught to one person unless that person already understands it! The church father Origen also tells us that Jewish boys were instructed in all the Scriptures, but certain biblical texts, including Ezekiel 1, were delayed until they reached full maturity.

present in his holy place, but now Ezekiel is seeing the glory in the land of the Chaldeans. This is an ominous sign that something is terribly wrong; we will learn later that it is a sign of judgment.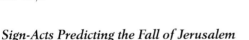

In 2:1–3:21, Ezekiel is formally called to be a prophet of YHWH. He is told to give his audience the complete message, whether they listen or not. It is his responsibility to speak faithfully, and it is *their* responsibility before God to obey (2:5, 7). In the vision, Ezekiel is presented with a scroll, which he must eat. This is symbolic of his need first to receive ("ingest") the message, and then to announce it to others. A similar image occurs with John in the book of Revelation (10:8–11). Finally, in 3:22–27, at the end of this section, God places restrictions on Ezekiel's speech. He must shut himself up in his house and will be "mute," able only to speak words of judgment until God opens his mouth (see 33:21–22).

Figure 11.2. *Ezekiel's Vision* by Bernard Picart (1693–1783) in the Kitto Bible

Sign-Acts Predicting the Fall of Jerusalem

▓ READ EZEKIEL 4–5 ▓

In this section, Ezekiel describes four sign-acts that depict the siege and conquest of Jerusalem as the climax of God's judgment against Judah. First, he makes a model of Jerusalem under siege (4:1–3). Next, he is commanded to lie on his left side for 390 days and then his right side for 40 days to signify the years of Israel's and Judah's respective punishments (4:4–8). Then, he describes his food while lying on his side: bread baked over dung, which is unclean (4:9–17). And finally, he cuts off his hair and beard and then burns, strikes, and

RECEPTION HISTORY

The Ancient Astronaut Hypothesis

The images of Ezekiel 1 have generated some *interesting* ideas (and that is an understatement). Some have seen the chapter as evidence that ancient astronauts visited the earth and were mistaken by primitive peoples (like Ezekiel) for gods. Erich von Däniken published the best-selling book *Chariots of the Gods?* in the late 1960s, promoting the theory.[b] Josef Blumrich, an engineer at NASA, first set out to prove von Däniken wrong, but then came to agree with him. In his short book *The Spaceships of Ezekiel*, Blumrich finds a spacecraft's central main body, four helicopters, and capsule for the crew in Ezekiel 1, and he explains how the ship might have functioned.[c] These literalistic readings are ridiculous, completely miss the point of the chapter, and fail to read it within the genre of the Prophets.

scatters the hair around the city (5:1–4). Only at the end of these dramatic sign-acts does he explain their meaning (5:5–17). The people of Jerusalem will die in the city, around the city, and in exile. This terrible suffering will satisfy God's fury and anger, and then they will know, God says, that "I am the Lord" (5:13, 15, 17).

Judgment on Israel

■ READ EZEKIEL 6–7 ■

Ezekiel's overwhelming, repeating message in these two chapters is that God is desolating the land because of the evil abominations of his people. He will kill many of them, but he will leave some alive and send them into exile. There, they will know that he is YHWH because he has kept his word to bring judgment. The prophets in the Old Testament frequently call the people to repent, but Ezekiel's message here is that it is too late to repent.[5] He says over and over, "The end has come. . . . The end is upon you. . . . It comes. . . . An end has come; the end has come. . . . Your doom has come. . . . Your doom has come. . . . The time has come; the day has arrived" (7:2, 3, 5, 6, 7, 10, 12). He "will bring the worst of the nations to take possession of their houses" (7:24). God's power and sovereignty are so great that he can use wicked people as instruments of judgment on other wicked people. 📖

A Vision of YHWH's Glory Leaving the Temple

■ READ EZEKIEL 8–11 ■

Typically, before a nation goes to war, it pulls its ambassador and staff out of the embassy in the capital city of the enemy country. Similarly, chapters 8–11 describe Ezekiel's vision of God's glory leaving the temple and the city of Jerusalem. God leaves before he brings judgment and catastrophe on his dwelling place. Ezekiel tells us in 8:1 that it is the sixth year (592 BC). The temple is still standing in Jerusalem; it will be six years before it is destroyed by the Chaldeans (586 BC).

The unit is structured as a chiasm in which the vision begins, is described, and then comes to an end (see fig. 11.3). In the vision, a heavenly being takes Ezekiel to Jerusalem (a distance of over 530 miles) and gives him a tour of wicked abominations in the temple. Ezekiel sees an idolatrous image and engravings on the temple walls that the elders are

📖 **LITERARY NOTES**

"I Would Do This Evil to Them"

In 6:10, God says that he will do "evil" to them. In English, that sounds like God is doing something immoral, against his character. However, the underlying Hebrew word (ra') refers to what is "bad" or "unpleasant." It can refer to moral evil, disaster, or whatever is undesirable.[d] In this context promising punishment for sin, use of ra' indicates that God will bring harm on the people. Such judgment does not undermine his moral perfection because it is completely within his rights as creator and covenant keeper.

worshiping (8:5, 10–12). Women are weeping for Tammuz, a Mesopotamian god, and people are worshiping the sun (8:14–16). There is wickedness and murder (11:2, 6). 🎨

Meanwhile, God's glory is departing from the temple. In 9:3, Ezekiel sees it lift up from its place in the holy of holies and move to the threshold. In 10:4, it fills the courtyard of the temple. In 10:18, it goes up from the temple to above the creatures and the heavenly "vehicle" (the same one that Ezekiel saw in chap. 1). The vehicle lifts into the air (10:19), and Ezekiel sees the glory leave the city and move off to the east toward Babylon (11:22–23). This vision explains why Ezekiel saw the glory in exile in chapter 1. God has removed his presence from the city in anticipation of his fierce judgment. Faced with such flagrant abuse of the covenant in his own house, God deserts the city where his presence was thought to be a given, and he himself chooses to be exiled.

It is difficult to imagine worse news for Ezekiel's audience. But there is a ray of hope. God says in 11:17–20 that he will gather his people back into the land, remove their abominations, and "remove the heart of stone from their flesh and give them a heart of flesh" (11:19). This transformation will ultimately lead to obedience and restoration of relationship with God (11:20).

Parables, Proverbs, Metaphors, and Sign-Acts (Part 1)

▓ READ EZEKIEL 12–14 ▓

Chapters 12–24 form another major unit in the book, consisting of a variety of vivid parables, sign-acts, and other images that, for the most part, announce judgment against Israel. For the sake of simplicity, we will break down this unit into six parts.

THINKING VISUALLY

The Structure of Ezekiel's Vision
Figure 11.3

8:1a—Ezekiel sits with the elders.

8:1b–2—The vision begins.

8:3—Ezekiel travels to Jerusalem in the vision.

8:4–11:23—Ezekiel sees abominations in Jerusalem.

11:24a—Ezekiel returns in the vision.

11:24b—The vision comes to an end.

11:25—Ezekiel reports to the other exiles.

Ezekiel begins in chapter 12 by describing a sign-act in which he packs his bags, digs a hole in the wall, and role-plays leaving for exile. The people are watching, and when they ask, "What are you doing?" he explains that the people of Jerusalem will go into exile soon (12:1–16). He then performs a second sign-act in which he eats and drinks while trembling with anxiety (12:17–20). This illustrates the stress that the people of Jerusalem will feel when their land is attacked. In chapter 13, he describes conflict with false prophets who have become God's enemies by speaking from their own minds. Finally, he announces that nothing will prevent God's judgment for their idolatry (14:12–23). 📖

Parables, Proverbs, Metaphors, and Sign-Acts (Part 2)

■ READ EZEKIEL 15–16 ■

This section contains two parables. Chapter 15 presents a parable of Israel as a vine. In the Old Testament, vines are usually used as images of something good and productive. In this case, however, Israel is a worthless vine that is only fit to be burned, and it will be even more worthless after that. Chapter 16 contains a vivid and shocking parable of Jerusalem as an unwanted infant, abandoned on the side of the road. God rescues, raises, and then marries her in a covenant relationship. This is symbolic of her history. Israel had no inherent value that caused YHWH to choose her above all other nations on the earth—it was simply his mercy and sovereign choice. Taking his abundant love and provision for granted, she turns to reckless and wild promiscuity. At least normal prostitutes receive payment, but she takes God's good gifts and gives them to all of her lovers in an ironic twist (16:33). Therefore, God will gather all her lovers (i.e., the nations) against her to strip her naked, stone her, and cut her to pieces (16:38–43). The meaning is obvious: because Israel is acting unfaithfully to God's covenant, her judgment will be the punishment for adultery. The nations she trusted will conquer her and plunder the adornment God gave her. However, God offers a note of hope even at the end of this severe story: "Yet I will remember my covenant with you" (16:60). The very covenant she has trampled is the one that binds God to her in relationship, and it will be the basis

LITERARY NOTES

Noah, Daniel, and Job

In Ezekiel 14:14 and 14:20, Ezekiel warns that judgment is inevitable. He says even if three well-known righteous men— Noah, Daniel, and Job—were in the land, their faithfulness to God would not be enough to avert disaster. They would simply save their own lives but would not provide cover for anyone else. This poses a problem for critical scholarship, which largely views the narratives in the book of Daniel as fiction written hundreds of years after Ezekiel, in the second century BC. This, along with a slight difference in the Hebrew spelling of the name, leads critical scholars to argue that this "Daniel" is not the Old Testament prophet by that name, but a wise man from Ugarit (modern Lebanon). But it would make no sense for that individual to exemplify righteousness, since he was a foreigner who worshiped other gods! It is preferable to understand this as the prophet Daniel, a contemporary of Ezekiel who had already gained a reputation for faithfulness like Noah and Job.

of his ongoing commitment to her. Then she will know that he is YHWH (16:62). 📖

Parables, Proverbs, Metaphors, and Sign-Acts (Part 3)

▦ READ EZEKIEL 17–18 ▦

Another vine parable in 17:1–10 describes a seed that was taken by an eagle to a place where it flourished until a second eagle pulled it up so that it withered. In 17:11–21 Ezekiel explains that the first eagle is the king of Babylon who made a covenant with Judah's king (the royal "seed"), causing him to flourish. But the king of Judah trusted in Egypt (the second eagle) instead, incurring disaster.

In chapter 18, Ezekiel addresses what was apparently a common proverb: "The fathers have eaten sour grapes, and the children's teeth are set on edge" (18:2). This proverb was quoted and debunked in Jeremiah 31:29–30, and Ezekiel's point is similar here. The people must not blame the previous generations for the consequences that they face. Rather, "the soul who sins shall die" (18:4). If they are righteous, they will live, and if they are wicked, they will die (18:5–13). The main point comes at the end of the passage: *God wants them to repent* because he takes no pleasure in killing the wicked (18:32).

Parables, Proverbs, Metaphors, and Sign-Acts (Part 4)

▦ READ EZEKIEL 19:1–20:44 ▦

In chapter 19, Ezekiel presents two more parables from God. The first, in 19:1–9, imagines two kings in Israel as lion cubs, taken into exile in Egypt and Babylon, respectively. The second parable, in 19:10–14, imagines Israel as a vine that was planted in a good place but was then dried up (by the Chaldeans) so that it was ruined. 📜

In chapter 20, the elders come to sit before Ezekiel to inquire of him, but God tells them (through Ezekiel) that he will not answer their inquiry. Rather,

---

LITERARY NOTES 📖

Sexual Violence in Ezekiel

Feminist scholars have given a great deal of attention to Ezekiel 16 (and also chap. 23) because of the sexualized violence contained there. They frequently charge that Ezekiel has a deviant mind or hates women. Furthermore, the male author and the (implied) male reader are aligning with the male husband in the text against the woman, Jerusalem. Why are the male lovers not being punished if they also are committing adultery with her? These scholars raise important questions, and the imagery is understandably troubling, especially to someone who has been mistreated sexually. However, it is important that we think carefully about Ezekiel's literary technique in at least four ways. (1) The parable never disguises that the *real* subject is Jerusalem, who has "relations" (political and religious) with foreign nations (the lovers). The nakedness and killing clearly refer to plundering and conquest. (2) It is a rhetorical trap. The husband represents God, but the wife represents . . . the reader! Even as we are tempted to "root" for the husband, we must remember that *our* sins are uncovered. (3) Ironically, Israel wanted to show her nakedness to her lovers, so God will do just that. She will actually get an abundance of what she asked for (see 16:43). (4) The offense of the image is the point. Jerusalem's sin is not a sterile, legal fact. It hurts God, who imagines himself as her husband. By using the metaphor of adultery to describe covenant breaking, Ezekiel imports all of the emotional pain, shame, and rejection into his indictment. He wants us to *feel* the horror of what God's people have done to him and, by extension, what we have done to him.

Ezekiel's Vine Imagery in the Gospel of John

This unit of Ezekiel contains three parables that present Israel as a vine (Ezek. 15:1–8; 17:1–10; 19:10–14). These are a likely background for the parable of the vine in John 15. Jesus says that he is the vine and we are the branches. Whereas in Ezekiel, Israel was a vine that failed to produce, Jesus is the true vine, who will produce fruit. If we abide in him, we will produce fruit as well because we are connected to what is true (15:5). If we do not abide in him, we will be thrown into the fire and burned (15:6). In Ezekiel's parables, the vines specifically symbolize Israel's sinful royal leadership. In John, Jesus is in conflict with the corrupt religious leadership of his own day.[e]

Ezekiel should recount the "abominations of their fathers" (20:4). Through his accurate—but selective—retelling of Israel's history, Ezekiel makes the case that there is no such thing as "the good old days" for Israel. They have been rebellious from the beginning. Therefore, God will enter into judgment with them once and for all, purging the rebels from among them. He will then take those who remain to his holy mountain, and they will know that he is YHWH (20:32–44).

Parables, Proverbs, Metaphors, and Sign-Acts (Part 5)

■ READ EZEKIEL 20:45–22:31 ■

Ezekiel continues his declaration of judgment against Israel with vivid imagery of God's unquenchable fire burning the land (20:45–49) and his sword that he is sharpening for the slaughter (21:8–10). His sword is actually in the hand of the king of Babylon, who will wield it on God's behalf (21:19). Death is coming because of Israel's many sins: they treat parents with contempt, practice extortion, exploit the poor and vulnerable, ignore the Sabbath, murder, practice false religion, commit sexual immorality, pay bribes, and cheat in business (22:6–12). This list is a direct violation of the law code in Leviticus 18–20 and 25.[6] They have fallen far short of what God commanded in his covenant with them. It is no surprise that the people are corrupt when they are led by violent, greedy, abusive leaders who act like wolves (22:23–31).

Parables, Proverbs, Metaphors, and Sign-Acts (Part 6)

■ READ EZEKIEL 23–24 ■

The messages of judgment conclude with two more parables, the first of which is about two adulterous sisters (23:1–49). One sister, "Oholah," is Samaria, the capital of the Northern Kingdom, and the other sister, "Oholibah," is Jerusalem. Like chapter 16, this story uses sexual imagery, but here it is even more graphic. It conveys a sense of shame over what the sisters have done and characterizes their insatiable desire to stray from YHWH. What Oholah/Samaria did was bad enough: she "lusted" after Assyria, impressed with that nation's power, and attempted to create an alliance. Therefore, YHWH gave her over to the Assyrians, and they killed her with the sword (an image of exile). However, the real tragedy of the parable is that Oholibah/Jerusalem saw what her sister did, failed to learn from her poor example, and became even worse! She "lusted" after the Assyrians, Chaldeans, and Egyptians (23:11–21). Therefore, YHWH will bring all of these nations against Jerusalem. They will strip her naked (i.e., plunder her) and put an end to her indecency (23:22–49). The second parable imagines Jerusalem as a boiling cauldron (24:1–14). This is a picture of the Chaldeans' siege of the city: the pressure and heat are building.

The book comes to a major turning point at 24:15–27. God tells Ezekiel that his wife will die, but he is not allowed to mourn for her in public with special clothing or food. When he grieves for his wife, he must do it privately and then get dressed and go about his business as usual. This would certainly provoke people to ask, "Why are you acting this way?" (24:19). The answer is that the delight of *their* eyes, Jerusalem, is going to "die" at the hands of the Chaldeans, but the people should not mourn, because it is a deserved consequence for rebellion against God. They had trusted in God's past favor toward Jerusalem as permanent insurance against his judgment. They had become proud that they were his special people, assuming he would never allow the city to be destroyed. But God hates sin, and his favor is not a given. He longs for his people to repent, but when they do not, the consequences are severe.

Prophecies against Foreign Nations

■ READ EZEKIEL 25–32 ■

The second half of the book of Ezekiel, chapters 25–48, is composed of messages of hope for God's people. The first unit in this part of the book contains Ezekiel's prophecies against foreign nations. He identifies the sin of these nations and proclaims God's judgment on them. First is Ammon, who cheered when God's temple was profaned and will be plunder for the nations (25:1–7). Second is Moab, who had contempt for God's people and will be given to desert tribes (25:8–11). Third is Edom, who took revenge on Judah and will be cut off (25:12–14). Then comes Philistia, who showed never-ending animosity toward God and will be destroyed (25:15–17). Tyre and Sidon come next in a lengthy passage that describes the pride of the king of Tyre (26:1–28:26). Finally, Egypt is also guilty of pride and will fall at God's hand (29:1–32:32).

We have seen these kinds of messages against foreign nations in Isaiah and Jeremiah as well, but in each book they serve a slightly different purpose. In Isaiah, they demonstrate that the nations are untrustworthy and that only YHWH can save. In Jeremiah, they demonstrate that God's justice will prevail and that he and his people will be vindicated. In Ezekiel, these messages anticipate God's victory over all threats to the full *restoration* of his people. In spite of his deadly judgments, God has still kept a people for himself. And they will be able to live in safety forever, knowing that God has destroyed his enemies and removed the danger. God's people will be secure because God's enemies—and their enemies—will be defeated.

The End of an Era

■ READ EZEKIEL 33 ■

In 3:16–21, as a part of Ezekiel's call narrative, God tells the prophet that he is like a "watchman" who is responsible to warn the people of the threat posed by their wicked ways. If Ezekiel is faithful, then he has completed his task whether the people listen or not. *They* are accountable for their response. Chapter 33 begins with the same watchman image (33:1–6). In his role as a prophet, Ezekiel is a watchman as well. If he does not deliver the word of judgment and give the wicked an opportunity to repent, then the wicked will die for their sin, but Ezekiel will also be held responsible! But if Ezekiel warns them and they do not repent, then they will bear the responsibility and Ezekiel will be delivered (33:7–20).

It is in the literary context of this conversation that an escapee arrives from Jerusalem and reports that the city is destroyed, including the temple (33:21). God's word from 24:26 has come to pass; he has brought about the final punishment for breaking the covenant. At the end of the chapter, we are reminded how God's people got themselves into this mess: They do not take God's word seriously. They love to listen to Ezekiel and gather around him to hear a word from YHWH (33:30), but they treat it like mere entertainment, as though he were a musician. They hear the word but will not obey it. Jerusalem has fallen, but more judgment is coming. When the land is devastated, "then they will know that a prophet has been among them" (33:33). This is a crucial warning to us as well. Do we read, study, and hear God's Word only because it is fascinating or inspirational? Do we treat it as one more way to stimulate our minds or satisfy our curiosity, without letting it actually having any bearing on our worldview and actions? It is not enough to appreciate God's Word—he requires that we obey it.

A New Shepherd

■ READ EZEKIEL 34 ■

The final major unit in the book, chapters 34–48, concerns messages of restoration for Israel and Judah. One scholar calls this unit "The gospel according to Ezekiel."[7] The prophet looks forward to a time when God will give his people a new shepherd, a renewed land, a renewed nature, a renewed people, and a renewed unity. We will explore these in the following sections.

Ezekiel begins by describing Israel's leaders as bad shepherds. They have been given a responsibility to lead and care for their sheep (the people of Israel), but instead they have only cared for themselves. Therefore, God will rescue his scattered sheep from these shepherds. He says, "I will seek the lost, and I will bring back the strayed, and I will bind up the injured, and I will strengthen the weak, and the fat and the strong I will destroy" (34:16). YHWH will himself shepherd them and will replace these wicked shepherds with a new shepherd: his servant David. But how can David be a new shepherd when he has been dead for hundreds of years? God is promising a future king from the line of David whose rule will bring security, blessing, and flourishing through a "covenant of peace" (34:25). This is another way of speaking about the new covenant that God will make with his people.

A Renewed Land

■ READ EZEKIEL 35:1–36:15 ■

Ezekiel 35:1–36:15 is a message directed to two different mountains. In the first half, Ezekiel directs God's word toward Mount Seir, which is in the territory of Edom. In the second half, Ezekiel speaks to the mountains of Israel. The Edomites descended from Esau, whereas the Israelites were descendants of Jacob. Thus, the two nations were "brothers" who were supposed to care for each other, but they had a long history of conflict. When the Chaldeans attacked Jerusalem, instead of helping their brothers, the Edomites took advantage of Judah and plundered them. Ezekiel announces judgment on Edom as a result. Because they did not hate bloodshed, it will pursue *them* (35:6). By contrast, Israel has suffered humiliation and violence from the nations (including Edom), but God will rescue his people, and they will no longer be disgraced (36:15). Israel will be inhabited and rebuilt, and its people will multiply.

In the Prophets, Edom came to be used as a symbol for all nations that oppose God. Judgment on Edom must take place so that God's people can be saved. The relationship between Edom and Israel, and the broader symbolism of that relationship, is the central topic of the book of Obadiah (see chap. 16).

A Renewed Nature

 READ EZEKIEL 36:16–38 ■

Israel had the incredible status of being God's special, chosen people among all the nations of the earth. This meant that they enjoyed God's care and protection, but it also meant that they had a particular responsibility to represent him well and to honor him, since he had attached his name to them. However, Israel failed at this. Because of their sins, they were unclean and offensive to God and dishonored his holy name (36:20). God's reputation was at risk, because everyone knew that Israel belonged to God, and yet they were under judgment.

Therefore, for the sake of God's name and reputation, he says he will act powerfully to enable his people to obey him and to live in a way that honors him. They have demonstrated over and over that they could not get this right, so now he will step in and do for them what they could not do for themselves. He says, "It is not for your sake, O house of Israel, that I am about to act, but for the sake of my holy name. . . . I will vindicate the holiness of my great name" (36:22–23). These are the things that he will do for them: He will bring them back into their own land (36:24). He will cleanse them and give them a new heart and a new spirit (36:25–26). This sounds very much like Jeremiah's promise of a "new covenant." God's Spirit will cause the people to obey his word, and he will make them live in abundance (Ezek. 36:27, 30). God concludes the passage by repeating, "It is not for your sake that I will act . . . ; let that be known to you" (36:32). God is concerned about his reputation and will not allow it to be dishonored. However, he is also gracious and will transform and renew his people so that they *can* honor him. ⬨

THEOLOGICAL ISSUES

A Woman in Her Menstrual Impurity

In Ezekiel 36:17, God says that Israel's sins are before him like a woman in her menstrual impurity. That statement may sound strange at best, since God made our bodies to function in certain ways. At worst, it might sound like an attack on women. Many rituals and laws in God's covenant with Israel are related to the fact that a holy God is living in the midst of his creatures, who also sin and do what is wrong. People who are defiled or "unclean" cannot be near a God who is not only absolutely righteous and without sin but also completely *other* than the humans he has created. In God's covenant with Israel, two things defile a person in close proximity to him. First, sin defiles a person and makes him or her unclean. Second, a person can become unclean by various things that are *not* sin: menstruation, giving birth, a nocturnal emission, touching a dead body, and so forth. In other words, *sin defiles a person, but not everything that defiles a person is sin.* In Ezekiel 36:17, God uses menstruation as an image of defilement not because it is sinful but because it temporarily kept a woman from God's presence and from participating in worship. Similarly, Israel's "blood" (i.e., murder and injustice) was polluting the land and separating the people from God.

A Renewed People

■ READ EZEKIEL 37:1–14 ■

In chapter 37, Ezekiel has another vision, in which the spirit of YHWH takes him to a valley filled with dry bones. Ezekiel emphasizes that the bones are totally dry and without any life at all (37:2). When he prophesies to the bones at God's command, the bones come back together into corpses, but they are still dead (37:7–8). It is only when God's breath comes into the corpses that they come to life and stand on their feet (37:10). One of the keys to understanding this vision is that the words "spirit," "breath," and "wind" all translate

Figure 11.4. The prophet Ezekiel's vision of the resurrection of the dead by Quinten Massys (1589)

the same Hebrew word, *ruah*. It is used nine times in this chapter as a wordplay to emphasize that it is God's power that brings hope and life.

The explanation of the vision comes in 37:11–14. The bones represent Israel: a dead, decayed nation with no hope at all. God is going to raise up his people and bring them back to the land. He says, "I will put my Spirit within you, and you shall live" (37:14). As New Testament Christians, we may be tempted to understand this story of life from death as a prediction of Jesus's resurrection or the resurrection of believers at the end of time. However, the authors of the New Testament never use Ezekiel's vision in this way. The focus is not on physical resurrection, but on God's ability to breathe new life into circumstances that seem *completely* hopeless in order to achieve his purposes. This is the resurrection of a *people*—a new Israel— back from the death of exile. The "whole house of Israel" is comprehensive in scope, but the promises here pertain to believing Israel, the true people of God, who will be gathered and given a future.

A Renewed Unity

■ READ EZEKIEL 37:15–28 ■

Following the vision of the dry bones in 37:1–14, Ezekiel relates a signact. God tells him to write "Judah" (signifying the Southern Kingdom) on one stick and "Joseph" (signifying the Northern Kingdom) on the other, and then to join them together in his hand to illustrate the reuniting of the nation. When the Chaldeans conquered Judah, they kept the exiles together, including Ezekiel himself. But when the Assyrians conquered the Northern Kingdom, they scattered the people, and those tribes as a coherent group were lost to history. Therefore, when Ezekiel performs this sign-act, the people wonder what it means (37:18).

Ezekiel explains that God will take the people of Israel from among the nations where they have been scattered and bring them into their own land, where they will be one unified people (37:21–22). He will cleanse them, and they will be his people, and he will be their God in a restored relationship (37:23). He will place a Davidic king over them forever and will make a covenant of peace with them, an everlasting covenant (37:26). The New Testament tells us that this Davidic king is Jesus Christ our Messiah, whose death and resurrection brought about the new covenant spoken of in Jeremiah.

But how do we make sense of the main point of the sign-act, which is that there will be one unified people? In Romans 9:23–25, the apostle Paul states that God is creating a people for himself, not only from the Jews but also from the gentiles. When the northern tribes were exiled by the Assyrians, they became "not my people" and were absorbed into the gentiles, separated from God.[8] However, God calls gentiles from all the nations so that they go from being "not my people" to being the children of the living God. A subset (or "remnant") of Israel will be saved (Rom. 9:27), and gentiles will be gathered into that group as well. In the end, there will be one people of God, collected from the nations, under the reign of the Davidic king Jesus Christ, transformed, and reconciled to God. This glorious future is not something that God's people could create for themselves any more than the dry bones could bring themselves back to life.[9] It is achieved only by God's great mercy and limitless power.

God's Restoration Is Tested

■ READ EZEKIEL 38–39 ■

In this section, Ezekiel depicts an attack on the restored people of God described in the previous chapter. God will bring them into a good land and cause them to live in safety and security. But in the "latter years"—that is, in the eschatological future—a great enemy named Gog will be the leader of a massive coalition of armies (38:7–9). The attack looks completely lopsided. The enemy's hordes will be like a cloud covering the land, coming against the people of God, who are "quiet" and live without any obvious defenses (38:9–11).

In fact, God's people *will* be outnumbered, but it is Gog who is at an extreme disadvantage because YHWH will fight on behalf of his people. YHWH is the one who is bringing Gog against his land in order to demonstrate to all the nations that his people truly are safe forever (38:16). One scholar writes, "[Ezek. 38–39] is a message of encouragement to all the saints of all times and places that no matter what the forces of evil may do, God's purpose and victory stands secure. If God can defeat the combined forces of Gog and his allies and turn them into fodder for the crows and carrion-eaters, how much more can he take care of us, whatever historical manifestation of the enmity of Satan we face."[10]

A Vision of the End

■ READ EZEKIEL 40–48 ■

In the final nine chapters of the book, Ezekiel describes his vision of the eschatological future when God and his people are restored to one another. The hand of YHWH comes on him and carries him in a vision to the land of Israel to show him what he must report to the exiles (40:1–2). This vision is like the vision in chapter 1, when he saw God's glory by the Chebar Canal, and it is like the vision in chapters 8–11, when he saw God's glory leave the temple because of the people's rebellion (43:3). Now, in this vision, Ezekiel sees a new temple, in a new city, on a new land, and God's glory is returning to dwell with his people once more!

First, God shows Ezekiel a new temple (40:1–47:12). He takes him on a guided tour of all of its parts: the wall, gates, side rooms, outer court, and perimeter. The temple is much larger and more glorious than the tabernacle or Solomon's temple, or even the temple Herod would build much later (see fig. 11.5). With such massive dimensions, it would not even fit on the Temple Mount in Jerusalem! The point here is that God's kingdom and dwelling place with his people is expansive.[11] Ezekiel's description of the temple, the Levites who work in it, and the surrounding area emphasizes that it is a *holy* place. He says, "This is the law of the temple: the whole territory on the top of the mountain all around shall be most holy" (43:12). This is because it represents the dwelling place of God with his people, as he had always intended. 🖎

God continues the vision by describing the renewed land that his people inherit (47:13–48:29). God's dwelling place is at the center. Although two and a half tribes had previously settled in the land east of the Jordan, in Ezekiel's vision, the promised land does not include that area. Rather, all twelve tribes receive territories within the promised land as given originally in Numbers 34:1–12 (see map 11.2).

The Sizes of the Tabernacle and the Jerusalem Temples

Figure 11.5

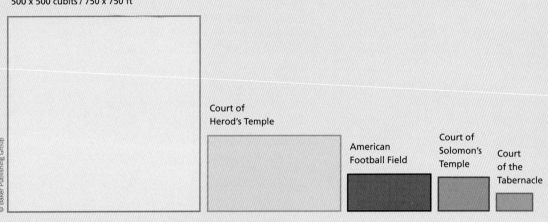

Court of Ezekiel's Temple,
500 x 500 cubits / 750 x 750 ft

Court of
Herod's Temple

American
Football Field

Court of
Solomon's
Temple

Court
of the
Tabernacle

© Baker Publishing Group

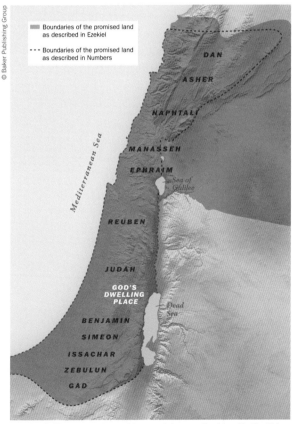

Boundaries of the promised land
as described in Ezekiel

Boundaries of the promised land
as described in Numbers

DAN
ASHER
NAPHTALI
MANASSEH
EPHRAIM
Sea of
Galilee
REUBEN
JUDAH
GOD'S
DWELLING
PLACE
Dead
Sea
BENJAMIN
SIMEON
ISSACHAR
ZEBULUN
GAD

Mediterranean Sea

© Baker Publishing Group

Map 11.2. The boundaries and layout of the promised land in Ezekiel 47–48

At the end of the book (48:30–35) Ezekiel describes a massive new city. His final words read: "And the name of the city from that time on shall be, The Lord is there." This encapsulates the message of this entire nine-chapter section. The visions of the temple, the land, and the city are likely not intended as blueprints for how they will physically appear in the future. Rather, the point is "theology in the form of geography."[12] The centerpiece of God's future restoration of his people is his own presence with them. He is *there*. His plan of salvation will have attained its goal when God dwells permanently with his people.

Implementation

Despite the length and complexity of the book of Ezekiel, there are a few obvious and important themes that run through the entire book. One of these is God's catchphrase "You will know that I am the LORD." In his revelation to Ezekiel, God uses variations of this expression seventy-one times (see table 11.3).

Fifty-one times, God states that people will know he is YHWH after he brings violent and terrible judgment. Seventeen times, he says this after announcing salvation (see the shaded references). And three times, he says they will know him after he reveals something (see the bold references).

At the beginning of this chapter, we noted how easily we fall into the temptation to worship a god made in our own image. Sometimes this involves thinking of God as we would like him to be: a softer God; a God who will not hold us accountable; a God who allows us to search for the "good life" wherever our imaginations take us. Ezekiel dispels these delusions and reveals the God who *is*. He is distinct from his creation. He expects his creatures to obey and worship him, and when they do not, he becomes angry. His judgment is real, terrible, and violent. Six times in the book he says, "My eye will not spare, and I will have no pity" (5:11; 7:4, 9; 8:18; 9:5, 10). God loves to show mercy, and he often waits to bring consequences until the last possible moment to allow people to repent. But when the time for mercy is past, he does not judge half-heartedly—his retribution is ferocious and unstoppable. This picture may seem incompatible with much that is said in our contemporary churches, at least in the West. Our typical expressions of faith are directed toward a soft god who might be confused with one's boyfriend or a generous uncle. When God brings judgment, however, we are faced with the undeniable reality of his unstoppable power and control. He is YHWH.

Ezekiel also tells us that we will know YHWH when he saves and delivers. As terrible as God's judgment is, his mercy is equally stunning. God is portrayed as one who loves his people with such intensity that he refuses to give up hope no matter how far they have strayed. In chapter 16 he describes Jerusalem's bold sins and incessant unfaithfulness. Shockingly, God is pictured as a humiliated, jilted husband. Even as he announces the consequences for her sin, he promises, "Yet I will remember my covenant with you in the days of your youth, and I will establish for you an everlasting covenant" (16:60). God's "yet" is a little word full of great hope that cannot be taken for granted. His love is always greater than our rebellion. He pursues us until we are exhausted from our wickedness, and then his transforming power gives us a fresh start. Twice he says in the book, "I will give them one heart, and a new spirit I will put within them. I will remove the heart of stone from their flesh and give them a heart of flesh" (11:19; cf. 36:26). God's work to make us new is celebrated and further explained in the New

Table 11.3. "You Will Know That I Am the Lᴏʀᴅ" in Ezekiel

Ref	Text	Ref	Text
5:13	"My anger [will] spend itself, and I will vent my fury"	26:5–6	*To Tyre:* "She shall become plunder for the nations"
6:7	"Slain shall fall in your midst"	28:22	*To Sidon:* "When I execute judgments in her"
6:9–10	"They will be loathsome in their own sight"	28:23	*To Sidon:* "The slain shall fall in her midst"
6:13	"When their slain lie among their idols"	28:24	Israel will be delivered from neighboring people
6:14	"I will . . . make the land desolate and waste"	28:26	Israel will dwell secure when I judge their neighbors
7:4	"I will punish you for your ways"	29:5–6	*To Egypt:* I will feed you to the animals
7:9	"I will punish you according to your ways"	29:9	*To Egypt:* They will "be a desolation and a waste"
7:27	"I will judge them"	29:16	*To Egypt:* They will never again be Israel's reliance
11:10	"You shall fall by the sword"	29:19–21	*To Egypt:* They will be destroyed by Babylon
11:11–12	"I will judge you"	30:8	*To Egypt:* "When I have set fire to Egypt"
12:15	"When I disperse them among the nations"	30:19	*To Egypt:* "I will execute judgments on Egypt"
12:16	"That they may declare all their abominations"	30:25	*To Egypt:* The king of Babylon will attack Egypt
12:20	The cities will be laid waste	30:26	*To Egypt:* "I will scatter the Egyptians"
13:9	False prophets will be cut off from the land of Israel	32:15	*To Egypt:* I will "strike down all who dwell" there
13:14	"You shall perish"	33:29	The land of Israel will be desolate
13:21	I will deliver from false *female prophets*	34:27	When I deliver them and they dwell securely
13:23	"I will deliver my people out of your hand"	34:29–30	"They shall . . . no longer suffer the reproach of the nations"
14:8	"I will . . . cut him off from the midst of my people"	35:4	*To Mount Seir:* "I will lay your cities waste"
15:7	The fire will consume them	35:9	*To Mount Seir:* "I will make you a perpetual desolation"
16:62	**"I will establish my covenant with you"**	35:11–12	*To Mount Seir:* "When I judge you"
17:20–21	"I will . . . enter into judgment with him"	35:15	*To Mount Seir:* "You shall be desolate"
17:24	I will exalt Israel over all others	36:11	"I . . . will do more good to you than ever before"
20:12	**"I gave them my Sabbaths, as a sign"**	36:23	"When . . . I vindicate my holiness"
20:20	**"Keep my Sabbaths holy"**	36:36	When "I have rebuilt the ruined places"
20:38	"I will purge . . . the rebels from among you"	36:38	When the waste cities are filled with people
20:42	"When I bring you into the land" (from exile)	37:6	When I resurrect you with skin and breath
20:44	"When I deal with you for my name's sake"	37:13	"When I . . . raise you from your graves"
21:5	I will draw my sword against all flesh	37:14	"I will place you in your own land"
22:16	You will be profaned	37:28	"When my sanctuary is in their midst forevermore"
22:22	You will be melted with the fire of my wrath	38:22–23	When I "enter into judgment with" Gog
23:49	"You shall bear the penalty for . . . sinful idolatry"	39:6	"I will send fire on Magog"
24:23–24	"You shall rot away in your iniquities"	39:7	I will make my holy name known
24:27	When you (Ezekiel) speak to them	39:21–22	When all nations see my judgment
25:5	*To the Ammonites:* You will be plundered	39:28	When I assemble them into their own land
25:7	*To the Ammonites:* "I will destroy you"		
25:11	*To Moab:* "I will execute judgments"		
25:17	*Of the Philistines:* When I bring my vengeance		

Testament (John 3:1–7; 2 Cor. 5:17; Gal. 6:15; Eph. 2:3–6). When God loves and pursues and saves us, then we know that he is YHWH.

Both judgment *and* salvation are important aspects of God's program. They are both good: he is not embarrassed to identify himself as a God of judgment, nor is he embarrassed to say that he loves us and will redeem us—even as we trample on his holiness. When we read the book of Ezekiel, we know that he is YHWH. And we are motivated to turn from our evil, trusting and following him.

Another key theme in the book of Ezekiel is the glory of God. The Hebrew word *kabod* (glory) occurs eighteen times in the book, in four clusters (see table 11.4). First, Ezekiel sees God's glory in the opening vision of the book and in his call narrative (chapters 1–3). The vision is unsettling: Why is God's glory in the land of the Chaldeans instead of the Jerusalem temple, where God has taken up residence? Second, in an extended vision Ezekiel sees God's glory depart from the temple because of Jerusalem's sin (chapters 8–11). Third, God speaks of his own glory in the context of defending his people from Gog and his terrible armies. Finally, in his last vision Ezekiel sees God's glory return to the new temple and once again dwell among his people in the new land. Ezekiel emphasizes that God's primary goal of salvation is not simply to rescue us from hell or from the power of sin. The goal of salvation is that God might be with us and live in relationship with us.

Table 11.4. God's "Glory" in Ezekiel

1:28	Vision = appearance of the likeness of the glory	Call narrative
3:12	Glory is in this place	
3:23 (2x)	Glory is on the plain (like by the Chebar River)	
8:4	Glory is in the temple (8:3)	Leaving the temple
9:3	Glory goes from the cherub to the threshold	
10:4 (2x)	Glory goes from the cherub to the threshold / Fills the whole court of the temple	
10:18	Glory departs from the threshold	
10:19	Glory rises up from the earth	
11:22	Glory hovers above the cherubim	
11:23	Glory departs from the city and stands over the mountain	
39:21	I will set my glory among the nations	Gog and his armies
43:2 (2x)	Glory was coming from the east, and the earth shone with his glory	Returning to the new temple
43:4	Glory enters the temple	
43:5	Glory fills the temple	
44:4	Glory fills the temple	

In the New Testament, Jesus is presented as a new temple because he is God among his people. John tells us that "the Word [Jesus] . . . dwelt among us, and we have seen his *glory*" (John 1:14). Later, Jesus tells the Jews, "Destroy this temple [i.e., Jesus's body], and in three days I will raise it up" (John 2:19). In 2 Corinthians, Paul says that *we* are the temple of the living God, because we are his dwelling place. Therefore, we should separate ourselves from what is evil (2 Cor. 6:16–17).

In Revelation 21:3, at the conclusion of redemptive history, when God's salvation has fully come to pass, a loud voice says, "The dwelling place of God is with man. He will dwell with them, and they will be his people, and God himself will be with them as their God." John further says, "I saw no temple in the [New Jerusalem], for its temple is the Lord God the Almighty and the Lamb" (Rev. 21:22). What a blessing to know that God *wants* to dwell with us! He is not a cruel or indifferent God. His great desire is to live with us and to love us forever.

Christian Reading Questions

1. Consider Ezekiel's use of violent and sexual imagery in the book. How is this a challenge for today's readers? How might it be particularly effective for today's readers?

2. Reread Ezekiel 3:16–21 and 33:1–6. Describe how Ezekiel's analogy of the prophet as "watchman" might be applied to teaching and preaching in the church today. How might this image strengthen our resolve in the face of challenges to our faith and ministry?

3. Identify some of the themes that weave throughout the long book of Ezekiel. What theological ideas keep recurring and connect the parts of the book together? How does the notion of "temple" relate to some of these repeated ideas?

4. In Ezekiel, God announces either salvation or terrible judgment and then says, "You shall know that I am the LORD." Why is it important that we know God as savior *and* judge? How do we relate the self-revelation of God in Ezekiel to the self-revelation of God in Jesus Christ?

CHAPTER TWELVE

Daniel

Orientation

In the 2016 film *Lion*, a five-year-old Indian boy becomes lost and separated from his family when he is trapped on a train that takes him a thousand miles from home. After finding his way to an orphanage, he is adopted by a loving Australian couple. But in spite of his good life in Australia, he is plagued by memories of his lost family and struggles to find a way to them once again. The film explores the internal tension that he feels between two families, two nations, and two cultures. It is a tension that has been felt throughout history by the people of God.

God had given Israel a land and a home after he brought them out of slavery in Egypt. It was a glorious covenant gift, where God protected and provided for them. It was the land of Joshua, Ruth, David, Solomon, Elijah, and Isaiah. It was the land of the temple and priesthood—where God manifested his presence in a particular way among his own special people. This land was deeply connected to the faith and identity of the people of God. It was home. But when Judah was conquered by the Babylonians, some of God's people were exiled to that foreign nation for the rest of their lives. They had a new home, with a new government, language, culture, and gods. They needed to remain loyal to their *true* home even as they were good citizens of their home in exile. They needed to remain distinctive as the people of God and hold on to their faith while living and working in a nation and culture that was sometimes hostile to that faith.

The book of Daniel comes from this time in Israel's history and explores these issues of loyalty,

HISTORICAL MATTERS

"Fact Sheet"—Daniel

Author: Daniel

Date: 605–536 BC

Location: Babylon

Political and social context: Daniel and his friends worked in the highest levels of the government of the Neo-Babylonian (and later, Persian) Empire. Exiles were generally treated well, but hostility emerged when their faith and values challenged those of the empire.

citizenship, and faith in a foreign land. It also explores God's authority over *all* nations and his ultimate plan to bring his people to their true home with him, saved and secure, forever.

The book begins in the third year of King Jehoiakim (Dan. 1:1). This was 605 BC, the same year that King Nebuchadnezzar and his army came west from Babylon and met Egypt in battle at Carchemish, a city in the region of modern Syria. Nebuchadnezzar defeated the Egyptian pharaoh and then pursued his army south toward Egypt, as indicated in map 12.1. The orange arrow represents Nebuchadnezzar's army. As he came through Judah, he stopped in Jerusalem and took tribute from King Jehoiakim in the form of sacred vessels from the temple (1:2; see 5:1–4). He also took some of the young people of Israel who were from the upper class, good looking, intelligent, and able to work in the government (1:3–4). Among those taken as captives were Daniel and his three friends Shadrach, Meshach, and Abednego. Daniel would live and prophesy in Babylon for twenty years before Nebuchadnezzar and his army would return to Jerusalem, conquer it, and destroy the temple in 586. Daniel lived through the entire period of the Neo-Babylonian dominance of Israel, from Nebuchadnezzar's victory at Carchemish in 605 to the rise of the new, Medo-Persian Empire in 539—a span of sixty-nine years. If he was in his late teens when he was taken to Babylon (1:1–4), he probably would have given his last dated prophecy when he was in his late eighties (10:1)! He was a contemporary of the prophet Ezekiel in the Babylonian Empire and is mentioned in Ezekiel 14:14, 20; 28:3.

The book of Daniel is arranged in chronological order with the exception that while the narratives (chaps. 1–6) present events in sequence, the visions (chaps. 7–12) overlap with them (see table 12.1). The events and visions in the book are clustered in three groups during the reigns of three kings. First, Nebuchadnezzar took Daniel into exile when he was a young man (chaps. 1–4).

Map 12.1. The Battle of Carchemish

© Baker Publishing Group

605 BC (Clash between Egyptians and Nebuchadnezzar)

Carchemish
Haran
Aleppo
Ugarit
Hamath
Tadmor
Byblos
Damascus
Tyre
Ashdod
Ashkelon
Gaza
Rabbah-bene-ammon
Jerusalem
Brook of Egypt
Mediterranean Sea

→ Pharaoh Neco
→ Nebuchadnezzar

Second, King Nabonidus spent considerable time away from Babylon, including a period of ten years. While he was gone, Belshazzar was regent, and he was the ruler who interacted with Daniel (chaps. 5, 7–8). Finally, the last events and visions in the book (chaps. 6, 9–12) occur during the first few years of the reign of Cyrus (also called "Darius the Mede").[1]

Questions of the authorship and genre of the book of Daniel are closely related to each other and have important implications for the meaning and message of the book. Generally speaking, there are two major positions: the traditional/evangelical position and the view of critical biblical scholarship.

The traditional view is that Daniel is the author of the book. Jesus considered Daniel to be a real, historical figure who had visions of the future that would be fulfilled (Matt. 24:15). Also, the Jewish historian Josephus

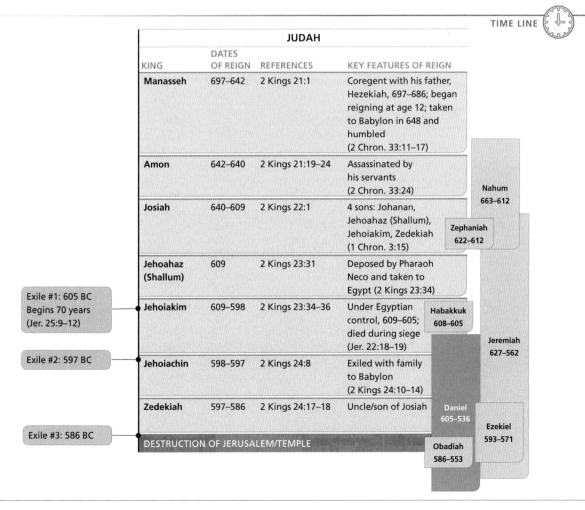

JUDAH			
KING	DATES OF REIGN	REFERENCES	KEY FEATURES OF REIGN
Manasseh	697–642	2 Kings 21:1	Coregent with his father, Hezekiah, 697–686; began reigning at age 12; taken to Babylon in 648 and humbled (2 Chron. 33:11–17)
Amon	642–640	2 Kings 21:19–24	Assassinated by his servants (2 Chron. 33:24)
Josiah	640–609	2 Kings 22:1	4 sons: Johanan, Jehoahaz (Shallum), Jehoiakim, Zedekiah (1 Chron. 3:15)
Jehoahaz (Shallum)	609	2 Kings 23:31	Deposed by Pharaoh Neco and taken to Egypt (2 Kings 23:34)
Jehoiakim	609–598	2 Kings 23:34–36	Under Egyptian control, 609–605; died during siege (Jer. 22:18–19)
Jehoiachin	598–597	2 Kings 24:8	Exiled with family to Babylon (2 Kings 24:10–14)
Zedekiah	597–586	2 Kings 24:17–18	Uncle/son of Josiah
DESTRUCTION OF JERUSALEM/TEMPLE			

Exile #1: 605 BC Begins 70 years (Jer. 25:9–12)

Exile #2: 597 BC

Exile #3: 586 BC

Nahum 663–612

Zephaniah 622–612

Habakkuk 608–605

Jeremiah 627–562

Daniel 605–536

Ezekiel 593–571

Obadiah 586–553

Table 12.1. Chronology of Daniel

	King	Dates (BC)	Events	Reference in Daniel
Babylonian	Nabopolassar	626–605	Chaldean who seized Babylon (626)	
	Nebuchadnezzar (Nebuchadrezzar)	605–562	Defeated Egypt at Carchemish; exiles Judahites (605)	Daniel 1—1st year of Nebuchadnezzar (1:1)
				Daniel 2—2nd year of Nebuchadnezzar (2:1)
			More exiles from Judah (597; 586)	Daniel 3—reign of Nebuchadnezzar (3:1)
				Daniel 4—reign of Nebuchadnezzar (4:1)
	Evil Merodach (Amel-Marduk)	562–560		
	Neriglissar	560–556		
	Labashi-Marduk	556 (3 months)		
	Nabonidus	556–539	Spent considerable time outside Babylon; Belshazzar served as regent in his absence*	Daniel 7—1st year of Belshazzar (7:1)
				Daniel 8—3rd year of Belshazzar (8:1)
				Daniel 5—Belshazzar dies (5:30) (fall of the Babylonian Empire)
Persian	Cyrus II (the Great)	539–530	Conquered Babylon (539)	Daniel 6—"Darius the Mede" (5:31–6:1)
				Daniel 9—1st year of Darius the Mede (9:1)
				Daniel 10–12—3rd year of Cyrus (10:1)†
	Cambyses II	530–522		

* Nabonidus was the true king, and Belshazzar was second in command. This is why Belshazzar was only able to offer that someone would be the "third ruler in the kingdom" for understanding the writing on the wall (Dan. 5:7).

† The mention of the "first year of Darius the Mede" in 11:1 refers to an event that occurred two years prior (it belongs with the end of chap. 10). Therefore, it does not indicate a new date for a new vision.

writes that Daniel "did not only prophesy of future events, as did the other prophets, but he also determined the time of their accomplishment."[2] According to this traditional view, the narratives report actual eyewitness events, and the visions and dream interpretations come from Daniel in the Babylonian and early Persian periods (in the sixth century BC).

Traditional evangelical scholars tend to identify the genre of the book as "prophetic-apocalyptic." This label highlights its connections with other Old Testament prophets but also recognizes that the book has apocalyptic elements. The apocalyptic literary genre is similar to prophecy in that it reveals information from God that would not otherwise be known. However, apocalyptic texts often relate visions containing a great deal of symbolism. An angel or other mediator typically helps the individual understand the vision and further explains what is revealed. Apocalyptic texts tend to be written in times of crisis or persecution to reveal God's work in the grand sweep of history, culminating with the eschatological triumph of the kingdom of God. Other biblical texts such as Isaiah 24–27, parts of Ezekiel, Zechariah, and the book of Revelation in the New Testament are apocalyptic.[3]

In the period of Jewish history between the Old and New Testaments, extrabiblical apocalyptic texts became very common. For example, the book of 1 Enoch (from the second century BC) describes a heavenly journey taken by Enoch (cf. Gen. 5:21–24), in which he is given revelatory tablets that review human history and divide it into periods of weeks. In the Apocalypse of Abraham (from the first century BC), the first eight chapters narrate Abraham's conversion from idolatry, while chapters 9–32 describe Abraham's heavenly vision, in which he is given a review of Israel's history, guided by an angel. These works have two significant features. First, they are pseudonymous, meaning that they were written by someone other than the person they claim as author. First Enoch does not really come from Enoch (who lived not long after Adam and Eve), and the Apocalypse of Abraham does not really come from Abraham; both of these works come from the much later Hellenistic period. Second, this means that whenever these books purport to describe events in the future (from the perspective of Enoch and Abraham), they are really describing the past (from the perspective of their actual authors). This is called *ex eventu* prophecy. According to the traditional evangelical view, these works are *imitations* of canonical apocalyptic literature like Daniel and Zechariah.

However, critical biblical scholars hold a second position on the authorship and genre of the book. Rather than viewing later Jewish apocalyptic works as imitations of canonical apocalyptic (like Daniel), they view Daniel as having the same features as those later apocalyptic works. In their view, the authorship of Daniel is *pseudonymous*: it was not written by Daniel in the sixth century BC but by an anonymous individual (or individuals) in the second century BC, when the Seleucid emperor Antiochus IV Epiphanes was persecuting the Jews. The narratives in chapters 1–6 are fictional legends,[4] and the visions in chapters 7–12, which claim to predict the future, are actually *ex eventu*, written after the events they describe. Figure 12.1 positions the two views on a basic time line. 🖉

Of these two views, the traditional perspective on the date and authorship of Daniel is more convincing. First, the book makes reference to Daniel writing down dreams (see 7:1) and the visions are presented in a first-person perspective. Critical scholars argue that pseudonymous authorship was an expected feature of the apocalyptic genre and that readers were not deceived. But this begs the question: Then why do it? The only reason to claim that an earlier, famous figure was responsible for a vision would be to enhance the book's authority and to claim that an overview of history is

The Date of Daniel

Figure 12.1

	Author of Daniel (traditional view)		Author of Daniel (critical view)	
Empire	Neo-Babylonia	Medo-Persia	Greece	Rome
Dates (BC)	626–539	539–333*	333–63[†]	63 BC-634 AD[‡]

* Anson F. Rainey and R. Steven Notley, *The Sacred Bridge: Carta's Atlas of the Biblical World* (Jerusalem: Carta, 2014), 296.

[†] Rainey and Notley, *Sacred Bridge*, 297.

[‡] In AD 634, Syria/Palestine was conquered by Muslim armies.

predictive and therefore God exercises control over all. But this would mean that a false claim was being used to enhance the sense of truthfulness![5] Furthermore, if the author *knows* that his claims of authorship and chronology are false, how then can he use these claims as an encouragement that his readers should be faithful to God even in the face of persecution and death? Second, the details of the narratives do not support a late date from the Maccabean period. While Daniel and his friends sometimes faced hostility and danger, Daniel is presented as a friend of each king, and there is no widespread persecution of God's people. Third, from a historical perspective, it is implausible that these features of the genre (i.e. pseudonimity and *ex eventu* prophecy) were misunderstood by the vast majority of scholars and pastors throughout Jewish and Christian history until the eighteenth century, who believed the author to be Daniel.[6]

If the book describes how God actually saved his people in history, then we can have hope in his ability to save us. If the book is accurate in its predictions of history, including those leading up to the first coming of Christ (e.g., chaps. 2 and 7), then we can have confidence in what it teaches about our future and God's final, eschatological victory. But if the narratives are fiction and the visions are contrived, then the book has little to offer us. One scholar writes, "The whole theological meaning of the book depends upon Yahweh's ability to deliver his people and declare the future before it takes place. If he cannot do these things, no one should 'stand firm and take action' and risk his life for Yahweh (Dan. 11:32)."[7]

Exploration

The book of Daniel takes place in Babylon—in exile—and does not have a specific interest in Israel's broken covenant or God's judgment and restoration in history. The exile is simply accepted as a fact of life, and the book models how God's people should live in that state. Therefore, the book is primarily concerned with the fourth and fifth prophetic phases (as we have been calling them). In the eschatological future, God will establish his kingdom, which will break all other kingdoms.

Several different features of the book of Daniel affect its structure. First, while most of the book is written in Hebrew, 2:4b–7:28 is written in Aramaic. The Aramaic portion is primarily concerned with history in Babylon, whereas the Hebrew portion speaks primarily of the fate of the Jewish people. Second, the book is divided by genre into narratives (chaps. 1–6) and visions (chaps. 7–12). Third, chapters 2–7 form a chiastic pattern (see table 12.2). In the chiastic arrangement, **chapters 2** (A) and **7** (A′) each contain visions regarding four kingdoms, **chapters 3** (B) and **6** (B′) both give examples of God's power to deliver his servants from persecution, and **chapters 4** (C) and **5** (C′) present stories of God's judgment on proud rulers. **Chapter 7** functions as a hinge in the book: it completes the chiasm in chapters 2–7, but it is also the first of the visions that conclude the book in **chapters 7–12**.

Table 12.2. The Structure of Daniel

Court Narratives						Daniel's Visions			
God's sovereignty over gentile empires						Vision 1	Vision 2	Vision 3	Vision 4
	A	B	C	C′	B′	A′			
Setting	Four-part image	Refuse: worship image	Humble King Nebuchadnezzar	Humble King Belshshazzar	Refuse: stop praying	Four beasts	Ram and goat	70 weeks	Final vision
chap. 1	chap. 2	chap. 3	chap. 4	chap. 5	chap. 6	chap. 7	chap. 8	chap. 9	chaps. 10–12
Hebrew	Aramaic						Hebrew		

Source: Adapted from J. Paul Tanner, "The Literary Structure of the Book of Daniel," *Bibliotheca Sacra* 160, no. 639 (2003): 269–82.

THINKING VISUALLY

The Five Phases: Daniel
Figure 12.2

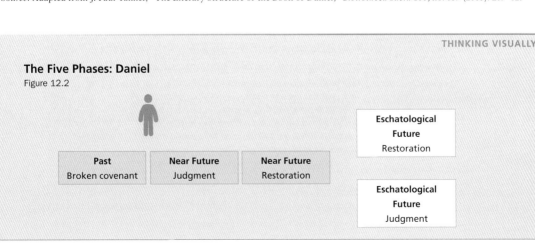

A New Life in Babylon

▓ READ DANIEL 1 ▓

The first chapter of the book introduces us to Daniel and his friends as well as their new situation in Babylon. Back in Jerusalem, they had a bright future ahead of them. Now they have been taken, against their will, to a foreign country almost a thousand miles away. New names, a new language, and a new culture have been forced on them. Surrounded by foreign, false religion, they are given jobs in the government that oppressed their home country and captured them. They are forced to decide: Where should they compromise, and where should they stand firm in this foreign land? When should they accept the traditions of their new land and participate in the culture as full members of society, and when will that violate their convictions and responsibilities to God?

In verses 8–21, they face their first crisis when they are given "the king's food" and wine (1:8). They have said "yes" to a pagan education, to their assigned roles, and even to their new names. In comparison to these fundamental markers of identity, food seems trivial.[8] But the commands of Moses teach that they must not eat unclean food, so this is a point where their new context is in conflict with their faith. Partly to protect the Babylonian eunuch who has responsibility for them, they propose a test: they will eat vegetables only (1:12). God honors them, and they are found to be significantly healthier than their fellow trainees (1:15, 20). This pattern of being tested, refusing to compromise (but not belligerently!), being vindicated by God, and ultimately bringing honor to God will be repeated in the narratives in the following chapters.

The Dream of the Four-Part Image

▓ READ DANIEL 2 ▓

Chapter 2 is divided into three parts. In verses 1–13, Nebuchadnezzar has a dream that troubles him. He demands that his magicians and enchanters must not only tell him the interpretation of the dream—they must reveal the dream itself or they will all be killed. They cannot, and therefore the king orders that all the wise men in Babylon be destroyed (1:12). Because Daniel and his friends are "wise men," they are also scheduled to be killed by the king's order. In verses 14–23, the four men pray for God's mercy, and God responds by revealing the interpretation in a night vision (2:19). In the final part of the chapter (2:24–49), Daniel reveals the interpretation to the king.

Table 12.3. Kingdoms in the Vision in Daniel 2

Empire	Neo-Babylonia	Medo-Persia	Greece	Rome	Kingdom of God
Dates (BC)	626–539	539–333	333–63	63 BC–AD 634	Inaugurated (by Jesus) during the Roman Empire and continues forever
Daniel 2	Gold head is Nebuchadnezzar (2:37–38)	Silver chest and arms are kingdom after (2:39)	Bronze middle and thighs are kingdom after (2:39)	Legs of iron and feet of iron and clay (2:40)	Stone that will break the other kingdoms (2:34–35, 44–45)

The king has dreamed about great empires coming in the future, symbolized by a large image made of various materials. The head, made of gold, represents Babylon (2:38). The chest and arms, made of silver, represent another, inferior kingdom (2:39). It is clear later in the book that this is Medo-Persia. The bronze middle and thighs represent a third kingdom, which we later learn is Greece (2:39). And a fierce fourth kingdom is represented by iron legs, but feet made of mixed iron and clay (2:40). When we piece together the biblical chronology, it becomes clear that this fourth kingdom is Rome, a historical nation that follows Greece but also becomes a symbol of all those who oppose God and his people. (See table 12.3.)

Daniel states that "in those days" (a reference to the eschatological future), God "will set up a kingdom that shall never be destroyed" (2:44). Nebuchadnezzar had dreamed of a large stone that broke the image into pieces. Now Daniel says that this stone, "cut from a mountain by no human hand," represents this new kingdom of God that will break all human kingdoms into pieces (2:44–45). Nebuchadnezzar responds by (temporarily) acknowledging that Daniel's God is the God of gods (2:47).

Faithfulness and a Fiery Furnace

■ READ DANIEL 3 ■

In chapter 2, Nebuchadnezzar has a dream about an image with a gold head that represents his own rule over Babylon. It cannot be a coincidence that in chapter 3, he makes an image entirely of gold and demands that everyone must worship it or die (3:1–7). By making the image of gold, the king is defying God and stating that his kingdom (gold) will *not* be replaced by silver, bronze, or iron.[9]

CANONICAL CONNECTIONS

Jesus Is the "Stone"

In Luke 20, Jesus tells a parable about wicked tenants (the Jewish leaders) who kill the heir of a vineyard (Jesus) in an attempt to take it for themselves. The owner of the vineyard (God) responds by destroying those tenants and giving the vineyard to others. Jesus concludes the parable by referencing two Old Testament passages in which a stone is a symbol for himself—God's Messiah. First, he quotes Psalm 118:22: "The stone that the builders rejected has become the cornerstone" (Luke 20:17). Then he alludes to Daniel 2:34 and 44–45, saying, "Everyone who falls on that stone will be broken to pieces, and when it falls on anyone, it will crush him." Jesus uses this stone imagery from the Old Testament to describe the terrible consequences of rejecting him as Messiah.

Out of loyalty to God, Daniel's friends, Shadrach, Meshach, and Abednego, refuse to worship the image, even though the decision carries a certain death sentence (3:11). Nebuchadnezzar asks poignantly, "And who is the god who will deliver you out of my hands?" (3:15). Their response is a model for God's people when they are faced with persecution or death for their faith. They are not belligerent, but they do speak with conviction. They answer that their God *is* able to deliver them from the furnace, "but if not, be it known to you, O king, that we will not serve your gods or worship the golden image that you have set up" (3:17–18). When they say, "but if not," they are not doubtful or uncertain—just the opposite. Even if God chooses not to save them, they will still serve him to the very end.

Filled with wrath, Nebuchadnezzar has them thrown into the furnace, which is so hot that his own men are killed by the flames. But not only do the three Jews survive, they are joined by a fourth individual who is unidentified (it is probably an angel). They come out unharmed, and Nebuchadnezzar again praises God and declares that no other god can "rescue in this way" (3:29). One scholar aptly summarizes the message of the story: "You're never alone in the flames, whether you walk out alive or not. This is a truth that has brought comfort and courage to all persecuted believers."[10]

The Humbling of King Nebuchadnezzar

■ READ DANIEL 4 ■

Chapter 4 tells a wild story in three scenes. In scene 1 (4:1–27), Nebuchadnezzar is at ease, prospering in his palace when he has a dream (4:4–5). Once again, his own magicians are unable to interpret it, so Daniel is brought in. The king dreamed that he was a large, strong, and beautiful tree, but an angel from heaven came down and called for the tree to be chopped down, leaving only the stump. The angel then says that Nebuchadnezzar will be driven away from humanity, eat grass like an ox, and be wet with dew for seven periods of time. What the king must learn (and we also) is that "the Most High rules the kingdom of men and gives it to whom he will" (4:17, 25, 32).

Scene 2 (4:28–33) occurs twelve months later. Nebuchadnezzar, on the roof of his palace, has not listened to Daniel's advice to humble himself. He looks at the great city around him and asks, "Is not this great Babylon, which I have built by my mighty power . . . for the glory of my majesty?" (4:30). The narrator says that "while the words were still in the king's mouth," a voice came from heaven announcing the fulfillment of his dream (4:31). In other words, what came next was no coincidence, but a rebuke for

Figure 12.3. Engraving of Nebuchadnezzar eating grass like an ox

his pride. He became like an animal, eating grass, with hair and nails that grew long (4:33).

Scene 3 (4:34–37) concludes the narrative. Nebuchadnezzar tells us, from a first-person perspective, that he has acknowledged that God is the King of all the earth, that God's dominion is everlasting, and that his kingdom endures from generation to generation. Having learned the lesson insisted on by the Most High, the king is restored to his position. Now he honors the King of heaven, "for all his works are right" (4:37). The theological point of this narrative is difficult to miss, for it is repeated three times: "The Most High rules the kingdom of men and gives it to whom he will" (4:17, 25, 32). Even Nebuchadnezzar, the most powerful ruler on earth and the enemy of Israel, has authority only by God's permission, and that power can be taken away and restored as God desires.

The Humbling of King Belshazzar

■ READ DANIEL 5 ■

Between the events of Daniel 4 and 5, more than twenty years pass, and three kings have been on the throne in Babylon. Daniel is probably in his eighties, and Belshazzar is ruling while the true king, Nabonidus, is away (refer to table 12.1 above). Belshazzar holds a great banquet for a thousand of his nobles. However, in an attempt to impress his guests, he calls for the golden vessels that had been taken from the temple in Jerusalem (5:2–3). Not only is this a celebration of their victory over Israel; it is intentional mockery of the God of Israel as inferior. The revelers become drunk from the vessels and praise their own false gods (5:4).

"Immediately"—the narrator connects Belshazzar's actions to God's response; it is not a coincidence—a hand appears and writes an unknown message on the wall, filling Belshazzar with fear (5:5–6). Once again, the magicians of Babylon are unable to interpret the writing. But the queen remembers that Daniel previously interpreted dreams for Nebuchadnezzar (5:10–11). When Daniel arrives, he reviews the story of how Nebuchadnezzar was unwilling to humble himself before God, so he was driven away like an animal (5:20–21). Daniel then condemns Belshazzar for not learning from Nebuchadnezzar's example, for drinking from the vessels of God's temple, and for praising false gods (5:22–23). The conclusion is a warning to all kings in authority and an encouragement to all under their authority: "But the God in whose hand is your breath, and whose are all your ways, you have not honored" (5:23). Proverbs 21:1 says something similar: "The king's heart is a stream of water in the hand of the LORD; he turns it wherever he will."

With God's help, Daniel reads the writing on the wall. It literally says, "Numbered, numbered, weighed, divided." God has numbered Belshazzar's ways, has found him wanting, and will divide his kingdom between two new empires: the Medes and the Persians (5:25–28). Belshazzar honors Daniel, but that very night he is killed in fulfillment of Daniel's prophecy. Darius the Mede takes power (5:30–31).

Faithfulness and a Den of Lions

■ READ DANIEL 6 ■

Daniel has earned a distinguished reputation as an official in Babylon. Not only is he competent, but he has integrity, and "no error or fault was found in him" (6:4). Therefore, when his envious colleagues want to complain against him, their only option is to find a problem with his faith. He has a reputation for that as well: he is unceasing in his daily prayers to God.

The officials plot against Daniel by appealing to the king's pride and persuading him to make a temporary ordinance that prohibits all prayer except to the king himself (6:6). That makes Daniel's faithful, daily prayer to God illegal and places him in conflict with his home in exile. Perhaps Daniel could cease praying and rationalize his decision by saying that it is only temporary—it does not constitute a denial of his faith. Or perhaps he could determine to pray secretly in his mind. But the issue is one of *loyalty*. It is significant that when Daniel hears of the command, he prays with his windows open toward Jerusalem (6:10). He is oriented toward his true home; he belongs to the people of God, not to Babylon.

When Daniel is discovered, his accusers identify him as "one of the exiles of Judah" (6:13). It is an accusation that his first loyalty is not to the king because he is an outsider. Daniel is guilty as charged—his loyalty to God is unwavering.

The king is distressed (6:14) because he values Daniel, but he is trapped by his own decree. He has Daniel thrown into a den of lions, where Daniel is sure to meet a terrible fate. Daniel does not know that he will be delivered; he is prepared to be killed for his faith. But God sends an angel, who shuts the mouths of the lions and delivers him (6:22). As with King Nebuchadnezzar, the Lord's intervention on behalf of his faithful servants leads Darius to acknowledge the King of heaven: "He is the living God, enduring forever; his kingdom shall never be destroyed and his dominion shall be to the end" (6:26–27; cf. 3:28–29; 4:2, 34–37). 👥 👥

The Dream of the Four Beasts

■ READ DANIEL 7 ■

Chapter 7 functions like a hinge in the structure of the book. In the chiastic pattern of chapters 2–7, it mirrors chapter 2, which describes Nebuchadnezzar's dream of the four kingdoms. But it is also the first of Daniel's visions in the book, introducing chapters 7–12.

Daniel has a dream (7:1–14), which is then interpreted for him by an angel (7:15–27). Just as Nebuchadnezzar's dream in chapter 2 predicted four coming kingdoms symbolized by four materials in a great image, Daniel's dream in chapter 7

Table 12.4. Kingdoms in the Visions in Daniel

Empire	Neo-Babylonia	Medo-Persia	Greece	Rome	Kingdom of God
Dates (BC)	626–539	539–333	333–63	63 BC–AD 634	Inaugurated (by Jesus) during the Roman Empire and continues forever
Daniel 2	Gold head is Nebuchadnezzar (2:37–38)	Silver chest and arms are kingdom after (2:39)	Bronze middle and thighs are kingdom after (2:39)	Legs of iron and feet of iron and clay (2:40)	Stone that will break the other kingdoms (2:34–35, 44–45)
Daniel 7	Lion with eagles' wings (7:4)	Bear, raised up on one side with ribs in its mouth (7:5)	Leopard with four heads and wings (7:6)	Terrifying beast with iron teeth and ten horns (7:7)	Eternal kingdom given to one like a son of man (7:13–14)

LITERARY NOTES

Animal Symbols

Daniel's visions use animals to symbolize empires in chapters 7 and 8. This seems strange at first glance, but we do the same thing in modern times. The USA is symbolized by a bald eagle, and Russia is sometimes called "the Bear." China is often symbolized by a giant panda, and India's animal is the tiger. If a modern writer were to warn about economic tension between the bald eagle and the giant panda, we would immediately understand her to be talking about the US and China. Perhaps if she were feeling poetic, she might say that an unfavorable trade deal with China meant that the eagle's wings were clipped (or something like that). In his vision, Daniel is seeing actual nations in the sequence of time, but the visions employ animal imagery to describe important aspects of those nations. Horns are powerful rulers. Wings symbolize speed. Sharp teeth represent fierce aggression and military power. Heavy use of this kind of symbolism—whether creatures, colors, shapes, or numbers—is a key feature of the apocalyptic genre.

CANONICAL CONNECTIONS

Jesus, the Son of Man

Jesus frequently refers to himself as the "Son of Man" in the Gospels. This is often a reference to his humanity (the way the prophet Ezekiel uses the title), but in a few key verses he uses the phrase to identify himself as Daniel's divine ruler who comes on the clouds, receives authority, and establishes God's kingdom forever. In Matthew 24:30 he says, "Then will appear in heaven the sign of the Son of Man, and then all the tribes of the earth will mourn, and they will see the Son of Man coming on the clouds of heaven with power and great glory." See also Matthew 26:64; Mark 13:24–27; 14:61–62; Revelation 1:7.

predicts the *same* four kingdoms with symbolic animals (see table 12.4). First, a lion with the wings of an eagle represents Babylon.[11] Second, there is a bear that is raised up on one side with three ribs in its mouth (7:5). The mention of one side being higher than the other is similar to the ram in 8:3, which the angel identifies as Medo-Persia (8:20). Third, the leopard with four wings and four heads represents Greece (7:6). The number four relates to the division of Alexander the Great's empire among his four generals, and similar imagery in chapter 8 is identified by an angel as Greece (8:21). Finally, there is a fourth, terrifying beast with great iron teeth and ten horns (7:7).

Daniel's attention turns from what is happening on the earth to what is happening above, in heaven, a cosmic perspective shift that is common to the apocalyptic genre. He sees the Ancient of Days (God) sitting on his throne (7:9) and "one like a son of man" coming with the clouds of heaven (7:13). To him is given a kingdom over all peoples that will not pass away. As in chapter 2, Daniel sees an eternal kingdom of God that will supersede all human kingdoms.

The Ram and the Goat

■ READ DANIEL 8 ■

In chapter 8, Daniel has another vision. He sees a ram with two uneven horns (similar to the bear raised up on one side in chap. 7) and a goat with a horn between its eyes (8:3–5). The goat attacks the ram and tramples it (8:6–7). Out of the horn comes a little horn, which gains influence, discontinues offerings, and overthrows the temple (8:9–11). An angel identified as Gabriel comes to interpret and explain the vision for Daniel (8:15–27). ⬚

This vision focuses on the second and third kingdoms to come in the future (see table 12.5). The ram with two horns symbolizes Media and Persia (8:20). Cyrus the Great expanded the Persian Empire across the known world from Greece, south to Egypt, and across to India (see map 12.2). The goat with the horn between its eyes represents Greece (8:21). Apparently, the great horn is a symbol of Alexander the Great (8:21b), while the four horns that arise from it

Angels in the Book of Daniel

The book of Daniel contains many references to angels. One appears in the fiery furnace in chapter 3, and one shuts the lions' mouths in chapter 6. Two angels are named in the book. Gabriel interprets Daniel's vision in chapters 8 and 9. He is also the angel who visits Mary to announce the birth of Jesus in Luke 1:19. Michael is the second named angel: a "prince" who fights for Israel against evil angels (Dan. 10:13, 21; 12:1). Michael is mentioned in Jude 9 and Revelation 12:7–9 as one of those who cast down Satan and his army.

Public Domain / Walters Art Museum purchase with funds provided by the W. Alton Jones Foundation Acquisition Fund, 1996

Figure 12.5. Michael and Gabriel from an illustrated Ethiopian manuscript (17th century)

Table 12.5. Kingdoms in the Visions in Daniel

Empire	Neo-Babylonia	Medo-Persia	Greece	Rome	Kingdom of God
Dates (BC)	626–539	539–333	333–63	63 BC–AD 634	Inaugurated (by Jesus) during the Roman Empire and continues forever
Daniel 2	Gold head is Nebuchadnezzar (2:37–38)	Silver chest and arms are kingdom after (2:39)	Bronze middle and thighs are kingdom after (2:39)	Legs of iron and feet of iron and clay (2:40)	Stone that will break the other kingdoms (2:34–35, 44–45)
Daniel 7	Lion with eagles' wings (7:4)	Bear, raised up on one side with ribs in its mouth (7:5)	Leopard with four wings (7:6)	Terrifying beast with iron teeth and ten horns (7:7)	Eternal kingdom given to one like a son of man (7:13–14)
Daniel 8		Ram with two horns, one higher than the other (8:3, 20)	Goat with horn between its eyes that becomes four horns (8:5, 8, 21)		

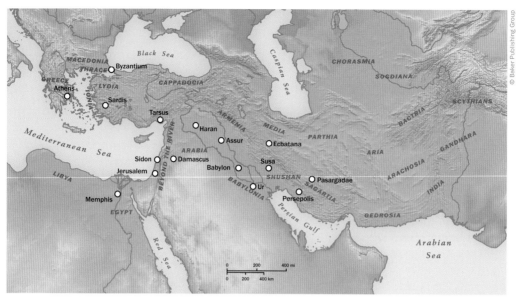

Map 12.2. Persian Empire

are his four generals: Cassander, Lysimachus, Seleucus, and Ptolemy. The little horn represents a fierce king to come—probably Antiochus IV, who ruled from 175 to 163 BC and persecuted the Jews. He is an archetype, or pattern, of recurring evil that persecutes and kills the people of God and culminates in the eschatological future. The interpretation of Daniel's vision ends with an encouragement that though this ruler will cause great destruction, God will place a limit on his power and will break his rule—"but by no human hand" (8:25). This last statement also described the kingdom of God in Daniel 2:34, 45.

The Seventy Weeks

■ READ DANIEL 9 ■

When chapter 9 opens, Daniel is reading Scripture and notes that the prophet Jeremiah predicted that Israel's exile would last for seventy years (9:2; see Jer. 25:11–12; 29:10). He wrestles over the future of God's people and prays that God would grant them mercy and forgiveness (9:3–19). As Daniel is praying, the angel Gabriel appears again to give Daniel insight and understanding (9:20–23). The vision itself (9:24–27) is notoriously difficult to understand. Readers throughout history have been challenged by its many interpretive problems and ambiguities. Saint Jerome, who lived in the fourth century, lists nine different possible interpretations and then writes, "Let the reader decide." One modern scholar writes, "The history of the [interpretation] of the 70 Weeks is the Dismal Swamp of OT criticism."[12] However, even if we aren't certain about every detail, the overall theological message is fairly clear.

Each of the seventy "weeks" (or "sevens") refers to seven years, for a grand total of 490 years. Scholars are divided on whether these 490 years should be understood literally or symbolically (as more flexible periods of time).[13] Gabriel tells Daniel that a total of seventy weeks are decreed from the end of Israel's exile to the time when God brings his salvation to completion (9:24). God will do six things, including putting an end to sin, atoning for iniquity, and bringing in everlasting righteousness. First, there will be a period of seven weeks from the command or permission to rebuild Jerusalem to the coming of an anointed one (9:25). Then there will be sixty-two weeks until an anointed one is cut off and the sanctuary is destroyed (9:26). The cutting off of an anointed one must refer to the death of Christ, followed by the destruction of the temple by the Romans. Finally, there will be one week when one makes a strong covenant with many and puts an end to sacrifice (9:27a). In the end, the enemy will be destroyed (9:27b). Table 12.6 below shows how Daniel's vision of the seventy weeks corresponds to, and confirms, his earlier visions of the time to come.

Table 12.6. Daniel's Vision of the Seventy Weeks

	Babylon 626–539 BC	Medo-Persia 539–333 BC	Greece 333–63 BC	Rome 63 BC– AD 634	Kingdom of God AD 33
Daniel 2	Gold head	Silver chest/ arms	Bronze middle	Iron legs/feet	Stone
Daniel 7	Lion	Bear	Leopard	Beast	Son of Man
Daniel 8		Ram: two horns	Goat: one horn		
Daniel 9		70 weeks (9:24) →			
		Word goes out (9:25a) (7 weeks) →	Troubled time (9:25b) (62 weeks) →		Anointed one cut off (9:26) (1 week) →

In this prediction, the first sixty-nine weeks are a preview of time in history, from the word to rebuild Jerusalem after the exile to the time that Jesus ("the anointed one") is "cut off" or crucified. The last (seventieth) week is symbolic of the last days, from the time of Jesus's first coming—when he is killed and rises again from the dead—to his second coming, when he returns and destroys evil once and for all. The main point of this vision is that we can have hope in our exile because the Lord of history will bring in his everlasting kingdom.[14]

Daniel's Final Vision

■ READ DANIEL 10–12 ■

The last unit of the book of Daniel, comprising chapters 10–12, reports events that occurred in the third year of Cyrus, or 536 BC. At this time, Daniel would likely have been in his late eighties. He has been mourning and fasting for three weeks when he sees a vision (10:2–7). When an angel arrives to encourage and strengthen Daniel (10:11–11:1), he explains that he was sent as soon as Daniel had prayed, but he could not come immediately because he was detained for twenty-one days by the "prince of the kingdom of Persia" (10:13). This is apparently a reference to an evil angel who had some jurisdiction over that particular land. However, the angel Michael came to fight off the evil angel and allowed the messenger to come to Daniel (10:13–14). Here, in the lead-up to the explanation of Daniel's vision, we are given a glimpse of warfare in the heavenly realms, which we cannot see but which has an effect on the events of this world.

The vision begins with a reference to coming kings of Persia (11:2), but then the remainder relates to Greece (11:2–45). The phrase "mighty king" refers to Alexander the Great (11:3); his kingdom will be divided among four rulers (11:4). After a discussion of the kings of the north and the south (11:5–20), the vision focuses on a "contemptible person" who will rule (11:21). This is Antiochus IV Epiphanes (11:21–12:1). This ruler is described in great detail, probably because he serves as a type, or pattern, of antichrist in the eschatological future (see table 12.7).[15]

As Daniel describes Antiochus, he uses phrases that indicate an eschatological time frame: "the time appointed" or "the appointed time" (11:27, 29, 35), "at the time of the end" (11:40), and "at that time" (12:1). He therefore blends together the events surrounding Antiochus in his (relatively) near future and those of the end of time in the eschatological future. Antiochus will be wicked and deceptive (11:21–23). He will attack God's people (11:30, 33) and profane the temple, setting up an "abomination that makes desolate" (11:31). In the end, he will be totally destroyed with no one to help him (11:45), and the people of God will

Table 12.7. Kingdoms in the Visions in Daniel

Empire	Neo-Babylonia	Medo-Persia	Greece	Rome	Kingdom of God
Dates (BC)	626–539	539–333	333–63	63 BC–AD 634	Inaugurated (by Jesus) during the Roman Empire and continues forever
Daniel 2	Gold head is Nebuchadnezzar (2:38)	Silver chest and arms is kingdom after (2:39)	Bronze middle and thighs is kingdom after (2:39)	Iron legs and feet of iron and clay (2:40)	Stone that will break the other kingdoms (2:34–35, 44–45)
Daniel 7	Lion with eagles' wings (7:4)	Bear, raised up on one side with ribs in its mouth (7:5)	Leopard with four wings and four heads (7:6)	Terrifying beast with iron teeth and ten horns (7:7)	Eternal kingdom given to one like a son of man (7:14)
Daniel 8		Ram with two horns, one higher than the other (8:20)	Goat with horn between its eyes that becomes four horns (8:21)		
Daniel 10–12		Persia (11:2)	Greece (11:2); divided toward the four winds of heaven (11:4); "a wicked ruler" (11:21)	Antichrist	

be delivered (12:1). These events in history anticipate a greater fulfillment in the eschatological future, on a worldwide scale, when God's people are persecuted and he delivers them once and for all.

God's people will not necessarily avoid physical death, but everyone whose name is written in "the book" will be delivered in the resurrection when "those who sleep in the dust of the earth shall awake, some to everlasting life, and some to shame and everlasting contempt" (12:1–2). The angel tells Daniel that these words are an encouragement to God's people in the future. Therefore, Daniel must "seal the

THEOLOGICAL ISSUES

Resurrection in the Old Testament

While Daniel 12:2–3 is perhaps the clearest evidence that resurrection was not a novel hope in the New Testament, there are other passages in the Old Testament that anticipate this destiny for humankind. In Psalm 16:10, David writes, "For you will not abandon me to Sheol." Isaiah says that God "will swallow up death forever . . . and . . . will wipe away tears from all faces" (25:7–8). In 26:19, he says, "Your dead shall live; their bodies shall rise. . . . And the earth will give birth to the dead." The very last verse in Isaiah speaks of eternity after death for the wicked, an eternity in which their "worm shall not die, their fire shall not be quenched" (66:24). While the picture of life after death in the Old Testament is more shadowy than what is illuminated in the New, resurrection has consistently been a beacon of hope for God's people and an urgent warning for the wicked to repent.

book, until the time of the end" (12:4, 9). As for Daniel himself, he has been a faithful servant. He must continue faithfully until the end, and then he will find rest (12:13). 🔳

Implementation

The people of God have always lived in the tension of having two different homes at the same time. We are born in physical bodies, under a human government, in a human economy, speaking a particular language and participating in a social culture. We have a certain loyalty to this world, and it *feels* like home. But when we commit ourselves to God, we join with his people, who come from every tribe and language, every era of history, and whose real home is in heaven. We have not yet even been there, but we catch glimpses of what it will be like. And it may not *feel* like home, but it is to that home that we pledge our ultimate loyalty. The old gospel hymn "This World Is Not My Home" expresses this tension:

> This world is not my home, I'm just a passing through;
> my treasures are laid up somewhere beyond the blue;
> the angels beckon me from Heaven's open door,
> and I can't feel at home in this world anymore.[16]

Daniel and his friends lived in a foreign land, in exile, which was sometimes hostile to their faith. We live in "exile" as well, and it is often hostile (1 Pet. 2:11–12). In the US and Europe, Christians who hold biblical ethical positions risk financial ruin. In Asia, the government closes churches and imprisons pastors. In Africa, Christian girls are kidnapped and taken to be child-wives for terrorists. And in the Middle East, Christians are taken to the beach and beheaded on video. Wicked people throughout history have sought to destroy the work of God and kill his followers. But the book of Daniel encourages us to stand firm, even to the point of death. In chapters 1–6, we find models of faithfulness in challenging circumstances, and we see that God can rescue. In chapters 7–12, we learn that God is not only the Lord of individuals (no matter how powerful) and nations (no matter how dominating); he is Lord of the entire scope of human history. While God's people expect to be persecuted, God is a *living* God, and he will ultimately deliver us—if not in this life, then in the next.

Even when we do not face persecution, it is important to remember that the authority of human rulers is *derived* from God. He can take it away. In Daniel 4–5, Nebuchadnezzar is warned several times, "The Most

High rules the kingdom of men and gives it to whom he will" (4:17, 25, 32; 5:21). This is an important warning against putting too much confidence in human authorities. We are tempted to feel great peace when certain rulers (perhaps from our political party) are in power, or to despair when other rulers (whom we do not like) are in power. But our trust must be in God. He raises up kings and tears them down (Rom. 13:1–7; 1 Pet. 2:13–17). In the eschatological future, even the wicked antichrist will be destroyed at the time God has appointed. We can live in great peace knowing that God is on *his* throne.

There is more good news from Daniel: all of history is leading to the kingdom of God. While human kingdoms come and go, only one kingdom will last forever. As Nebuchadnezzar says, "His kingdom is an everlasting kingdom, and his dominion endures from generation to generation" (4:3, 34). This is the stone, not made by human hands, that smashes all other kingdoms (2:34–35). However, we should not think that the kingdom of God will simply be an improvement over human kingdoms—it will be fundamentally different. It will be ruled by the Son of Man—God's Messiah—who will come on the clouds (7:13). He will come to bring an end to transgression and to atone for sin (9:24). The New Testament teaches that this kingdom of God began during the Roman Empire when Jesus Christ became incarnate, was crucified, rose again from the dead, and took his rightful place at God's right hand. He is the Son of Man, and the promises of the kingdom are already being fulfilled. Now, living in the "last days," we await the full realization of Jesus's kingdom, when God rescues his people from evil and dwells with them in peace and security forever.

The book of Daniel gives us a new perspective on citizenship, suffering, and power. It gives us hope and challenges us to be faithful to our ultimate Lord no matter what it may cost. And it exalts Jesus as our Savior and King, painting a picture of an enduring kingdom that stretches across the entire world. Daniel's book insists that the story of God's people is not a random mess that ends in disaster, but the unfolding of an intentional plan that points forward to the day when the faithful will rise and shine "like the stars forever and ever" (12:3).

Christian Reading Questions

1. Does it matter whether one holds the traditional or critical view of the date and authorship of Daniel? Are these simply two different

theories? What theological and interpretive implications come with each perspective?

2. How do the stories in Daniel 1–6 encourage the believer who lives in hostile territory away from his or her home with God? Summarize some of the ways that these chapters model authentic faith and the proper response to challenges.

3. What does the book of Daniel teach about the coming kingdom of God, which comes after earthly kingdoms? Identify three or four key ideas. How does this view of the kingdom of God hold out hope to God's people in exile?

4. Do Christians today have a sufficient sense that this world is not our home? Examine the following passages in the New Testament on this topic: Romans 12:2; Philippians 3:20; Hebrews 13:14; James 4:4; 1 John 2:15. Can you find others? Why might this be an important conviction to cultivate? How do we reconcile it with the fact that "God so loved the world" (John 3:16)?

CHAPTER THIRTEEN

Hosea

Orientation

Sometimes a novel or film contains such a vivid scene that it comes to symbolize the contents of the entire work. In the film *Saving Private Ryan*, the violence and tension of the opening scene when the soldiers storm the beach on D-Day are well known even to those who have not seen it. It encapsulates the horror of war and how director Steven Spielberg presents that experience. Or, even if you have not seen the film *Big*, also starring Tom Hanks, you may be familiar with the scene in which his character plays a giant piano in the toy store. It captures the whimsy and wonder of a man who is really a playful child. In the same way, even those who are not very familiar with most of the contents of the twelve "Minor" Prophets *do* know the story of Hosea's unfaithful wife.

God calls his prophet Hosea to marry a sexually promiscuous woman as a sign of God's own covenant "marriage" with his people, Israel. Just as Hosea's wife sleeps around with other men, Israel is promiscuous too—worshiping other gods and failing to love God exclusively. Imagine Hosea's anguish as his own personal life and the drama of his broken home become part of a prophetic message. However, the story really grabs our attention when God calls Hosea to go out, find his wife again, and bring her home even though she is loved by another man. Hosea obeys and "buys" his wife with some silver and some food and takes her home. In the same way, although Israel's rebellion is great and they show no signs of changing their behavior right now, God will seek out his people and love them, giving them hope for the future.

Many readers do not realize that the description of Hosea's marriage and family comprises only about *nine* verses total in a book of fourteen chapters! There is much more to say about God's relationship with Israel and his plans for the future. But the image of a prophet pursuing his unfaithful wife captures our imaginations and gives us an interpretive grid for the entire book.

We are told very few biographical details about Hosea except for the name of his father (Beeri) and the brief narrative of his wife and children, because they directly relate to his prophetic oracles. Hosea's wife was named Gomer (1:3). Together they had two sons and a daughter. The children's names are also prophetic sign-acts, which we will discuss below.

The superscription to the book (1:1) dates Hosea's prophetic ministry to the days of Uzziah, Jotham, Ahaz, and Hezekiah, kings of Judah; and Jeroboam II, king of Israel. It is somewhat strange that although Hosea was a prophet to the Northern Kingdom, his book is primarily dated by kings of *Judah*. He only mentions one king of Israel, Jeroboam II, who ruled during the beginning of Hosea's ministry (see the time line of Hosea).

Hosea is the only writing prophet in the Old Testament who was a native of the Northern Kingdom. (Amos was also a prophet in Israel, but he was from Judah.) At the beginning of Hosea's ministry, the nation was stable and prosperous, but as the years went by, it became less stable and was threatened from outside. King Jeroboam II was succeeded by a series of weak kings, who came to power either by assassination or by appointment from the Assyrian Empire. Zechariah was king for only six months, and Shallum ruled for only one month before he was assassinated (2 Kings 15:13–14). It is possible that Hosea ignores the later kings of Israel because he views them—or even the Northern Kingdom itself—as illegitimate. Although God predicted that Israel would separate from Judah and allowed it to do so (see 1 Kings 11:31), God's desire was that all twelve tribes would be united, with the center of worship in Jerusalem.

The kings' and people's response to these mounting problems was *not* to trust God but to turn to idols, political alliances, and other resources. Finally, in 722 BC, the Assyrians conquered the Northern Kingdom, exiled many of its inhabitants, and brought in exiles from other nations that the Assyrians had conquered. Hosea does not mention this earth-shattering, nation-dissolving event, so his ministry must have concluded before 722. The book refers several times to Judah as well. Israel and Judah are often mentioned together: they were one covenant people, guilty of the same sins, destined for the same judgment, and both loved by God.

Hosea faced significant religious challenges in Israel. First, Israel worshiped God in a way that he had

HISTORICAL MATTERS

"Fact Sheet"—Hosea

Author: Hosea, the son of Beeri

Date: 755–725 BC

Location: Northern Kingdom (with reference to Judah)

Political and social context: Hosea prophesied during a time of great instability in the Northern Kingdom, in the years immediately preceding its conquest and exile by the Assyrian Empire.

JUDAH

KING	DATES OF REIGN	REFERENCES	KEY FEATURES OF REIGN
Uzziah/ Azariah	792–740	2 Kings 14:21; 2 Chron. 26:3	Coregent with his father, Amaziah, 792–767; began reigning at age 16 (2 Kings 14:21); struck with leprosy for offering incense in 750, then lived in a separate house while his son governed (2 Chron. 26:16–21)
Jotham	750–735	2 Kings 15:32–33	Coregent with Uzziah, 750–740; removed from the throne in 735
Ahaz	735–715	2 Kings 16:1–2	16 years counted from death of Jotham in 732 (2 Kings 15:38)
Hezekiah	729–686	2 Kings 18:1–2	Coregent with father, Ahaz, 729–715; Sennacherib attacked Judah in 701 BC (2 Kings 18:13)

Isaiah
740–695

Micah
742–686

ISRAEL

KING	DATES OF REIGN	REFERENCES	KEY FEATURES OF REIGN
Jeroboam II	793–753	2 Kings 14:23	Coregent with Jehoash, 793–782
Zechariah	753–752	2 Kings 15:8	Assassinated by Shallum (2 Kings 15:10)
Shallum	752	2 Kings 15:13	Assassinated by Menahem (2 Kings 15:14)
Menahem	752–742	2 Kings 15:17	Made an alliance with Pul, king of Assyria (2 Kings 15:19–20)
Pekahiah	742–740	2 Kings 15:23	Assassinated by Pekah (2 Kings 15:25)
Pekah	752–732	2 Kings 15:27	Reigned in Gilead, 752–740, overlapping with Menahem; reigned over united Israel, 740–732; assassinated by Hoshea (2 Kings 15:30)
Hoshea	732–722	2 Kings 15:30; 17:1	Appointed by Tiglath-pileser III

Jonah
792–753

Amos
767–753

Hosea
755–725

Map 13.1. The golden calves at Dan and Bethel

not commanded. As discussed above in chapter 3, the first king of Israel, Jeroboam I (930–909), had set up worship sites with golden calf idols at Dan (in the north of Israel) and Bethel (in the south of Israel) when the ten tribes of the Northern Kingdom separated from Judah (see 1 Kings 12:28–29 and map 13.1). God had commanded Israel to make pilgrimage and offer sacrifices in the temple in Jerusalem, but the people of Israel were required to worship at Dan and Bethel. This essential conflict meant that there was systemic sin in the Northern Kingdom—the people's sacrifices were necessarily illegitimate from God's perspective. Second, Israel worshiped the true God in combination with idols and the false gods of the surrounding peoples. This blending of two different belief systems is called *syncretism*. The people associated God with golden calf idols and imagined that a Canaanite goddess was his wife.[1] While some of their beliefs may have been based on God's revelation in his Word, they were mingled with falsehood. Third, they worshiped Canaanite fertility deities directly. All of this violated the clear commands that God had given in his covenant with Israel.

The most significant fertility deity in the region around Israel was Baal, a god mentioned seven times in the book of Hosea.[2] Baal was worshiped widely in the ancient world, from Egypt to Mesopotamia,[3] and he was a particularly important deity in Phoenicia, a nation that had significant economic, cultural, and religious influence on the Northern Kingdom due to its proximity. Baal was thought to have power over clouds, lightning, and storms, and therefore power to cause rain, making the soil fertile and producing a good harvest.[4] For the ancient farmer who struggled to grow enough food to feed his family, it was a great temptation to serve Baal in the hopes of ensuring a successful crop. By serving Baal and other fertility gods, worshipers sought to go around YHWH and gain some control over the natural world so that it would provide not only the necessities of life but also security and wealth.[5] This "pull" that the Israelites felt between popular fertility religion, which promises near-instant gratification for personal gain, and God, their creator and covenant partner, is an important background for Hosea's accusation of covenant unfaithfulness in the book.

Exploration

Hosea addresses three of the five phases in God's dealing with Israel: (1) past accusation, (2) judgment in the near future, and (5) ultimate restoration in the eschatological future (see fig. 13.2). He heavily emphasizes the sins of the Northern Kingdom and the coming destruction of the nation as a result. Hosea does not hold out any hope for restoration in the near future. However, in the eschatological future, God will forgive and establish his people in peace and security.

These three phases form a repeating pattern in the book that gives it structure. Chapters 1–3 are the introduction to the book. **Chapters 1** and **3** present the sign-act of Hosea's marriage and the names of his children as a picture of God's relationship with Israel. These chapters form endcaps around chapter 2, which applies the sign-act to Israel. **Chapter 2**, in the center, uses the imagery from the sign-act of mother, children, husband, adultery, lovers, and gifts to explore Israel's relationship with God: first in an accusation of Israel's unfaithfulness (2:2–8), then in an announcement of coming judgment (2:9–13), and finally in describing the hope that God will ultimately restore his people and bring them back to himself (2:14–23).

Chapters 4–14 contain detailed oracles in which Hosea continues the three-part structure that he has established in the first three chapters.[6]

Figure 13.1. Bronze figurine of a Baal (14th–12th century BC)

THINKING VISUALLY

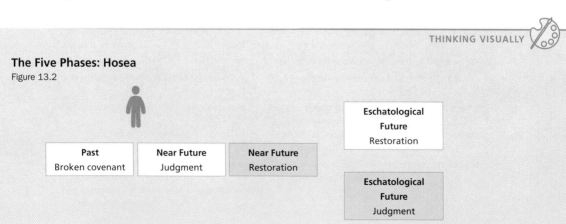

The Five Phases: Hosea
Figure 13.2

Past	Near Future	Near Future
Broken covenant	Judgment	Restoration

Eschatological Future
Restoration

Eschatological Future
Judgment

Table 13.1. The Structure of Hosea

		Superscription (1:1)		
Application of the sign-act	Sign-act	Gomer and Israel are two adulterous wives, but there is hope (1:2–2:1)		
	Accusation	She goes to adulterous lovers for gifts (*rib*) (2:2–8)	Accusation (*rib*): idols, political schemes, and manipulative worship (4:1–8:14)	Accusation (*rib*): Israel is not like their father Jacob (11:12–12:14)
	Temporary judgment	YHWH will take away her gifts and leave her desolate (2:9–13)	YHWH will destroy Israel's food, children, cult sites, and the nation itself (9:1–10:15)	YHWH has become Israel's enemy (13:1–16)
	Ultimate restoration	YHWH will put away her lovers and establish a new relationship (2:14–23)	YHWH's resolve and Israel's repentance will lead to relationship (11:1–11)	Relationship will be restored through repentance (14:1–8)
	Sign-act	Gomer and Israel are two wives, awaiting full reconciliation (3:1–5)		
				Postscript (14:9)

Source: Adapted from Eric J. Tully, *Hosea: A Handbook on the Hebrew Text* (Waco: Baylor University Press, 2018).

CANONICAL CONNECTIONS

Marriage as a Metaphor in the Prophets and the New Testament

Marriage is an ideal analogy for God's covenant with Israel in the book of Hosea. In the ancient Near East, idol worship was apparently imbued with sexual imagery and rituals because of the fertility deities. And a marriage covenant, like God's covenant with Israel, consists of both loving relationship *and* the expectation of exclusive loyalty. Isaiah calls God Israel's "husband" (54:5). Jeremiah describes Israel's early love for God as being like that of a bride (2:2–3). Ezekiel 16 presents an extended allegory, similar to the sign-act in Hosea, in which God marries Jerusalem but she becomes an extravagant "whore" who has sexual relations with anyone who passes by. In the New Testament, marriage is used to symbolize the relationship *fulfilled*: the church is the "bride" of Christ— presented to him in purity (see Mark 2:19–20; 2 Cor. 11:2; Eph. 5:21–33; Rev. 19:7; 21:2, 9).

The Hebrew word *rib* (translated in the ESV with "plead," "controversy," or "indictment") occurs in 2:2, 4:1, and 12:2 to initiate three sections of accusation against Israel. In chapters 4–11, Hosea makes his first case against Israel: first with accusation (**chaps. 4–8**), then temporal judgment (**chaps. 9–10**), then ultimate restoration (**chap. 11**). In chapters 12–14 he makes a second, shorter case, with accusation (**chap. 12**), temporal judgment (**chap. 13**), and ultimate restoration (**chap. 14**).

The Sign-Act (Part 1)

■ READ HOSEA 1:2–2:1 ■

The book opens with God's command for Hosea to marry a promiscuous woman. Nothing in the book says that she was technically a prostitute; perhaps her flagrant promiscuity was a lifestyle rather than a profession. Her behavior represents Israel's unfaithfulness. Israel too was "married" in a covenant relationship to God but "slept around" with other gods.

Figure 13.3. The Jezreel Valley in Israel

Hosea and Gomer have three children together. God instructs Hosea to give each child a name that will function as a sign-act for a particular message that he has for Israel. Their first child, a son, is named "Jezreel," which is the name of a valley and a city in the Northern Kingdom (1:4). This is the location of a bloody episode in which God instructs King Jehu to kill the house of King Ahab for their wickedness (see 1 Kings 21:17–24; 2 Kings 9:7; 10:30). However, Jehu apparently goes beyond what God had commanded and brutally exterminates anyone who might have a claim to the throne. God, through Hosea, recalls this episode as an image of how Israel itself will be destroyed.

Hosea and Gomer next have a daughter, whom they name "No Mercy," for God will no longer have mercy on Israel (1:6). Their third child is another son, named "Not My People" (1:9). The people of Israel have broken the covenant, so now God considers that covenant to be (temporarily) annulled: the relationship is broken. Imagine being one of Hosea's children and living your life with a name that signifies God's anger and judgment! In chapter 7 we discussed the wide variety of sign-acts used by the prophets. Some were simple object lessons; others came at great personal cost to the prophet. Hosea's sign-acts involved his intimate life and family, embodying the prophetic message in an especially personal way.

The unit ends on a hopeful note. In the eschatological future, God will reverse the message of the children's names. There will be a new people of God that comes out of Israel, so numerous that they cannot be counted (1:10). They *will* be God's people (1:10) and will have received mercy (2:1).

The Sign-Act Applied to Israel

■ READ HOSEA 2:2–23 ■

Here Hosea uses the family and adultery imagery from the sign-act in chapter 1 to illustrate God's relationship with Israel in the past, near future, and ultimate future. As noted above, this chapter establishes the thematic and structural pattern for the rest of the book, like a basic table of contents.

As a part of his covenant with Israel, God had given Israel all kinds of blessings, including abundance and security. In Hosea 2:2–8, the prophet accuses Israel of taking those gifts, given in love, and using them to acquire "lovers"—false gods. In a strange twist, not only does Israel use God's gifts to support her unfaithfulness; she is unfaithful because she wants even more gifts! Israel, personified as an adulteress, says that she goes after lovers because she thinks *they* are the ones who give her bread, water, wool, flax, oil, and drink (2:5). She considers her fruitful vines and fig trees to be "wages" that her lovers have given to her (2:12). When she does decide to return to God, it is because she thinks life was better with him (2:7). In other words, her decision to give herself to the true God or false gods is simply a mercenary calculation as to who will supply what she wants. She is not committed to God as her covenant partner.

In 2:9–13, Hosea announces temporal judgment in the near future. Because Israel cares more about the blessings than her relationship with God, he will take back all of his good gifts: the grain, wine, wool, and flax (2:9). He will put an end to her festival days (2:11) and destroy her vines and fig trees (2:12). In 2:13 he says, "I will punish her for the feast days of the Baals," when she "went after her lovers and forgot me."

Although Israel allows her desire for blessing and security to lead her into "adultery," this does not mean that her desires are illegitimate. She is simply looking in the wrong place. God *wants* to give her these things, but she must look to him alone. In 2:14–23, Hosea predicts that when Israel is reconciled to God, he will give his gifts once again. This section is located in the eschatological future with "in that day" (2:16), "on that day" (2:18), and "forever" (2:19). He will restore her vineyards (2:15; a reversal of 2:12), give her peace with animals (2:18), and restart the mechanism of the natural world so that it produces for Israel once again (2:21–23). He summarizes this good news with another reversal of the names of Hosea's children: "Jezreel" (repopulation of the land), "mercy," and "You are my people" (2:22–23).

The Sign-Act (Part 2)

■ READ HOSEA 3 ■

In chapter 3, Hosea returns to the sign-act once again. God commands him to go and love his wife, even though she is an adulteress. In the same way, God loves the people of Israel even though they turn to other gods (3:1). However, in another hint that judgment is coming, Hosea is not to have sexual relations with his wife for a time, just as Israel will be temporarily separated from God (3:4). In the "latter days" (the eschatological future), however, Israel will return to God and be in relationship with him once more (3:5).

Accusation against Israel (Part 1)

■ READ HOSEA 4 ■

Following the first three introductory chapters, Hosea begins his first case against Israel in chapter 4. Israel has committed sins of omission against God: they have no faithfulness, covenant love, or knowledge of God (4:1). They are also guilty of sins of commission: there is swearing, lying, murder, stealing, adultery, and bloodshed (4:2). This list comes from the Ten Commandments, the essential summary of covenant obligations.

One of the reasons that Israel has turned away from God is that they have bad spiritual leadership. Hosea speaks to a wicked priest in 4:4 and a bad prophet in 4:5. The priests and the people have participated in the same sins, so they will experience the same punishments from God (4:9). They "play the whore" and worship Baal in an attempt to increase their fertility and multiply, but it will have the opposite effect.

LITERARY NOTES

"I Will Destroy Your Mother"

Hosea mentions his audience's "mother" in 2:2, 5, and 4:5. At first glance, it may seem like Hosea is speaking to his own children about their mother (his wife), Gomer. But chapters 2 and 4 do not refer directly to the sign-act of Hosea's family; they are directed to Israel. One scholar makes a good argument that Hosea is using the image of a "mother" to refer to the leadership, institutions, and culture of the nation.[e] The people look to their "mother" for guidance, but the secular and spiritual leaders are wicked failures, leaving the people vulnerable.

LITERARY NOTES

"Beth-aven"

In Hosea 4:15, the prophet tells the people of Israel not to go up to "Beth-aven." This name occurs again in 5:8, 10:5, and 10:8. It is a substitute for the Hebrew name Bethel. Bethel is an important religious site throughout the history of Israel. It is the place where their ancestor Jacob sees the vision of the staircase to heaven and builds a memorial pillar. After this he names it "Bethel," which is Hebrew for "House of God." But Bethel becomes one of two sites where Jeroboam places his golden calves, establishing it as an epicenter of idol worship and sin against God in the Northern Kingdom. Highlighting the tragic irony of the town's fall, Hosea calls it "Beth-aven," which means "House of Sin" in Hebrew. It is a clever play on words designed to condemn the location and the activities that take place there.

Ephraim/Israel

The name Ephraim occurs thirty-seven times in the book of Hosea. It is sometimes connected with Israel (e.g., 5:3, 5, 9) and sometimes compared to Judah (e.g., 5:12, 13). Ephraim was the name of Joseph's second son, who became the father of one of the twelve tribes of Israel (Gen. 41:52). Later, it was the name of the territorial center of the Northern Kingdom; perhaps we might consider it the "heartland."[f] It included prominent cities and was the administrative hub of the nation.[g] In the Prophets, the name is often used as a metonymy to refer to the entire Northern Kingdom. Hosea uses the names "Ephraim" and "Israel" synonymously.

Hosea 6:6 in the Book of Matthew

In the time of the New Testament, eating with other people was usually reserved for intimate friends and, at the very least, suggested that one approved of others at the table.[h] In Matthew 9, Jesus causes something of a scandal because he is having dinner with tax collectors and sinners. The Pharisees question this, and Jesus responds that it is the sick (i.e., sinners) who need a doctor (i.e., himself), not those who are healthy. He then quotes Hosea 6:6: "I desire mercy, and not sacrifice." He is likely using "sacrifice" to represent the broad system of ritual worship commanded by God. The Pharisees do not understand the heart of God, who prefers to show *mercy* to those who acknowledge their sin rather than those who think they are *already* fulfilling the requirements. Jesus quotes from Hosea 6:6 again in Matthew 12:7 when the Pharisees criticize him and his disciples for picking grain on the Sabbath. Because they are focused on their own specific rules, they misunderstand what is more important in God's will. Doing what is right is more important than rituals.[i]

Accusation against Israel (Part 2)

■ READ HOSEA 5 ■

Hosea's accusation continues in chapter 5. Now he turns his attention from the spiritual leadership to the secular leadership. He announces judgment on the king, who has had a role in slaughter (5:1–2), and the princes, who are corrupt (5:10). The government officials are involved in idolatry—but not the idolatry that we normally picture, involving idols, rituals, and sacrifices. It is the idolatry of putting their trust in alliances with powerful foreign nations. Rather than looking to God for security when they are in trouble, they go to Assyria to ask for help (5:13). Before we are too quick to judge, we should be honest about how tempted *we* are to put our hopes in the victory of a particular political party, the security that comes with a well-equipped fire department, or the comfort of having a modern hospital close by. While these things are blessings, they can become idols if we put our trust in what is tangible instead of in the power of God.

Accusation against Israel (Part 3)

■ READ HOSEA 6 ■

We are not told who is speaking in 6:1–3. Someone is proposing that Israel should return to God, for he can heal them. The difficulty is that it is immediately followed by more accusation of sin in verses 4 and following. Hosea may be highlighting that the people are fickle, illustrating their false and empty repentance. Alternatively, it may be Hosea himself speaking and urging the people to repent, using the plural "we" because he is one of the people. In either case, the effect of these verses is to further condemn the people. They are *not* repenting, though they should. In the remainder of chapter 6, Hosea describes the people's refusal to turn from their sin. Even the priests join them in bloody acts of murder (6:9)!

Accusation against Israel (Part 4)

■ READ HOSEA 7 ■

Hosea uses several metaphors to describe Israel's trust in politics and national alliances. He first says that Israel's political leaders are like an overheated oven operated by an incompetent baker (7:3–10). A baker who fails to stir the fire, knead the dough, or keep the oven at the right temperature will surely burn the cake or make something inedible (7:4, 6). In the same way, the hearts of the leaders are inflamed with drunkenness, conspiracies, and murder (7:5, 7). Therefore, Israel is "a cake not turned," ruined because it is baked on one side and raw on the other (7:8).

In the second metaphor, Hosea compares Israel to a fickle dove that flies here and there without clear direction or intention (7:11). They go to Egypt and then to Assyria to get help with their problems rather than submitting to God. In response, he will trap them like birds (7:12).

Hosea's third metaphor pictures Israel as a bow that does not shoot straight (7:16). They are aiming at the wrong thing, turning to others instead of to God. Therefore, instead of getting help from Egypt, they will be mocked there (7:16).

Accusation against Israel (Part 5)

■ READ HOSEA 8 ■

At the beginning of chapter 8, Hosea sounds the alarm: an enemy is attacking! Ironically, Israel has gone to foreign nations for help (see chap. 7), so now God will bring foreign nations to destroy them (8:3). The remainder of chapter 8 is a summary of Hosea's accusation against Israel; we might use the analogy of a prosecuting attorney's closing argument after presenting evidence in court. Israel has demonstrated a consistent refusal to submit to God. They have attempted to rule themselves and set up their own kings (8:4). They have made idols to worship (8:4–6). They have attempted

LITERARY NOTES

"Egypt" in Past, Present, and Future

Hosea refers to Egypt in three different ways in the book. Recalling the past, he uses Egypt as a reminder that God brought Israel out of slavery (2:15; 11:1; 12:9, 13; 13:4). God has shown himself to be gracious and powerful, so why is Israel treating him with contempt? In the present, Egypt is an illegitimate object of Israel's trust. Israel attempts to make alliances and gain favor with Egypt so that when trouble comes, Egypt will come to help (7:11, 16; 12:1). Hosea also speaks of Egypt as a threat looming in Israel's future. He says in 8:13 and 9:3, "They shall return to Egypt." In 9:6 he says, "Egypt shall gather them." In these cases, the prophet is using Egypt as a symbol of captivity and exile. He is not saying that Israel will literally return to slavery under a pharaoh; rather, they are going into captivity in Assyria (11:5). By using Egypt in this way, Hosea intensifies the irony and tragedy of what is about to take place. After all that God did to save them from slavery in Egypt and give them the land he'd promised, their unrepentant sin will take them back to captivity in a foreign land once more.

alliances with foreign nations, even their enemy Assyria (8:9). The conclusion is grim: God will set fire to their cities and destroy their strongholds (8:14).

Judgment on Israel (Part 1)

■ READ HOSEA 9 ■

Hosea is in the middle of his first case against Israel (chaps. 4–11). In chapters 4–8 he presented evidence that Israel had broken covenant with God in a number of different ways. Although God had promised his people abundant crops, wealth, and security, they had turned away from him. To add insult to injury, they had given credit for his gifts to false gods and believed that those deities would be more effective than God at giving the good things they desired. Tragically, because those gods are false and cannot actually do anything, and because Israel has angered God, they have not improved their situation but have instead brought great harm to themselves.

In 9:1–9, Hosea grimly declares that God will take away their food. They have "played the whore" at the threshing floor, presumably in an attempt to increase the yield of their crops (9:1). But now God will ensure that they do not have enough (9:2). Their land will fail them, and they will eat unclean food when they go into exile in Assyria (9:3).

In 9:10–17, Hosea has more bad news: God will disrupt their childbearing. They have sought after fertility deities in order to have more children, but now God will work against them so that there is "no birth, no pregnancy, no conception" (9:11). Notice that the prophet mentions these three stages of childbearing in *reverse* order, as though God is undoing the natural process. Once God is working against them, they cannot possibly succeed. He says in 9:12 and 9:16 that *even if* they were somehow to produce children, he would kill the children. This sounds incredibly harsh, but God will not allow the people to overrule him and avoid the consequences that they deserve.

Judgment on Israel (Part 2)

■ READ HOSEA 10 ■

Hosea continues his declaration of judgment in chapter 10. He has already said that God will take away

---

CANONICAL CONNECTIONS

"They Came to Baal-peor"

In Hosea 9:10, the prophet alludes to the time when Israel "came to Baal-peor." This is an allusion to an event described in Numbers 25. When Israel comes to the edge of the promised land to receive it as a gift from God, they camp at Shittim, on the plains of Moab, across from Jericho. There, at Baal-peor, they engage in sexual immorality with the women of Moab and worship Moabite gods. As a result, God commands that the twenty-four thousand guilty men must be killed. This whole episode is a great scandal in Israel's history, mentioned later in passages such as Deuteronomy 4:3 and Psalm 106:28. Here Hosea is saying that this current generation is just like their fathers. They have "consecrated themselves to the thing of shame" (9:10).

their food (9:1–9) and their children (9:10–17). Now he says that God will destroy their places of worship, where they have "cheated" on him (10:1–8). God made Israel flourish in wealth because he was committed to them. But the more they had, the more they wanted, so they built altars to other gods (10:1). Now God will destroy these illegitimate sites (10:2). The calf idol at Bethel, which was supposed to help the people, will itself be taken captive to Assyria (10:6). 〽

Hosea concludes this section by predicting that the nation itself will be destroyed (10:9–15). He makes three brief allusions to the past. First, the "days of Gibeah" (10:9–10) is a reference to a terrible gang rape, slaughter, and civil war (see Judg. 19–20). Next, Hosea alludes to the beginnings of Israel as a nation, when God taught them to do right, but they rebelled (10:11–12). Third, he speaks of a time when "Shalman destroyed [the city of] Beth-arbel" (10:14). Although scholars today cannot identify this historical event, Hosea's audience must have been aware of it. His point with these references to the past is that some things never change. Israel is guilty of the same sins as generations past, and they should expect the consequences promised long ago. Hosea says ominously, "Thus it shall be done to you, O Bethel, because of your great evil" (10:15).

God Will Restore His People in the End

■ READ HOSEA 11 ■

We have seen that the book of Hosea is structured in a repeating, threefold pattern of accusation, announcement of temporal judgment, and prediction of ultimate restoration. Chapter 11, the climax of the book, is also structured in this same pattern. Hosea begins with accusation in 11:1–4, in which he reviews Israel's past. The current generation stands condemned because God did nothing to deserve his people's rebellion. From the very beginning he led them out of slavery, treated them like a son, taught them, led them gently, and fed them. But from the very beginning, they responded by giving their devotion and sacrifices to the Baal gods. They "did not know" that he healed them (11:3). Their ignorance of who God really is leads to straying from him. And because they stray, they become even more ignorant.

In 11:5–7, Hosea announces judgment: God will send his people into exile in Assyria. He will devastate their cities with war and "devour them" (11:6). One emphasis in this chapter is that the people are *determined* to rebel against him. God says in 11:5 that they "refused to return" and in 11:7 that they are "bent on turning away."

But a great surprise comes in 11:8–11. Although God's people are stubborn and resolved to be unfaithful, he is even more determined to forgive and love them! Just as he finishes announcing judgment, he suddenly says, "How can I give you up?[!] . . . My heart recoils within me; my compassion grows warm and tender" (11:8). God's justice demands that he punish Israel, but he loves them and grieves to see them in such a ruined state. He will not allow that to be the end of the story.

There was a teacher in my high school who had a very challenging student in her math class who finally earned a failing grade. The teacher said to the student, "You have been *trying* to fail all year, and I have been trying to help you succeed. And you won." But God's word here is the opposite: He says to Israel, "You are determined to rebel, and I am determined to love you and make you my special people. I *will* win and forgive you in the end." Therefore, he says in 11:9 that he will not execute his burning anger. In the end, he will bring his people home from exile (11:10–11). This did not

CANONICAL CONNECTIONS

"Out of Egypt I Called My Son"

In Hosea 11:1, God refers to Israel in the *past* when he says, "Out of Egypt I called my son." This allusion back to the exodus is an opportunity for Hosea to show that although Israel was in captivity (Egypt) and is going back into captivity (Assyria), God made a covenant relationship with them and cared for them. This same pattern is fulfilled in Jesus. In Matthew 2:15, when Jesus is a little child, he and his family go to Egypt to escape King Herod, and when the danger is past, they return to the land of Israel. Matthew writes, "This was to fulfill what the Lord had spoken by the prophet, 'Out of Egypt I called my son.'" Matthew is not claiming that Hosea 11:1 is a predictive prophecy (it is not). He is using the quotation like a *hyperlink* to take his readers back to Hosea's entire argument in Hosea 11:1–11. Jesus is following the pattern of Israel's history by entering into the place of his people's captivity and rebellion and emerging on the other side; Jesus will be the means by which God accomplishes the plan of love and restoration that he announced in Hosea.

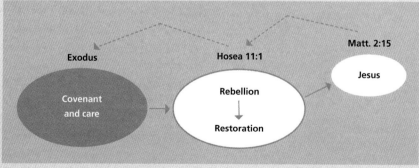

Figure 13.4. Matthew's Use of Hosea 11:1

happen in history—the tribes taken to Assyria were lost. God is speaking here of the eschatological future and the true people of God. We had a preview of all this in Hosea's sign-act when he finds his sexually promiscuous wife and brings her home. In the same way, God will find his people, forgive them, and restore them to himself. 📜

Accusation against Israel

■ READ HOSEA 12 ■

In chapter 12, Hosea begins a second case against Israel, returning to accusation. Whereas the previous cycle in chapters 4–11 is lengthy and detailed, chapters 12–14 are shorter and more emotionally charged. Hosea again highlights the sins that we have seen previously in the book: lies and deceit (11:12), multiplying violence and making covenants with Egypt and Assyria (12:1), dishonest business practices and oppressing the poor (12:7), and sacrifices to false gods (12:11).

The core of the chapter consists of two allusions to Israel's ancestor Jacob in 12:4–6 and 12:13–14. Jacob had a reputation as a deceiver. Even when he was in the womb, he grabbed his brother, Esau, by the heel in an attempt to get ahead (12:3; Gen. 25:26). Hosea's point in alluding to these events is that Jacob sinned in order to benefit himself, and his descendants—the people of Israel—have done the same. Jacob was finally humbled and submitted himself to God (Hosea 12:4b). Now it is time for Israel to follow his example (12:6).

Judgment on Israel

■ READ HOSEA 13 ■

Chapter 13 begins (13:1) and ends (13:16) with the declaration that Israel is "guilty." Although God has cared for them from the beginning, they forget him. Therefore, he will be like a ferocious wild animal that lies in wait for the people of Israel and attacks without mercy (13:7). Like a mother bear robbed of her cubs or like a lion, he will tear them open (13:8). The God who made a loving covenant relationship with his people at Mount Sinai has become their enemy. All the power that he wielded for their benefit will now be turned against them—truly a terrifying thought. Who could possibly save them from his anger (13:9–10)? 📜

CANONICAL CONNECTIONS

"O Death, Where Are Your Plagues?"

In his announcement of judgment, Hosea personifies death and Sheol (the place of the dead) and summons them to come for Israel: "O Death, where are your plagues?" and "O Sheol, where is your sting?" (13:14). Death is called on to bring judgment on God's people. But in 1 Corinthians, the apostle Paul picks up on this language to celebrate God's victory over death through Christ's resurrection. With a few slight differences in wording, Paul quotes Hosea 13:14 and turns it into a taunt *against* death.[k] He writes, "Death is swallowed up in victory. O death, where is your victory? O death, where is your sting?" (1 Cor. 15:54–55). Death, the cruel judgment against God's people in Hosea, is now powerless to defeat the person who trusts in Christ.

God Will Restore His People in the End

■ READ HOSEA 14 ■

In the last chapter of the book, Hosea looks into the future, past the judgment to come (cf. chap. 13) to a time when God finally restores his people to himself. "It is too late to ward off the destruction now, but in the eschatological future they can look forward to a renewed relationship with [God] and a complete renewal of the land."[7] That is, if they repent and put their whole trust in him.

Hosea begins chapter 14 by calling on Israel to do just that. He says, "Return, O Israel, to the LORD your God" (14:1–3). In response, God will freely love and heal them (14:4). Hosea uses metaphors from nature to describe Israel's renewal: they will take root, spread out shoots, flourish like grain, blossom like the vine, and be like wine (14:5–7). This imagery is particularly significant in the book of Hosea because these are the very gifts that the people longed for and hoped to receive from their false gods. But they will only receive them when they turn to the *true* God.

In the last verse, which is a postscript to the entire book, the author turns to us, the readers, and tells us to "understand these things" (14:9). With a cluster of words usually associated with Wisdom literature, he reminds us that if *we* want the good life, if *we* want to live a life of success, wealth, and security, then we must recognize that these things are only to be found when we walk in the ways of God.

Implementation

The book of Hosea makes many important contributions to Christian theology, but we will focus on three key, distinctive emphases. First, the book reminds us that before we can submit to God and follow him, we have to know him as he truly is. Hosea says repeatedly in the book that Israel does not know God (4:1; 5:4). They do not know that God is the one who gave them the gifts of nature (2:8) and healed them (11:3). It is because the people do not know God that they are destroyed (4:6). They have rejected knowledge of him, which has led them into every other kind of error, false perspective, and sinful action. Their ignorance is so profound that even when God brings judgment on them, they still do not "know" (7:9).

It is a common conception that religious practice consists of rituals and rules, saying the right things, avoiding certain activities, and participating in institutions such as houses of worship. But none of these are as important to God as knowing him (6:6). The book of Hosea casts our relationship with God as a *marriage* relationship. In a book that begins with the image of Hosea pursuing Gomer (chaps. 1, 3) and ends with God's intimate, restored relationship with his people (chap. 14), it is impossible to miss God's desire to know his people and to be known by them. Hosea looks forward to a time when God will betroth (another marriage term) his people to himself, and they will "know the LORD" (2:20). And now, after the first coming of Jesus Christ, we are living in that future time. Jesus is the climax of God's self-revelation, and we have an unprecedented opportunity to know him as he truly is: a God who cannot look on sin because he is holy and who will do whatever it takes to restore his people to wholeness because he is loving. Jesus brings us the clearest picture yet of who God is. In the future, however, we look forward to Jesus's second coming, when all is made clear and we know God face-to-face. We will know God fully, and we will be fully known (1 Cor. 13:12). It is only by knowing God as he truly is and coming to him through Jesus Christ that we can find true peace and success (Hosea 14:9).

A second theological emphasis in the book concerns God's gifts to his people and the nature of idolatry. God generously promised to give his people good gifts as a result of his covenant with them. It was not wrong for Israel to desire a "good life" and security from enemies. They only wanted those things that God planned to give them. But when their desires became disordered, apostasy followed. Furthermore, they refused to come to God for good things and turned to idols, over which (they thought!) they had more control.

This is an important warning for us to consider our own idols. Few of us have been tempted to worship a golden statue of a calf or burn incense to a tree. That form of idolatry, described in the Bible, feels so foreign that we are tempted to give ourselves a pass. But the question we must ask is, What or whom do I trust to get what I want? For some of us, it is politics. When our party or politician wins, we feel peace and hope for the future, but when the other side wins, we are filled with despair. Some of us trust in science and technology to improve our lives with communication, entertainment, and security. We trust in our social networks and contacts. We trust in our financial resources: our paycheck, 401(k) account, or rising home values. All of these things are physical and tangible, and everyone else is trusting in them for the good life! But Hosea condemns us when he says, "You have trusted in your own way!" (10:13).

It is true that, in this life, following Jesus Christ often results in difficulty, suffering, and even death. God calls us to die to ourselves and to prioritize nothing higher than him. However, to reject God is to gain permanent death and to follow God is to inherit life everlasting. Therefore, Hosea reminds us that the *ultimate* choice is not between faith in God and success in life, as though God were a miser who tries to prevent blessing. "Every good gift and every perfect gift is from above, coming down from the Father of lights, with whom there is no variation or shadow due to change" (James 1:17). The choice is actually between God *and* blessing, on the one hand, and rebellion against God *and* death on the other. Only God is the giver of life and abundance. Our own search for the good life apart from him will only end in misery.

A third emphasis in the book of Hosea is that even as we are determined to sin, God is determined to restore. Hosea remarks that the people of Israel were dominated by a "spirit of whoredom" (5:4) and "bent" on apostasy (11:7). There was no indication that Gomer, or Israel, had any intention of repenting. They lived wildly with their "lovers." Yet God was determined to seek them out and save them (3:5; 6:4; 11:8).

All of us share the rebellious "spirit" and "bent" that eroded Israel's devotion. Do we have the ability to cure ourselves of even the smallest sin? Do we demonstrate day after day that our hearts are committed to God and that we serve him above all else, even ourselves? Broken and burdened with the baggage from a lifetime of sinning and being sinned against, have we any chance of fixing ourselves? What we need is transformation: a grace that forgives and restores apart from our own ability to obey. This drastic action is accomplished by Jesus Christ. In Christ, God's holiness is satisfied. And in Christ, God reclaims his people for himself. One scholar writes, "[God's] people put him in a bind; he is torn between two passions, justice and mercy. But the gospel is that this conflict has been resolved on the cross by Jesus, who willingly took the judgment his people earned so that a just God did not have to 'give them up' [Hosea 11:8]."[8] This hope enables Hosea to look into the future and describe a restored relationship between God and his people. Under the God who heals, satisfies, and loves them freely, Israel will again "blossom" and "flourish" (14:4–8).

Christian Reading Questions

1. Having read the book of Hosea, go back and reread 2:2–23. Describe how these verses set up the themes and structure of the entire book.
2. What kinds of idolatry tempt Hosea's audience? Do we struggle with those same kinds of idolatry today? If not, what would be comparable examples from the modern world? In other words, how can we

trace the same heart attitudes in ourselves as in Hosea's ancient listeners and readers?

3. Reread Hosea 6:6 and compare it to an earlier prophetic statement in 1 Samuel 15:22. How would you describe the central concern in these statements? What fundamental sin are they warning against?

CHAPTER FOURTEEN

Joel

Orientation

When we think about the end of the world, or the "latter days," it is difficult to imagine what it would be like to be there. We know that God has interrupted human history in the past—when he parted the Red Sea for the Israelites or tore down the walls of Jericho—but what would we experience if he came to judge the world one final time during our lifetime? We may have ridiculous images in our minds from video games or sensational stories we have read. Or we may struggle to take the "day of the LORD" very seriously at all. It sounds so far away. It sounds unreal or abstract. It sounds spiritual and intangible.

We saw in the previous chapter that Hosea uses the sign-act of his marriage to a promiscuous wife as a way of illustrating Israel's unfaithfulness and God's unrelenting love. The prophet Joel explores God's final answer to humanity's rebellion: the day of YHWH, when God will judge the entire earth once and for all. Rather than a dramatic sign-act, Joel uses a tragic current event as a concrete picture of what is to come. A locust plague has devastated the land, bringing with it poverty and starvation. In Joel's time, this event represented the judgment of God for covenant unfaithfulness. But the locust plague also functions as a pattern or prototype of a greater event in the future. It is as though Joel is saying, "You know the terror and devastation of a locust plague up close and personal. It is as real as your ravaged backyard and your empty stomach! Now, prepare for something far, far worse that will be just as real." But there is good news, too, for God's forgiveness in history is also a preview of his ultimate forgiveness and rescue in the day of YHWH.

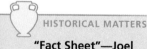

HISTORICAL MATTERS

"Fact Sheet"—Joel

Author: Joel, the son of Pethuel

Date: uncertain

Location: Judah

Political and social context: A locust plague has devastated the land and agriculture of Judah. The prophet Joel promises that if the people repent of their sin, God will restore the land in the near future.

The superscription of the book (1:1) tells us only the prophet's name, Joel, and the name of his father, Pethuel. "Joel," which means "YHWH is God," was a common name in ancient Israel; at least fourteen other individuals named Joel are mentioned in the Old Testament.[1] Joel's location is not explicitly stated in the book, but the contents suggest that his prophecy was directed to the Southern Kingdom (see 2:1, 15; 3:1, 6).

Apart from Joel's name and probable location, we know nothing for certain about the background or historical circumstances of his ministry.

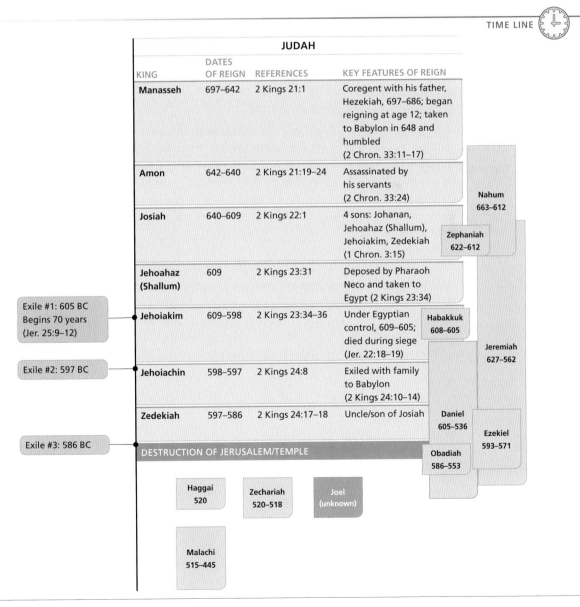

JUDAH			
KING	**DATES OF REIGN**	**REFERENCES**	**KEY FEATURES OF REIGN**
Manasseh	697–642	2 Kings 21:1	Coregent with his father, Hezekiah, 697–686; began reigning at age 12; taken to Babylon in 648 and humbled (2 Chron. 33:11–17)
Amon	642–640	2 Kings 21:19–24	Assassinated by his servants (2 Chron. 33:24)
Josiah	640–609	2 Kings 22:1	4 sons: Johanan, Jehoahaz (Shallum), Jehoiakim, Zedekiah (1 Chron. 3:15)
Jehoahaz (Shallum)	609	2 Kings 23:31	Deposed by Pharaoh Neco and taken to Egypt (2 Kings 23:34)
Jehoiakim	609–598	2 Kings 23:34–36	Under Egyptian control, 609–605; died during siege (Jer. 22:18–19)
Jehoiachin	598–597	2 Kings 24:8	Exiled with family to Babylon (2 Kings 24:10–14)
Zedekiah	597–586	2 Kings 24:17–18	Uncle/son of Josiah

Exile #1: 605 BC Begins 70 years (Jer. 25:9–12)

Exile #2: 597 BC

Exile #3: 586 BC

DESTRUCTION OF JERUSALEM/TEMPLE

Nahum 663–612

Zephaniah 622–612

Habakkuk 608–605

Jeremiah 627–562

Daniel 605–536

Ezekiel 593–571

Obadiah 586–553

Haggai 520

Zechariah 520–518

Joel (unknown)

Malachi 515–445

Joel 265

One scholar calls the book "practically undatable."[2] Several general time periods have been suggested. A minority of scholars argue that the book is preexilic. Possible support for this view is the fact that the twelve so-called Minor Prophets are arranged in roughly chronological order from Hosea to Malachi, and Joel comes between Hosea (eighth century BC) and Amos (eighth century BC). This might suggest that Joel is early like those books. However, the most common view among scholars is that Joel is one of the later prophetic books, from the Persian period.[3] Perhaps this is why there is no mention of a king in Judah. However, Joel's unidentified historical setting does not obscure his message. It is the book's chronological ambiguity that allows it to develop themes that unite the Minor Prophets.[4] 🕐

Exploration

Of the five phases of history that the Old Testament prophets address (see chaps. 6 and 7), the prophet Joel speaks to four of them. In figure 14.1, the stick figure represents the prophet Joel's chronological position as he looks to the future. Joel makes no formal accusation of the sins of Judah in the past. He vividly describes the judgment that the people are already experiencing in the present. This becomes a pattern to describe eschatological judgment in the distant future. In light of this great and terrible day of YHWH that is coming, Joel calls the people to repent and looks forward to restoration in the near future, which he then uses as a pattern of God's ultimate restoration for his people at the end of time. These four phases underlie the structure of the book of Joel, illustrated in table 14.1.[5] 📖

The book begins in **1:1–20** with a description of a terrible locust plague. This present disaster is an omen of ultimate destruction in the distant future (see 1:15). The prophet then uses locust *imagery* in **2:1–11** to describe

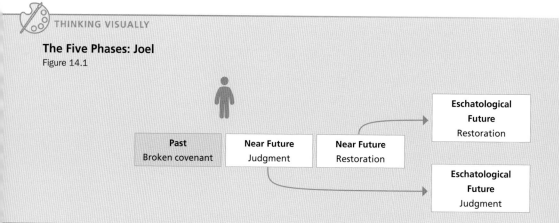

THINKING VISUALLY

The Five Phases: Joel
Figure 14.1

Table 14.1. The Structure of Joel

	Near Future	Distant Future
Judgment	1:1–20 Locusts: a preview of the day of YHWH • Locusts • Day of YHWH (1:15) • Economic catastrophe	2:1–11 Announcement of the day of YHWH • Devastating army • Day of YHWH (2:1b, 2a, 11b) • Final catastrophe; there is no escape
Call to Repent	2:12–17 Call to repentance: "Return to me with all your heart"	
Restoration	2:18–27 Reversal of the locust disaster	2:28–32 The Spirit and salvation for all who call upon YHWH
		3:1–21 Judgment for the enemies of God and blessing for the people of God

an overwhelming army in the coming day of YHWH (see 2:1–2, 11). But in 2:12 there is a transition—"yet even now"—which returns the focus to the present time. Joel calls for repentance (2:12–17), a call that functions as a transition between judgment in the first part of the book and restoration in the second part of the book. Joel then announces that the results of repentance will be restoration in the near future (2:18–27). The present calamity will be reversed, and the land will be healed. This restoration becomes a pattern for the eschatological restoration in the distant future (2:28–32), a time period designated as "afterward" (2:28), "in those days" (2:29), and the "day of the Lord" (2:31). The book concludes in 3:1–21 with the promise that "in those days" (3:1; cf. 3:18: "in that day")—the eschatological future—God will destroy his enemies and dwell with his people forever.

The Locust Plague

▓ READ JOEL 1 ▓

The prophet does not mention the word "covenant" in the book, but, as with all of the prophets, that relationship is the foundation of his message. God refers to himself as "the Lord," which is his covenant name (cf. Exod. 3:13–17). He calls Joel's audience "my people" (2:26, 27; 3:2) and refers to the land as "my land" (1:6; 3:2). And though Joel does not accuse the people of specific covenant sins, their culpability is implied by the fact that they are experiencing God's judgment. Moses had even warned that locust plagues would be among the covenant curses (Deut. 28:38).

Figure 14.2. A cloud of locusts

Figure 14.3. Locust plague

Chapter 1 begins with a rhetorical question: "Has such a thing happened in your days, or in the days of your fathers?" (1:2). Joel's readers had likely experienced locust plagues before. Farmers always face the risk of ruined crops from bad weather, insect pests, or (in the ancient world) marauding armies. But this is a unique disaster. Joel commands the people to tell their children about it, because understanding the significance of the event is necessary for the future people of God.

Modern locust plagues can give us some idea of the terror and loss that ancient Judah experienced. In 1890, a swarm of locusts descended on Algiers, French Algeria. According to one eyewitness, "The larvae marched over the ground in columns often more than 50 miles wide; and a field of barley after an hour presented the appearance of having been mown."[6] In the winter and spring of 2020, locusts swept into Kenya, Somalia, and Ethiopia, ravaging crops and farmland. Farmers attempted to frighten them away by banging metal pans, whistling, or throwing stones, but it was futile, and they watched in frustration as the locusts ate everything.[7]

In Joel's time, the loss from the locust plague has been total. The crops that are left by some types of locusts are ravaged by others (1:4). The people's vines and fig trees and fields are ruined (1:7, 10). The food is gone and the storehouses are empty. Even the animals are starving (1:16–18).

Joel urges the population to come out of their stupor and turn their sorrow into repentance. They should "awake" and "weep" and "lament" (1:5, 8–10). The priests should put on sackcloth, and the elders should gather and cry out to God (1:13–14). In 1:15, Joel connects the present experience to the day of YHWH, which is "near." This present disaster is not the day of YHWH, but it gives us a concrete illustration of what that day will be like.

The Day of YHWH

■ READ JOEL 2:1–11 ■

We come to a new section in 2:1–11, which is bracketed by the phrase "the day of the LORD" in 2:1 and 2:11. Here Joel transitions from a description of present circumstances to a warning of the distant future. He says of this coming time, "Nothing has been like it, and will not be again" (2:2). While he does not mention locusts specifically, he uses the *imagery* of a locust plague to describe the army of God, swarming over the land and bringing total destruction. The plague that the people have already experienced is a foretaste of what is to come. 📜

Joel describes the day of YHWH as "a day of darkness" (2:2). A place that had been like the garden of Eden will become a wasteland (2:3). With cruel efficiency, the destroyers will enter the city and cannot be stopped (2:8). This is the army of God, moving at his command (2:11).

Call to Repentance

■ READ JOEL 2:12–17 ■

At the end of the previous section, Joel asks, "For the day of the LORD is great and very awesome; who can endure it?" (2:11). The answer to that question comes in 2:12–17: in order to endure, all must repent of their sin and fall on the mercy of God. In 2:12, Joel calls on the people to return to God with fasting, weeping, and mourning. Unfortunately, Israel's history was filled with dramatic displays of sorrow and repentance, but it was obvious that the people were not serious because their *actions* did not

CANONICAL CONNECTIONS

"Like the Appearance of Horses"

In Joel 2:4, the prophet merges the imagery of locusts, horses, and an eschatological army: "Their appearance is like the appearance of horses, and like war horses they run." The apostle John makes a similar connection in the book of Revelation, perhaps drawing from the book of Joel. In Revelation 9, an angel opens the shaft of a bottomless pit, and locusts emerge with power like scorpions (9:3). In this case, however, they do not harm the grass, green plants, or trees; they harm the people who do not belong to God (9:4), whom they torment for five months (9:5). Their appearance is like that of horses (9:7; a possible allusion to Joel 2:4), and their teeth are like lions' teeth (9:8; a possible allusion to Joel 1:6).[a] For both Joel and John, the warrior locusts offer a warning that brings God's future judgment close enough to make our skin crawl.

Figure 14.4. Locusts

Holger Kirk / Shutterstock.com

change. God is not looking for ripped clothing as a showy demonstration; he wants their hearts to be broken over their sin so that they truly turn from it (2:13a).

Joel provides a strong motivation to repent of sin: we can expect God to respond favorably. "Return to the Lord your God," he says, "for he is gracious and merciful, slow to anger, and abounding in steadfast love; and he relents over disaster" (2:13b). God does not overlook sin, nor is he weak and unwilling to punish it. But he has told us that mercy is part of his essential character. It is who he is. He loves to forgive and welcome sinners back with open arms. In other words, if we know that God will be merciful, we have every reason to repent quickly and authentically.

Reversal of the Disaster

■ READ JOEL 2:18–27 ■

Assuming that the people have repented or will repent, Joel moves directly to an announcement of restoration in the near future. In 1:10 he had described the destruction of the grain, wine, and oil. Now God promises to replenish those very same things (2:19; cf. 2:24). The pastures will be green, and the trees and vines will bear fruit (2:22). Most importantly, the people's relationship with God will be restored: "You shall know that I am in the midst of Israel, and that I am the Lord your God and there is none else. And my people shall never again be put to shame" (2:27).

Spirit and Salvation

■ READ JOEL 2:28–32 ■

Joel's announcement of restoration in the near future serves as an illustration for a greater restoration in the distant, eschatological future. This restoration will include several events. God's Spirit will be poured out abundantly and broadly. God says, through Joel, that the Spirit will not be constrained by any of the typical social divisions but will be poured out on "all flesh"— on sons, daughters, old, young, and on servants as well

(2:28–29). This outpouring will include all God's true people, from all the nations. As one author writes, "Joel envisages a sociological overhaul: the distinctions . . . are swept aside."[8]

When God breaks into history at the end of time, there will also be wonders in the heavens, blood, fire, and smoke (2:30). "The sun shall be turned to darkness, and the moon to blood" on "the great and awesome day of the LORD" (2:31). These signs echo the plagues in Exodus 10, when God powerfully brought his people out of slavery in Egypt. There will be upheaval and an undoing of the natural order, but "everyone who calls on the name of the LORD shall be saved" (2:32).

Judgment and Refuge in the End

■ READ JOEL 3 ■

The promised day of YHWH is a day of terror or hope depending on a person's status before God. In 3:1–15, Joel focuses first on God's final judgment, which he will bring to the nations on behalf of his people (3:2, 12). God's people will have suffered for hundreds and thousands of years at the hands of wicked rulers and oppressive empires, waiting for justice. But in the end, God will relieve his people of suffering and give them safety by destroying the wicked once and for all.

In the last verses of the book, 3:16–21, Joel announces further blessing. God will be a refuge and stronghold for his people (3:16). He will not only reverse the previous disasters but will also give them even more than they had before (3:18–21; see fig. 14.5).

Implementation

Joel is a short book, but it presents a complex and sophisticated picture of the day of YHWH that both warns us of the consequences of defiance

"I Will Pour Out My Spirit on All Flesh"

In Acts 2, the followers of Jesus are gathered together on the day of Pentecost. There is a sound of rushing wind, a tongue of fire appears on each of them, and they are filled with the Holy Spirit. They are Jews and people from many different nations, but they speak in other languages and yet can understand one another (Acts 2:1–6). Peter stands up and explains that what they have seen is the fulfillment of Joel's prophecy. He quotes Joel 2:28–32, ending with "Everyone who calls upon the name of the Lord shall be saved" (Acts 2:17–21). God offers his salvation and his Holy Spirit to *anyone* from any tribe, nation, language, or social group who puts his or her faith in Jesus, the Lord and Messiah.[b]

Joel 2:32 in the Book of Romans

In Romans 10, Paul is in the midst of making the argument that it is not obedience to the law that saves. Rather, "If you confess with your mouth that Jesus is Lord and believe in your heart that God raised him from the dead, you will be saved" (10:9). A few verses later, Paul quotes Joel 2:32: "for 'everyone who calls on the name of the Lord will be saved'" (10:13). What is the "name of the Lord"? It is the name "Jesus Christ," the only name that can save. And because faith in that name is the only way of salvation, God's grace is open to everyone—from every nation—not just Jews who have the law of Moses.

Reversal of Past Disaster
Figure 14.5

Past Disaster		Future Blessing
Sweet wine cut off (1:5)		Wine will drip from mountains (3:18)
Creek beds dried up (1:20)		Creek beds will flow with water (3:18)
Temple without offerings (1:9)		Temple will have a fountain (3:18)
Judah is a wilderness (2:3)		Enemies will be a wilderness (3:19)
Disaster for generations (2:2)		Judah will be inhabited for generations (3:20)

Adapted from James Nogalski, *Redactional Processes in the Book of the Twelve* (New York: de Gruyter, 1993), 42.

against God and encourages us to keep the faith, knowing that God will protect and reward his people in the end.

A key theological takeaway from Joel is that repentance must be authentic and complete. In his two main calls for repentance (1:13–14 and 2:12–17), Joel urges his hearers to take no prisoners in identifying sin and its consequences, rejecting it, and turning back to God. One of the most well-known verses in Joel is 2:13, "Rend your hearts and not your garments." In ancient Israel, ripping one's clothing was a sign of sorrow. It is easy to *look* sorry or *sound* sorry for what we have done. It is even easy to *feel* sorry, especially when we are caught or facing unpleasant consequences. But what is needed is a kind of personal defeat. With brutal honesty, we reckon with a godly sorrow that cuts through excuses all the way to the heart; and we determine, with God's help, to be done with that sin once and for all.

As we noted previously, Joel continues in 2:13 with an assurance that God will receive the people's confession with mercy and kindness and that he will not stay angry. That guarantee offered to Judah not only still stands today but is even more certain! For now Jesus Christ has been revealed in the flesh to bear God's wrath and offer forgiveness. He has died for us on a painful cross, climactically demonstrating the lengths to which he would go to rescue sinners. God always takes his time in getting angry and is lightning quick to offer kindness—a kindness that is meant to lead us to repentance (Rom. 2:4).

Joel also teaches Christians today that the reality and finality of the day of YHWH should inform our perspective about life in this world. If the day of YHWH involves incredible destruction and suffering that cannot be avoided except by turning from sin and back to God in faith, then we must be faithful in passing on the warning to future generations. Joel's command to the elders applies to us as well: "Tell your children of it, and let your children tell their children, and their children to another generation" (1:3).

A reality check about a certain and imminent future builds faith in God and cautions us to take him seriously. His judgment will come out of Zion (2:1; 3:16), and the only way to avoid it is to repent and call on the name of YHWH, a name that we know to be "Jesus Christ."

However, Zion will also be a place of refuge for God's people (2:23, 32; 3:17, 21). Joel paints a picture of a glorious future that is vivid and concrete, defined by abundance, safety, God's presence, and unending life. For those who know God, the day of YHWH is not something to fear; it is a day of justice, when all things will finally be set right. Regardless of what our passport says or what nation we call home, our *true home* as Christians is Mount Zion, the heavenly Jerusalem, the city of the living God, with Jesus, the mediator of the new covenant (Heb. 12:22, 24). This offers real hope, encouraging us to stay the course and remain faithful, no matter the cost.

Christian Reading Questions

1. If someone were to ask you, "What will the day of the LORD be like?" how would you answer that person from the book of Joel? In your own words, identify four or five key points that the prophet makes about this great day.

2. Like many other books, Joel teaches that God is "gracious and merciful, slow to anger, and abounding in steadfast love" (2:13). Read other similar statements in Exodus 3:2; Numbers 14:18; Nehemiah 9:17; Psalms 86:15; 103:8; 145:8; and Jonah 4:2. How is this "grace formula" used in each context to make a broader point?

CHAPTER FIFTEEN

Amos

Orientation

As we have seen in previous chapters, God's covenant with Israel at Mount Sinai obligates the people to observe a wide variety of requirements. Perhaps we could group these in two main categories. First, the people are to maintain exclusive loyalty to God, worship him exactly as he instructs, and refuse to serve any of the gods of the surrounding peoples. The stipulations with this vertical orientation govern the relationship between the people and God. We saw in chapter 13 that the prophet Hosea focuses primarily on this vertical aspect of the covenant, accusing the people of worshiping other gods and worshiping the true God in ways that he rejects.

A second category of the covenant stipulations has a horizontal orientation, governing the relationships between people within the covenant community. God has formed a special people for himself, and he expects that just as he has treated them with kindness and love, they will treat each other with love, righteousness, and justice as well. The king over them was to take the lead and set the example, but love and justice toward one another was the responsibility of all community members. When God delivered this covenant through Moses, the people enthusiastically accepted these obligations and committed themselves to obeying them all, including the horizontal demands of justice (see Exod. 24:7–8).

One scholar defines the Old Testament notion of justice as "the claim of all persons to full and equitable participation in the structures and dealings of the community, and especially to equity in the legal system."[1] Positively, this means that people treat each other fairly. Everyone has access to the same resources and privileges of society. Negatively, justice means avoiding corruption and "fixing" laws for one's own benefit. It means refusing to testify falsely. It means refusing to rig the economic system to enrich oneself at the expense of others. Justice also means correcting a situation when it has gone wrong, such as releasing a person falsely imprisoned or returning money that has been wrongly taken.

Map 15.1. The geography of Amos

The prophet Amos, our subject for this chapter, is very concerned with justice. He focuses primarily on the people's failure to fulfill the *horizontal* obligations of the covenant, accusing the people of mistreating and oppressing one another. Some enjoy lavish lives of luxury while others starve. The people enslave and take advantage of each other for their own profit. Some have manipulated business practices to become rich quickly while others are deprived of basic necessities. These injustices are wrong not just because they hurt people; they are wrong because they are offenses against the fundamental nature of God, who is just, true, and good.

Over the course of nine chapters, Amos relentlessly condemns the Northern Kingdom for their rejection of God's covenant, promising that God will act against them in judgment. Initially, the book might seem depressing. And yet Amos's words actually highlight the goodness of God, who cares deeply about justice and the plight of the vulnerable. Furthermore, the book ends with a note of hope. God offers people of all nations a wonderful future in a land that will be transformed by one who comes from the house of David.

The superscription to the book (Amos 1:1–2) tells us that the prophet Amos was one of the "shepherds" (Hebrew: *noqed*) from a town called Tekoa, which was ten miles south of Jerusalem. Though he was from the Southern Kingdom, God called Amos to a prophetic ministry in the Northern Kingdom. The book mentions the capital city of Samaria (3:12; 4:1; 6:1) as well as the worship sites at Dan and Bethel (3:14; 4:4; 5:5; 8:14). It may be that Amos was based in Bethel, just across the border from Judah (see 7:12–13) (see map 15.1).

Early scholars sometimes assumed that Amos was a poor shepherd, and perhaps this was why he cared deeply about social justice. However, elsewhere the same word, "shepherd," describes the king of Moab, who had over one hundred thousand lambs and one hundred thousand rams (2 Kings 3:4). Amos may have been a wealthy "rancher" with great flocks and herds. In any case, he worked in agriculture and was not a professional prophet (7:14). Poverty or riches made no difference: he was interested in social justice because he was compelled to proclaim the word of the Lord.

HISTORICAL MATTERS

"Fact Sheet"—Amos

Author: Amos

Date: 767–753 BC

Location: Northern Kingdom

Political and social context: In the mid-eighth century, the Northern Kingdom was wealthy, prosperous, and secure. The society was marked by oppression of the poor, social injustice, and complacency in their relationship with God as well as continued unorthodox worship practices.

Amos 1:1 also tells us that Amos prophesied in the days of Uzziah, king of Judah, and Jeroboam, the son of Joash, king of Israel. This would put Amos in the middle of the eighth century BC (see the time line of Amos), making him one of the earliest writing prophets in the Old Testament. At this time, the great Assyrian Empire was occupied in the east, so Israel was free to flourish in trade and commerce.[2] They became extremely wealthy and successful. Amos provides examples of this decadence: seasonal homes and palaces rich with ivory decorations (3:15), women addicted to wine (4:1), frivolous feasting (6:4), and anointing with precious oils (6:6). However, in many cases this wealth was not gained honestly. The rich oppressed the poor, sold them into debt slavery, and turned the needy away instead of helping them.

Exploration

Amos addresses four of the five phases of prophetic history (see chaps. 6 and 7). In figure 15.1, the stick figure represents the prophet Amos's chronological location. He looks back to the past at the ways Israel has broken God's covenant. In the near future, Israel will face certain judgment as their land is destroyed and they are taken into exile. There will be no restoration in the near future. At the end of the book, Amos gives glimpses of an ultimate judgment in the distant, eschatological future, before finally announcing that God will transform nature to give his people a restored, glorious home forever.

In the past, many Bible scholars doubted that the book of Amos had a literary structure at all. One scholar writes, "[Amos] has too little story,

THINKING VISUALLY

The Five Phases: Amos
Figure 15.1

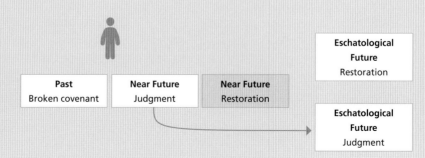

ISRAEL

KING	DATES OF REIGN	REFERENCES	KEY FEATURES OF REIGN
Jeroboam II	793–753	2 Kings 14:23	Coregent with Jehoash, 793–782
Zechariah	753–752	2 Kings 15:8	Assassinated by Shallum (2 Kings 15:10)
Shallum	752	2 Kings 15:13	Assassinated by Menahem (2 Kings 15:14)
Menahem	752–742	2 Kings 15:17	Made an alliance with Pul, king of Assyria (2 Kings 15:19–20)
Pekahiah	742–740	2 Kings 15:23	Assassinated by Pekah (2 Kings 15:25)
Pekah	752–732	2 Kings 15:27	Reigned in Gilead, 752–740, overlapping with Menahem; reigned over united Israel, 740–732; assassinated by Hoshea (2 Kings 15:30)
Hoshea	732–722	2 Kings 15:30; 17:1	Appointed by Tiglath-pileser III

Amos 767–753

Jonah 792–753

Hosea 755–725

JUDAH

KING	DATES OF REIGN	REFERENCES	KEY FEATURES OF REIGN
Uzziah/ Azariah	792–740	2 Kings 14:21; 2 Chron. 26:3	Coregent with his father, Amaziah, 792–767; began reigning at age 16 (2 Kings 14:21); struck with leprosy for offering incense in 750, then lived in a separate house while his son governed (2 Chron. 26:16–21)
Jotham	750–735	2 Kings 15:32–33	Coregent with Uzziah, 750–740; removed from the throne in 735
Ahaz	735–715	2 Kings 16:1–2	16 years counted from death of Jotham in 732 (2 Kings 15:38)
Hezekiah	729–686	2 Kings 18:1–2	Coregent with father, Ahaz, 729–715; Sennacherib attacked Judah in 701 BC (2 Kings 18:13)

Isaiah 740–695

Micah 742–686

too little train of thought, and too little internal coherence to hold interest for more than a few verses or, at most, a chapter."[3] However, the book does have a coherence and order (see table 15.1).

Table 15.1. The Structure of Amos

		Superscription: "The words of Amos . . . which he saw" (**1:1**)
		Judgment on the nations (**unexpected inclusion of Israel**) (**1:2–2:16**)
Words		Words of punishment for Israel's sins (**3:1–15**) Words of condemnation of Israel's women, worship, and stubbornness (**4:1–13**) Words of warning against complacency: "Seek the LORD and live" (**5:1–6:14**)
Visions		Visions of Israel's imminent destruction (**7:1–8:3**) A vision of Israel's ultimate destruction (**8:4–9:10**)
		Restoration of Israel (**unexpected inclusion of the nations**) (**9:11–15**)

Note: My understanding of the structure is influenced by Duane A. Garrett, *Amos: A Handbook on the Hebrew Text* (Waco: Baylor University Press, 2008), 7; Billy K. Smith and Frank S. Page, *Amos, Obadiah, Jonah*, New American Commentary 19b (Nashville: Broadman & Holman, 1995), 33–34.

The superscription in 1:1 introduces the "words" of Amos that he "saw." These two words anticipate the two major sections of the book: first "words" (**3:1–6:14**) and then "visions" (**7:1–9:10**). There is also a frame around these words and visions. The book opens with oracles of accusation against the nations, and *Israel* is surprisingly included (**1:2–2:16**). It ends with hope and restoration for Israel, and the *nations* are surprisingly included (**9:11–15**). This frame ties Israel and the nations together: God's judgment and salvation are for the entire world.

Judgment on the Nations . . . and Israel

■ READ AMOS 1:2–2:16 ■

The book begins with oracles against the nations. However, Amos's real purpose is to spring a rhetorical trap for his audience. He lists the sins of Damascus/Aram (1:3–5), Gaza/Philistia (1:6–8), Tyre (1:9–10), Edom (1:11–12), Ammon (1:13–15), Moab (2:1–3), and Judah (2:4–5). For each city or nation, he uses the repeating pattern "for three transgressions . . . and for four, I will not revoke the punishment" and then lists the ways that they have abused and exploited weaker people for their own gain. The consequences will fit the crime: God will take away their security and wealth. We might imagine the listeners or readers in the Northern Kingdom cheering as they hear their enemies and neighbors condemned . . . but then they find themselves at the end of the list! In 2:6 the prophet proclaims, "For three transgressions of *Israel* and for four, I will not revoke the punishment." They may be God's chosen people, but they are just as guilty as the surrounding nations and are included in the list with the same literary pattern.[4] The trap is enhanced by the geographical order in which these nations are addressed (see map 15.2). The order is (1) to the northeast, (2) to the southwest, (3) to northwest, then (4) to southeast, crossing over Israel in the shape of an "X." He then addresses close neighbors to the east (5–6) and then Judah (7) before finally hitting Israel (8) like a bull's-eye.

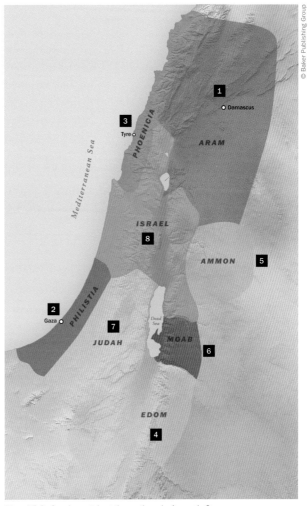

Map 15.2. Oracles against the nations in Amos 1–2

Words of Punishment for Israel's Sins

■ READ AMOS 3 ■

Amos continues the indictment of the Northern Kingdom he began in chapter 2. He says in 3:2, "You only have I known of all the families of the earth; therefore I will punish you." It is *because* they are his special people that he brings judgment. He is not picking on them at random; he is holding them accountable to the covenant. They are not exempt from judgment because they are his people . . . they are more guilty! Given their history with God and his special revelation to them, their sin is all the more outrageous. He says, "They do not know how to do right" (3:10). Therefore, he will tear down their idolatrous altars and destroy their extravagant houses of ivory.

Words of Condemnation of Israel's Women, Worship, and Stubbornness

■ READ AMOS 4 ■

In chapter 4, Amos addresses the women of Samaria as a representation of the entire nation. He calls them "cows of Bashan," wealthy women who

Ivory

Ivory was not found in Israel. It had to be imported from the tusks of elephants in Syria or hippopotamuses in Africa. Therefore, it was a very expensive luxury for the upper class. Amos uses it as an example of excess. While the poor were barely getting enough food, the rich had manipulated the economy so that they could collect large amounts of money for lavish decorations. Amos mentions "houses of ivory," which likely refers to ivory decorations on walls and furniture (3:15; 6:4). When archaeologists excavated the palace of King Ahab (who lived one hundred years before Amos) in Samaria, they discovered elaborate ivory carvings (see fig. 15.2).[a]

Figure 15.2. Ivory furniture inlay of a sacred tree

crush the needy while lying around demanding that their husbands bring them another drink (4:1). They are like fattened animals who will be taken away into exile on hooks. In the remainder of the chapter, the prophet uses a repetitive list to show that although God has withheld food (4:6), rain (4:7–8), and crops (4:9), killed their young people (4:10), and overthrown their cities (4:11), they have refused to return to him. They are so stubborn that the consequences do not break their will to rebel, so God has become their enemy (4:12–13).

Words of Warning against Complacency

■ READ AMOS 5–6 ■

Amos begins this unit with a short obituary for Israel: the nation is fallen, never to rise again (5:1–3). Chapters 5 and 6 describe the coming judgment, interweaving a few important themes. First, Amos reminds them of what they can and must do to avoid judgment. If they seek YHWH, they will live (5:4, 6, 14). Second, he connects their punishment to what they have done to others: "Because you trample on the poor . . . , you have built houses of hewn stone, but you shall not dwell in them; you have planted pleasant vineyards, but you shall not drink their wine" (5:11). Third, a major part of the problem is that they are complacent in their relationship with God. They believe that because they are his covenant people, nothing bad will happen to them. They eagerly anticipate the day of YHWH, believing that it will be good news for them. But Amos warns them that while the day of YHWH *is* good news for the true people of God, for them it will be "darkness, and not light" (5:18, 20). It will be like fleeing from a lion only to run right into a bear (5:19).

Perhaps the people think they are keeping God happy with their worship habits. But God says that he hates and despises their feasts, assemblies, offerings, and songs (5:21–23). Why is that? Because their worship is accompanied by unfair taxes on the poor, corruption, and oppression of the vulnerable. God prefers "justice" (5:24).

"Let Justice Roll Down like Waters"

Martin Luther King Jr. quoted from Amos 5:24 in his famous address delivered at the March on Washington on August 28, 1963. The following is a portion of a transcript of this famous speech, including responses from the crowd, with the Amos quotation in bold:

> We can never be satisfied as long as our children are stripped of their selfhood and robbed of their dignity by signs stating "for whites only." [*applause*] (*Yes, Hallelujah*) We cannot be satisfied as long as a Negro in Mississippi cannot vote and a Negro in New York believes he has nothing for which to vote. (*Yeah, That's right, Let's go*) [*applause*] No, no, we are not satisfied and we will not be satisfied until *justice rolls down like waters* (*Yes*) and *righteousness like a mighty stream.* [*applause*][b]

With his powerful rhetoric and moving words, King used Amos 5:24 well, recognizing the importance that God places on justice for those who have been denied it.

Stephen's Sermon before Being Martyred

In Amos 5:25–27, the prophet accuses the people of failing to obey God by sacrificing in the wilderness after they came out of Egypt; they worshiped other gods instead. Since that time, they have learned nothing: they disobeyed then and they disobey now.[c] Many years later in Acts 7, Stephen has been accused of blasphemy by false witnesses in the Jewish council. Before he is martyred by stoning, he preaches a lengthy sermon demonstrating that the Jews have rejected Jesus Christ, making a case that from the beginning, Israel has rebelled against God's leaders. In Acts 7:42–43, Stephen quotes Amos 5:25–27 to show that Israel's early idolatry in the wilderness continued up to the time of the prophets and throughout their entire history.[d] Stephen traces a sustained pattern of disobedience and judgment up to his very own generation, enraging his Jewish accusers by highlighting their continuity with the disobedient generations Amos condemns.

A Modern Version of Amos 6:4–7

In an attempt to show the modern relevance of Amos's cries for justice, blogger Samantha Field has rewritten portions of the text with modern references. Below, the ESV translation of Amos 6:4–7 is on the left, and her modern update is on the right:[e]

Woe to those who lie on beds of ivory	You assemble your Ikea furniture
and stretch themselves out on their couches,	And lounge on Ethan Allen[.]
and eat lambs from the flock	You dine on lambs shipped from New Zealand
and calves from the midst of the stall,	And feast on veal and filet mignon.
who sing idle songs to the sound of the harp	Your hipsters strum away on their guitars, and you Christian-ize "Take me to Church" and "Hallelujah."
and like David invent for themselves instruments of music,	And wear T-shirts that parody Facebook and Coca-Cola for your pride.
who drink wine in bowls	Your youth groups chug gallons of milk for a contest,
and anoint themselves with the finest oils,	And you teach girls to obsess over "modest is hottest."
but are not grieved over the ruin of Joseph!	But you do not grieve over the black and brown children gunned down by police, And their sisters, handcuffed, who have to watch them die.
Therefore they shall now be the first of those who go into exile, and the revelry of those who stretch themselves out shall pass away.	Therefore you will go into exile: your lock-ins and potlucks will end.

Visions of Israel's Imminent Destruction

■ READ AMOS 7:1–8:3 ■

Amos has three successive visions of judgment. After his vision of locusts (7:1–3), he intercedes for Israel, and God relents. He intercedes again after a vision of fire (7:4–6), and once again God relents. However, in his third vision, he sees the Lord holding a plumb line, a tool consisting of a weight at the end of a string (7:7–9). If a builder stands in the middle of a crooked house, the walls may all look straight if they are *all* crooked because he has no way to get an objective perspective. But a plumb line always hangs straight and will give an objective assessment. In the same way, a culture or society can become so crooked with sin and evil that it looks normal and right. It becomes difficult to assess what is true if everyone is practicing falsehood. In Amos's vision, God holds the plumb line of his word, truth, and character in the midst of the people and finds that they are crooked. This time, Amos does not intercede, and God announces that they will be destroyed, like a wall that needs to be torn down (7:8).

Amos 7:10–17 contains the only narrative in the book. Because Amos is predicting the doom of the Northern Kingdom, Amaziah (the priest at Bethel) views Amos as a traitor and his words as a conspiracy against the king (7:10). He tells Amos to go back to Judah and prophesy there because this is the king's turf (7:13). However, because Amaziah has tried to silence the word of YHWH, Amos prophesies doom against him and his family (7:17).

Amos records a fourth vision in 8:1–3 that drives home the reversal of Israel's fortunes. His chosen rhetorical device is a play on words: the Hebrew word for "summer fruit" (*qayits*) (8:1) sounds very similar to the word for "end" (*qets*) (8:2). As in the vision of the plumb line, Amos does not intercede for Israel, and God does not relent.

A Vision of Israel's Ultimate Destruction

■ READ AMOS 8:4–9:10 ■

Following more descriptions of Israel's sin and injustice in 8:4–6, Amos again describes terrible judgment that is coming on Israel (8:7–9:10). YHWH is no longer content to send them into exile; he will hunt the people down and destroy them (9:4). Because he is the great God over all the earth, who can possibly escape from him (9:5–6)? Amos illustrates this with a sifting metaphor (9:9). An ancient farmer would use a sieve to separate the grain (which he wanted to keep) from other debris (which he wanted to remove) (see fig. 15.3). As he shook the sieve, the grain would fall through, and the pebbles and dirt would stay in the sieve to be thrown out.

The primary meaning of this metaphor is that it will be *impossible* for the wicked to escape judgment. God says, "No pebble shall fall to the earth" (9:9). In other words, no wicked person (a "pebble") who is sifted out for destruction will accidentally fall down with the good grain to be saved. But the metaphor also suggests that the righteous will be saved. God will separate them out from the wicked to be preserved. Amos tells how this can be accomplished in the final verses of the book. 📜

Figure 15.3. An ancient sieve from Amarna, Egypt

© Baker Publishing Group. Courtesy of the British Museum, London, England.

Restoration of Israel . . . and the Nations

■ READ AMOS 9:11–15 ■

After almost nine chapters of indictment and judgment, Amos finally comes to some good news in the last five verses of the book. In the context of all this darkness, they shine out like a spotlight: God has plans for mercy and salvation on the other side of judgment. In Amos's time, the line of David is not a great "house"; it is sad and decrepit like a rundown shack, but God will raise it up (9:11). It is through the line of David that God's plan of salvation will be offered to all nations (9:12). It is not the entire world that will be saved, but only those who are called by his name (9:12). In the eschatological, distant future, God will transform nature and restore the fortunes of his people, and they will never be uprooted again (9:13–15). 📜

CANONICAL CONNECTIONS

"I Will Never Forget Any of Their Deeds"

In Amos 8:7, God responds to the people's pride and unwillingness to address their sin. Therefore, he says, "Surely I will never forget any of their deeds." What a terrible thought! If God is holy, demanding absolute perfection, and he is omniscient, never forgetting the smallest sin, what hope is there for anyone? There is no hope of expunging sin. They cannot pay it off, and it will not disappear over time (perhaps like a traffic ticket falling off one's record). But there is hope. In Jeremiah 31:34, God says that when he establishes the new covenant, "I will forgive their iniquity, and *I will remember their sin no more.*" The author of Hebrews quotes from Jeremiah 31:34 and celebrates God's "forgetfulness," which has been accomplished by the finished work of Christ (Heb. 8:12; 10:17).

CANONICAL CONNECTIONS

Amos 9:11–12 quoted in Acts 15:15–18

Acts 15 records a debate in the early church concerning whether gentile believers in Jesus needed to become Jews—circumcised and obedient to the law of Moses—to be saved (15:5). When Paul and Barnabas come to Jerusalem, they report that God has given the Holy Spirit to gentiles just as he did to Jews and has cleansed their hearts by faith (15:8–9). The apostle James concludes that God has saved some gentiles for himself (15:14), and this was anticipated by the prophets (15:15). As proof, he quotes Amos 9:11–12. His wording is slightly different because he quotes from the Greek Septuagint version, but it has essentially the same meaning. His point is that the Davidic Messiah was *always* intended to bless the nations and incorporate them into the people of God. The early church is seeing Amos's proclamation happen before their eyes: gentiles are coming to faith in Christ. There is no need for them to become Jews first, because God's plan has always been to invite the whole "remnant of mankind" to seek him.[f]

Implementation

Amos's condemnation of Israel's sins is good news because it shows that there is a living God who cares about justice for the oppressed.[5] Justice is not just an ideal or social norm that develops in progressive societies; it is *God's* concern, rooted in his character, and an obligation in light of our relationship with him.

In order to apply Amos's words in our own context, we need to clarify a few things. First, we should note that Amos does not condemn wealth. Rather, he condemns the *wicked* wealthy who oppress the righteous poor. He condemns those who are envious, gluttonous, and corrupt. Prosperity through honest means is a gift from God to be valued, but luxurious excess at the expense of others is sinful.[6]

Second, in ancient Israel, wealth was dependent on the land, and there was only so much land available. Therefore, the balance between wealth and poverty was a zero-sum situation. If one person became rich and owned the land, another became poor. Today, Western free-market economies are not necessarily zero sum. A person can start a business or invent something and become incredibly wealthy without oppressing the poor. In fact, creating something new often provides well-paying jobs for many people, lifting them up as well. So we need to be careful not to draw a one-to-one correspondence between wealth and oppression.

Third, the ways that we use the word "justice" are affected by our political outlook. One author with a left-leaning view of economics defines justice as fair, equitable, and impartial treatment with access *to the same outcomes*.[7] But someone else who leans toward the free-market would focus on access *to the same opportunities*. As we discuss social justice, we must have charity toward those of different political persuasions, always seeking to test all ideas by Scripture and to reflect God's values in our complex economies and political realities.

Amos is concerned with injustice that arises from acts of "omission" (failing to help when a need is known) as well as "commission" (actively harming the poor or vulnerable). Exploiting others in any way is a great offense to God, and Christians should be the first to demand justice and ensure that every person is treated as he or she deserves. The New Testament is even more explicit about the relationship between the true worship of God and the ways that we treat other people. Jesus links together loving God and loving neighbor (Matt. 22:37–40). He goes right to the heart of ethnic stereotypes and class distinctions in his parable of the good Samaritan (Luke 10:25–37). James continues the connection between right worship and just deeds: "Religion that is pure and undefiled by God the Father is this: to visit orphans and widows in their affliction, and to keep oneself unstained from the world" (1:27). James also warns against treating people in our churches with partiality (2:1–13). The demand for justice is not the gospel, but it is *required* by the gospel because it is so important to God (2:14).

Christian Reading Questions

1. Why do you think the issue of "justice" is so important in our political and social conversation today? How does the book of Amos support contemporary discussions of justice? How does it challenge and adjust them?
2. Compare Amos 5:21–24 with Isaiah 1:10–17. They sound similar. How are they actually unique in their respective contexts?
3. The prophet Amos uses the fascinating image of a plumb line in 7:7–9. How does the book of Amos function as a plumb line in the crooked nation of Israel? What ideas, which seem so certain and undeniable, does it correct?

CHAPTER SIXTEEN

Obadiah

Orientation

The book of Obadiah is strange among the Prophets. It is the shortest book in the Old Testament, with only 388 words (in Hebrew) in 21 verses. That's about one page in a typical Bible. Not only that, but the book is not addressed to Israel but to Edom, a foreign nation that was a neighbor of Israel and Judah (v. 1). What relevance could this tiny book, concerned with a tiny, ancient nation, have for us today?

In 1917, a British poet named Siegfried L. Sassoon was serving as a soldier in World War I. He had already been wounded twice and was given orders to return to fight in the trenches. He refused and wrote a letter to his commanding officers, beginning, "I am making this statement as an act of willful defiance of military authority because I believe that the war is being deliberately prolonged by those who have the power to end it."[1] Sassoon's letter was circulated widely, published in newspapers, and even read aloud in the British House of Commons. Through this letter, which was read far more widely than he had intended, Sassoon's particular situation became a symbol of the terrible cost of the war as a whole. His statements to his commanding officers were relevant to soldiers everywhere, military families, politicians, and all of us who are interested in history.

Whereas Sassoon's letter was accidently circulated to a wider audience, the Old Testament prophets *intended* for their oracles against foreign nations to be read by Israel and Judah, as well as by God's people throughout time. Though Obadiah addresses a

HISTORICAL MATTERS

"Fact Sheet"—Obadiah

Author: Obadiah

Date: 586–553 BC

Location: Concerns the nation of Edom, a neighbor to the southeast of Judah

Political and social context: When the Babylonian army conquered Jerusalem after a two-year siege, they inflicted terrible destruction and suffering on the city. The Edomites, who descended from Esau, the brother of Israel, celebrated Judah's suffering and even participated in ransacking the city.

specific situation in ancient Edom, through this prophet God is revealing his character as well as his sovereign purposes for all nations.

The broader relevance of Obadiah is enhanced by the fact that Edom is regularly used in the Old Testament, and especially the Prophets, as a symbol of all nations who defy God and oppress his people. For example, in Isaiah 34:2 the prophet warns that YHWH is enraged against "all the nations" and then says next that his "sword . . . descends for judgment upon Edom" (Isa. 34:5). Similarly, in Amos 9:12 God says that he will raise up the booth of David "that they may possess the remnant of Edom and all the nations." Malachi 1:2–5 also uses Edom as a paradigm of God's sovereign judgment among all nations.

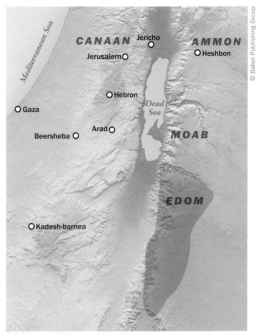

Map 16.1. The location of Edom

Edom's history with Israel goes back to the very beginning. We saw in chapter 2 that God had a particular family line in mind through which he would eventually bring about salvation for the world. He chooses Abraham out of all the people of the earth to be the father of his people and makes a covenant with him. Then he chooses Isaac rather than Ishmael (Abraham's son with his wife's servant Hagar). When Isaac has twin sons, God unexpectedly chooses the younger son, Jacob, rather than Esau. In Genesis 25:23, YHWH says to Rebekah, the mother of Jacob and Esau, "Two nations are in your womb, and two peoples from within you shall be divided; the one shall be stronger than the other, the older shall serve the younger." Jacob's name is later changed to "Israel," and as God foretold, he becomes the father of the twelve tribes and the line of God's Messiah. Esau becomes the father of the people of Edom, whose territory was southeast of Judah (see map 16.1). (The territory was later home to the builders of the famous ruins of Petra and is now part of the modern nation of Jordan.)

Just as Jacob and Esau clash from the time they are in the womb (Gen. 25:22), their descendants are hostile toward one another. When the Israelites travel from the wilderness to the promised land, the Edomites refuse them passage (Num. 20:14–21), but God instructs the Israelites not to fight (Deut. 2:1–8). King Saul fights against and defeats Edom (1 Sam. 14:47), as does King David (2 Sam. 8:11–14), and the Edomites revolt against King

Solomon (2 Kings 8:20). So there is a long history of animosity between the people of Israel and the people of Edom.

The greatest act of hostility between these estranged nations comes in 586 BC when the Babylonian army wages the final campaign against Judah. As the Babylonians attack the fortified cities of Judah, the Edomites refuse to support their neighbor and brother and instead attack Judean forts near their territory.[2] During the two-year Babylonian siege of Jerusalem, the people suffer terribly from starvation and disease. The book of Lamentations describes hunger so severe that mothers eat their own children (2:20). When the defenses are broken and the Babylonian soldiers pillage and destroy the city, one might expect the Edomites to assist their brother Judah in whatever way they can. Instead, they stand aloof, happy to see Judah fall, and even

TIME LINE

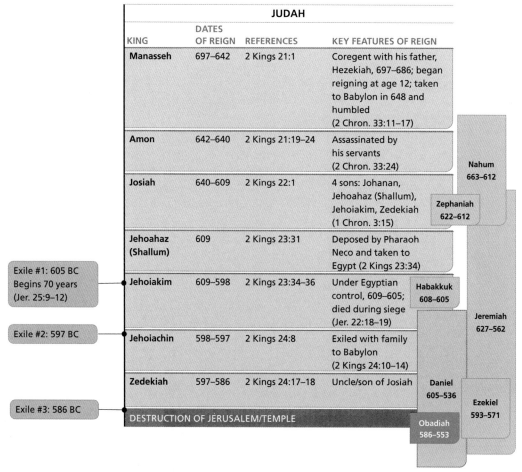

JUDAH			
KING	DATES OF REIGN	REFERENCES	KEY FEATURES OF REIGN
Manasseh	697–642	2 Kings 21:1	Coregent with his father, Hezekiah, 697–686; began reigning at age 12; taken to Babylon in 648 and humbled (2 Chron. 33:11–17)
Amon	642–640	2 Kings 21:19–24	Assassinated by his servants (2 Chron. 33:24)
Josiah	640–609	2 Kings 22:1	4 sons: Johanan, Jehoahaz (Shallum), Jehoiakim, Zedekiah (1 Chron. 3:15)
Jehoahaz (Shallum)	609	2 Kings 23:31	Deposed by Pharaoh Neco and taken to Egypt (2 Kings 23:34)
Jehoiakim	609–598	2 Kings 23:34–36	Under Egyptian control, 609–605; died during siege (Jer. 22:18–19)
Jehoiachin	598–597	2 Kings 24:8	Exiled with family to Babylon (2 Kings 24:10–14)
Zedekiah	597–586	2 Kings 24:17–18	Uncle/son of Josiah
DESTRUCTION OF JERUSALEM/TEMPLE			

Nahum
663–612

Zephaniah
622–612

Habakkuk
608–605

Jeremiah
627–562

Daniel
605–536

Ezekiel
593–571

Obadiah
586–553

Exile #1: 605 BC Begins 70 years (Jer. 25:9–12)

Exile #2: 597 BC

Exile #3: 586 BC

participate in the looting. Psalm 137:7 describes the Edomites as cheering on the Babylonians, shouting, "Lay it bare, lay it bare, down to its foundations!" Other passages also describe Edom taking advantage of Judah's situation to take revenge on them for past conflicts (see Lam. 4:21–22; Ezek. 25:12–14).

Though we are not given any explicit historical context in the book of Obadiah, it is this event that is apparently the background of the prophet's message. In verses 11–14, Obadiah indicts Edom for not only refusing to support Jerusalem when an enemy army attacked but also participating in that attack. While some scholars have suggested that Obadiah refers to an event in the preexilic period[3] or to the late postexilic period,[4] the most likely possibility is that the Babylonian conquest of Jerusalem in 586 BC is in view.[5] 🕐

Exploration

The book of Obadiah is structured to make a connection between specific historical events (vv. 1–14) and God's judgment and salvation in the distant, eschatological future (vv. 15–21). The prophet describes the sins of Edom in the past in **verses 1–4**, followed by an announcement of judgment on Edom in the near future (**vv. 5–10**). In **verses 11–14**, he goes back to the past once again to further indict Edom for the specific ways that it exploited Judah on the day of Judah's judgment. It is important to keep in mind that the Babylonian conquest of Jerusalem was God's intentional judgment on Judah for breaking covenant. Yet Edom took advantage of the situation to take revenge, and for that they are condemned. In **verses 15–21**, the prophet moves to the distant, eschatological future. First, he announces judgment on all nations (patterned on Edom), and then restoration for God's people in YHWH's kingdom. As we will see below, the word "day" is a key word in

Table 16.1. The Structure of Obadiah

Superscription	Past Accusation	Judgment in the Near Future	Eschatological Judgment in the Distant Future	Eschatological Restoration
v. 1a "The vision of Obadiah"	vv. 1b–4 Indictment of Edom: pride	vv. 5–10 Judgment for Edom		
	vv. 11–14 Indictment of Edom: Judah's "day" in history		vv. 15–18 Judgment for the nations: a "day" in the future	vv. 19–21 YHWH's kingdom

Figure 16.1. The mountains of Seir in Edom

the book. Judah's historical "day" (and Edom's involvement in it) becomes a pattern for the ultimate day of YHWH. Thus, Obadiah addresses four of the five phases in God's plan of redemption (see fig. 16.2).

Indictment and Judgment for Edom

■ READ OBADIAH 1–10 ■

The land of Edom was situated in a dry wilderness that made agriculture somewhat challenging. However, the mountainous terrain meant that it was highly defensible. As the book of Obadiah begins, the prophet critiques Edom for their prideful belief that they are untouchable: "The pride of your heart has deceived you, you who live in the clefts of the rock, in your lofty dwelling, who say in your heart, 'Who will bring me down to the ground?'" (v. 3). God's answer is, "From there I will bring you down" (v. 4).

Obadiah views the coming destruction as an already-completed event—a done deal. "Esau has been pillaged" (v. 6). "Your allies have driven you to your border; [they] have deceived you" (v. 7). Ironically, this is exactly what

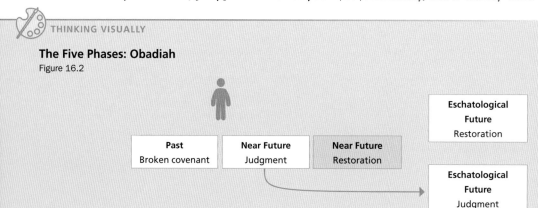

THINKING VISUALLY

The Five Phases: Obadiah
Figure 16.2

Edom did to Judah (vv. 11–14)! Though the ultimate "day of the LORD" lies in the future, Edom will receive a preview in the near future. God says in verse 8, "Will I not on that day . . . destroy the wise men out of Edom, and understanding out of Mount Esau?" A reckoning is coming for Edom, and no military defenses or "wisdom" can avert it.

Indictment: Judah's "Day" in History

▓ READ OBADIAH 11–14 ▓

It was God who brought the Babylonian army against Judah and Jerusalem, as judgment for violating his covenant and rebelling against him. It was the ultimate covenant curse, promised in Deuteronomy 28. If the "day

---

CANONICAL CONNECTIONS

Obadiah and Jeremiah

In Jeremiah's "oracles against the nations," he addresses Edom in a lengthy section (49:7–22). Interestingly, the first six verses of Jeremiah contain wording very similar to Obadiah 1–8. The following table aligns the two passages, with similar wording in **bold**.

Jeremiah 49:14–16	Obadiah 1–4
I have heard a message from the LORD, and an envoy has been sent among the nations: "Gather yourselves together and come against her, **and rise up for battle!** For **behold, I will make you small among the nations, despised** among mankind. The horror you inspire has deceived you, and the **pride of your heart, you who live in the clefts of the rock,** who hold the height of the hill. Though you make **your nest** as high **as the eagle's, I will bring you down from there, declares the LORD.**	Thus says the Lord GOD concerning Edom: **We have heard a report from the LORD, and a messenger has been sent among the nations:** "Rise up! Let us **rise against her for battle!**" **Behold, I will make you small among the nations; you shall be utterly despised. The pride of your heart** has deceived you, **you who live in the clefts of the rock,** in your lofty dwelling, who say in your heart, "Who will bring me down to the ground?" Though you soar aloft **like the eagle,** though **your nest** is set among the stars, **from there I will bring you down, declares the LORD.**
Jeremiah 49:9–10	Obadiah 5–6
If grape gatherers came to you, would they not leave gleanings? **If thieves came by night,** would they not **destroy** only enough for themselves? But I have stripped **Esau** bare; I have uncovered his hiding places, and he is not able to conceal himself. His children are destroyed, and his brothers, and his neighbors; and he is no more.	If thieves **came to you,** if plunderers **came by** night—how you have been **destroyed!**— would they not steal only enough for themselves? **If grape gatherers came to you, would they not leave gleanings?** How **Esau** has been pillaged, his treasures sought out!
Jeremiah 49:7	Obadiah 8
Concerning Edom. Thus says **the LORD** of hosts: "Is **wisdom** no more in Teman? Has counsel perished from the prudent? Has their wisdom vanished?	Will I not on that day, declares **the LORD,** destroy the **wise** men out of Edom, and understanding out of Mount Esau?

It is likely that Jeremiah borrowed from Obadiah, even though Obadiah addressed the time period at the very end of Jeremiah's prophetic ministry. First, Jeremiah has a tendency to borrow from earlier books. Second, Obadiah seems to be a more unified speech, whereas the wording in Jeremiah is more scattered.[a]

of the LORD" is the ultimate time of judgment, then Judah was experiencing a preliminary "day" of judgment. God says that this was the "day" that strangers carried off Judah's wealth (v. 11), the "day" of his misfortune (v. 12), the "day" of his calamity (v. 13), and the "day" of his distress (v. 14). However, whereas Edom might have shown compassion on Judah because Judah was experiencing judgment and great suffering, instead they piled on with increasing directness. They gloated (v. 12), they entered the gates of Jerusalem (v. 13a), they looted the wealth of the city (v. 13b), and then they cut off Judah's survivors and prevented them from escaping (v. 14). Throughout this section, the prophet is describing events that have already taken place, but he speaks as if he is watching the events unfold in real time.[6] He says, "Do not gloat . . . ; do not rejoice. . . . Do not enter. . . . Do not stand at the crossroads." This heightens the sense of their guilt; it is as though he is shouting to them from the sidelines of history, "No! Don't do it! You'll regret this."

Eschatological Judgment in the Distant Future

■ READ OBADIAH 15–18 ■

In verse 15, Obadiah says, "For the day of the LORD is near upon all the nations." This is a pivot from a "day" in the past to the distant, eschatological future. It is also a transition from condemnation and judgment on Edom in particular to judgment on all nations who have defied God. Table 16.2 shows each occurrence of the word "day" in Obadiah and gives an idea of how the prophet is encouraging us to view the eschatological day of YHWH through the lens of God's actions in the past.

Table 16.2. The Word "Day" in Obadiah

Verse	Occurrence of "day"	Time
8	"Will I not on that **day** . . . destroy . . . Edom?"	Future
11	"on the **day** that you stood aloof"	Past
11	"on the **day** that strangers carried off his wealth"	Past
12	"the **day** of your brother"	Past
12	"the **day** of his misfortune"	Past
12	"in the **day** of their ruin"	Past
12	"in the **day** of distress"	Past
13	"in the **day** of their calamity"	Past
13	"in the **day** of his calamity"	Past
13	"in the **day** of his calamity"	Past
14	"in the **day** of distress"	Past
15	"for the **day** of the LORD is near"	Future

Obadiah continues, "As you [singular] have done, it shall be done to you" (v. 15). In other words, just as Edom helped destroy Jerusalem, Edom itself will be destroyed. One scholar rewrites this sentence as, "If you wish to know what to expect, remember exactly what you did to the Judeans!"[7] In verse 16, the prophet switches to the plural "you" and says, "For as you have drunk on my holy mountain, so all the nations shall drink continually." Here he is speaking to the people of Jerusalem. The image of drinking is used elsewhere in the Old Testament to denote receiving judgment. Just as Jerusalem has experienced judgment, all nations will experience judgment in the great day of YHWH.

Verses 17–18 predict that the people of Israel will ultimately emerge victorious over Edom in the sibling rivalry, according to God's sovereign choice. Mount Zion will be the epicenter of God's redemptive work.

Eschatological Restoration in the Distant Future

■ READ OBADIAH 19–21 ■

God's people had previously lost their land to various oppressors, but in his description of God's final restoration, Obadiah repeats the word

CANONICAL CONNECTIONS

"The Day of the LORD upon All Nations"

Obadiah's important emphasis on the nations is shared with Joel and Amos. In the following table, the text is aligned with color coding to show the common wording.

Amos 9:12	Obadiah 15	Joel 2:32
. . . that they may possess the remnant of Edom and all the nations who are called by my name, . . .	For the day of the LORD is near upon all the nations.	For in Mount Zion and in Jerusalem there shall be those who escape, as the LORD has said, . . .
	Obad. 17	**Joel 3:2**
	But in Mount Zion there shall be those who escape, . . .	I will gather all the nations and bring them down to the Valley of Jehoshaphat.
	Obad. 19–20	**Joel 3:14**
	Those of the Negeb shall possess Mount Esau, and those of the Shephelah shall possess the land of the Philistines; they shall possess the land of Ephraim and the land of Samaria, and Benjamin shall possess Gilead. The exiles of this host of the people of Israel shall possess the land of the Canaanites as far as Zarephath, and the exiles of Jerusalem who are in Sepharad shall possess the cities of the Negeb.	For the day of the LORD is near in the valley of decision.

It may be that Obadiah borrowed the key word "possess" from Amos, who lived about two hundred years previously. Joel likely came later than Obadiah and perhaps borrowed from Obadiah 15 and 17 (but in reverse order). This shared wording is one example of the thematic and theological connections between the twelve Minor Prophets.

Mount Zion

Like other Old Testament prophets, Obadiah identifies "Mount Zion," a reference to the temple mount in Jerusalem, as the place where God will save his people. The New Testament picks up this motif from the Prophets. In Romans 11:26, Paul quotes Isaiah 59:20: "The Deliverer will come from Zion." First Peter 2:6 quotes Isaiah 28:16: "Behold, I am laying in Zion a stone, a cornerstone . . . , and whoever believes in him will not be put to shame." (Peter identifies that "stone" as Christ.) The author of Hebrews calls Zion "the city of the living God, the heavenly Jerusalem" (12:22), and John says in Revelation 14:1, "Then I looked, and behold, on Mount Zion stood the Lamb, and with him 144,000 who had his name and his Father's name written on their foreheads." Mount Zion is the image of God's victory over sin and evil, and it is the place of safety for his people.

Edomites among the People of God? A "Twist" Ending

Obadiah's prophecy of the destruction of Edom was at least partially fulfilled in 553 BC when the nation was conquered by the Babylonians. The irony is thick: the Edomites had celebrated the Babylonians' victory over Jerusalem, and now they were conquered by that same nation. But later, when Arabs encroached on formerly Edomite territory from the east, the descendants of Edom who remained moved toward Israelite territory and their new territory became known as Idumea. They were absorbed into the Jewish nation and lost their own national identity. However, eventually, these people of Esau/Edom encountered Jesus Christ in his earthly ministry and some were saved (see Mark 3:7–8).[b] Although God had not chosen Esau to continue his covenant and promised line, and although Edom was under judgment, God showed his mercy in the end.

"possess" six times to show that all of the promised land will be returned—from Samaria in the north to the Negeb wilderness in the south, with Mount Zion at the center. This land is symbolic of the permanent home that God will give to his people when their oppressors are finally destroyed once and for all. We might call verse 21 "a tale of two mountains." On the one hand is "Mount Esau," which represents the nations hostile to God. It will be ruled by "Mount Zion," the place of God's salvation and the home of his people.

Implementation

Obadiah uses the specific historical situation of Edom's crimes against Judah as a means of talking about ultimate realities that apply to God's people everywhere and throughout time. The structure of the book sets up the comparison between past and future, and Obadiah explicitly invites us to consider the future on the basis of what God has done in the past (see v. 15). In this way, Edom becomes a symbol for all enemies of God who are rejected because of their rebellion and oppression of God's people, and Judah becomes a symbol for the true people of God. We are not simply *reading* Edom and Judah as symbols of broader realities; Obadiah *intends* them as symbols. In the past, Edom exalted themselves. But in the future, Edom (and all nations) will fall. In the past, God's people were humiliated and exploited. But in the future, they will be exalted and delivered.

Interestingly, the book does not call Edom to repentance, nor does it offer any hope for Edom or the nations in the near future. It functions as an "open letter" intended for God's people, to bring them encouragement and hope. As Christians who serve the living God, we see at least three reasons for hope in this book. First, Obadiah teaches us that God is sovereign—not only over the affairs of Israel, not only over the affairs of the region around Palestine, but over all of history. His people were small and seemingly defenseless against a powerful Babylonian army. How could they ever be avenged? Edom was known for a strong defense in the rocks. Who could ever bring them down? But there is a living God who has complete control over great nations and small peoples. He ensures that what is right will eventually come to pass. Obadiah warns us not to let our own achievements in science, technology, education, military power, or anything else make us proud. No nation can stand before God.

Second, though God's people are oppressed now, we can look forward to relief in the future. We are presently scattered across the world: some of us live in free nations while some of us suffer under oppressive regimes. But when God puts down his enemies, there will be no more humiliation, and we will be invited into God's good land in the new heavens and the new earth. One scholar writes of the book of Obadiah, "The church can be assured that, however much she is made to suffer by her enemies, she will never be completely abandoned. The Lord will bring judgment on those who mistreat the church, the bride of Christ."[8] Another writes, "The Christian, therefore, will see in Obadiah's prophecy . . . [the] hope of God's intervention on behalf of his people to rescue them from helplessness in the face of mortal danger, and to guarantee them a bright future of reward for their faithfulness (1 Pet. 4:12–14). The success of early powers arrayed against God's purposes can only be temporary, and the ultimate victory of God's people is assured."[9]

Finally, Obadiah is clear that rebellion against God is futile and hopeless, but God is merciful. There is no way to "beat" God; one can only join him on the terms he sets. When Judah broke the covenant, God brought the Babylonians. When Edom broke faith with Judah, God destroyed that nation. But God will preserve a people for himself who will be victorious and

THINKING VISUALLY

Hope for God's Salvation at the End of Time
Figure 16.3

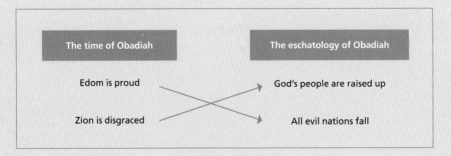

The time of Obadiah — The eschatology of Obadiah

Edom is proud — God's people are raised up

Zion is disgraced — All evil nations fall

exalted. What makes them so special? Why should they inherit the land and live under God's good rule while others are ruined and shattered? It is only because they have accepted God's gift of mercy through the finished work of Jesus Christ. He calls his people from the kingdom of darkness into a kingdom of light (Col. 1:12–14; 1 Pet. 2:9). Though God will destroy Edom and *all* wicked nations, he is reconciling the world to himself—from *all* nations, *all* those who would submit to the lordship of Christ and follow him in faith.

Christian Reading Questions

1. The background of the book of Genesis is crucial for understanding the book of Obadiah because Obadiah is based on the relationship between Jacob and Esau. Can you think of ways that the theology and stories of Genesis have formed a background to other Old Testament Prophets that we have studied thus far (Isaiah–Amos)?
2. How does Edom's sin of pride (v. 3) influence all of its other sins in the book? How does the conclusion to the book relate to Edom's (and the world's) pride?
3. In your own words, describe how Obadiah uses events in his own time period in order to communicate effectively about the eschatological future. What other prophetic books use a similar strategy?

CHAPTER SEVENTEEN

Jonah

Orientation

Christopher Watts was cheating on his wife. He had tried to cover up the extramarital affair, but early one morning in August 2018 when his pregnant wife returned home from a business trip, they got into an argument. In the end, Christopher strangled his wife to death. Because his two young daughters saw what had happened, he smothered them to death and hid all three bodies at the company where he worked. Two days later, he was arrested for the murders of his wife, daughters, and unborn child, and he was eventually sentenced to five life sentences without the possibility of parole.[1]

But the story doesn't end there. In 2019, Christopher Watts was interviewed at the federal prison where he is serving out his sentence. He said that he has found a relationship with God and has experienced God's amazing grace. Now he reads the Bible frequently and sends passages of Scripture to his parents. What a wonderful testimony of God's mercy!

This kind of transformation raises questions for us: Does this mean that God has forgiven Christopher of these horrific crimes? He will live and die in prison, but what about God's justice? An elementary school teacher named Stephanie called in to a popular Christian podcast and said: "After following the news closely, back when [Christopher Watts] was originally suspected of this heinous crime, my reaction to his so-called finding God was *anger*. Is it wrong for me to not want this man, who committed unspeakable acts, to know *my Jesus*? Do you believe *someone like him* can truly repent and enter the kingdom of God?" The podcast host responded, "God is free to be gracious to whom he will be gracious. . . . This means that an entire lifetime of sinning and stealing from others, and probably worse, can be forgiven one hour before you die."[2]

Stephanie's struggle is a real one. We love grace when it is given to us. We love to sing about "amazing grace" and "grace that is greater than all our sin." But grace also means that people who have done *terrible* things to others are forgiven instead of facing justice. It means that God's anger toward the worst sins evaporates when someone repents. If we really understand grace, it becomes something of a problem. This "problem" of grace is explored in the book of Jonah.

The book of Jonah begins without a superscription—no background or date or information about the author. This book is unlike other prophetic books; it is mostly narrative, with one poetic prayer and one short, five-word prophetic oracle (3:4). In most prophetic books, a faithful prophet represents God to a sinful nation. The book of Jonah is about an *unfaithful* prophet interacting with unbelievers who relate with God *better* than he does. He represents Israel—and all of us—and gives us an opportunity to confront our own twisted attitudes and perspectives.

 TIME LINE

ISRAEL			
KING	DATES OF REIGN	REFERENCES	KEY FEATURES OF REIGN
Jeroboam II	793–753	2 Kings 14:23	Coregent with Jehoash, 793–782
Zechariah	753–752	2 Kings 15:8	Assassinated by Shallum (2 Kings 15:10)
Shallum	752	2 Kings 15:13	Assassinated by Menahem (2 Kings 15:14)
Menahem	752–742	2 Kings 15:17	Made an alliance with Pul, king of Assyria (2 Kings 15:19–20)
Pekahiah	742–740	2 Kings 15:23	Assassinated by Pekah (2 Kings 15:25)
Pekah	752–732	2 Kings 15:27	Reigned in Gilead, 752–740, overlapping with Menahem; reigned over united Israel, 740–732; assassinated by Hoshea (2 Kings 15:30)
Hoshea	732–722	2 Kings 15:30; 17:1	Appointed by Tiglath-pileser III

Amos
767–753

Jonah
792–753

Hosea
755–725

Outside the book of Jonah, there is one reference to a prophet named Jonah, son of Amittai; he served God during the reign of Jeroboam II (2 Kings 14:25). If this is the same individual, which seems likely, then the story takes place in the middle of the eighth century BC and Jonah was likely the earliest prophet for whom we have a prophetic book (see the time line of Jonah).

The story of Jonah is very concise, highly literary, and not generally concerned with historical specifics. However, it is important to understand one aspect of the historical background that is assumed by the author. The Assyrian Empire (and Nineveh, one of its major cities and later the capital) had a reputation for military conquest, barbarism, and cruelty. King Assurnasirpal II, who reigned about a hundred years before Jonah, boasts of skinning his victims, erecting them on stakes, and draping their skins over the city walls.[3] He writes of his enemies, "I burned many captives from them. I captured many troops alive: I cut off of some of their arms (and) hands; I cut off of others their noses, ears, (and) extremities. I gouged out the eyes of many troops. . . . I hung their heads on trees around the city. I burnt their adolescent boys (and) girls. I razed, destroyed, burnt (and) consumed the city."[4]

King Shalmaneser III (about seventy-five years before Jonah) commissioned a bronze relief for his palace. It depicts a captive with his hands and feet amputated, another captive impaled on a stake, and heads placed on stakes around the city walls (see fig. 17.1). It was to Nineveh, in Assyria, that God called Jonah. Jonah's reluctance to proclaim God's word to this city and Jonah's reason for his reluctance are the key to the book.

Does the lack of historical details in the book of Jonah mean that it is fiction? Many scholars think so, stating that it is like a parable: the events did not happen, but the lesson is true. Proponents of this view cite the facts that only Jonah is named in the book and the book includes sensational details such as a fish swallowing a man, animals fasting in sackcloth, and a plant that grows in one day.

"Fact Sheet"—Jonah

Author: Unknown

Date: 792–753 BC

Locations: Jonah's journey takes him from the Northern Kingdom to a ship on the Mediterranean Sea and then to Nineveh, a great city in the Assyrian Empire.

Political and social context: The Assyrians had a reputation not only for wickedness and brutality in general but for the oppression of God's people in Israel. As a great military "superpower," the empire was feared across the ancient Near East. God called Jonah to go to Nineveh and speak against it for its evil.

Figure 17.1. Bronze relief from the palace of Shalmaneser III (852 BC)

© Baker Publishing Group

In my view, however, the book of Jonah is historical narrative. There is no formal indication that it is fiction; it simply tells a story like other parts of Scripture. Jonah being swallowed whole by a fish is no more ridiculous than food falling from the sky (Exod. 16), a talking donkey (Num. 22), or city walls that fall down of their own accord (Josh. 6). Sometimes God acts in human history with miraculous intervention. In the New Testament, Jesus makes a point that depends on the historicity of Jonah, stating that "the men of Nineveh will rise up at the judgment with this generation and condemn it, for they repented at the preaching of Jonah" (Matt. 12:41). Jesus is not merely referring to a story (i.e., a legend); he says that the men of Nineveh *will* rise up in the future. In the same way as other biblical books, the book of Jonah presents history in a highly selective and vivid way to make a powerful theological point. It not only presents the kind of thing God might do; it presents what God *did* do in the past.

Exploration

Typically, at this point we would discuss what aspects (or phases) of redemptive history Jonah addresses. These are not applicable to the book of Jonah because it does not have typical prophetic oracles.

The macrostructure of the book can be seen in table 17.1. This structure highlights the correspondences between different parts of the narrative. There are two main events; the correspondences between the two events and Jonah's reaction to each one can be seen in the vertical columns. In **chapter 1**, Jonah is on a ship, running away from the task that God has given him to do. God sends a storm to capsize the boat and kill him, and the sailors on the boat are likely to be killed as well. But the sailors learn who God is and turn to him in faith. At Jonah's request, they throw him overboard, and the storm stops. But the story does not end there: Jonah is swallowed by a huge fish. Jonah's experience with the fish in **chapter 2** is his response to the events in chapter 1. He is delighted that God has shown him mercy, but his words are ironic and inappropriate in light of the sailors' faith in God and the fact that God delivered them as well.

Table 17.1. The Structure of Jonah

Jonah's Call	Event	Jonah's Response
Call to go to Nineveh (1:1–2)	"Sinful" sailors are delivered from death (1:3–16)	Jonah is thankful that he is shown mercy (2:1–10)
Call to go to Nineveh (3:1–2)	"Sinful" Ninevites are delivered from death (3:3–10)	Jonah is angry that the Ninevites are shown mercy (4:1–11)

In **chapter 3**, Jonah announces that the city of Nineveh will be over-thrown in forty days. The Ninevites repent zealously, and God changes his mind. **Chapter 4** relates Jonah's response to the events in chapter 3. Jonah is furious that God has shown the Ninevites mercy. They deserved to die for their wickedness! Jonah's words are ironic and inappropriate again, this time in light of the mercy that God has shown *him*.

Sinful Sailors Are Delivered from Death

■ READ JONAH 1 ■

The book opens with God's call to Jonah. He instructs him to travel to Nineveh, a massive, important Assyrian city to the east of Israel. Their evil has come up before God, and he wants Jonah to "call out against it" (1:2). This sounds like a typical prophetic call, and we expect Jonah to obey be-cause that's what God's prophets do. It is a great surprise, then, when Jonah gets up and makes a run for it! Rather than traveling east to Nineveh, he heads west to the port city of Joppa on the Mediterranean coast and finds a ship heading to Tarshish (1:3) (see map17.1). The location of ancient Tarsh-ish is uncertain, but it was likely in the region of modern-day Spain, the *op-posite* direction from Nineveh and the farthest point in the known world. In other words, Jonah is trying to go as far from Nineveh as he possibly can.

Why does Jonah refuse to go to Nineveh? The narrator does not tell us. We might guess that he is deterred by the great distance to Nineveh (six hundred miles or thirty days of walking), except that Jonah is willing to go even farther, to Tarshish. Is it because of Nineveh's reputation for violence?

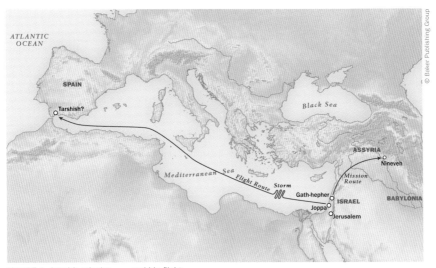

Map 17.1. Jonah's mission . . . and his flight

Is Jonah afraid that he will be persecuted and killed for condemning their sins? The problem with this guess is that Jonah is ready to die rather than go to Nineveh later in chapter 1. No, Jonah runs for an entirely different reason—but we do not learn his true motive until the climax of the story in chapter 4.

Once Jonah is on the ship and out to sea, God sends a great storm that threatens to capsize the ship. Jonah (the prophet of God) and the sailors on the ship (who do not believe in God) respond very differently. The sailors frantically call on their gods for help and try to save the ship, but Jonah is *asleep* (1:5). This shows that he does not care if he or the sailors live or die. The captain (leader of the pagans!) rebukes Jonah (God's prophet!) for not calling on his God (1:6). The sailors, who do not want to die, desperately try to find the cause of the storm. They cast lots to identify the one responsible, and the lots indicate Jonah. However, as they interrogate him, Jonah hesitates to speak and does not volunteer information (1:8–10). Finally, preferring to die rather than go to Nineveh, Jonah recommends that they throw him overboard to certain death. The sailors—who by now are shown to be good men—care about Jonah's life and do not want to kill him, but they finally throw him overboard, and the storm ends abruptly (1:14–15). Realizing that Jonah's God is the true God, they offer sacrifices and vows to him. They have come to faith in the God of Israel (1:16). 📖

Poor Jonah! He is trying to run away from serving God, but even on the journey—and apparently against his will—God uses him to draw unbelievers to himself. The sailors want to be saved, and God has mercy on them. But God reveals his mercy not through Jonah the prophet but in spite of him. God wants to show mercy to these unbelievers, and not even Jonah's rebellion will stop him from doing so.

Jonah Is Thankful That He Is Shown Mercy

■ READ JONAH 2 ■

As chapter 1 ends, we assume that Jonah is dead—How could he not be? He has been thrown into the ocean. In addition, God has stopped the storm (1:15), indicating that his anger at Jonah has been satisfied. However, Jonah is *not* dead. God appoints a large fish to swallow him (1:17). We may be fixated on how disgusting it would be to lie in a fish's digestive track and consider this to be a punishment. However, the fish is God's way of saving

LITERARY NOTES

"Fear" and Fearing God

The word "fear" is repeated several times in Jonah 1 and is an important key to the narrative. In the beginning, the sailors "fear" the storm, but Jonah does not (because he wishes to die; 1:5). In 1:9, Jonah identifies himself as a "fearer" of YHWH. He means that he is a follower of YHWH, identified by faith in him. But this is ironic because he is currently disobeying God! In 1:10, the sailors "fear" when they understand the connection between Jonah's disobedience and the storm, realizing that Jonah's God is the creator of heaven, earth, and sea. Finally, in 1:16, the sailors "fear" YHWH himself, which leads to worship and vows to follow him in the future. Jonah, the bad prophet, has been killed for disobedience (so we think), while the unbelieving sailors have become "fearers" of the Lord!

Jonah's life; it is a lifeboat that saves him from drowning.

Chapter 2 is Jonah's prayer of thanksgiving to God. He was sinking into the depths, surrounded by waves (2:3) and seaweed (2:5), but God saved him (2:6). Jonah's conclusion is that "salvation belongs to the Lord!" (2:9). This prayer sounds great at first glance, as though Jonah has learned his lesson. But on closer inspection, some of his words are deeply inappropriate, given the context in chapter 1. He says in 2:3, "You [God] cast me into the deep." But God did not cast him anywhere; he ended up in the ocean because he was rebelling against God's word! He says in 2:4, "I am driven away from your sight." But why does he use the passive sense of the verb (implying that someone else drove him away) when he was the one who ran? Jonah prayed to YHWH when he was fainting away (2:7), but why didn't he pray and repent when he was still on the ship? Finally, in 2:8 Jonah complains about "those who pay regard to vain idols." But in chapter 1, it is the idol-worshiping sailors who show greater faith and obedience than he does. One scholar says, "These are the right words coming out of the wrong mouth."[5]

This is not a prayer of repentance. Jonah is thankful that God has shown him mercy and kept him alive, but his words—juxtaposed to chapter 1— show that he is just as narrow and stubborn as before. As if in response to Jonah's prayer, the fish "vomits" him out on dry land, back on the coast of Israel (2:10). The word "vomit" is often used in the Old Testament to refer to the promised land vomiting out the Israelites when they rebel against God; this may be a poignant play on words.

Sinful Ninevites Are Delivered from Death

■ READ JONAH 3 ■

In 3:1–2, God repeats his command to Jonah to go to Nineveh (see 1:1–2). This time, Jonah obeys. However, we will see in chapter 4 that he

Jonah and the Whale by Pieter Lastman

Pieter Lastman played an important role in the development of Dutch painting and was Rembrandt's teacher. His painting *Jonah and the Whale* captures the moment when Jonah is spewed out of the fish after having been inside it for three days and three nights. The work seeks to capture the crucial turning point when Jonah recognizes the power of God but has not yet reached the safety of land. Lastman foregrounds Jonah, twisted and nude.[a]

Figure 17.2. *Jonah and the Whale* by Pieter Lastman

Public Domain / Wikimedia Commons

foreign people) repented quickly. By contrast, Jesus is the ultimate prophet and Son of God, who performs miracles! And yet his listeners from the covenant people of Israel refuse to believe.[6] The book of Jonah forces us to confront our own narrow-minded conceptions of grace. It is good for us, yes. But is it also intended for people (gasp!—even foreigners?) who are *really* bad?

Why is God so intent on forgiving even the worst of us? Jonah knows the right answer: it is because God is "gracious . . . and merciful, slow to anger and abounding in steadfast love, and relenting from disaster" (4:2). And this grace and mercy are ultimately demonstrated in the death of Christ, when God forgives a world of bad people at great cost to himself. Paul says in Romans 5:8, "But God shows his love for us in that while we were still sinners, Christ died for us." A few verses later, he acknowledges that grace is strong enough for even the worst sin. For "where sin increased, grace abounded all the more" (5:20).

In some ways, it is only when we acknowledge the "problem" of grace and wrestle with its full implications that we understand it fully. God's grace means that evil people are forgiven and do not experience judgment. It means that an innocent man, Jesus Christ, pays a terrible penalty for sins that he did not commit. It means that our enemies escape God's wrath if they turn to him. All of this seems unjust and wrong when we count ourselves among the deserving. But we are overcome with thankfulness for this mercy when we realize that *we* were his enemies, and yet he welcomes us into his family through Christ.

Christian Reading Questions

1. Give specific examples of how the author of the book of Jonah depicts the sailors (chap. 1) so that we identify with them and hope the best for them. What is the purpose of this literary strategy?

2. Have you, or has someone close to you, struggled over the problem of God's mercy? Do you think the author of the book of Jonah wants us to relate to Jonah's struggles with God or reject them? Or both?

3. Is God's mercy a violation of his justice? How does the gospel of Jesus Christ inform our thinking on that question? Read 2 Corinthians 5:1–15 and find other New Testament passages that relate to this question.

4. In chapter 4, Jonah tells God twice that he wishes he were dead. What has provoked such a strong reaction in Jonah? Can you think of ways that Jonah's statements relate to the themes of the book?

CHAPTER EIGHTEEN

Micah

Orientation

In our day, a *contract* is a legally binding agreement between two parties. I might have a contract with my internet service provider, my landlord, or my insurance agent in which we both promise to carry out certain obligations over a set amount of time. These contracts have significant financial and social implications. Therefore, we cannot simply agree to the terms with a fist bump or a thumbs-up emoji in a text message. We must sign a formal agreement that will hold up in court so that both parties are protected.

Ancient Near Eastern covenants were similar to our contracts in that they involved concrete obligations for the two parties. As with contracts, the stakes were significant. And like contracts, covenants could also end up in "court" in order to prove that one party had failed to meet the obligations and to announce the consequences. Archaeologists and historians have found examples of literary documents called "covenant lawsuits" that function in this way. They follow the same literary pattern as the original covenant agreement, but they show that the agreement was broken and what will happen as a result.

We have seen in previous chapters that one of the major roles of God's prophets is to serve as "covenant prosecutors" who indict God's people for breaking their special covenant relationship with him. Not only did God pattern his relationship with Israel after an ancient Near Eastern covenant, but his prophets used

HISTORICAL MATTERS

"Fact Sheet"—Micah

Author: Micah

Date: 742–686 BC

Location(s): Micah lived and ministered in the Southern Kingdom, but he addresses both Israel and Judah.

Political and social context: Micah prophesied at a pivotal time in the history of Israel and Judah. He experienced the defeat of the Northern Kingdom as well as an intense Assyrian attack on Jerusalem and God's miraculous protection of the city. His book describes rampant injustice and violence in Israel and Judah, the exploitation of the weak, and the worship of idols. He announces imminent destruction but also salvation for those who are faithful to the Lord.

Map 18.1. The location of Moresheth-gath, Micah's hometown

the literary form of the "covenant lawsuit" to prosecute Israel for breaking the covenant. The prophet Micah is one of the clearer examples of this rhetorical technique. God has a case against his people. Micah announces the lawsuit at the beginning of his book: "Hear, you peoples . . . and let the Lord God be a witness against you" (1:2). Later, he uses court imagery to make his case, beginning with the summons, "Hear what the Lord says" (6:1–2). The verdict of Micah's case against Israel, Judah, and the nations of the earth is *Guilty!* They are sentenced to destruction and death. But God will save some of them, and he will rule over this "remnant" in peace and justice forever.

In the superscription, we learn that the book contains the word of the Lord to Micah (1:1). The prophet's name is actually a sentence in Hebrew: *Mi* (Who is) + *c* (like) + *ah* (the Lord?). It is a rhetorical question expecting a negative answer: no one is like the Lord! Micah was from Moresheth-gath (1:14), which was about twenty-five miles southwest of Jerusalem in Judah (see map 18.1).

The book is dated to the "days of Jotham, Ahaz, and Hezekiah, kings of Judah," in the second half of the eighth century. Micah was a contemporary of the prophet Isaiah in Judah and the prophet Hosea in Israel. During his long ministry, he saw the conquest and exile of Israel in 722 BC and God's miraculous salvation of Judah during the time of Hezekiah in 701 BC (see Isa. 37). Though he lived in Judah, Micah addresses the people of both Israel and Judah.

Exploration

The book of Micah is structured as summarized in table 18.1. The book is arranged in four cycles of judgment and then salvation. One obvious indicator of the structure is repetition of the word "remnant," which anchors each salvation section (2:12; 4:7; 5:7–8; 7:18). This word does not occur anywhere else in the book of Micah.

Each cycle relates to a different theme. The first cycle relates to the *promised land* (1:2–2:13). Because Israel and Judah have committed injustice, idolatry, and violence *in the land*, God will destroy the land and send them

ISRAEL

KING	DATES OF REIGN	REFERENCES	KEY FEATURES OF REIGN
Jeroboam II	793–753	2 Kings 14:23	Coregent with Jehoash, 793–782
Zechariah	753–752	2 Kings 15:8	Assassinated by Shallum (2 Kings 15:10)
Shallum	752	2 Kings 15:13	Assassinated by Menahem (2 Kings 15:14)
Menahem	752–742	2 Kings 15:17	Made an alliance with Pul, king of Assyria (2 Kings 15:19–20)
Pekahiah	742–740	2 Kings 15:23	Assassinated by Pekah (2 Kings 15:25)
Pekah	752–732	2 Kings 15:27	Reigned in Gilead, 752–740, overlapping with Menahem; reigned over united Israel, 740–732; assassinated by Hoshea (2 Kings 15:30)
Hoshea	732–722	2 Kings 15:30; 17:1	Appointed by Tiglath-pileser III

Amos
767–753

Jonah
792–753

Hosea
755–725

JUDAH

KING	DATES OF REIGN	REFERENCES	KEY FEATURES OF REIGN
Uzziah/ Azariah	792–740	2 Kings 14:21; 2 Chron. 26:3	Coregent with his father, Amaziah, 792–767; began reigning at age 16 (2 Kings 14:21); struck with leprosy for offering incense in 750, then lived in a separate house while his son governed (2 Chron. 26:16–21)
Jotham	750–735	2 Kings 15:32–33	Coregent with Uzziah, 750–740; removed from the throne in 735
Ahaz	735–715	2 Kings 16:1–2	16 years counted from death of Jotham in 732 (2 Kings 15:38)
Hezekiah	729–686	2 Kings 18:1–2	Coregent with father, Ahaz, 729–715; Sennacherib attacked Judah in 701 BC (2 Kings 18:13)

Isaiah
740–695

Micah
742–686

Table 18.1. The Structure of Micah

	Indictment and Judgment	Salvation
Cycle #1	1:2–2:11 Israel and Judah are evil in the land, so they will lose the land	2:12–13 . . . but God will regather a remnant
Cycle #2	3:1–12 Israel's and Judah's leaders are wicked, so they will be ruined	4:1–8 . . . but God will rule perfectly over a remnant
Cycle #3	4:9–5:1 Without leadership, Israel and Judah will be defeated	5:2–15 . . . but God's king will lead a remnant to victory
Cycle #4	6:1–7:6 YHWH has a case against Israel	7:7–20 . . . but God will plead the case of the remnant and forgive

Note: Though the cyclical structure of the book of Micah is well established, I was particularly influenced by Kenneth H. Cuffey, *The Literary Coherence of the Book of Micah: Remnant, Restoration, and Promise* (New York: Bloomsbury T&T Clark, 2019), 213–53.

into exile. However, God will regather a remnant of his people in the future. The second cycle focuses on *leadership* (3:1–4:8). The rulers, prophets, and priests of Israel and Judah are evil; therefore, God will ruin them. In the near future, however, God himself will rule perfectly over a remnant of his people. The third cycle concerns *defeat and victory* (4:9–5:15). Micah predicts siege, destruction, and exile for Jerusalem because the people have no leaders to guide them. But this will not be the end of the story. In the distant future, God will reveal his messianic king, born in Bethlehem, who will lead the remnant to victory. The fourth cycle contains Micah's *covenant lawsuit* against Israel (6:1–7:20). Fortunately, there is long-term hope: God will plead the case of a remnant of people who belong to him and will remove their sins completely. One scholar describes these repeating cycles in the book as "a symphony in which similar themes are repeated and intensified before finally building to a crescendo."[1]

The literary structure of the book relates to the five prophetic phases of history. Micah addresses four of these (see fig. 18.1). Micah indicts Israel

THINKING VISUALLY

The Five Phases: Micah
Figure 18.1

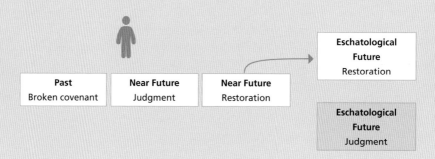

and Judah for breaking the covenant in the **past**, and he announces judgment in the **near future**. (The stick figure in fig. 18.1, which represents Micah, is located in the midst of the "judgment" phase because he has witnessed God's judgment on Israel and he anticipates, in the near future, God's judgment on Judah.)

The nature of God's restoration and salvation is developed progressively in the course of the four cycles. In cycle #1, the remnant includes those people from Judah whom God will restore from exile in the *near future* (2:12). But the historical remnant in the near future then becomes a pattern for God's ultimate salvation in the distant, *eschatological future*. In cycle #2, the remnant includes those from Israel, Judah, and the nations who will live under God's perfect rule (4:7). In cycle #3, a remnant will be delivered by a Davidic, messianic king (5:7–8). In cycle #4, the remnant is the true people of God, who experience God's forgiveness and perfect rule for all time (7:18) (see fig. 18.2).

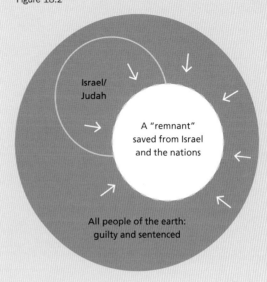

The "Remnant" in the Eschatological Future
Figure 18.2

Israel/Judah

A "remnant" saved from Israel and the nations

All people of the earth: guilty and sentenced

Israel and Judah Are Evil in the Land, So They Will Lose the Land

■ READ MICAH 1:2–2:11 ■

Micah begins by announcing YHWH's case against Israel and Judah. YHWH, the king of all the earth who reigns in his holy temple, is coming to judge his people, and the mountains will melt in his presence (1:2–4). In 1:5–7, the prophet describes the sins of the Northern Kingdom. It is filled with idols and cult sites. Therefore, Samaria will be conquered and will become a heap of ruins in the open country (this came to pass in 722 BC). Micah turns his attention to Judah in the next set of verses (1:8–16). Judah has participated in the same sins as Israel, so it will participate in the same judgment (1:13).

Micah was the first of the prophets to announce the destruction of Jerusalem and the temple—it must have been shocking for his listeners. The false prophets criticize him, saying, "One should not preach of such things; disgrace will not overtake us!" (2:6). But Micah's response is that God's own people have become the enemy. If they had walked uprightly, Micah would not have to give them the bad news (2:7–8).

. . . But God Will Regather a Remnant

■ READ MICAH 2:12–13 ■

At the end of the first cycle, Micah suddenly shifts to an oracle of restoration. Although Israel and Judah will lose the promised land and go

---

© Baker Publishing Group

HISTORICAL MATTERS

Refugees Come to Jerusalem

The artist's reconstruction of Jerusalem in figure 18.3 shows the size and shape of the city during the early days of Micah's ministry. You can see the original city of David—a peninsula in the midst of valleys to the east, south, and west—as well as the Temple Mount to the north. But in the time of King Hezekiah, the city grew dramatically when the Northern Kingdom was conquered by Assyria and refugees fled south to Jerusalem and Judah. Figure 18.4 illustrates the new size and shape of Jerusalem due to the expansion of the city onto the western hill. Hezekiah built a broad wall around this part of the city to enclose it and protect it from Assyrian invasion.

Figure 18.3. Jerusalem in the time of Solomon

into exile as a result of their sin, God will gather a remnant and bring them back from exile. God is imagined as a shepherd who collects his sheep into the fold, a safe pasture. If exile is like a prison, God will be one who breaks open the gates and leads his people to safety (2:13).

Israel's and Judah's Leaders Are Wicked, So They Will Be Ruined

■ READ MICAH 3:1–12 ■

The focus of the second literary cycle in the book is leadership.[2] The rulers and officials of Israel are supposed to ensure justice; instead, when the people come to them for help, these leaders oppress them even further. Micah uses graphic imagery of slaughtering an animal: the leaders eat

Figure 18.4. Jerusalem in the time of Hezekiah

The Preacher's Temptation

Before we are too quick to judge the priests and prophets of Judah, we should recognize what a strong temptation there always is to modify a message or soften it so that we do not offend people. Why should we warn people—the people who give money to the church!—that they are sinning against God? It is easier to give an encouraging word and then get texts and emails telling us what a good preacher we are. It is easier to preach against generic sins "out there" in the world than to tackle the blind spots of the people in our own congregation. In certain periods of history, it was easy to preach against sexual sin and difficult to preach against racism. In our own time, it is easy to preach against racism but hard to preach against sexual sin. The prophet Micah provides us with a model for speaking truth under the pressure of cultural agendas: filled with the Holy Spirit and dependent on the full counsel of God's word, he spoke what was true even when it was difficult to hear.

The Book of Micah, One Hundred Years Later

Jeremiah 26 tells us about a time one hundred years after Micah's era when the prophet Jeremiah preaches against Jerusalem. When the priests and prophets react by trying to kill Jeremiah, the officials and elders defend him and argue that he does not deserve death. They quote what is now Micah 3:12 as an example of a past prophet who spoke against Jerusalem and was not killed (26:18). Rather, King Hezekiah repented, and YHWH relented of the disaster he had planned (26:19). This episode provides some interesting extra context for Micah 3:12. First, Micah does not indicate specifically *when* he spoke the words of verse 12, but Jeremiah 26 locates them in the time of Hezekiah. Second, Micah does not indicate that his word against Jerusalem is conditional and might be averted. And yet judgment was temporarily averted because of Hezekiah's humble response.[a]

the people's flesh, flay their skin, break their bones, and chop them up like meat in a pot (3:3).

One would hope that the religious leaders would be better, but the prophets and seers lead the people astray and adapt their oracles to whatever will get them personal gain (3:5). As a result, when they seek God, he will give them no answer (3:7). Micah contrasts himself with these fakes: he is filled with the Spirit of YHWH, represents justice, and declares Israel's sin to them (3:8).

Micah goes on to indict the rulers, priests, and prophets even further. They are corrupt and act only for their own gain (3:9–12). The rulers take bribes, the priests teach for payment, and the prophets are mercenary. Because of the failed leadership, Zion will "be plowed as a field" and will become a heap of ruins (3:12). This reminds us of the prophet's dire prediction for Samaria (1:6).

. . . But God Will Rule Perfectly over a Remnant

■ READ MICAH 4:1–8 ■

The second cycle concludes with an oracle of restoration that will take place in the eschatological future—in "the latter days" (4:1) and "in that day" (4:6). Although the leaders of Israel and Judah are wicked failures in the present, one day God himself will rule perfectly over his people. Zion, the epicenter of God's authority, will be lifted up above all else (4:1). People from all nations will stream to Zion to be taught by God and to submit to his rule (4:2–4). There will be justice on a global scale (4:3). Peace will be assured, and with no more need for weapons, they will be destroyed. Others who worship false gods are destined for destruction, but God will take the weak and the lame and make them a remnant who belong to him (4:7).

We should not miss the radical nature of these claims. Injustice and war have plagued humanity throughout history, and they cannot be solved by human means. Totalitarian governments arise with total power to balance injustices and bring peace; then these governments become the oppressors because the fundamental problem is the human heart. But all these problems *will* be solved when God reigns over his people.

Without Leadership, Israel and Judah Will Be Defeated

■ READ MICAH 4:9–5:1 ■

In the third cycle of the book, Micah wonders where the leaders are who are to protect Judah (4:9). Zion should groan like a woman in labor, for she is about to give birth to exile (4:10a). Even now, hostile nations are gathered against Jerusalem, bringing siege and humiliation (5:1). But throughout this short section, Micah also sprinkles glimpses of hope for the future. God's plans are not ruined: he has hope for his people on the other side of judgment. They will be rescued (4:10b) and will triumph over their enemies at the end (4:13).

. . . But God's King Will Lead a Remnant to Victory

■ READ MICAH 5:2–15 ■

In the previous section, Micah pronounced the defeat of Jerusalem because it had no leaders (4:9). Now, he predicts that God will provide the people with the *ultimate* leader: a messianic king. This ruler will come from Bethlehem, a small village not even large enough to be worth mentioning among the clans of Judah (5:2). In the US, we expect our leaders to come from important places like New York, Los Angeles, or Chicago—not a small town like Lake Triangle, Connecticut. But Bethlehem's size is not important. The key is that it is the city of David, and it was to David that God promised a future king who would sit on his throne forever (2 Sam. 9). The prophet states that this ruler was foretold from long ago (5:2); thus Micah indicates that the ruler has supernatural origins. He will shepherd the people of God in great strength and will bring peace to the whole earth (5:4–5).

Whereas in Micah's present, Jerusalem will be defeated because of failed leaders, this Davidic king will ensure victory for the remnant of God's people. He will execute vengeance and establish what is right, destroying weapons of war, cutting off false prophets and fortune-tellers, and bringing an end to false

The Adoration of the Mystic Lamb

On the altar in Saint Bavo's Cathedral in Belgium rests a piece of art made by Hubrecht and Jan van Eyck called *The Adoration of the Mystic Lamb*. Created in 1432, it celebrates Jesus as the Lamb of God. In the center, the archangel Gabriel tells Mary that she has been chosen to be the mother of Jesus. In the panel above Mary, the prophet Micah watches with expectation (see fig. 18.5). The text on the ribbon above him says in Latin, "Ex te mihi egredietur qui sit dominator in Israhel" (Out of you [Bethlehem] shall come forth unto me that is to be ruler in Israel).

Figure 18.5. The prophet Micah in *The Adoration of the Mystic Lamb*

religion (5:10–15). God's fierce, unstoppable victory is bad news for those who defy God and will not submit to him, but it is good news for God's people, who will not be hurt anymore.

YHWH Has a Case against Israel

■ READ MICAH 6:1–7:6 ■

In the fourth cycle, Micah argues a covenant lawsuit on behalf of God. It is important to track who is speaking in each verse in order to understand the setup. In 6:1a, the prophet introduces the oracle to his listeners: "Hear what the LORD says." In 6:1b, God speaks to Micah and commands him to serve as prosecutor (with singular verbs), instructing, "Arise, plead your case." Micah then turns in 6:2 (rhetorically, using a plural verb) to the mountains that will serve as the jury in the case: "Hear, you mountains, the indictment of the LORD." Finally, in 6:3 God speaks to the people of Judah: "O my people, what have I done to you?"

If we imagine a courtroom scene, God is the plaintiff—he is the one who has the complaint against his people. Micah is the prosecuting attorney who will prove their guilt. The defendant on the stand is Judah. Nature is the jury. (Usually in ancient Near Eastern covenants, the gods are witnesses, but in the Bible other witnesses must be found, as there are no other gods.) The prophet announces the verdict of the case: "Guilty!" God serves in a second role as well: the judge who determines the sentencing.

In a surprise twist, the indictment begins not by describing Judah's sins against God but with God asking how *he* has wronged *them* (6:3–5). Of course, God has done nothing wrong, so this accentuates their guilt. God has rescued them from Egypt, given them leaders, and performed righteous acts. They have no excuse for their rebellion.

In response to this indictment, Micah characterizes the attitude of the people by putting words in their mouths (6:6–7). He presents a hypothetical objection against God so that it can be refuted. The people say, "What more could God want from us? Is all our worship not good enough?" With increasingly extreme suggestions, they ask, "Does God want more burnt offerings? Thousands of rams? Ten thousand rivers of oil? Human sacrifice of our own children?" In other words, will *nothing* please YHWH? This is an attempt to throw blame back on God.

The prophet's answer is simple: religious ritual, no matter how extreme, is no substitute for loyalty and obedience. It is obedience that indicates faith, and the obedience that God is looking for is justice (doing what is right, without corruption, toward

Figure 18.6. Drawing of a courtroom

God and others), covenant love, and humble relationship with him. That God desires this of his people is neither a riddle nor a mystery. He has made it clear in his Word: "He has told you, O man, what is good" (6:8). The section goes on to continue the indictment with a list of specific sins (6:11–7:6).

. . . But God Will Plead the Case of the Remnant and Forgive

⬛ READ MICAH 7:7–20 ⬛

In the salvation section of the fourth and final cycle in the book, the prophet acknowledges sin and describes a radical shift in the courtroom analogy: YHWH will switch from plaintiff to defense attorney, pleading the case of his people and forgiving them (7:9). God will trample the enemies of his people and make them secure (7:10–11).

The final three verses of the book are a climax of praise to the God who forgives. Micah's name means "Who is like YHWH?" Now in 7:18 he asks, "Who is a God like you, pardoning iniquity and passing over transgression for the remnant of his inheritance?" Micah is not a universalist—God pardons the sin of the *remnant*, those who have come to him humbly and in faith. God will cast their sins into the depths of the sea (7:19).

Implementation

The key question in the book is also the name of the prophet, the book's title, and its key verse: "Who is like you?" We cannot see God and do not hear his voice audibly—What is he like? One scholar summarizes:

Throughout the collection of Micah's speeches the audience . . . learns a great deal about this God. He is a God who takes his covenant with his people seriously (1:5), who will brook no rivals to transcendence (1:6–7), and who controls the nations—even the dreaded Assyrian army (1:6–16). Yet he is concerned with the plight of the "little people" and their exploitation at the hands of the covetous rich (2:1–3, 8–9; 3:1–3), with telling the truth (2:6–11; 3:5–8), with a just society and the importance of human rights (6:6–8), with the terrible blight of war in the world (4:1–5), and with what it means to be human (6:6–8).[3]

We must not take for granted that he is also a God who pardons sin and passes over transgression. He does not hold on to anger forever. He is compassionate and faithful. In this book, we learn not only what he is like; we learn that there is no one like him! He is a God worthy of worship and praise, deserving of a total-life commitment that costs all we have.

Who is like God? He revealed himself to us most fully when he sent his son, Jesus Christ, to be born in Bethlehem to be our good ruler (Mic. 5:2; Luke 1:32–33). Human rulers often do more harm than good: we look to them for justice and get oppression instead. So we look forward to Christ's return, when he will reign over us in Zion and extend his grace and healing to the entire world (Luke 24:47). His people are the new temple—living stones—built up into a spiritual house (1 Pet. 2:5). He will shepherd them in the strength of YHWH (Mic. 5:4). He rules with gentleness, but not weakness; he reigns in majesty and power. This is good news in a world in which Christians are constantly persecuted and even killed for their allegiance to him. He will be their "peace" (Mic. 5:5).

While we wait for God's perfect rule under imperfect and even oppressive authorities, we are called to live out the values of his kingdom by loving justice and doing mercy *now* (Mic. 6:8). Christ redeems us from darkness into light (Eph. 5:8; 1 Pet. 2:9). He saves us from the dominion of sin *for* good deeds. Paul says in 1 Corinthians, "Do you not know that the unrighteous will not inherit the kingdom of God?" (6:9). "The unrighteous" include those who are sexually immoral, idolaters, adulterers, those who practice homosexuality, thieves, the greedy, drunkards, revilers, and swindlers (6:10). "And such were some of you. But you were washed, you were sanctified, you were justified in the name of the Lord Jesus Christ and by the Spirit of our God" (6:11). Having been purchased by Christ, we are called to live in the light of his kingdom, obeying his word, doing justice toward others, and loving mercy.

Christian Reading Questions

1. To what does "the remnant" refer in the book of Micah? Who is included in the remnant? Who is not a member of the remnant? How would you relate Micah's "remnant" theology to other prophetic books that we have studied thus far?

2. The book of Micah continues to show the contrast between true and false prophets that was emphasized in the book of Jeremiah. Compare Jeremiah 23:16–17 with Micah 2:6 and 3:5. Why do these books associate good news with false prophecy and bad news with true prophecy? Does the temptation to preach good news (no matter what) have any implications for the church today?

3. In Micah 6:6–7, the people ask Micah what God wants from them, including the sacrifice of their own children. What do you think lies behind this exaggeration? Why are the people (as presented by Micah) being so extreme? Can you think of other passages in the Old Testament Prophets in which worship is used as an attempt to manipulate God?

CHAPTER NINETEEN

Nahum

Orientation

Although many of us live in safety and freedom, countless people throughout history have lived under a brutal dictator or been subject to constant threat of torture and death by a foreign nation. During World War II, Nazi Germany initiated a conflict that led to the death of millions, as well as the starvation and suffering of millions more. European Jews were displaced, then imprisoned and tortured in death camps. When Germany finally surrendered, people all over the world danced in the street and kissed random strangers in celebration. Adolf Hitler committed suicide in his bunker, but no one mourned him. When evil is conquered, we celebrate not only because the abstract principle of justice has been preserved but also because the victims of that evil are finally free from danger.

In the book of Nahum, the prophet proclaims doom on the city of Nineveh, the capital of Assyria. The king and people of Nineveh have oppressed and brutalized the surrounding nations, but now God will overthrow that city with violence and destruction. This is great news! There will be justice, and Nineveh's victims—including the people of God—will breathe a sigh of relief. And this event will point to even better news for all people at all times. There is a God who sees the injustice in the world, and he will act to ensure that right is done.

The superscription to the book (1:1) tells us only two things. We know that Nahum (whose name, appropriately, means "comfort" in Hebrew) is from Elkosh, but the location of this town is unknown. We also learn that the book is an oracle concerning Nineveh. The prophet addresses Nineveh

Figure 19.1. Lachish reliefs from Sennacherib's palace in Nineveh

and its king directly throughout the three chapters and does not mention any specific events or locations in Judah. However, in the same way that Obadiah rhetorically spoke to Edom while his real audience was God's people, Nahum's message is actually for the people of Judah and those throughout the ages who belong to God and have been mistreated by God's enemies.

We already saw in chapter 17, on the book of Jonah, that Assyria had a reputation for savage cruelty in war. Assyrian kings bragged of skinning their captives, cutting off appendages, and making piles of human heads. In 722 BC, after the time of Jonah, Assyria invaded the Northern Kingdom, conquered its capital, Samaria, and sent the people into exile, where they were lost to history. About twenty years later, in 701 BC, just fifty years before the time of Nahum, Assyria invaded Judah (see Isa. 36–37; 2 Kings 18–19). King Sennacherib's army had conquered all the towns of Judah, including the second-most-important city, Lachish. As a monument of the battle, the king commissioned carvings on his palace walls that illustrated the battle. These carvings, now in the British Museum in London, show Judahite captives with their feet and hands amputated, impaled on wooden spikes, with heads "decorating" the city walls (see fig. 19.1).

Nineveh was extremely wealthy, was apparently impervious to attack, and commanded the greatest army in the world. Who could stand up to this great evil? One scholar writes, "The Assyrian empire could not have looked stronger. From Egypt to Elam they

HISTORICAL MATTERS

"Fact Sheet"—Nahum

Author: Nahum

Date: 663–612 BC

Location: The book concerns Nineveh, the capital of the mighty Assyrian Empire in the east.

Political and social context: Assyria had dominated and troubled Israel and Judah for many years. Now Nahum assures God's people that they will find relief when the God of salvation becomes the God of justice and rightly destroys his enemies.

dominated all the nations of the world. Yet Nahum does not hesitate to declare their doom."[1]

The earliest Nahum could have prophesied seems to be 663 BC, since he refers to the *past* conquest of the Egyptian capital of Thebes, which occurred in that year (see 3:8). Nahum says that the Assyrian Empire is currently at "full strength" (1:12), suggesting that he wrote prior to the death of King Assurbanipal in 627 BC, when the Assyrian Empire began to decline. In any case, the latest possible date of the book is 612 BC, when Nineveh fell to the Medes and the Babylonians. That future event is predicted throughout the book.

TIME LINE

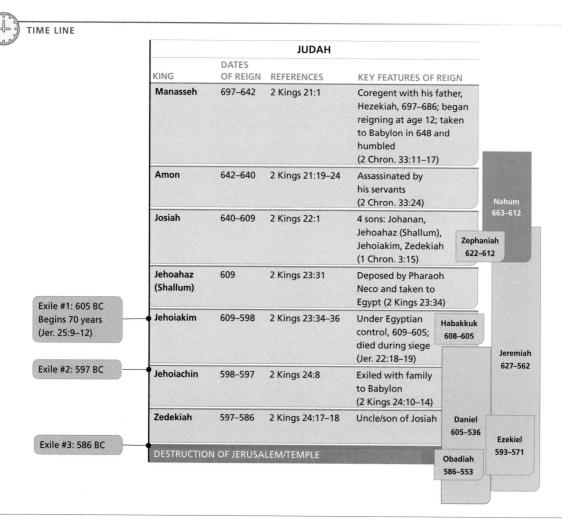

JUDAH

KING	DATES OF REIGN	REFERENCES	KEY FEATURES OF REIGN
Manasseh	697–642	2 Kings 21:1	Coregent with his father, Hezekiah, 697–686; began reigning at age 12; taken to Babylon in 648 and humbled (2 Chron. 33:11–17)
Amon	642–640	2 Kings 21:19–24	Assassinated by his servants (2 Chron. 33:24)
Josiah	640–609	2 Kings 22:1	4 sons: Johanan, Jehoahaz (Shallum), Jehoiakim, Zedekiah (1 Chron. 3:15)
Jehoahaz (Shallum)	609	2 Kings 23:31	Deposed by Pharaoh Neco and taken to Egypt (2 Kings 23:34)
Jehoiakim	609–598	2 Kings 23:34–36	Under Egyptian control, 609–605; died during siege (Jer. 22:18–19)
Jehoiachin	598–597	2 Kings 24:8	Exiled with family to Babylon (2 Kings 24:10–14)
Zedekiah	597–586	2 Kings 24:17–18	Uncle/son of Josiah

DESTRUCTION OF JERUSALEM/TEMPLE

Exile #1: 605 BC Begins 70 years (Jer. 25:9–12)

Exile #2: 597 BC

Exile #3: 586 BC

Nahum 663–612

Zephaniah 622–612

Habakkuk 608–605

Jeremiah 627–562

Daniel 605–536

Ezekiel 593–571

Obadiah 586–553

Exploration

The book of Nahum consists of three movements of disproportionate lengths. First, Nahum praises the great God of heaven, who takes vengeance on his adversaries (**1:2–8**). This hymn is the theological grid through which we are meant to read the entire book. Second, the prophet announces the death of the king of Assyria near the beginning and end of the book in **1:9–15** and **3:15b–19**. Third, those verses form a frame around the main part of the book (**2:1–3:15a**), which describes the downfall of Nineveh (see table 19.1).

Table 19.1. The Structure of Nahum

1:1 Superscription	
1:2–8 God takes vengeance on his adversaries	
1:9–15 Though the Assyrians are numerous, their king will perish	
2:1–7 A description of Nineveh's doom • Description of battle • Stripping of Nineveh (2:7) • Her handmaids mourn	**3:1–7** The justice of Nineveh's doom • Description of battle • Stripping of Nineveh (3:5) • No one mourns
2:8–10 Nineveh will be sacked • Nineveh is a pool of water • "No end" to the plunder (2:9) • The people are afraid	**3:8–11** Nineveh will be sacked like Thebes • Thebes's strength was her water fortress • "No end" to Thebes's allies (3:9) • The people will go into hiding
2:11–13 Nineveh devoured other nations like prey	**3:12–15a** Nineveh will be devoured
	3:15b–19 Though the Assyrians are numerous, their king will perish

The center section, describing Nineveh's fall, is itself divided into three sets of corresponding panels. The first set of panels (**2:1–7 and 3:1–7**) describes the battle for Nineveh. They both contain the Hebrew word *galah* (to strip), which portrays the plundering of the land. The second set of panels (**2:8–10 and 3:8–11**) focuses on the sacking of Nineveh and its comparison to the sacking of Thebes. Both sections speak of water in relation to the cities' defenses, and they contain the Hebrew phrase *'en qetseh* (there is no end) to describe the richness of Nineveh and Thebes. They also mention the fear of the people in the battle. The third set of panels (**2:11–13** and 3:12–15a) uses the imagery of devouring and being devoured to describe Nineveh's fall and the poetic justice of the destroying city itself being destroyed.

The book of Nahum has a focused message that relates to only two prophetic "phases" (see fig. 19.2). When Nineveh is destroyed, Judah will be free of its terrors. That event in history teaches us something about God's power and desire for ultimate justice in the world he has created. In the end—the eschatological future—not only Nineveh but every adversary of God will be defeated in judgment, and those who belong to him will be safe. 🎨

God Takes Vengeance on His Adversaries

■ READ NAHUM 1:2–8 ■

Nahum's opening hymn describes God with the words "jealous . . . avenging . . . avenging . . . wrathful . . . takes vengeance . . . and keeps wrath" (1:2). However, it is not as though God is inherently angry or unstable, exploding randomly and wrecking everything around him. He is "slow to anger" (1:3). The point is that God is patient and merciful, but when he does become angry, it is justified and he is purposeful. His anger is directed at "the guilty." Though Nahum focuses in the book on historical Assyria, God's justice has a global scope; it is for "the world and all who dwell in it" (1:5). One scholar writes, "As this hymn presents punishment and deliverance of consequences of either opposing or trusting God, it makes clear that God is not simply on the side of all Judeans, nor is he the enemy only of Assyria; all people will have to give an account of whether they have trusted him or have instead rebelled against him."[2] God's anger is not like a conventional bomb that falls randomly; it is like a laser-guided missile that targets only evil and avoids collateral damage.

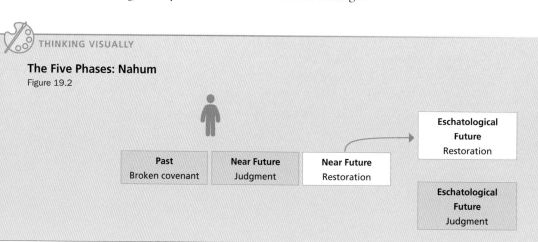

🎨 THINKING VISUALLY

The Five Phases: Nahum
Figure 19.2

Past	Near Future	Near Future	Eschatological Future
Broken covenant	Judgment	Restoration	Restoration

Eschatological Future
Judgment

Though the Assyrians Are Numerous, Their King Will Perish

■ READ NAHUM 1:9–15 ■

Having announced God as the righteous judge on a global scale, Nahum now turns to the Assyrian Empire and its king. The effect of this narrowed focus is that Assyria functions as a concrete, historical illustration of God's character and action. His judgment is not just a theoretical concept—it is real and results in actual destruction of the wicked and actual deliverance of their victims. Nahum asks the people of Assyria in 1:9, "What do you plot against the LORD?" In 1:11 he refers to the king: "From you [Assyria] came one who plotted evil against the LORD, a worthless counselor." In Hebrew, the word "you" is always marked as either masculine or feminine, singular or plural. This allows us to track the addressee in complex passages like this one. Therefore, we can see in 1:12–13 that Nahum turns to Judah (feminine singular) and says, "Though I have afflicted you, I will afflict you no more." But in 1:14 he turns back to the king of Assyria (masculine singular) and announces his death, for he is "vile."

In 1:15, Nahum quotes from Isaiah 52:7, announcing a messenger who brings good news of peace to Judah. Specifically, this good news is that "never again shall the worthless pass through you; he is utterly cut off." Given this, what do we do with the fact that Judah *was* conquered again, about twenty-five years later, by the Babylonians? One possible answer is that, in context, Nahum refers only to Assyria, who would never trouble Judah again. A second possibility is that the quotation is drawing on its original context in Isaiah. There, Isaiah urges his audience to celebrate because God has finally announced his ultimate, effective salvation (52:8–10). Immediately following this is Isaiah's final "Servant Song" (52:13–53:12), which describes a coming messianic figure who will save people from their sin. From the New Testament, we know that this figure is Jesus Christ (cf. Acts 8:32–35). It may be that Nahum uses this quotation to connect God's immediate victory over Assyria (in history) to the eschatological future, when he defeats evil once and for all through his messianic servant, Jesus.

A Description of Nineveh's Doom

■ READ NAHUM 2:1–7 ■

The prophet turns next to a description of the actual fall of Nineveh. Although this event will come in the future, he uses the present tense and describes the event as though it is happening now, with detailed, concrete images. He facetiously calls on the people of Nineveh to defend their city: "Station soldiers on the ramparts! Watch the road! Dress for battle!" (2:1,

A Flood in Nineveh?

The ancient city of Nineveh (modern Mosul, Iraq) sat on the east bank of the Tigris River with a tributary running through its center. Nahum's description of the city's fall mentions a flood in 1:8, 2:6, and 2:8. This is probably not purely figurative imagery. An ancient historian named Diodorus writes that during the siege of Nineveh, heavy rains swelled the Tigris, breaking the defensive wall and flooding the city.[c] This would have "softened" the city's defenses and allowed the invaders to enter much more easily.[d] Another possibility is that the Medes and Babylonians flooded the city *after* it fell as a symbol of its defeat.[e]

Map 19.1. Nineveh

my translation). He describes the enemy soldiers and chariots coming through the city walls and the city flooding. Why is God bringing such destruction, which causes even the slave girls to lament (2:7)? The answer is at the beginning of this section in 2:2. Assyria has plundered God's people in Israel, and now God is plundering Assyria.

Nineveh Will Be Sacked

▓ READ NAHUM 2:8–10 ▓

Now Nahum turns our attention from the city of Nineveh to the invading army. They call out, urging each other to plunder the silver, gold, and all precious treasure (2:9). The kings of Assyria have collected massive amounts of treasure by robbing other nations; now it will be stolen from them.[3] As a result, the city will be desolate. The formerly proud inhabitants of the mighty, wealthy city will be pale as they anguish over what they have lost. This is a good reminder to those of us who feel safe behind our high-tech military, abundant financial resources, and bustling infrastructure. Nothing stands a chance against God's wrath when it is unleashed.

Nineveh Devoured Other Nations like Prey

▓ READ NAHUM 2:11–13 ▓

As a conclusion to the first half of the book and the first three structural panels, Nahum compares Assyria to a lion that feeds on others. In the modern world, this metaphor may lose some of its impact because we are not normally in danger from lions—they are kept safely in cages in a zoo. But in the ancient world they were a real threat, unpredictable and constantly

The Fall of Nineveh

In 1829 John Martin produced the mezzotint (a print made from an engraved copper or steel plate), reproduced in figure 19.3, depicting the fall of Nineveh in the book of Nahum. In the background, we can see the invading army swarm through the breach in the wall that has been made by the flooded river. "Under a convulsive sky the doomed Ninevites scatter like ants" while their king prepares to burn on a funeral pyre.[f]

Figure 19.3. *The Fall of Nineveh* (1829) by John Martin

prowling. Just as a lion returns to its den after killing its prey, Nineveh was the home base of a fierce army. It tore open its prey to feed its cubs and filled its den with torn flesh (2:12). But now that home base is gone because God declares, "Behold, I am against you" (2:13).

The Justice of Nineveh's Doom

■ READ NAHUM 3:1–7 ■

This first unit in the second half of the book parallels 2:1–7 in describing the fall of Nineveh in detail. The prophet predicts that there will be "heaps of corpses, dead bodies without end" (3:3). Many cities were attacked in the ancient world, but this invasion of Nineveh will not be a coincidence of history, as though the enemy might easily have chosen another target. The primary reason for the attack will not be Nineveh's great wealth or strategic value; it will be God's justice. God says again, "I am against you" (3:5). Her

LITERARY NOTES

Assyria the Lion

It is appropriate for Nahum to imagine Assyria as a lion, for Assyrian kings frequently imagined *themselves* as lions in their writings. For example, Adad-Nirari II (early ninth century BC) called himself a "potent lion."[g] Sargon II (eighth century BC) said he was a "wild lion who is lordly with frightfulness," boasting, "I did not see an adversary to overwhelm me."[h] These kings used the imagery of lions to depict their great strength, but Nahum announces that the mighty have fallen. Other Old Testament prophets also use the lion as an image of Assyria (Isa. 5:29; Jer. 50:17).[i]

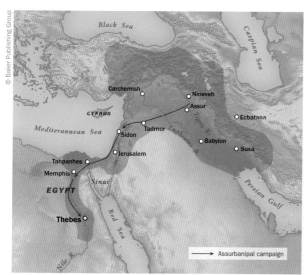

Map 19.2. The Assyrian conquest of Thebes

victims will not be sorry when she is made into a shameful spectacle (3:6–7). This is long overdue.[4]

Nineveh Will Be Sacked like Thebes

■ READ NAHUM 3:8–11 ■

God's people may ask, Is God *really* going to be able to take down a city as secure and powerful as Nineveh? Nahum answers this implied question by using the example of Thebes, the capital of Egypt, which was also thought to be invulnerable to attack. It was located hundreds of miles from the Egyptian border, surrounded by various rivers and lakes, and additionally protected by allied nations. And yet the Assyrian king Assurbanipal *was* able to defeat Thebes (see map 19.2). Her infants were slaughtered and her men taken away in chains (3:10). Is Nineveh any better off than Thebes (3:8)? If this happened to Thebes, it can and will happen to Nineveh, rest assured. Nahum says, "You [Nineveh] also will be drunken; you will go into hiding; you will seek a refuge from the enemy" (3:11).

Nineveh Will Be Devoured

■ READ NAHUM 3:12–15A ■

In the previous, corresponding unit (2:11–13), Nahum states that Nineveh devours others like a ferocious lion. In this short section, he returns to this imagery but flips it: Nineveh, the devourer, will be devoured! The Hebrew word *akal* ("to eat" or "to devour") occurs four times in these four verses (3:12, 13, 15 [2x]). 🔳

Though the Assyrians Are Numerous, Their King Will Perish

■ READ NAHUM 3:15B–19 ■

The book comes to a conclusion with some sharp, somewhat surprising statements from the prophet. First,

---

THEOLOGICAL ISSUES

"Your Troops Are Women"

In 3:13, Nahum describes the vulnerability of the Assyrians by saying that their soldiers "are women." Is this a sexist insult toward women? It is important to remember that warfare in the ancient world consisted of physically overpowering the enemy and wielding heavy weapons and armor. Brute physical strength was a major advantage. This is why it was noteworthy that King Saul was a big man (1 Sam. 9:2) and that the giant Goliath had massive metal weapons (1 Sam. 17:4–7). Because they were at a physical disadvantage, women in biblical times did not fight in combat (see the exception of Deborah in Judg. 4). Rather, women were often the victims of terrible abuse and mistreatment by enemy soldiers (as they sometimes are in the modern world), before whom they were defenseless. Nahum's metaphor certainly does not imply that all women are weak and defenseless in general. He is simply reflecting the terrible reality of warfare.

he mocks the people of Nineveh: "Multiply yourselves like the locust!" (3:15). Locusts or grasshoppers may have impressive numbers, but all it takes is a strong wind to blow them away. Second, Nahum rhetorically speaks to the king of Nineveh (with masculine singular pronouns): "There is no easing your hurt. . . . All who hear the news about you clap their hands over you" (3:19). Why do the peoples rejoice? Because they have all been the victims of his "unceasing evil."

Implementation

It may seem counterintuitive, but this book about the defeat and suffering of an ancient city is primarily a book of hope for the people of God. It teaches that God judges evil and brings justice. He is gracious and loves to show mercy, but he is not weak. We must not imagine God as a confused old man who is not quite aware of what is going on and fails to defend his people. Rather, Nahum presents him as a strong warrior. He is patient with those who do evil, but his patience has limits. When his wisdom dictates that the time for patience has passed, he arises and judges sin. It is not loveless or evil to want justice—justice is a fundamental aspect of God's character, and when we long for it, we long for who God is. When we are treated unfairly, exploited, robbed, or harmed, we want justice—and rightly so. When someone preys on young children, when a dictator slaughters thousands in war, or when a person steals what someone else has worked for, we want justice! And God wants it too. It is a fundamental part of his character. God dealing with evil Nineveh is meant to encourage his victimized people because it means that he will hold all powers accountable for what they have done.

The book also illustrates a judgment that is ultimately retributive, not restorative. God does not "turn up the heat" only to bring people to himself in repentance. In the end, for those who do not repent, there is suffering and death—no second chances. This sobering truth should cause us to evaluate ourselves. We cannot outwit him; our only hope is to submit to him and repent, throwing ourselves on his mercy. The good news of the gospel is that on the cross, Jesus Christ absorbed God's full wrath on behalf of anyone who will take refuge in him. For the believer, "there is therefore now no condemnation for those who are in Christ Jesus" (Rom. 8:1). But those who are *not* in Christ Jesus are in terrible danger. There is no defense against God's anger when it comes.

How do we reconcile the message of this book with the book of Jonah, which also concerned the people of Nineveh but ended with restoration rather than retribution? If Jonah teaches us to love God's mercy (even for wicked people) and Nahum teaches us to love God's judgment (which brings relief to victims), how do we handle this tension? The Bible teaches both of these truths, and not only in these two books. Wisdom demands that we must grow in both directions simultaneously. Just as God is astonishingly merciful and *also* hates sin with white-hot intensity, we must learn to show mercy even at great cost to ourselves but *also* long for God's name to be vindicated by the destruction of evil. When we lack mercy or flirt with sin, we are weak in faith. But strong faith, rooted in Scripture, loves mercy *and* judgment because both are important to God. Trusting him to do what is right and developing godly discernment to imitate him, we can clap our hands with Nahum when evil is defeated (3:19).

Christian Reading Questions

1. The end of this chapter briefly addresses the tension between the perspectives of Jonah and Nahum. Jonah is a negative example, because he does *not* want mercy for Nineveh. But Nahum urges us to celebrate God's judgment on Nineveh. Are they opposite perspectives? In what other ways can the two books be reconciled?

2. Why do you think Nahum goes into detailed descriptions of the destruction of Nineveh instead of using a general summary? How do the details affect us as readers, and how is this related to the message of the book?

3. In your own words, describe how the message of the book of Nahum relates to the gospel of Jesus Christ.

CHAPTER TWENTY

Habakkuk

Orientation

The Latin proverb *Aegrescit medendo* means "The remedy is worse than the disease." Imagine burning down your house in order to rid it of termites or cutting off your arm to cure poison ivy. No one would do that, even though termites and poison ivy are unpleasant and difficult to remove. We all sense that the "fix" should not make things even worse. This was Habakkuk's concern about God's response to injustice and evil in Judah at the end of the seventh century BC. When Habakkuk asks God to intervene and punish Judah, God responds that he will send a wicked pagan army. To Habakkuk, this remedy is worse than the disease. If the goal is justice and righteousness, how can it be right for God to use evil to accomplish his purposes? How can Habakkuk make sense of God's sovereignty and human responsibility? And, as a native of Judah, what about the suffering that Habakkuk must endure when he is living there? Must the righteous suffer along with the wicked? These are not curiosities for scholars to argue about as if they were merely an intellectual puzzle; they are serious problems of faith. The goodness of God and the possibility of true justice are on the line. These big issues are addressed in the three short chapters of Habakkuk. Ultimately, the book is about maintaining faith in God even in very difficult circumstances, even when that faith itself *is* the challenge.[1]

The superscription tells us only that this book is the "oracle that Habakkuk the prophet saw" (1:1). The word that's translated "oracle" is the same one that describes messages of Isaiah (13:1; 23:1), the book of Nahum (1:1), units in Zechariah (9:1; 12:1), and the book of Malachi (1:1). We are given no details about the prophet himself, nor any historical context or date for his ministry. These must be discerned from statements within the book. Because the poem in chapter 3 contains musical and liturgical

Habakkuk in Bel and the Dragon

It is not uncommon for ancient writers to create fantastic backstories for well-known individuals in the Bible. A later Jewish text called Bel and the Dragon, which is an addition to the book of Daniel, identifies Habakkuk as the son of Joshua, the son of Levi (v. 1). According to this fictional story, Habakkuk is on his way to deliver soup and wine to harvesters in the field when an angel of the Lord tells him to deliver the food instead to Daniel, who is in a pit of lions (cf. Dan. 6). When Habakkuk replies that he does not know Daniel's location, the angel grabs Habakkuk by the hair and transports him to the lions' den. After Daniel eats, the angel returns Habakkuk to his original location (vv. 33–39).

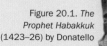

The Prophet Habakkuk

Between AD 1423 and 1426, the celebrated artist Donatello completed a sculpture of the prophet Habakkuk, which was then placed in the front of the bell tower of the cathedral in Florence, Italy. Donatello sought to infuse the sculpture with a sense of life and vitality. It is said that while he was working on it, he would say to the sculpture, "Speak, speak or be damned!"[a]

Public Domain / Wikimedia Commons

Figure 20.1. *The Prophet Habakkuk* (1423–26) by Donatello

notations like a psalm, some have suggested that Habakkuk was on staff at the Jerusalem temple—perhaps as one of the temple singers.[2]

In 1:6, God tells Habakkuk that he is "raising up the Chaldeans." This is our best clue to the time period. In the eighth century, the Assyrian Empire was in control of the ancient Near East, including Israel and Judah. After Assyria conquered Samaria and exiled many from the Northern Kingdom in 722 BC, Judah remained alone, subject to the empire. However, as we saw in our discussion of the book of Nahum, in the late seventh century the Assyrian Empire began to decline in power as the Chaldeans in Babylon grew in strength. In 605 BC, the Babylonians decisively defeated the Egyptians at the Battle of Carchemish. While they were in the area, they took control of Judah and exiled some people, including the prophet Daniel. Later they returned to deal with rebellions in 597 and 586 BC, when they destroyed Jerusalem (see the overview in chap. 3).

Therefore, if Habakkuk is anticipating the rise of the Babylonians, his ministry probably dates to a few years before 605, when they became powerful and invaded Judah. This time period would also correspond to the reign of Jehoiakim (609–598 BC), a period in which Judah was known for wickedness (2 Kings 24:1–3; Jer. 26; 36). Based on this information, we can tentatively date Habakkuk to 608–605 BC (see the time line of Habakkuk).

Exploration

Table 20.1 presents the structure of the book of Habakkuk. The book begins with a dialogue in two parts (1:2–2:5). In the first part, Habakkuk asks if God is going to do anything about the sin and injustice in Judah (**1:2–4**), and God responds that he is bringing the Chaldeans to attack Judah (**1:5–11**). For Habakkuk, this seems to make things worse, which prompts a second round of dialogue. Habakkuk asks how it can be right to send the wicked Chaldeans. Will they be punished for *their* evil? What about that justice? (**1:12–2:1**). God answers by promising a vision, commanding the righteous person to live in faithfulness while he or she waits (**2:2–5**).

This response from God is a key turning point in the book, and it sets up the second half in two more parts. First, Habakkuk further explains the vision, declaring five "woes" on the wicked, confident that God will act and bring justice (**2:6–20**). Second, Habakkuk prays a prayer of faith in which he admits that what is coming on Judah will be difficult to endure, but he has

HISTORICAL MATTERS

"Fact Sheet"—Habakkuk

Author: Habakkuk

Date: 608–605 BC

Location: Judah, after the Northern Kingdom had come to an end

Political and social context: The prophet Habakkuk complains that the land of Judah is characterized by violence and injustice so that "the law is paralyzed" (1:4). In this context, he announces that God is bringing the Chaldean army from Babylon as judgment. The prophet himself struggles over this news because the Chaldeans have a fierce and violent reputation (1:8–9).

TIME LINE

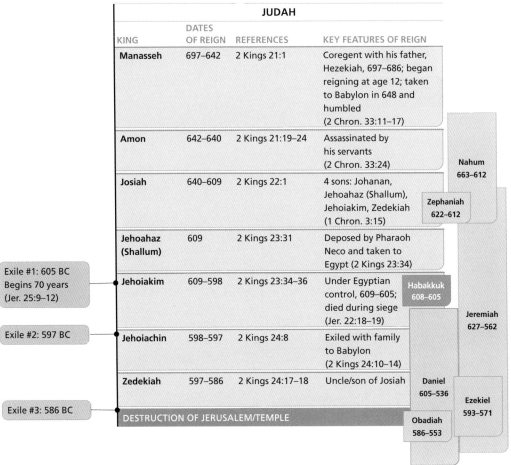

JUDAH			
KING	DATES OF REIGN	REFERENCES	KEY FEATURES OF REIGN
Manasseh	697–642	2 Kings 21:1	Coregent with his father, Hezekiah, 697–686; began reigning at age 12; taken to Babylon in 648 and humbled (2 Chron. 33:11–17)
Amon	642–640	2 Kings 21:19–24	Assassinated by his servants (2 Chron. 33:24)
Josiah	640–609	2 Kings 22:1	4 sons: Johanan, Jehoahaz (Shallum), Jehoiakim, Zedekiah (1 Chron. 3:15)
Jehoahaz (Shallum)	609	2 Kings 23:31	Deposed by Pharaoh Neco and taken to Egypt (2 Kings 23:34)
Jehoiakim	609–598	2 Kings 23:34–36	Under Egyptian control, 609–605; died during siege (Jer. 22:18–19)
Jehoiachin	598–597	2 Kings 24:8	Exiled with family to Babylon (2 Kings 24:10–14)
Zedekiah	597–586	2 Kings 24:17–18	Uncle/son of Josiah
DESTRUCTION OF JERUSALEM/TEMPLE			

Nahum 663–612

Zephaniah 622–612

Habakkuk 608–605

Jeremiah 627–562

Daniel 605–536

Ezekiel 593–571

Obadiah 586–553

Exile #1: 605 BC Begins 70 years (Jer. 25:9–12)

Exile #2: 597 BC

Exile #3: 586 BC

Table 20.1. The Structure of Habakkuk

1:1 Superscription	
1:2–11 First conversation • Habakkuk: Judah is unjust! (1:2–4) • YHWH: The Chaldeans will bring justice (1:5–11)	
1:12–2:5 Second conversation • Habakkuk: Sending the Chaldeans is unjust! (1:12–2:1) • YHWH: Wait for the vision to be fulfilled and live in faithfulness (2:2–5)	2:6–20 The vision: five "woes" on the destroyer 3:1–19 Habakkuk's prayer of faith

Note: On the structure, I am influenced by David G. Firth, "Habakkuk," in *ESV Expository Commentary*, vol. 7, *Daniel–Malachi*, ed. Iain M. Duguid, James M. Hamilton, and Jay Sklar (Wheaton: Crossway, 2018), 537.

confidence in God's goodness and will trust him (**3:1–19**). This corresponds to God's command to live in faithfulness.

Habakkuk addresses three of the five phases that we have seen in other prophetic books. He accuses Judah of breaking covenant and sinning against God in the past. He also calls for judgment on Judah and reports God's promise that judgment is coming in the near future. This leads to a broader indictment and assurance of judgment on the Chaldeans in the more distant future, a pattern that gives all God's people hope that though the righteous have to wait, eventually (even in the eschatological future) God will judge evil and justice will be done.

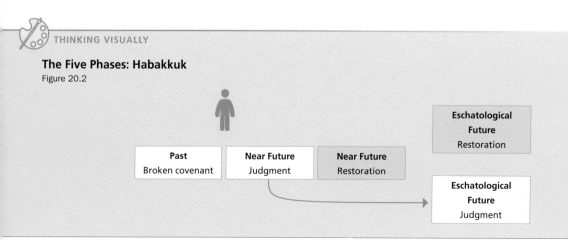

THINKING VISUALLY

The Five Phases: Habakkuk
Figure 20.2

Habakkuk's First Conversation with YHWH

■ READ HABAKKUK 1:2–11 ■

Following the superscription in 1:1, we join a conversation in progress. The prophet Habakkuk is crying out to God over the sins of Judah. Like other prophets, Habakkuk is distressed over the sin and covenant unfaithfulness among his own people—the people of God. He sees violence, wrongdoing, destruction, and strife. Furthermore, the "law is paralyzed" so that justice is perverted. However, Habakkuk's primary complaint is that God does not hear his cries (1:2) and looks "idly" at wrong (1:3). How can God see the sin of Judah and not do anything about it? When will he act to judge what is evil?

In 1:5–11, God responds that he *is* bringing judgment against Judah, in the form of the fierce Chaldean army. God admits that this is a surprising move; Habakkuk will hardly believe it (1:5). The reason for the shock is that the Chaldeans themselves are wicked—more wicked than Judah! In 1:6–11 God describes their evil character. They are thieving, unjust, violent, "guilty men" who worship their own strength.

Habakkuk's Second Conversation with YHWH

■ READ HABAKKUK 1:12–2:5 ■

When God responds that the Chaldeans will be his tools of judgment against Judah, Habakkuk raises a second objection in 1:12–2:1. Previously, he could not understand how God could see Judah's sin and not deal with it. Now he asks how God can look at the Chaldeans "and remain silent when the wicked swallows up the man more righteous than he" (1:13). The cure is worse than the disease! How can a holy God stand by while the Chaldeans conquer and destroy God's own people, who are comparatively better? In the first conversation, Habakkuk was worried about God's apparent lack of justice. Now that concern has been intensified. Confused and struggling to accept God's response, Habakkuk states that he will station himself at his "watch post" and wait to see what God will say (2:1). He is using the image of a solider standing guard at a fortress—but instead of looking intently for some sign of the enemy, he is looking intently for some answer from God that will make sense of what he has been told. 👥

God offers a double response to Habakkuk's second objection. First, he gives Habakkuk a vision that awaits fulfillment in the future (2:2–3). We are not told the content of the vision in these verses, but it seems likely that it consists of the five "woes" against the Chaldeans in verses 6–20 (see below). God assures Habakkuk that though he will have to wait for justice to be done, it *will* happen (2:3).

The second part of God's answer is that "the righteous shall live by his faith" (2:4). (It is also possible to translate the Hebrew, "The righteous shall live by its faithfulness," referring to the vision. In other words, the righteous person will live knowing that the vision of justice will come to pass.) The word translated "faith" or "faithfulness" here refers to commitment to God as well as to ongoing trust in God. In contrast to the proud person (2:4a, 5), the righteous person maintains faith in God even when the situation is incredibly difficult. Habakkuk may be alluding to Genesis 15:6, which says that Abraham "believed the LORD, and he counted it to him as righteousness," using the same two words, "righteous" and "belief/faithfulness." If he has Genesis in mind, then Habakkuk is encouraging his listeners to follow the example of Abraham, who did not just believe in God once, but lived a whole life of obedience.[3]

The Vision: Five "Woes"

■ READ HABAKKUK 2:6–20 ■

Although it is not explicitly stated, it seems that the oracles in this section make up the vision that God promised. Habakkuk should be encouraged that although the Chaldeans will be successful in the short term, eventually they will be doomed because of what they have done—if not in the near future, then certainly in the eschatological time to come. The oracles consist of five woes. The word "woe" (Hebrew: *hoy*) expresses a cry or a howl that something terrible has happened or will happen. It is used for warnings and sometimes for mourning the dead. Habakkuk uses it in 2:6, 9, 12, 15, and 19 to divide this section into smaller units.

In the first woe, 2:6–8, Habakkuk announces that because the Chaldeans have plundered many other nations, everyone who remains will plunder them. In the second woe, 2:9–11, he says that they have harmed others while assuming that they were safe from any danger, but danger will come back to them in the end. Third, in

2:12–14, the prophet says that the Chaldeans have used violence to build their cities and empire, but God owns and rules the earth. Their work will have been "for nothing." Fourth, in 2:15–17, Habakkuk uses the imagery of drunkenness to show that although the Chaldeans have abused and humiliated others, it is they who will be humiliated. Finally, in the fifth woe (2:18–20), Habakkuk attacks the idolatry of the Chaldeans; they trust in gods of wood and metal who have no life or power. By contrast, "the LORD is in his holy temple; let all the earth keep silence before him" (2:20). This final verse is a fitting conclusion to the entire oracle. The Chaldeans seem fierce and unstoppable, but they are only allowed to do what they do by the great God who rules in power over the entire earth. When his patience is exhausted and his will is done, he will destroy the Chaldeans and nothing will stand in his way. 📖 👥

Habakkuk's Prayer of Faith

■ READ HABAKKUK 3:1–19 ■

In 2:2–4, God responded to Habakkuk's complaint of injustice by giving him a vision of the future and the instruction to live by "faithfulness." Habakkuk presents the vision in the remainder of chapter 2. Chapter 3 is a song of faithfulness in which Habakkuk acknowledges the judgment coming on Judah and is realistic about the suffering to follow, but he also puts his trust and confidence in God. Christians throughout the ages

The "Cup" in YHWH's Right Hand

In the Old Testament, the word "cup" is used in the typical sense of something that holds liquid for someone to drink. It also frequently appears as a metaphor for the judgment and wrath of God (see Ps. 75:8; Isa. 51:17; Jer. 25:15). Perhaps the idea is that God's anger and judgment will cause the people to "stagger and go out of their minds."[f] In Habakkuk 2:16, the prophet introduces the metaphor of drunkenness and then uses the "cup" of YHWH to represent his wrath. The Chaldeans have made others drunk in order to take advantage of them (2:15), and now God's cup will come around to them in judgment.

Pesher Habakkuk among the Dead Sea Scrolls

The famous Dead Sea Scrolls were discovered about thirteen miles east of Jerusalem, near Qumran, a community inhabited by Jews who had separated themselves from mainstream Judaism.[9] Among the finds were 225 scrolls of biblical texts, as well as other writings related to the sect's teachings and theology. These extrabiblical texts included biblical commentaries called *pesharim*. The most famous and best preserved of these is Pesher Habakkuk, which provides commentary on Habakkuk 1:2–2:20 (see fig. 20.3). Rather than interpreting biblical books according to the author's original context, interpreters read the text allegorically in light of their own circumstances. For example, in Habakkuk 1:4, where Habakkuk says that "the wicked surround the righteous," the writers of Pesher Habakkuk identify the righteous as their own leader, the "Teacher of Righteousness."[h] When Habakkuk announces the coming of the "Chaldeans" (1:6), the Qumran community interpreted this to refer to the Romans, who had invaded Palestine in 63 BC. In this way, the commentators attempted to make the book immediately and directly relevant for themselves.[i]

Public Domain / Wikimedia Commons

Figure 20.3. A page from Pesher Habakkuk

have drawn strength from this prayer as they have faced their own hardship and loss.

Habakkuk begins by asking God for mercy in the midst of his wrath (3:2). He then meditates on God's glory and total rule over creation. However, God's acts of power are not just a show for his own amusement. He comes for the salvation of his people, to crush the head of the wicked (3:13). When God is angry, he is still good. He is angry for the sake of justice and righteousness, always justified in what he does. With this theological foundation in mind, Habakkuk turns his attention to the coming judgment. He is terrified and fully expects to experience starvation and destitution (3:16–17). However, even in the midst of hardship, he will rejoice in YHWH and take joy in his salvation (3:18–19).

Implementation

Like other short prophetic books, the book of Habakkuk has a greater theological weight and significance than one might assume based on its length alone. Let us consider three key issues it addresses. First, Habakkuk contributes to a biblical understanding of the sovereignty of God. We know from other parts of Scripture that God cannot be tempted by evil (James 1:13) and that he is never the author of evil (Ps. 5:4). He hates wickedness (Ps. 45:7), and in him there is no darkness at all (1 John 1:5). However, God can and does use the actions of evil people to accomplish his purposes. God will use the Chaldeans without being morally responsible for their evil, and they in turn will not be immune to justice when they have finished his work (see also Isa. 10:5, 12). Just as we struggle over this tension of God's sovereignty and the freedom of the human will, it seemed unjust to Habakkuk. But like Habakkuk, we must continue to trust God and have confidence in him. We can be certain of this: in our worst times, God is completely good and completely in control of the situation.

Second, Habakkuk shows us that it is okay to wrestle with God. Sometimes, when God reveals truth, it is not easy to accept or understand. His thoughts and ways are higher than ours (Isa. 55:8–9), and our perspective is perverted by pride and sin. One of the amazing things about the Old Testament is that it encourages us to be honest when we do not feel like God is managing things properly. We saw an example of this in the book of Jonah when God patiently reasoned with Jonah even though he was so obviously out of line. The prophet Habakkuk also has problems with the way God is running his universe. He struggles with the lack of justice in society and wonders why God is slow to act. Then, when God announces that he will act, Habakkuk thinks God's plans are even more unjust. Rather than letting his doubts fester and drive a wedge between him and God, Habakkuk brings them to YHWH in an act of faith. The book presents the struggling prophet's dialogue with a patient God for our benefit. Amazingly, our great God, who made the heavens and the earth, is willing to dialogue with one small, angry prophet. And he is gentle, knowing that the truth will be hard to hear. God is similarly eager for us to come to him with what troubles us; we will find the same gentleness and faithfulness that inspired the confident faith of Habakkuk.

Third, the book urges us to cling to God even in the midst of challenges. As we listen in on the conversation between Habakkuk and God, we gain a fresh perspective. Despite appearances, God *is* good. Sometimes we must determine to remain loyal to him while we endure suffering, even when our confidence in him is temporarily shaken. In the Gospel of John, when many of Jesus's disciples were leaving him in a difficult season, Peter said to Jesus, "Lord, to whom shall we go? You have the words of eternal life" (John 6:68). Similarly, Habakkuk feels that God is being unjust, and yet he calls him "the God of my salvation" (3:18). To whom else would he go? This God is the maker of all things and has demonstrated his mercy and kindness over and over. Habakkuk will live in faithfulness with the tension and mystery. He will not demand all the answers as a condition for his faith. He will live joyfully, trusting that God knows what he is doing, even when it is difficult to accept.

Christian Reading Questions

1. What is your reaction to the presentation of the first two chapters of Habakkuk, in which God and the prophet engage in a dialogue? The prophet is unhappy with God, and God responds to his complaints. Where else in the Prophets have we seen God's willingness to dialogue with his people? How can this interaction be an encouragement to people in the church today?
2. Compare Habakkuk's first complaint against God (1:2–4) and his second complaint (1:12–2:1). How are they related? How do the same values underlie both of Habakkuk's concerns?

3. Describe how Habakkuk's prayer of faith (3:1–19) is related to his complaints in chapter 1. What has Habakkuk learned about God? Does his prayer in 3:1–19 ignore his earlier concerns?

CHAPTER TWENTY-ONE

Zephaniah

Orientation

Is a military invasion good news or bad news? That depends on who you are and your relationship to the ones invading. Early on the morning of June 6, 1944, "D-Day," a massive group of naval and amphibious forces from the US, Great Britain, and Canada crossed the English Channel and approached the beaches of France, which was occupied by German troops. The invasion force consisted of 5,000 ships and landing craft, 11,000 support aircraft, and 156,000 soldiers; they were there to liberate Europe from Adolf Hitler's Nazi Germany.[1] As the German soldiers stood in their fortified bunkers and saw the Allied ships appear on the horizon, what were they thinking? US battleships began to pound their positions with massive, destructive shells, aircraft bombed them, and thousands of Allied soldiers streamed ashore.

Was this invasion good news or bad news? Of course, for the Germans, it was terrible news. In the next few hours, many of them would die, and their side would eventually be defeated. However, for the people of Paris, the invasion was the best news they had received in a long time. They cheered when they heard news reports on the radio and knew that the occupation of their nation would likely be over soon. One invasion was viewed from two very

Figure 21.1. German soldiers in World War II

different perspectives. For the occupier, it meant defeat. For the occupied, it meant liberation.

The book of Zephaniah tells of the coming day of YHWH, when God will break into human history and "invade" with terrible destruction, holding the world accountable for its rebellion against him. Is this day something that we should fear or celebrate? Again, it depends. For those who persist in evil and have not reconciled to God, this day will be their ultimate defeat. But for those who belong to God, the undoing of the earth and the defeat of wickedness will mean liberation, freedom, security, and hope.

The superscription to the book (1:1) traces the prophet Zephaniah's ancestry back five generations. It is unusual for a prophet's lineage to go into such detail, but we are likely given this information in order to draw attention to Zephaniah's great-great-grandfather, King Hezekiah (cf. 2 Kings 18–20; Isa. 36–39). Hezekiah is well known for attempting widespread religious reforms in Judah in order to purge the land of idolatry and unorthodox ritual practices and return it to the faithful, biblical worship of God. Zephaniah, therefore, was of royal ancestry. Unlike the prophet Micah, who has a particular interest in the common people, Zephaniah seems to be more familiar with the ruling class and the leadership of Judah. His main concern is with princes, judges, prophets, and priests.[2]

The first verse of the book also tells us that the prophet was active during the days of Josiah, king of Judah, who initiated religious reforms like those of Hezekiah. Since Josiah was king between 640 and 609 BC, this is the general time frame of Zephaniah's prophetic work. But can we be more precise?

In his eighteenth year (622 BC), Josiah gave orders to refurbish the temple in Jerusalem (2 Kings 22:3). In the process, the workmen discovered the book of the law, which had been hidden and neglected for years. When the book was read to him, Josiah tore his clothes in repentance and sorrow. Determined that Judah would obey God, he began reforms to remove idols, tear down altars, destroy ritual sites, and depose false priests (2 Kings 23). If Josiah's actions are any indication of the book's contents, it is likely that the discovered book was Deuteronomy. And because the book of Zephaniah contains extensive language from the book of Deuteronomy,[3] Zephaniah must have had access to this book *after* it was discovered in 622 BC.[4] Zephaniah also looks forward to the destruction of Nineveh (cf. 2:13), which occurred in 612 BC. Therefore, his ministry was probably between 622 BC and 612 BC (see the time line of Zephaniah).

We might speculate that Zephaniah was involved in Josiah's reforms, urging him to do the right thing and to seek after God.[5] One scholar writes, "Even if [King Josiah's] major policies were instituted in a relatively short period of time, he still would have needed the strong supporting confirmation of a contemporary word from the Lord to make his policies even remotely acceptable to the public. Very possibly this supporting word came from Zephaniah the prophet."[6]

King Josiah's reforms ultimately revealed a difficult truth. The king could decide that Judah would obey God, removing idols and killing wicked priests, but he could not change the hearts of the people. The reforms would be only external, while the people were actually no more faithful to God than they had been before. In this light, Zephaniah's discussion

TIME LINE

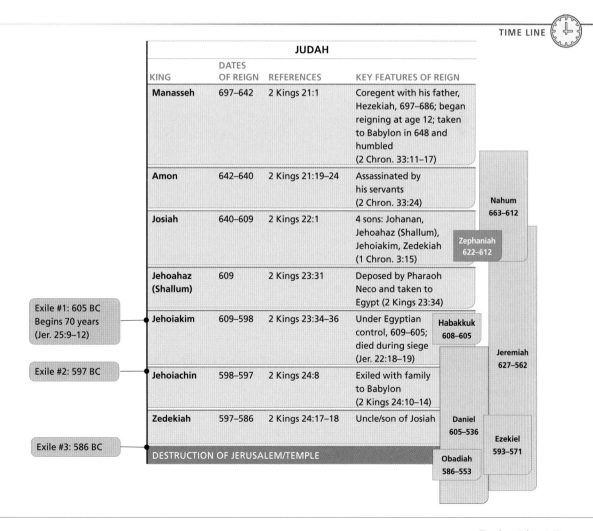

JUDAH			
KING	DATES OF REIGN	REFERENCES	KEY FEATURES OF REIGN
Manasseh	697–642	2 Kings 21:1	Coregent with his father, Hezekiah, 697–686; began reigning at age 12; taken to Babylon in 648 and humbled (2 Chron. 33:11–17)
Amon	642–640	2 Kings 21:19–24	Assassinated by his servants (2 Chron. 33:24)
Josiah	640–609	2 Kings 22:1	4 sons: Johanan, Jehoahaz (Shallum), Jehoiakim, Zedekiah (1 Chron. 3:15)
Jehoahaz (Shallum)	609	2 Kings 23:31	Deposed by Pharaoh Neco and taken to Egypt (2 Kings 23:34)
Jehoiakim	609–598	2 Kings 23:34–36	Under Egyptian control, 609–605; died during siege (Jer. 22:18–19)
Jehoiachin	598–597	2 Kings 24:8	Exiled with family to Babylon (2 Kings 24:10–14)
Zedekiah	597–586	2 Kings 24:17–18	Uncle/son of Josiah
DESTRUCTION OF JERUSALEM/TEMPLE			

Nahum 663–612

Zephaniah 622–612

Habakkuk 608–605

Jeremiah 627–562

Daniel 605–536

Ezekiel 593–571

Obadiah 586–553

Exile #1: 605 BC Begins 70 years (Jer. 25:9–12)

Exile #2: 597 BC

Exile #3: 586 BC

of a righteous remnant is significant. Although the people of Judah were God's people according to the covenant, only some of them truly sought God and worshiped him in truth. And only these would be saved from the coming judgment.

Exploration

Zephaniah mentions the sins of Judah, but his primary purpose is not to indict his audience or convince them that they've broken God's covenant. He does not demonstrate their guilt or give many examples. Nor does Zephaniah announce judgment and restoration in the near future. He is entirely concerned with the eschatological future, when the day of YHWH will bring global judgment for the wicked and permanent restoration for the remnant.

The structure of the book is presented in table 21.1. The shaded boxes represent announcements of judgment, while the white boxes represent oracles of salvation. The first section, **1:2–6**, is a general introduction to the book and an announcement of God's global judgment. In the eschatological future, the status quo will come to an end. God will end business as usual when he stops human history and calls all people to account. In **1:7–18**, this time of judgment is identified as the "day of the LORD," and references to that day occur in various forms (e.g., "that day," "that time," "a day of . . . ," "day of the wrath of the LORD") sixteen times in a range of twelve verses (vv. 7, 8, 9, 10, 12, 14, 15, 16, and 18). Zephaniah then issues a call to repentance in **2:1–4**. This new section is marked by a shift from declarations to commands. Surprisingly, we learn that God's judgment *is* avoidable if the humble seek him before his wrath comes. If they do, they will not be included in God's judgment and will instead find that the day of YHWH

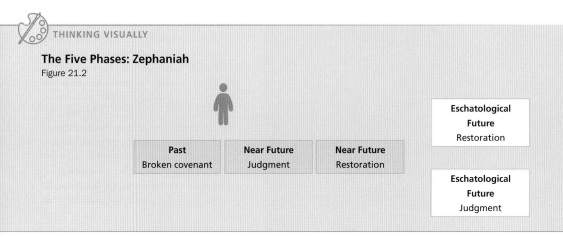

THINKING VISUALLY

The Five Phases: Zephaniah
Figure 21.2

Past	Near Future	Near Future
Broken covenant	Judgment	Restoration

Eschatological Future
Restoration

Eschatological Future
Judgment

Table 21.1. The Structure of Zephaniah

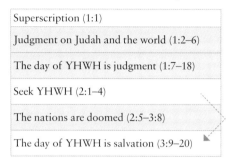

Superscription (1:1)
Judgment on Judah and the world (1:2–6)
The day of YHWH is judgment (1:7–18)
Seek YHWH (2:1–4)
The nations are doomed (2:5–3:8)
The day of YHWH is salvation (3:9–20)

is a day of salvation (illustrated by the black arrow). Next, **2:5–3:8** extends Zephaniah's discussion of the day of YHWH to the nations around Judah, and he includes Jerusalem as a wicked city as well. Finally, the last section (**3:9–20**) offers an alternative to the preceding day of YHWH. In the midst of judgment, God will preserve and transform a remnant of people for himself. For these people, the day of YHWH is not fearful, but joyous. The book concludes with a hymn of praise to God, who saves his people.

Judgment on Judah and the World

■ READ ZEPHANIAH 1:2–6 ■

The book of Zephaniah begins with an announcement of God's judgment against all creation. He will destroy not only humans—though they are the focus—but all created things, including animals (1:2–3). In verses 4–6, God focuses his attention on Judah and its capital city, Jerusalem. The inhabitants of Judah are God's special people, in a covenant relationship with him. However, they "do not seek the LORD or inquire of him" (1:6). They worship Baal and follow idolatrous priests. Therefore, just as Judah and Jerusalem have been singled out for God's special favor, now they will be singled out for his particular attention in judgment. They bear a greater responsibility because they are his people.

The Day of YHWH Is Judgment

■ READ ZEPHANIAH 1:7–18 ■

Zephaniah calls for silence because he is announcing "the day of the LORD" (1:7). The previous section announced judgment on the world in general (1:2–3) and on Judah (1:4–6); the present section announces

CANONICAL CONNECTIONS

The Undoing of Creation

In Genesis 1, the description of God's creation mentions first fish, then birds (1:20–21), then land animals (1:24–25), then humans (1:26). Zephaniah, however, uses exactly the reverse order in his description of God's devastating judgment: humans, land animals, birds, and fish (1:2–3). It is as though God will undo what he did at the first. He has built the world; now he will take it apart again.[a]

CANONICAL CONNECTIONS

Houses and Vineyards

In 1:13, Zephaniah predicts that one result of the terrible day of YHWH is that the people of Judah will build houses but not live in them and will plant vineyards but not drink their wine. We have seen similar statements previously in the book of Amos (5:11; cf. 9:14–15). Both Amos and Zephaniah (along with Micah 6:15) are drawing on the book of Deuteronomy (28:30, 39). These verses are part of the original covenant curses that God said would come on those who betray him. God is making good on his promise to judge his people when they break the covenant.

CANONICAL CONNECTIONS

Imagery from Mount Sinai

In Zephaniah 1:15, the prophet speaks of the day of YHWH as "a day of darkness and gloom" and "a day of clouds and thick darkness." This wording is identical to Joel 2:2. In the next verse, Zephaniah 1:16, the language of "a day of trumpet blast and battle cry" is very similar to Joel 2:1. Perhaps one of these prophets drew on the other. If, as I suggest, the book of Joel is late, then perhaps Joel is alluding to Zephaniah. Another possibility is that both prophets are drawing on imagery from God's appearance at Mount Sinai in the book of Exodus, which involved darkness, cloud, and trumpets (cf. Exod. 19:16).[b]

RECEPTION HISTORY

Dies Irae

The poem *Dies Irae* (Latin for "day of wrath") is a reflection on judgment that is heavily influenced by Zephaniah 1:14–18. First printed in 1485, it has been chanted for hundreds of years as a part of church liturgies, and every major hymnbook in Great Britain and the US has represented it in some form.[c] Thus, it has been extremely influential on Christian faith. The poem begins as follows:

That day of wrath, that dreadful day,
shall heaven and earth in ashes lay,
As David and the Sibyl say.

What horror must invade the mind,
when the approaching Judge shall find
and sift the deeds of all mankind!

The mighty trumpet's wondrous tone
shall rend each tomb's sepulchral stone
and summon all before the Throne.[d]

the day of YHWH in reverse order: first against Judah (1:7–13) and then against the world (1:14–18).

The prophet compares the coming day to a sacrifice (1:7–8). This would have been a vivid image for an ancient audience who had firsthand experience seeing an animal slaughtered, with blood pouring out and its carcass burning on an altar. The prophet warns that God will not be sacrificing a bull or a sheep—he will kill and burn the wicked of the earth! We can all imagine a fugitive trying to hide from danger wherever he can: behind a wall, in a hole, or in a locked storage room. In verse 12, Zephaniah gives us the terrifying image of God himself searching through Jerusalem for his enemies so that he can destroy them. There will be no safe place to hide. The day of YHWH is "near"; it will be a "bitter" time of wrath, distress, anguish, ruin, devastation, darkness, and gloom (1:14–15).

God is not bringing distress on mankind because he is fundamentally angry and destructive. It is because "they have sinned against the LORD" (1:17). No one will escape the consequences that he or she has stored up: "In the fire of his jealousy, all the earth shall be consumed; for a full and sudden end he will make of all the inhabitants of the earth" (1:18).

Seek YHWH

■ READ ZEPHANIAH 2:1–4 ■

Suddenly, after a chapter of describing God's fierce judgment, there is an unexpected twist at the beginning of chapter 2: the judgment can be avoided by those who repent. Zephaniah calls on Judah (and, by extension, the readers of his book) to gather together and seek YHWH. There is no way to stop

the day of YHWH; it *is* coming. But if a person
seeks YHWH, he or she can be hidden from
God's anger in that time (2:3). There are two
stipulations. First, a person must seek YHWH
before the day of judgment arrives (2:2). After
the day comes, it will be too late. Second, a person must be humble and demonstrate faith by
seeking what is right and obeying God (2:3). For
the humble person, that future day can be a time
of salvation. This anticipates the last section of
the book, which we will discuss below.

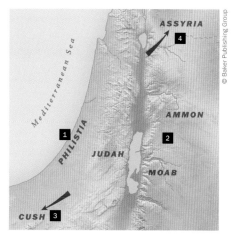

Map 21.1. Zephaniah's oracles against the nations

The Nations Are Doomed

■ READ ZEPHANIAH 2:5–3:8 ■

Zephaniah's oracles against the nations surrounding Judah begin with
a "woe"—a cry that something terrible has happened or will happen (see
the discussion of Hab. 2:6–20 above). His words in this section are organized by the four points on a compass (see map 21.1). To the west, YHWH
declares that he is against the Philistines (2:5–7). The Ammonites and
Moabites are to the east (2:8–11). They have mistreated God's people, and
in response the remnant of God's people will plunder and possess Ammon
and Moab. To the south, God declares that he will slay Cush by his sword
(2:12). And to the north, he says he will stretch out his hand against Assyria
(2:13–15). (Assyria is actually directly east of Judah, but one travels there
by first going north and then east around the Arabian Desert.)

In 3:1, Zephaniah turns his attention next to an "oppressing city." At
first glance, since the passage follows the discussion of Assyria in the
previous verses, it seems like he is speaking about Nineveh. However, he
must be talking about Jerusalem because he calls the city the dwelling
place of God (3:5). The rhetorical effect is clear: the Philistines, Ammonites, Moabites, Cushites, and Assyrians are pagan nations who obviously
do not acknowledge God—and Jerusalem is just like them! She is just as
guilty. She is oppressive, accepts no correction, and does not trust in God
(3:1–2). Her officials exploit the people, and her prophets and priests are
false (3:3–4). Tragically, Jerusalem should have seen the judgment that God
brought against other nations and learned from the example. Instead, "all
the more they were eager to make all their deeds corrupt" (3:7). Because
Judah has acted just like the oppressing nations around her—even though
she should know better—she will face the same judgment in the day of
YHWH.

The Day of YHWH Is Salvation

■ READ ZEPHANIAH 3:9–20 ■

Up to this point, Zephaniah has described the day of YHWH as a time of darkness, gloom, punishment, and destruction. Even in chapter 2, when he calls the reader to seek YHWH, the day is still something to be saved *from*. However, in the last section of the book, 3:9–20, we get a completely different perspective on this inevitable day. For those who have humbled themselves before God and belong to him, the day of YHWH will be a time of relief and salvation.

We can summarize Zephaniah's positive description of the day in four categories. First, it will be a day of *transformation*. God will change the speech of the peoples, enabling them to call on him and serve him (3:9). This suggests that without his enabling power, they will not be able to escape their own sin and rebellion. They will no longer be proud (3:11–12) and will reflect God's character as those who do justice and tell the truth (3:13). Second, it will be a day of *forgiveness*. God says, "On that day you shall not be put to shame because of the deeds by which you have rebelled against me" (3:11). He will have taken away the judgments against his people (3:15). Third, he will *remove all evil*. In six verses in this section, he states that he will remove the proud and any who oppress them and make them afraid (3:11, 13, 15, 16, 18, 19). As we have seen in other prophetic books, God's people will only be safe and at rest when God has destroyed his enemies and there is none left to mistreat them. Finally, it will be a day of *restoration*. God will save the lame, gather the outcast, and turn shame into praise (3:19). He says, "I will make you renowned and praised among all the peoples of the earth, when I restore your fortunes before your eyes" (3:20).

The joy of this day is depicted in singing. God's people will sing and praise (3:14, 19). And God himself will sing over his people—those in whom he delights—for he has rescued them for himself. In one of the most beautiful verses in all of Scripture, Zephaniah paints a vivid picture of God bursting with joy over his people: "The LORD your God is in your midst, a mighty one who will save; he will rejoice over you with gladness; he will quiet you by his love; he will exult over you with loud singing" (3:17).

Implementation

The prophet Zephaniah refers to the day of YHWH twenty-two times in his book (see table 21.2). One scholar writes, "There is a compelling

Table 21.2. Zephaniah's References to the Day of YHWH

The day of YHWH is judgment	1:7	The **day** of the LORD is near.
	1:8	On the **day** of the LORD's sacrifice— "I will punish . . ."
	1:9	"On that **day** I will punish . . ."
	1:10	"On that **day** . . . a cry will be heard."
	1:12	"At that **time** . . . I will punish the men . . ."
	1:14	The great **day** of the LORD is near . . . ; the sound of the **day** of the LORD is bitter.
	1:15	A **day** of wrath is that **day,** a **day** of distress and anguish, a **day** of ruin and devastation, a **day** of darkness and gloom, a **day** of clouds and thick darkness,
	1:16	a **day** of trumpet blast and battle cry.
	1:18	Neither their silver nor their gold shall be able to deliver them on the **day** of the wrath of the LORD.
Seek YHWH	2:2–3	. . . before the **day** passes away like chaff— before there comes upon you the **day** of the anger of the LORD. Seek the LORD.
The nations are doomed	3:8	"Therefore wait for me . . . for the **day** when I rise up to seize the prey."
The day of YHWH is salvation	3:9	"For at that **time** I will change the speech of the peoples."
	3:11	"On that **day** you shall not be put to shame."
	3:16	On that **day** it shall be said to Jerusalem: "Fear not, O Zion."
	3:19	"Behold, at that **time**, I will deal with all your oppressors."
	3:20	"At that **time** I will bring you in, at the **time** when I gather you together; . . . I will make you renowned."

simplicity about Zephaniah's message: he has only one topic, and he never digresses from it."[7]

Although Zephaniah's one topic is the day of YHWH, he gives us two very different perspectives on it. And these perspectives depend entirely on our status before God. If we do not belong to God, we *should* fear his day, and we should be motivated to humble ourselves before him while we still have time.

There are five verses in the book in which Zephaniah issues commands directly to the reader. The first four verses are addressed to those who are not in a saving relationship with God. In 1:11, Zephaniah urges us to "wail" when we see judgment, because we are also potential targets of God's wrath. We must understand the danger of remaining enemies of God. In 2:1 he calls us to "gather together" before the judgment arrives so that we can honestly assess our situation. If God's day comes, it will be too late, and we will be lost. The only hope for those who stand at odds with God lies in the third set of commands in 2:3: "Seek the Lord. . . . Seek righteousness; seek humility." This is the key to salvation from that terrible day. It is a matter of defecting from one people to another, abandoning God's enemies and joining his people by humbling ourselves before him. In 3:8, he issues another command: we must wait for the day when he pours out his burning anger on all the earth.

On the other hand, if we already belong to God, we have nothing to fear from the day of YHWH. The fifth and final verse containing commands is 3:14, in which God says, "Sing aloud . . . shout . . . ! Rejoice and exult with all your heart . . . !" The day of YHWH will be a time of salvation, when we find firsthand that God is merciful. He does not leave his people as slaves to sin but transforms them to be what he created them to be: whole, and in a loving relationship with him for all time.

When Zephaniah tells us in 2:3 to "seek the Lord," how does one do that? The New Testament tells us that we must call on Jesus Christ, God's crucified Son, and place our trust in him. The book of Zephaniah looks forward to Christ, who executes both aspects of the day of YHWH. It is Christ who performs the judgment on that day, slaying the wicked and defeating them permanently (cf. 2 Pet. 3:10; Rev. 19:19–21). It is also Christ who saves us from that same judgment. Christ, on the cross, has already absorbed the great and terrible day of YHWH in our place (cf. 2 Cor. 5:21). Zephaniah's description of judgment is horrific, but Christ, the spotless lamb of God, bore it in its entirety. If we turn from our sin and put our trust in him, we can have certainty that we will be forgiven, adopted as sons and daughters, and made a part of the "remnant" that he has created for himself. We can also have certainty that we will be "hidden" in the time of God's anger. The choice between the two experiences of the day of YHWH is ours to make. God will not wait forever—seek him now.

Christian Reading Questions

1. Make a list of the images that the prophet Zephaniah uses for God's judgment. What does each image contribute to Zephaniah's depiction of the day of YHWH?

2. Reread Zephaniah 2:1–4 and consider the prophet's call to seek YHWH. What can we learn about repentance from these verses? What kinds of actions or attitudes are *excluded* from true repentance?

3. What is the point of Zephaniah's oracles against the nations (2:5–3:8) within his overall message? Compare Zephaniah's oracles against the nations to those in Isaiah, Jeremiah, Ezekiel, Amos, and so forth.

4. Compare Amos 5:18–20 with Zephaniah 3:9–20. Is the day of YHWH good news or bad news? What determines a person's experience in it?

CHAPTER TWENTY-TWO

Haggai

Orientation

When I graduated from seminary, I did not receive my actual diploma at the commencement ceremony. On that Friday evening when I walked across the stage in front of family and friends, I shook the president's hand and someone handed me a royal blue display folder. It was attractive enough, but it was empty! After years of hard work—taking quizzes, toiling over final exams, and writing papers—I was told that I would have to wait for up to six weeks for my actual diploma to arrive in the mail. While I waited, I found the empty display folder somewhat disappointing. I could not frame it or show it off. I was not even sure what the real diploma would look like. Though it may have been disappointing as the reward for years of work, that blue folder also represented a promise. Every time I looked at it, I knew that my actual diploma was on the way.

In the time of the prophet Haggai, the people of Judah had finally been given permission to return to the promised land from exile in Babylon. When they arrived, life was . . . disappointing. They came for new lives, but they struggled to grow enough food. They hoped to rebuild the temple, but it was small and unimpressive compared to what it had been. And their leader, Zerubbabel, was subservient to the Persian Empire, which was in control of the region. Haggai promises that ultimate restoration is coming, but the people will have to wait for it. In the meantime, the disappointments that they experience will serve as visible promises for the glorious future that God has in store.

HISTORICAL MATTERS

"Fact Sheet"—Haggai

Author: Haggai

Date: 520 BC

Location: Jerusalem, in Yehud, the Persian province that contained the bulk of what had been the territory of Judah

Political and social context: God's people who had been exiled to Babylon have returned to Jerusalem to settle and rebuild the temple, with support from the Persian Empire. However, the work on the temple has been stopped for years, and the people are struggling with poverty, starvation, and pressure from antagonistic neighbors.

The prophets Haggai, Zechariah, and Malachi lived and served in a very different time than the preexilic and exilic prophets we have discussed to this point. Although we briefly looked at the postexilic historical context in chapter 3, let us review some key events that form the background to the book of Haggai. Because of the covenant unfaithfulness of Judah and Jerusalem—God's people—God brought the Chaldeans against them to remove them from the land. In 586 BC, the Chaldeans conquered Jerusalem, broke down the city wall, destroyed the temple, and exiled a sizable portion of the social upper class to Babylon. The people of Judah were in exile for about seventy years,[1] and at the end of this time the Persians took control of Babylon. In 538 BC, Cyrus the Great, king of the Persian Empire, issued an edict allowing the exiles to return to their own land and to rebuild the temple of God (Ezra 1:1–4; Isa. 44:28). The exiles returned to Judah, now the Persian province of "Yehud," in multiple waves. The first two returns were led by Sheshbazzar and Zerubbabel (governors appointed by the Persians), and later two more returns were led by Ezra and Nehemiah.

When the exiles returned to their homeland, they were disheartened for several reasons. First, they did not have self-rule and were under the control of the Persian Empire. Second, they were few in number[2] and were surrounded by antagonistic neighbors. Third, the people were not growing sufficient food, so they were poor and starving. Fourth, Jerusalem was much smaller than it had been in preexilic times. It was dilapidated and defenseless, without a city wall (see map 22.1).

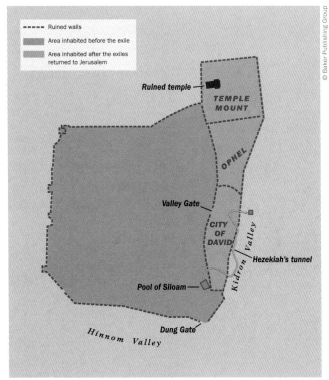

Map 22.1. Jerusalem in the time of Haggai

© Baker Publishing Group

---- Ruined walls

Area inhabited before the exile

Area inhabited after the exiles returned to Jerusalem

Ruined temple

TEMPLE MOUNT

OPHEL

Valley Gate

CITY OF DAVID

Kidron Valley

Hezekiah's tunnel

Pool of Siloam

Dung Gate

Hinnom Valley

Haggai the Prophet

We are told nothing about Haggai in the Bible except that he was a prophet (Hag. 1:1). Unlike some superscriptions in other prophetic books, the opening verse of this book does not even tell us the name of the prophet's father. Later Christian tradition held that Haggai was a priest. However, others have pointed to Haggai 2:11 as evidence that Haggai was *not* a priest, since he asked the priests for their perspective on holiness and uncleanness.[a]

The first exiles to return from Babylon arrived in Jerusalem in 538 BC. Two years later, in 536 BC, the Jewish leadership laid the foundations of the temple (Ezra 3:8–10; 5:14–17).[3] At that point, difficulties arose, including challenges from local adversaries who claimed that building the temple was illegal. The Jews became discouraged and were afraid to continue the project (Ezra 4:4). Given the hardships of life, they prioritized their own homes and farms, and as a result, the work on the temple stopped for sixteen years. However, in 520 BC, the prophets Haggai and Zechariah confronted the people for their disordered priorities and urged them to complete the temple (cf. Ezra 5:1–2; 6:14). The people began to build again in 520 BC, and they dedicated the rebuilt temple in 515 BC (cf. Ezra 6:15–18) (see fig. 22.1).

The book of Haggai contains five superscriptions, which date Haggai's oracles to the last few months of the second year of King Darius, which was 520 BC (see table 22.1).

Table 22.1. The Dates of Haggai's Oracles

Reference	Year	Month	Day	Date
1:1	2nd year of Darius	6th	1st	Aug. 29, 520
1:15	2nd year of Darius	6th	24th	Sept. 21, 520
2:1	[2nd year of Darius]	7th	21st	Oct. 17, 520
2:10	2nd year of Darius	9th	24th	Dec. 18, 520
2:20	[2nd year of Darius]	9th	24th	Dec. 18, 520

Source: Carol L. Meyers and Eric M. Meyers, *Haggai, Zechariah 1–8: A New Translation with Introduction and Commentary*, Anchor Bible 25B (New Haven: Yale University Press, 1987), xlvi–xlvii. Table adapted from a class handout by Sagar Mekwan, Trinity Evangelical Divinity School, fall semester, 2018.

THINKING VISUALLY

The Time Line for Rebuilding the Temple
Figure 22.1

First return → | Temple foundation laid (Ezra 3:10) → | The work stops (Ezra 4:24) | Haggai and Zechariah prophesy ↓ | Temple dedicated (Ezra 6:15) ↓

538 536 520 515

Exploration

Haggai is primarily concerned with two chronological horizons. First, he addresses the present, which is marked by the people's disobedience (not building the temple) and the consequences for it (unsuccessful farming). Second, he looks forward to God's restoration in the eschatological future, when there is a temple with a greater glory and rule under God's Davidic king. (See fig. 22.2.)

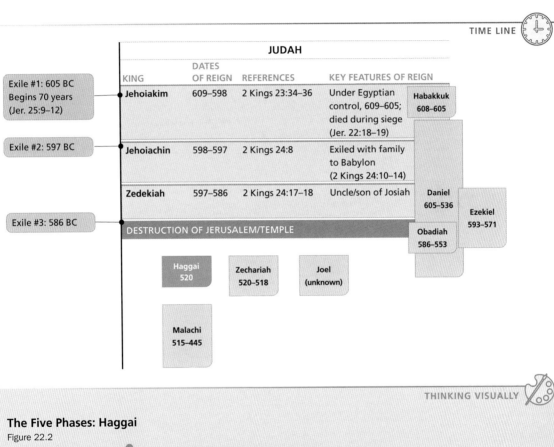

JUDAH			
KING	DATES OF REIGN	REFERENCES	KEY FEATURES OF REIGN
Jehoiakim	609–598	2 Kings 23:34–36	Under Egyptian control, 609–605; died during siege (Jer. 22:18–19)
Jehoiachin	598–597	2 Kings 24:8	Exiled with family to Babylon (2 Kings 24:10–14)
Zedekiah	597–586	2 Kings 24:17–18	Uncle/son of Josiah

Exile #1: 605 BC Begins 70 years (Jer. 25:9–12)

Exile #2: 597 BC

Exile #3: 586 BC

DESTRUCTION OF JERUSALEM/TEMPLE

Habakkuk 608–605

Daniel 605–536

Obadiah 586–553

Ezekiel 593–571

Haggai 520

Zechariah 520–518

Joel (unknown)

Malachi 515–445

THINKING VISUALLY

The Five Phases: Haggai
Figure 22.2

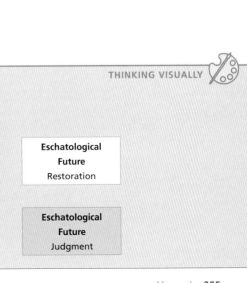

Present	Present	Near Future
Broken covenant	Judgment	Restoration

Eschatological Future
Restoration

Eschatological Future
Judgment

The structure of the book can be discerned in two ways: by the sections marked with dated superscriptions and by repeated phrases (see table 22.2). In the left-hand column, the first and last sections (**1:1–11 and 2:10–19**) both contain accusations of disobedience. In both cases, God has responded to the people's sin by making the land infertile. In the middle sections (**1:12–15 and 2:1–5**), God assures them, "I am with you," first as a motivation to rebuild the temple and then as an encouragement when it turns out to be a disappointment. In the final sections, Haggai transitions twice from present discouragement to eschatological hope (marked by the arrows in table 22.2). In response to the discouragement of the temple, he says that in the eschatological future, it will have a greater glory. In response to the discouragement of present sin, he says that in the eschatological future he will restore the Davidic line, from which the Messiah will come.

Table 22.2. The Structure of Haggai

Date	Present Discouragement	Eschatological Hope
2nd year 6th month 1st day	1:1–11 Accusation: the people have not built the temple (therefore, no fertility)	
2nd year 6th month 24th day	1:12–15 The people obey and build the temple YHWH's encouragement: "I am with you"	
[2nd year] 7th month 21st day	2:1–5 The rebuilt temple is a disappointment YHWH's encouragement: "I am with you" →	2:6–9 ("will shake the heavens") A greater glory
2nd year 9th month 24th day	2:10–19 Accusation: the people are unclean (therefore, no fertility) →	2:20–23 ("about to shake the heavens") A signet ring

Accusation: The People Have Not Built the Temple

■ READ HAGGAI 1:1–11 ■

Through the prophet Haggai, God's word comes to Zerubbabel and Joshua, the leaders of the Jews who have returned from exile. God accuses the people of saying that "the time has not yet come to rebuild the house [i.e., temple] of the Lord" (1:2). They no doubt plan to get around to it later, but for now there are more pressing matters, such as their own houses (1:4). In response to this lack of obedience, God says that though they expected to flourish in the land, he is frustrating their efforts and ensuring that their food, drink, clothing, and economy are all scanty and failing (1:5–11). The language here in Haggai recalls the covenant curses in Deuteronomy (Hag. 1:6 // Deut. 28:38; Hag. 1:10 // Deut. 7:13; 11:13–15; 28:51).

What was so important about the temple? God's temple in Jerusalem was a constant reminder that he had chosen that city as the place of his particular presence and salvation. Therefore, the temple was closely connected to God's covenant relationship with his people. By not prioritizing the temple, the restored community was demonstrating a lack of interest in God's place among his people.

The People Obey and Build the Temple

■ READ HAGGAI 1:12–15 ■

Whereas the previous section was a verbal confrontation, this section is historical narrative. In response to Haggai's word, Zerubbabel, Joshua, and all the rest of the people obey God and determine to work on the temple. We saw in chapter 4 that a prophet is essentially a "messenger" from God to his people. Here, Haggai is actually called a "messenger" as he brings an encouraging word from YHWH: "I am with you" (1:13). In discouraging, fearful times, there could be no greater comfort than that the God of Israel who created all things is with them to encourage, protect, equip, and reward. His presence will motivate them to follow through and complete the work.

The Rebuilt Temple Is a Disappointment

■ READ HAGGAI 2:1–5 ■

According to the superscription in 2:1, Haggai gives this prophetic oracle about one month after the work on the temple restarted. Although this new temple will not be completed for five more years, the people must be able to see—perhaps from the dimensions and the foundations—that this temple will be inferior to the previous one, which had been built by Solomon (1 Kings 6). YHWH draws attention to what is obvious, saying, "How do you see it now? Is it not as nothing in your eyes?" (2:3). Solomon's temple was large and beautiful, with costly materials, precious metals, and the careful design of craftsmen. The author of 1 Kings tells us that it took well-organized and heavily resourced workers seven years to build (6:38). By contrast, the second, rebuilt temple in the time of Haggai was small and poor.

Despite the disappointment, there is good news. YHWH again says, "Work, for I am with you. . . . My Spirit remains in your midst. Fear not" (2:4–5). The new temple may be unimpressive, but God will still honor his covenant with his people and will strengthen them by his Spirit.

A Greater Glory

■ READ HAGGAI 2:6–9 ■

In the previous section, God's first response to the disappointing temple was that he would be with them (2:4). In this section, he gives a second response: he has something far better planned for them. He signals that he is referring to the distant, eschatological future when he "will shake the heavens and the earth" (2:6; cf. Isa. 13:13; Joel 3:16). It is true that he says this will take place "in a little while," but the Bible often speaks of eschatological realities as imminent or coming soon (cf. Rom. 16:20; Heb. 10:37; Rev. 1:1).

In that time, he will not only shake the heavens; he will also shake the nations in order to plunder them of their treasures. One almost gets the idea of shaking a man upside down so that everything in his pockets falls out! The nations will bring their treasures to the temple so that it has a greater glory in the future than it ever did in the past (2:9). We saw in the book of Isaiah a similar vision: the nations will bring their wealth to Jerusalem in order to submit to God and become a part of his people (Isa. 45:14; 60:5–11).

Accusation: The People Are Unclean

■ READ HAGGAI 2:10–19 ■

The superscription in 2:10 tells us that Haggai proclaimed the oracle in this section two months after the previous one. He suddenly changes topic and asks the priests technical questions about how holiness and uncleanness are transferred. This only makes sense in light of the instructions in the book of Leviticus. In the first question, he asks if a garment carrying holy food can transfer holiness to other food. The answer is no (cf. Lev. 6:27). The second question asks if a person who is unclean due to touching a dead body can transfer uncleanness to food. The answer this time is yes (cf. Lev. 11:28; 22:4). Haggai is not asking these questions because he is curious; he is using the analogy to make a larger point about the Jews. They have returned from exile and are supposed to be set apart as holy to YHWH. Instead, they are unclean because of sin and are making everything else unclean, such as their offerings and worship. As a result, God is preventing them from prospering.

A Signet Ring

■ READ HAGGAI 2:20–23 ■

Haggai pronounced this oracle on the same day as the previous section (cf. 2:10 and 2:20). In response to the spiritual uncleanness of the people, God says again that he will "shake the heavens and the earth" (2:21). This time, the references to the nations describe judgment: God will "destroy the strength of the kingdoms" and ruin their weapons of war. But while God destroys other kingdoms, he will preserve and advance his own kingdom. In 2:23 he announces that he has chosen Zerubbabel and will make him like a signet ring. To us, that statement may not sound very significant, but to Haggai's audience it was full of hope and promise. Previously, the prophet Jeremiah had given a prophecy concerning King Jehoiachin, the last king of the line of David and Zerubbabel's grandfather. God said that even if King Jehoiachin (also called "Coniah") were his "signet ring," God would tear him off and send him into exile (Jer. 22:24–30). Now, that displeasure is reversed. Zerubbabel will be a signet ring, representing the preservation of the Davidic line and God's plans for a future messianic king who will rule his people in victory, security, and prosperity.

Implementation

In chapter 7, "The Persuasive Strategies of the Prophets," we discussed how the prophets sometimes use present realities as analogies for eschatological realities that are difficult to comprehend. We find two examples of this in the book of Haggai.

First, the temple was disappointing. The people had finally returned from exile, but when they rebuilt the temple, it was a poor substitute for what stood there previously. Yet Haggai says that the disappointing temple in postexilic history is a token for a new temple that God will build in the eschatological future. He will bring in the treasures of the nations and give the temple a far greater glory. In the New Testament, we learn more about what God has in mind—not a physical building that contains God's presence, but a body of believers who are filled with God's fullness. Paul says to the believers in Corinth, "Do you not know that you [plural] are God's temple and that God's Spirit dwells in you?" (1 Cor. 3:16; cf. 6:19; 2 Cor. 6:16). He says in Ephesians 2:20–22 that all who belong to Christ are a temple, built on the foundation of the apostles and prophets, with Jesus Christ as the chief cornerstone: "In him you also are being built together into a dwelling place for God by the Spirit" (2:22; cf. 1 Pet. 2:5–7). This future temple, consisting of people from every nation, will have far greater glory than a lackluster brick building because God will fully dwell with his people once again. We are that temple if we belong to him through Christ.

Second, Haggai speaks to an unclean people who are dominated by a foreign power. Zerubbabel was governor in a disappointing time. And yet their hope is not cut off. God had "torn off" King Jehoiachin and sent him into exile, but now he announces that Zerubbabel will be like a signet ring. In other words, he will be a temporary token of a far greater leader to come in the future. As the continuation of the Davidic line, Zerubbabel was an ancestor of Jesus Christ (Matt. 1:12–13; Luke 3:27). Jesus solves the problems that ancient Jews—and we—face in our disappointing world. He is a priest—through his work on the cross, he removes uncleanness so that we can be in relationship with God without the barrier of sin (Heb. 2:17). He is also a king—his rule has begun now, but in the future his kingdom will come in full. Poverty, insecurity, and subjugation will be history, and we will enjoy him forever.

Christian Reading Questions

1. When the people disobey God, why does he respond by removing the fertility from their land (see 1:1–11; 2:10–19)? See if you can provide examples of this same response from God in earlier, preexilic prophets.

2. Reread Haggai 1:2–6 and describe the primary sin of the people. What have they done wrong? What have they *not* done wrong? How can we avoid simplistically condemning them, while at the same time recognizing that they have failed in their faithfulness to God?

3. Although Haggai lived over five hundred years before Christ, he says that the eschatological future will begin "in a little while" (2:6). Compare Romans 16:20, Hebrews 10:37, and Revelation 1:1. Why do you think the biblical authors often speak of the eschatological future as coming soon?
4. How can the book of Haggai give us hope in disappointing circumstances?

CHAPTER TWENTY-THREE

Zechariah

Orientation

In the period after their exile in Babylon, the Jews were back home in Jerusalem but not fully *home*. They were rebuilding the temple and reestablishing their society and culture, but they were still under foreign domination. They were subject to the Persian government and military officials who were gentiles and pagan idolaters. There was instability in the empire, and they were vulnerable to attack and interference from outsiders. The economy was poor and they were barely surviving. In the face of all this, they needed hope: hope that God was still sovereign over history, hope that God knew them as his own people and would save them from their enemies.

The church today exists in a similar situation. We are home, living in the world that we were born into, the only world we have ever known. But if we belong to Christ, it is not our true home. We live in a world dominated by evil powers. We live in hostile enemy territory, subject to persecution and abuse. In some nations, Christians are imprisoned and killed for their faith. Churches are torn down and pastors are beaten. In the West, Christians are under increasing pressure from a secular society with a worldview and values that are not compatible with God's Word. Like the ancient Jews in Jerusalem, we need hope as well. The book of Zechariah provided that hope for people in its own time, and it continues to gives us hope as well. Zechariah calls us to repentance and looks forward to a future when God's Messiah will cleanse us from sin, restore his people, defeat his enemies, and rule over

HISTORICAL MATTERS

"Fact Sheet"—Zechariah

Author: Zechariah, the son of Berechiah, the son of Iddo

Date: 520–518 BC

Location: Jerusalem

Political and social context: Many exiles have returned from Babylon to Jerusalem and the Persian province of Yehud (formerly "Judah") to rebuild the temple and resettle in the land. However, it is a discouraging time of economic difficulty, military insecurity, and spiritual confusion. The prophet Zechariah, alongside his contemporary Haggai, encourages the people to remain faithful to YHWH now as they wait for his glorious victory and rule in the future.

a peaceful world forever. God's sovereign will cannot be stopped, and he works for the benefit of his people.

The book of Zechariah contains three superscriptions, which date Zechariah's oracles to the same time as the prophet Haggai (see table 23.1). Zechariah's first oracle takes place during the events of the book of Haggai (between the dates stated in Hag. 2:1 and in 2:10), but the rest of Zechariah takes place after the book of Haggai. Both Haggai and Zechariah are among the last books of the Old Testament, prior to Malachi (see the time line of Zechariah).

Table 23.1. The Dates of Zechariah's Oracles

Reference	Year	Month	Day	Date*
Haggai 1:1	2nd year of Darius	6th	1st	Aug. 29, 520
Haggai 1:15	2nd year of Darius	6th	24th	Sept. 21, 520
Haggai 2:1	[2nd year of Darius]	7th	21st	Oct. 17, 520
Zechariah 1:1	2nd year of Darius	8th		Nov. 520
Haggai 2:10	2nd year of Darius	9th	24th	Dec. 18, 520
Haggai 2:20	[2nd year of Darius]	9th	24th	Dec. 18, 520
Zechariah 1:7	2nd year of Darius	11th	24th	Feb. 15, 519
Zechariah 7:1	4th year of Darius	9th	4th	Dec. 7, 518

Source: Table adapted from a class handout by Sagar Mekwan, Trinity Evangelical Divinity School, fall semester, 2018.

* Carol L. Meyers and Eric M. Meyers, *Haggai, Zechariah 1–8: A New Translation with Introduction and Commentary*, Anchor Bible Commentary (New Haven: Yale University Press, 2008), xlvi–xlvii.

TIME LINE

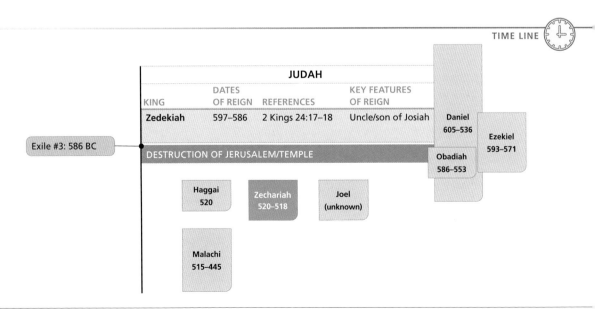

We have already discussed the historical background and postexilic situation in the time of Haggai and Zechariah (see chap. 22), so we will not repeat it here. Both prophets mention the two most important Jewish leaders of the time: Joshua, the high priest, and Zerubbabel, the governor appointed by the Persians. Zechariah was from a priestly family, like Jeremiah and Ezekiel (according to Zech. 1:1, he was the grandson of Iddo, a priest in exile; cf. Neh. 12:4). Whereas Haggai's book is mostly concerned with present realities, Zechariah spends more time discussing God's plans for the future.[1]

The book of Zechariah is difficult to understand—perhaps one of the most difficult in the Old Testament. Rashi, the renowned medieval Jewish interpreter, wrote of the book, "We shall never be able to discover the true interpretation until the Teacher of Righteousness arrives" (presumably he means the Messiah or Elijah the prophet). Another Jewish scholar, Abrabanel, wrote that "expositors however skilled" were unable to discern its meaning.[2] Unlike standard preexilic prophetic literature, Zechariah contains apocalyptic visions and oracles, which depend on visions, symbolism, and interpretation by angelic guides. Previously, in chapter 12, we saw that the book of Daniel also contains these same features. Apocalyptic literature often focuses on God's complete control over history, a strong contrast between good and evil, and God's ultimate victory.

We should add a brief word about the unity of the book. The various superscriptions mentioned above only identify Zechariah the prophet as the source of the material. However, in the last several hundred years, certain aspects of the book have led critical biblical scholars to argue that chapters 1–8 and chapters 9–14 come from different authors and different time periods. Chapters 1–8 contain dated superscriptions, concerns about rebuilding the temple, and visions, whereas chapters 9–14 do not contain any of these elements. Some scholars have suggested that Haggai and Zechariah 1–8 were originally one work, while Zechariah 9–14 is connected to Malachi (the superscription "The oracle [Hebrew: massa'] of the word of the LORD" is found in Zech. 9:1, 12:1, and Mal. 1:1).

While it is true that there are some differences in content and language between chapters 1–8 and 9–14, there are many similarities as well. There is no reason to assume that the same author (Zechariah) could not write in different literary styles. In addition, all fourteen chapters have been passed down as one book in every manuscript that we possess.[3] Recent scholars, both evangelical and critical, tend to acknowledge the literary unity of the book.

Exploration

Zechariah is primarily concerned with eschatological restoration (for God's people) and eschatological judgment (for God's enemies) in the distant future. The book also refers a few times to the Jews' sins in the past (e.g., chap. 1); judgment in the historical, near future (likely chap. 11); and relief and restoration for the Jews in the near future, including completing the temple (e.g., chaps. 4 and 6) (see fig. 23.1).

The book is structured in five sections of various lengths, illustrated in table 23.2. Although the meaning of the contents is sometimes obscure, the various divisions of the book are clear. Following the introduction in **1:1–6**, a superscription in 1:7 marks the second unit, which comprises visions that Zechariah sees at night and discusses with an angel. Another superscription in 7:1 marks **7:1–8:23** as a distinct unit, in which Zechariah addresses his contemporaries. They ask a question about fasting or feasting at the beginning of the section (7:3), and it is answered near the end (8:18–19). The last two sections of the book, indicated by distinctive superscriptions in 9:1 and 12:1, describe God's future plans for his people and the world.

Introduction

■ READ ZECHARIAH 1:1–6 ■

It is significant that in a book filled with hope and descriptions of God's salvation, the prophet begins by calling the people to repent. Repentance and commitment to God are always necessary to receive his good gifts. Zechariah describes how previous generations rejected the prophets and refused to listen to God's word (1:2, 4–5). However, the current generation does not need to make the same mistake and has the opportunity for a fresh start. The words of the earlier prophets came to pass; God says, "Did they not overtake your fathers?" (1:6). This is a reminder that the people (and

THINKING VISUALLY

The Five Phases: Zechariah
Figure 23.1

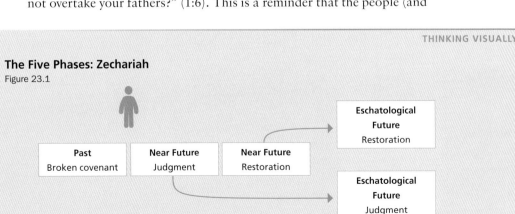

Table 23.2. The Structure of Zechariah

Introduction (1:1–6)

Eight visions and a sign-act (1:7–6:15)
- Vision 1: A man and horses (1:7–17)
- Vision 2: Four horns and four craftsmen (1:18–21)
- Vision 3: A measuring line for Jerusalem (2:1–13)
- Vision 4: The clothes of Joshua the high priest (3:1–10)
- Vision 5: A lampstand and olive trees (4:1–14)
- Vision 6: A flying scroll (5:1–4)
- Vision 7: A woman in a basket (5:5–11)
- Vision 8: Four chariots (6:1–8)
- A sign-act: A crown for Joshua the high priest (6:9–15)

An address: God will restore his people (7:1–8:23)

The first oracle (9:1–11:17)
- The victorious king will come to Jerusalem (9:1–17)
- God will protect his people from wicked shepherds (10:1–11:17)

The second oracle (12:1–14:21)
- Jerusalem will be attacked and defended (12:1–13:9)
- YHWH will be King over all the earth (14:1–21)

now the readers of the book) should take seriously what Zechariah has to say as well.

Vision 1: A Man and Horses

> READ ZECHARIAH 1:7–17

Chapters 1–6 contain eight visions that Zechariah sees at night. He is apparently awake, as the angel rouses him in 4:1 in order to show him the next vision. As we discussed in chapter 7, the visions are presented in a compelling way that engages us as readers. We experience the imagery along with Zechariah. If we find it confusing . . . so does he! He often asks the angel to explain it to him. The imagery that is explained is typically the most important part of the vision; we should not feel pressure to find a significance for every aspect of what Zechariah sees, since some of it is simply part of the overall image and may not have symbolic importance.[4]

In the first vision, Zechariah sees a man riding a red horse, with other horses nearby in a valley. When Zechariah asks what he is seeing, the man in the vision answers that they have been sent out by God to patrol the earth and do reconnaissance (1:10). The angel then cries out, "O LORD of hosts, how long will you have no mercy on Jerusalem and the cities of Judah?" (1:12). The reference is to the seventy years of exile. When will it end? When will God restore Jerusalem? God responds that he *does* care about Jerusalem. The temple will be rebuilt, and he will show mercy. The

The Horses in the Valley

The imagery of the first vision may be connected to Persian horses and a well-known palace garden in the Persian Empire. If so, then they are depicting God's place of authority in heaven in similar ways. Zechariah and his listeners and first readers would have been familiar with Persian couriers on horseback who took messages throughout the empire and brought back word to the king. In 1:10, it is God who sends out horses to patrol his realm (the earth) and ascertain the situation.[a]

Figure 23.2. *The Vision of Zechariah*, by an unknown artist. The painting is a miniature from about AD 1300. Zechariah, on the left, stands next to an angel who points to the man mounting a red horse.

judgment of exile has been a break in God's relationship with his people, but he will "again" (a word used four times in 1:17) comfort and choose Jerusalem.

Vision 2: Four Horns and Four Craftsmen

■ READ ZECHARIAH 1:18–21 ■

Zechariah next sees a vision of four horns. The angel explains that these horns have driven God's people from Judah and Jerusalem into exile in distant lands. One scholar suggests that the four horns are two animals—each with two horns—and the two animals represent the Assyrian and Babylonian Empires.[5] Next, YHWH shows Zechariah four craftsmen, who represent God's authority over the nations that have scattered his people. As we mentioned above, Zechariah's audience was in an extremely vulnerable position: living in a city without defensive walls, surrounded by hostile people, without an army, and subjected to the whims of the Persian government. This vision gives great hope that God will protect and avenge those who belong to him.

Vision 3: A Measuring Line for Jerusalem

■ READ ZECHARIAH 2:1–13 ■

Zechariah's third vision consists of a man with a measuring line. As we saw in the first vision, somehow Zechariah can converse with the

Satan

The word that we translate "Satan" in English is *hassatan* in Hebrew, which means "the adversary." The use of the definite article ("the") in 3:1–2 suggests that in this context *hassatan* is not a proper name but rather a title. From the perspective of the entire biblical canon, we can identify this individual as the devil, the enemy of God and his people. He was apparently behind the serpent who tempted Eve in the garden of Eden (Gen. 3:1; cf. Rev. 12:9; 20:2). In the book of Job, he accuses God of buying Job's favor (Job 1:6–12). In the New Testament, he tempts Jesus (Matt. 4:1–11), is the enemy of God's kingdom (12:26), and seeks to undermine the faith of God's people (Mark 4:15; 1 Cor. 7:5; Eph. 6:11; 1 Pet. 5:8). In the future, he will be thrown into the eternal lake of fire along with his angels (Matt. 25:41).

"The Branch"

Isaiah and Jeremiah also call God's future Messiah a "branch," using the same Hebrew word (*tsemah*). Isaiah 4:2 says, "In that day the branch of the Lord shall be beautiful and glorious." Isaiah 11:1, with a different Hebrew word, uses similar imagery of a branch that comes from the line of David. Jeremiah 23:5–6 says of the eschatological future, "Behold, days are coming . . . when I will raise up for David a righteous Branch, and he shall reign as king and deal wisely." In Jeremiah 33:15–16, the prophet says that this righteous Branch will be called "The Lord is our righteousness." This predicts that the Messiah will not only be a wise king, he will also deal with the problem of sin and make us righteous before God. In hindsight—from the perspective of the New Testament—this is a stunning prediction.

individuals in his visions. He asks the man where he is going, and the response is that he will measure Jerusalem (2:2). Apparently, measuring the city assumes that its size will not change. So the angel who is serving as Zechariah's guide prevents the man from measuring, because the city will experience massive growth due to the people who will flock to it (2:4).

This vision anticipates Zechariah's short oracle in 2:6–13. He calls on God's people to leave exile and return to Jerusalem to be a part of YHWH's program of restoration (2:7). Then, using this call in his own time as a pattern for the eschatological future, he predicts a time when people from many nations will come to Jerusalem because they want to join themselves to YHWH (2:11). And they will not remain as foreign visitors—they will be God's people, and he will dwell among them. Throughout the Prophets, we have seen that Jerusalem is viewed as the epicenter of God's redemption, and believers from the nations come into it (Isa. 56:6–8; 66:20–21; Mic. 4:2; cf. Zech. 8:20–23).

Vision 4: The Clothes of Joshua the High Priest

■ READ ZECHARIAH 3:1–10 ■

Zechariah sees a vision of Joshua the high priest standing in filthy (the Hebrew word means "excrement" or "vomit") clothing (3:3). Satan is there to accuse Joshua, who, in his priestly role, represents all the people and their status before God. The angel gives a command to clothe Joshua in clean garments, symbolizing the removal of his guilt (3:4). Following this symbolism of cleansing and forgiveness, the angel makes three promises to Joshua (and thus to all God's people) in verses 6–10. First, God will send a messianic servant, whom he calls "the Branch" (3:8). The image of a branch comes from the idea that God will cause the Messiah to sprout from the line of David. This same Hebrew word is also used as a symbol for the Messiah in Isaiah and Jeremiah. Second, God will remove the sin of the land in a single day (3:9). Third, the land will flourish and be at peace (3:10).

The imagery and promises look forward to an individual who fills both priestly and royal roles. On the one hand, he will remove sin like a priest; on the other, he will bring peace and prosperity to the land like a ruler. From the perspective of the New Testament, we know that this anticipates Jesus the Christ (Messiah), who removed sin on the cross in a single day and someday will usher in his perfect kingdom. Like the sin of Joshua the high priest, our sin is rank as we stand before God, but Christ cleanses us completely when we put our faith in him.

Figure 23.3. *Zechariah Sees the Menorah*, a drawing by Jan Luyken and Pieter Mortier

Vision 5: A Lampstand and Olive Trees

■ READ ZECHARIAH 4:1–14 ■

During the same night that Zechariah has had the first four visions, the angel comes again and rouses him. Perhaps he has been asleep, or perhaps the angel is preparing him for another visionary experience. This time, Zechariah has a vision of a gold lampstand with seven lamps beside two olive trees (4:2–3). The golden lampstand would have been familiar to Zechariah—one stood in the holy place of the tabernacle (cf. Exod. 25:31) in order to provide light inside the tent (Exod. 25:37), and later, a similar lampstand was used in the temple (cf. 1 Kings 7:49). In this vision, the combination of a lampstand and two olive trees has an uncertain meaning, so Zechariah asks the angel to explain (4:4). The angel responds that Zerubbabel *will* complete the rebuilding of the temple, "not by might, nor by power," but by God's Spirit (4:6–9). It is an encouragement to the entire worshiping community. God will accomplish his plans for them, now and in the future.[6]

Zechariah then asks about the identity of the two olive trees, and the angel responds that they are "two anointed ones who stand by the Lord" (4:14). Unfortunately, this ambiguous answer does not provide us with a certain identification of the individuals. Are they heavenly figures? Do they represent the prophets Haggai and Zechariah? Perhaps the best suggestion is that they represent Zerubbabel (who is mentioned in the passage) and Joshua the high priest.

Vision 6: A Flying Scroll

■ READ ZECHARIAH 5:1–4 ■

The sixth vision features a large, flying scroll. It is huge: twenty cubits by ten cubits, which equates to thirty feet by fifteen feet (9 meters by 4.5

meters). Perhaps this large size ensured that no one would miss it.[7] It is a curse on the whole land, holding people accountable for their sin and declaring judgment—even reaching the guilty in the privacy of their homes (5:4). Even the best human ruler can never really purge evil from the land; at best he or she can resist it. But in the eschatological future, God will purge the land of all wickedness.

Vision 7: A Woman in a Basket

■ READ ZECHARIAH 5:5–11 ■

Like the previous vision, Zechariah's seventh vision also deals with purging evil from the land. He sees a large basket with a woman sitting inside. The woman represents sin (5:6) and wickedness (5:8). The basket will carry her away to the land of Shinar—a region around Babylon where the Jews had been in exile—and keep her there permanently (5:11). Shinar is imagined as the place of refuse, the holding area for everything we want to remove from our towns and cities—perhaps the equivalent of a landfill or a toxic waste dump today. God will tolerate no evil in his presence. Either it will be forgiven by his Messiah, or he will eradicate it and banish it from the land. He will ultimately reject all those who reject his salvation and continue in wickedness.[8]

Vision 8: Four Chariots

■ READ ZECHARIAH 6:1–8 ■

In his eighth and final vision, Zechariah sees four chariots, pulled by red, black, white, and dappled horses. (These multicolored horses recall the first vision, in 1:7–17.) The angel explains that the chariots have gone out in different directions ("the four winds of heaven") to patrol the earth (6:5–7). In many other passages in the Old Testament, chariots are associated with God as a divine warrior who has victory over his enemies (cf. Pss. 18:10; 68:17; 104:3; Isa. 66:15). The present passage focuses on the "north country" and the "south country." These may be references to Babylon (since one goes north from Palestine to get there) and Egypt (to the south) since these were the two nations where the Jews had been exiled.[9] The point of the vision is God's total dominion over the entire world, especially over those enemies who had oppressed his people.

A Sign-Act: A Crown for Joshua the High Priest

■ READ ZECHARIAH 6:9–15 ■

At God's instruction, Zechariah performs a sign-act with silver and gold that had been brought back from Babylon. He makes a crown, a symbol of royalty, and places it on the head of Joshua the high priest (6:11). Zechariah merges the offices of priest and king and prophesies of another individual to come who will fulfill both of these roles. "The Branch," whose name prophetically signifies the Messiah (cf. 3:8 above), will build the temple of YHWH and rule on his throne. "And there shall be a priest on his throne" (6:13). The prophet cannot be talking about either Joshua the high priest or Zerubbabel since neither ruled as a king. Although Zechariah may not have fully understood it, it is clear from the New Testament that he is talking about Jesus Christ, who is both priest and king. The temple he builds will be the people of God, as we saw in the book of Haggai (cf. Eph. 2:22).

An Address: God Will Restore His People

■ READ ZECHARIAH 7:1–8:23 ■

A superscription in 7:1 indicates a new section in the book, containing oracles that came to Zechariah about two years after the night visions and sign-act in chapters 1–6. This passage begins with a question in 7:3: "Should I weep and abstain in the fifth month, as I have done for so many years?" The people had fasted during the seventy years of exile. Now that it was at an end, did they need to continue?

Chapter 7 focuses on the failures of earlier generations and what God requires of his covenant community. Their ancestors had "refused to pay attention and turned a stubborn shoulder" to the prophets (7:7, 11). But God wants his people to do justice; show kindness and mercy toward the vulnerable; protect the widow, fatherless, and immigrant; and care for the poor (7:8–14).

Chapter 8 turns to restoration and renewal. The Jews' ancestors had hard hearts, so God sent them into exile. But God has a new age in store for his people. He has returned to Jerusalem, which will be faithful and holy to him (8:3). He looks forward to a time in the eschatological future when old men and women sit in the streets and children play: an image of a city marked by peace and joy, without fear of harm. Instead of bringing covenant curses on his people, the land will be fruitful and the remnant of God's people will flourish and be blessed (8:12). In 8:18–19, God answers the initial question in 7:3. Should the people fast? No, the regular fasts will be transformed into cheerful feasts! In those days, people from other nations will see the relationship that the Jews enjoy with God and will seek to join him as well, saying to each other, "Let us go at once to entreat the favor of the Lord and to seek the Lord of hosts; I myself am going" (8:21). Therefore, Israel will fulfill its God-given role as a nation of priests, bringing people from many other nations to God (cf. Exod. 19:6 and the discussion in chap. 2).

The Victorious King Will Come to Jerusalem

■ READ ZECHARIAH 9:1–17 ■

We mentioned above that the book of Zechariah is difficult; the last six chapters are especially so. One scholar states that "attempts to discern some overall literary pattern in their arrangement . . . have been unsuccessful."[10] The overall focus of these chapters is the eschatological future, but it is difficult to place the events on a specific time line. One wonders if they are intended to be arranged and understood in chronological order, or if they are presented with another effect in mind. For example, think of a classic painting of a battle. The events are arranged on a large canvas, perhaps a mural on a wall or ceiling of a building. The scene is very active, with fighting, suffering, death, victory, and defeat, and yet the painter makes no attempt to portray the chronology of the events or how they relate to each other. It looks as though they are all happening at the same moment—like a snapshot in time. Our eyes move back and forth across the scene, taking it all in. The purpose is not to give us a detailed chronology but to evoke a sense that is abstract and visceral: legitimacy, power, victory, glory, joy. See, for example, *The Battle of Milvian Bridge* (fig. 23.4). Romano's painting does not tell us who these individuals are, who died first, or who killed whom. And yet we get a sense of the chaos of battle and also victory. Perhaps this is analogous to the oracles in this last part of Zechariah. We should seek to understand as much as we are able, and some of it is quite specific, but the key is to appreciate the effect that the oracles have on us: confidence in God's great victory, relief that his enemies will be destroyed, and an anticipation of the glory that awaits his people. These chapters are the most quoted of the Prophets in the passion narratives of the New Testament and were very influential on the book of Revelation.

In the first major oracle, indicated by a superscription in 9:1, Zechariah begins by presenting YHWH as a divine warrior. He marches south from Syria (Hadrach and Damascus) to Phoenicia on the coast (Tyre and Sidon) to the Philistine cities and finally to Jerusalem, where he sets up his camp. This is the typical route that an ancient invading army would take through the land (see map 23.1). As God moves through enemy territory, he systematically defeats the historic enemies of Israel—none can oppose him. They are terrified and cannot stand before the awesome power of the God of Israel. However, along the way, he is also gaining new followers! Even in Philistia, there will be "a remnant for our God; it shall be like a clan in Judah" (9:7).

Figure 23.4. *The Battle of Milvian Bridge* (1520–24), by Giulio Romano. This fresco, found in one of the rooms of the Vatican, shows the battle (Oct. 28, 312) between Roman emperors Constantine and Maxentius. Constantine had a dream in which a cross appeared in the heavens; he was told that he would be victorious if he used it as a standard.

In Jerusalem, God presents his king: "Rejoice greatly, O daughter of Zion! Shout aloud, O daughter of Jerusalem! Behold, your king is coming to you" (9:9). Who is this king? At first glance, we might think it is YHWH himself, as he has been the subject of the previous section and YHWH is called "king" later, in 14:9. However, two details in the text suggest that this king is another individual. First, YHWH speaks in this section in the first person ("I") but refers to the king in the third person ("he") (see 9:8–10). Second, the expression "having salvation" in 9:9 is passive, meaning that this individual relies on YHWH for his victory, not on his own military power or strategy. The king is humble and enters Jerusalem on a donkey. In 9:10, we learn that after God destroys all weapons of war, the king will rule "from sea to sea, and from the River to the ends of the earth." This is a quotation from Psalm 72:8, which speaks of God's Messiah and his global rule. In summary, these verses look forward to a time when God presents his messianic king in Jerusalem, riding on a donkey, as a prelude to his final victory over his enemies and his perfect rule over the entire world. 🕮

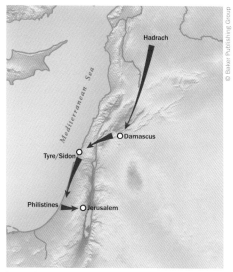

Map 23.1. The King comes to Jerusalem

Jesus the King

Each Gospel writer alludes to or quotes Zechariah 9:9 when Jesus enters Jerusalem on a donkey (Matt. 21:1–11; Mark 11:1–10; Luke 19:28–38; John 12:12–15). Jesus deliberately enters Jerusalem this way to trigger their memory of Zechariah's prophecy. It is noteworthy that the crowds recognize the prophetic fulfillment even though they presumably saw people riding donkeys into Jerusalem every day.[b] In Zechariah, God promises that he will reveal his messianic king in Jerusalem. The Gospel writers all say, *Here he is!* Jesus is the king who comes in peace and who will be vindicated by God. At his second coming, he will rule from sea to sea.

LITERARY NOTES

Who Are the Three Shepherds?

It is impossible to be certain about the identity of the three shepherds destroyed by Zechariah. There have been at least forty different suggestions as to who they are.[c] The last three kings of Judah: Jehoiakim, Jehoiachin, and Zedekiah? Foreign kings who ruled over Israel and Judah? Enemy nations: Assyria, Babylonia, and Persia? Biblical figures: Moses, Aaron, and Miriam? Postexilic priests?[d] Later Jewish groups: Pharisees, Sadducees, and Essenes? One scholar suggests that the number "three" is symbolic for totality: the good shepherd will remove *all* unworthy leaders from power.[e]

CANONICAL CONNECTIONS

Thirty Pieces of Silver

In the Gospel of Matthew, Judas agrees to betray Jesus for the price of thirty pieces of silver. But when he sees that Jesus is condemned, he changes his mind and tries to return the money. Because it is blood money, the priests cannot return the money to the temple treasury; instead, they use it to buy a potter's field. At this point in the story, Matthew quotes from and combines two Old Testament passages: Jeremiah 32:6–9 (buying a field) and Zechariah 11:12–13 (thirty pieces of silver). According to standard practice at the time, he only attributes the passage to Jeremiah, the first of the two Old Testament prophets. Matthew sees a pattern in the biblical text: just as Jeremiah and Zechariah were rejected as God's faithful prophets by a sinful people, Jesus Christ was rejected as well.[f]

God Will Protect His People from Wicked Shepherds

■ READ ZECHARIAH 10:1–11:17 ■

In this section, Zechariah turns his attention from the messianic king in the future to wicked leaders in his own time. They are pictured as shepherds over the flock of God (10:3). He promises that he will bring back his people ("the house of Judah" and "the house of Joseph") from the nations where they are scattered in exile (10:6–12), but he will destroy the wicked shepherds (11:1–3). God then asks Zechariah to be a shepherd for God's people. Apparently this is a temporary task, because the people are "doomed to slaughter" (11:4), and God will no longer have any pity on them (11:5). The people reject Zechariah, and he becomes impatient with them and destroys the three shepherds (11:8). For his work as shepherd, Zechariah is paid thirty pieces of silver; YHWH tells him to throw away the money as a sign of rejection (11:12–13).

It is difficult to understand what is being described here or who is represented by these three shepherds. The overall point is that God is a good leader who plans to restore his flock. However, because the people are unresponsive, he will allow the nations to oppress them once again for a period of time.[11]

Jerusalem Will Be Attacked and Defended

■ READ ZECHARIAH 12:1–13:9 ■

In 12:1 we find a final superscription, "The oracle of the word of the Lord," which is identical to the one in 9:1 above and also in Malachi 1:1. Chapters 12–14 make up the last major unit of the book, divided into two parts, both of which are focused on the eschatological future. (The phrase "on that day" occurred only twice in chaps. 9–11, but it occurs seventeen times in chaps. 12–14.)

In the first section, 12:1–13:9, God declares that all nations will gather against Jerusalem, but they will only hurt themselves, for he will protect the city and destroy those who oppose it (12:2–9). There will be great salvation for God's people. God's certain victory is connected to an intriguing statement in 12:10: "When they look on me, on him whom they have pierced, they shall mourn for him." This will lead to "a fountain opened for the house of David and the inhabitants of Jerusalem, to cleanse them from sin and uncleanness" (13:1). Interestingly, Isaiah 53:5 also speaks of the "piercing" (different Hebrew word) of God's servant so that he can atone for sin. And Ezekiel uses similar imagery of sprinkling with clean water to cleanse God's people from sin and give them a heart of flesh (36:25–26).

It sounds like God is saying that *he* will be the one who is pierced. But how is that possible? There is also a strong connection to the house of David (see 12:10, 12). It is a mystery that can only be understood in the future with the coming of Jesus Christ. As David's offspring *and* as God incarnate, Jesus died painfully on the cross and was pierced to atone for the sin of all who would come to him in faith.

In 13:7, God again speaks about the death of a coming individual, but now the imagery shifts to that of a shepherd (recalling chaps. 10–11). God says, "Awake, O sword, against my shepherd. . . . Strike the shepherd, and the sheep will be scattered." Who is this shepherd? In chapter 11, the shepherd was the prophet Zechariah, but here in chapter 13 this reference to a slaughtered shepherd follows the discussion of the one "they have pierced" in 12:10. The combination of prophecies in this chapter suggests the shepherd is not Zechariah or an individual in his own time but the coming Messiah. It is YHWH who strikes him with

"On Him Whom They Have Pierced"

A number of events involved in Jesus's crucifixion are fulfillments of Old Testament prophecy. The soldiers divide Jesus's clothes (John 19:24 cites Ps. 22:18). Jesus is thirsty on the cross (John 19:28–29 cites Ps. 69:21). The soldiers do not break Jesus's legs on the cross (John 19:36 cites Exod. 12:46). And when a soldier sees that Jesus is already dead, he pierces his side with a spear (John 19:37 cites Zech. 12:10). John sees the piercing of Jesus on the cross as a confirmation that Jesus was the Messiah. Zechariah's prophecy is picked up again in Revelation 1:7: "[Jesus] is coming with the clouds, and every eye will see him, even those who pierced him."

"A Fountain Opened"

William Cowper was an English poet who lived from 1731 to 1800. After he was institutionalized for insanity, he became serious about his Christian faith and wrote a number of hymns. One of these, written after a bout of depression, was "There Is a Fountain Filled with Blood," which draws on the text of Zechariah 13:1.[9] It begins, "There is a fountain filled with blood, drawn from Immanuel's veins, and sinners plunged beneath that flood, lose all their guilty stains." Verse 2 continues, "The dying thief rejoiced to see that fountain in his day; and there have I, as vile as he, washed all my sins away."

"Strike the Shepherd and the Sheep Will Be Scattered"

After Jesus's last supper with his disciples, they all go out to the Mount of Olives, just outside Jerusalem. Jesus warns them of his coming arrest, saying, "You will all fall away because of me this night." He then quotes from Zechariah 13:7: "For it is written, 'I will strike the shepherd, and the sheep of the flock will be scattered'" (Matt. 26:31). Jesus understood Zechariah 13:7 as a direct prophecy about his own death and the resulting, temporary scattering of his disciples.

his own sword. Isaiah 53:10 says something similar: "It was the will of the Lord to crush him." 📜

YHWH Will Be King over All the Earth

📜 READ ZECHARIAH 14:1–21 📜

Just as God predicted in chapter 12, he states again that he will gather all nations against Jerusalem. There will be great suffering: conquest, plunder, rape, and exile (14:2). But then YHWH will fight against the nations and will take his stand on the Mount of Olives to the east of Jerusalem. The mountain will split open, creating a valley so that God's people can escape (14:4–5).

The need for abundant water was always a major concern for ancient cities. Jerusalem's water supply came from a spring that was just outside the city wall and was later directed into the city via a tunnel. But Zechariah predicts that in the future, "living waters" will flow out of Jerusalem (14:8). There will be geographic upheaval: the surrounding area (which is now mountainous) will be turned into a plain, and Jerusalem will be raised up. Perhaps this is so that the living waters can flow down.[12] 📜

The book concludes with great news for God's people. Those who are wicked from the nations will be judged (14:12–15). The remnant of people from the nations—those who survive—will turn to God in faith and will come to Jerusalem to worship him (14:16–19). Jerusalem will be holy and purged of all evil (14:20–21).

CANONICAL CONNECTIONS

"Living Water"

In the Gospel of John, Jesus is traveling through Samaria with his disciples when he meets a woman at a well. He asks her for a drink, which surprises her because he is a Jew and she is a Samaritan. Jesus responds, "If you knew the gift of God, and who it is that is saying to you, 'Give me a drink,' you would have asked him, and he would have given you living water" (4:10). When the woman asks where he would get such water, Jesus replies, "Whoever drinks of the water that I will give him will never be thirsty again. The water that I will give him will become in him a spring of water welling up to eternal life" (4:14). The book of Revelation also uses the image of living water. At the end of time, Jesus will be his people's shepherd (another image in Zechariah), "and he will guide them to springs of living water" (7:17).

Implementation

Zechariah gives his original readers—and readers today—a vision of hope for the future. Although God created the world good, our sin and wickedness make it a difficult and painful place to live. Our sin plagues and enslaves us. By our actions, we hurt each other, and we are separated from our good God, who created us to be in relationship with him. The nations are in constant warfare against each other, and human power is often used to abuse and mistreat God's people. What a sad state of affairs! And yet what has been is not what always *will* be. God has a future in store for his people that is utterly different from what our experience in a world of sin has always been. It is a future of hope, victory, safety, and joy. Knowing that end strengthens our resolve to press on in our faith, trusting in God.

This great hope will be accomplished by God's power (in general) and by his Messiah (specifically). Of all the Old Testament prophets, Zechariah is perhaps the most vivid in his predictions of God's coming Messiah. He looks forward to a "Branch" (3:8; 6:9–15) who is a blend of priestly and kingly roles. From the New Testament, we know that Jesus Christ is the Messiah who fills both of these roles. As a priest, Jesus would build the temple of God's presence (his people) and atone for sin. Zechariah reveals that Jesus would be "pierced" on the cross (12:10) so that his blood would be the fountain to cleanse from sin (13:1). The author of the book of Hebrews describes Jesus's priestly role when says, "After making purification for sins, [Jesus] sat down at the right hand of the Majesty on high" (1:3). Later he says, "We have such a high priest, one who is seated at the right hand of the throne of the Majesty in heaven" (8:1; cf. 10:12).

But Zechariah also looks forward to Jesus's role as king—he would be a priest who sits on a *throne* (6:13). In contrast to the wicked shepherds of Zechariah's day (chap. 10) and even Zechariah's own stint as a frustrated shepherd of God's people (11:4), Jesus is the "good shepherd" who leads his flock in strength and gentleness, and whose sheep recognize his voice (John 10:11, 27). He entered Jerusalem on a donkey, presenting himself as a king who relied on God and would bring peace (Zech. 9:9). Someday, "his rule will be from sea to sea, and from the River to the ends of the earth" (9:10). Zechariah looks forward to what we are now seeing in the New Testament era: people from all nations are seeking YHWH and joining themselves to his people through Jesus Christ (2:11; 8:20–23). In the realm of Christ the King, the world will be restored, the people will be safe, enemies will be defeated, wickedness will be purged from the land, and—best of all—God will dwell with his people.

As we discussed in chapter 7, Zechariah does not distinguish between events at the time of Jesus's first and second comings. For example, he speaks of Jesus entering Jerusalem on a donkey (our past) and a few verses later describes his worldwide reign as king (our future). On one hand, this merging of time periods helps us see God's revelation as a whole. It gives us a unique perspective because the events are all parts of one plan of salvation. But on the other hand, we have a perspective that Zechariah did not have. For us, Zechariah's predictions of Jesus's first coming have already come to pass. Jesus *did* come and atone for sin, just as he said. Therefore, as we wait for Jesus's second coming, we should have confidence that those predictions by Zechariah will come true as well. God has already proved himself as one who keeps his promises. For those of us for whom this world is "home away from home" and currently under the dominion of evil, this is good news! When we are mistreated for our faith and struggle in a sinful world, we must not lose hope. God sees, and someday he will set all things right.

Christian Reading Questions

1. The books of Daniel and Zechariah both address God's people away from their true home with him. Compare the messages of the two books and how they offer hope to those who live in "hostile territory" in the world.
2. Which of the eight visions (1:7–6:8) do you find most compelling and most encouraging? Which vision do you find the most difficult to comprehend?
3. Trace the theme of God's Messiah in the book of Zechariah. Summarize the imagery that is used to describe this coming ruler, what he will do, and how we might identify him.
4. A number of Old Testament prophets address the problem of wicked shepherds who lead God's people astray. Choose two or three of the following passages and compare and contrast the descriptions of these shepherds and how God will deal with them: Jeremiah 23:1–4; 50:6–19; Ezekiel 34; Zechariah 10:1–11:17.

CHAPTER TWENTY-FOUR

Malachi

Orientation

Malachi is the last of the Old Testament prophetic books, the last book in the Old Testament, and therefore the last book before the coming of Jesus Christ. Malachi represents the end of an era. After the book of Malachi, there will be a little more than four hundred years of prophetic silence—no new authoritative Scripture until God reveals himself further in Christ. What are God's parting words to his people before this period of waiting? As we will see, the prophet Malachi is concerned about the same things as other Old Testament prophets: he wants the people to honor God, treat each other with righteousness and justice, and wait faithfully for God to act on their behalf.

The superscription to the book (1:1) is short and gives us three pieces of information. First, the book is "the oracle of the word of the LORD." This is the same heading that appears in Zechariah 9:1 and 12:1, leading some scholars to suggest that the book of Malachi is either one work with Zechariah 9–14 or that it is a kind of appendix added to the Prophets. However, the word "oracle" appears in other prophetic books as well, and the book of Malachi has its own distinctive structure and message. Second, Malachi 1:1 tells us that the book is "to Israel." In the period before the exile, "Israel" often referred to the Northern Kingdom in contrast to Judah. But following the exile, it refers to the nation as a whole. Finally, 1:1 attributes the book to "Malachi," which is Hebrew for "my messenger." We do not know anything else about this prophet, and some scholars have suggested that it is a title rather than a proper name. However, every other prophetic book in the Old Testament is connected to a prophet's name.[1]

Our only evidence for the date of Malachi's ministry comes from the contents of the book. He mentions a "governor" in 1:8, which would

"Fact Sheet"—Malachi

Author: Malachi

Date: 515–445 BC

Location: Jerusalem

Political and social context: Following the time of Haggai and Zechariah, the temple has been rebuilt, but the people's spiritual fervor has fizzled out. The people of Israel are discouraged and careless in their worship, mistreating each other while they continue to be controlled by the Persian Empire.

suggest that the Persians are still in power. His references to sacrifices and offerings suggest that the temple has been rebuilt (cf. Haggai and Zechariah), putting Malachi after 515 BC. The social conditions that he describes, such as the problem of intermarriage with women outside the faith, seem to indicate that he was a contemporary of Ezra and Nehemiah. Therefore, we can date Malachi to between 515 and 445 BC (see the time line of Malachi).

Unlike other prophets who faced crisis and change, Malachi lived during an "uneventful waiting period, when God seemed to have forgotten his people."[2] Zerubbabel (the governor from the house of David) and Joshua the high priest (who figured prominently in Haggai and Zechariah) had both died without seeing God's promises realized. The rebuilt temple was completed, but new generations were turning away from YHWH.[3] It was a time of great discouragement, but Malachi sought to restore the people's faith in God.

Exploration

Malachi deals with three of the five phases of prophetic vision. He addresses past and present breaches of the covenant with God, including the Jews' direct sins in their worship as well as social injustices. He does not

TIME LINE

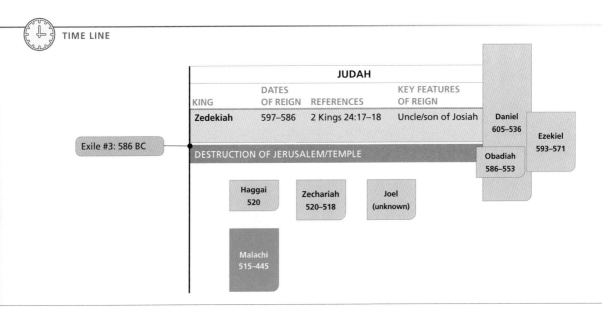

JUDAH						
KING	DATES OF REIGN	REFERENCES	KEY FEATURES OF REIGN			
Zedekiah	597–586	2 Kings 24:17–18	Uncle/son of Josiah	Daniel 605–536		Ezekiel 593–571
Exile #3: 586 BC						
DESTRUCTION OF JERUSALEM/TEMPLE				Obadiah 586–553		
	Haggai 520	Zechariah 520–518	Joel (unknown)			
	Malachi 515–445					

address the near future; instead, he looks to the eschatological future when God will judge the wicked and save his people. At the end of this prophetic era, Malachi encourages the people to live in light of God's unfolding redemptive plan.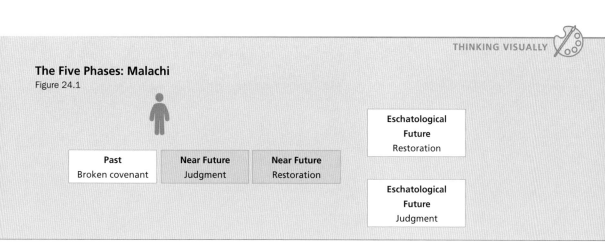

The book is structured around six "disputations" or miniarguments between God and the people. Each unit has four elements. First, God makes some kind of accusation. Second, the people question or challenge him. Third, God responds to their question. And fourth, he or Malachi applies his response more fully. These are not records of actual conversations between YHWH and the people. Rather, the prophet is speaking for YHWH, presenting what the people *would* say in response, and revealing how YHWH would answer them. It is an accurate presentation of the people's perspective, allowing Malachi to put Israel's distorted perspective into words so that it can be evaluated and critiqued (see persuasive stategy 10 in chapter 7). The structure of the book is represented by table 24.1.

The first (**1:2–5**) and sixth (**3:13–4:3**) disputations both discuss the contrast between the righteous and the wicked. It is rebellious to suggest that there is no difference between those who walk closely with God and those who do evil. The second (**1:6–2:9**) and fifth (**3:6–12**) disputations deal with failing to honor God with half-hearted worship. These two disputations also have two questions from the people. The third (**2:10–16**) and fourth (**2:17–3:5**) disputations address issues of social virtue and integrity. In the approximate center of the book (**3:1–5**), God announces that he will send a messenger who will prepare the way for him. This anticipates the conclusion of the book (**4:4–6**), in which Malachi again states that this messenger—called "Elijah"—will prepare for the day of YHWH.

THINKING VISUALLY

The Five Phases: Malachi
Figure 24.1

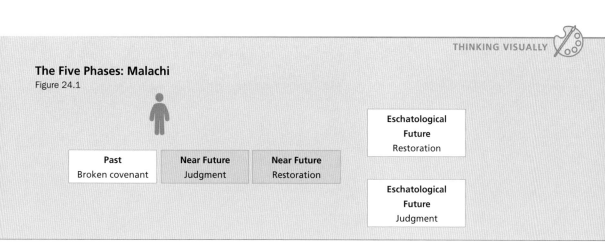

Table 24.1. The Structure of Malachi

Disputation	Verses	Statement	Question	Response
1	1:2–5	"I have loved you."	**"But you say, 'How have you loved us?'"**	"I have loved Jacob but Esau have I hated." *(distinction between the righteous and the wicked)*
2	1:6–2:9	"Where is my honor?"	**"But you say, 'How have we despised your name?'"** **"But you say, 'How have we polluted you?'"**	You present defiled offerings upon my altar.
3	2:10–16	YHWH will not accept your offering	**"But you say, 'Why does he not?'"**	You have divorced the wife of your youth.
4	2:17–3:5	"You have wearied the LORD with your words."	**"But you say, 'How have we wearied him?'"**	You accuse God of injustice. **"I send my messenger, and he will prepare the way before me."**
5	3:6–12	"You are robbing me."	**"But you say, 'How shall we return?'"** **"But you say, 'How have we robbed you?'"**	You are withholding tithes and contributions.
6	3:13–4:3	"Your words have been hard against me."	**"But you say, 'How have we spoken against you?'"**	You say that it is useless to serve God. *(distinction between the righteous and the wicked)*
	4:4–6	Conclusion		

Disputation 1: "How Have You Loved Us?"

■ READ MALACHI 1:2–5 ■

The first disputation begins with the simple statement that YHWH loves Israel. Surprisingly, the people respond by asking *how* YHWH has loved them. This is not a request for information but an accusation that YHWH has not loved them well. YHWH responds by reminding them of two things. First, he chose ("loved") Jacob—the father of Israel—but rejected ("hated") Esau, even though Esau was the firstborn (1:2–3). His choice of a covenant partner does not depend on merit but on his sovereign will. Second, his judgment of the Edomites (the descendants of Esau) is deserved and is a demonstration of his love for his own people (1:4–5). God's love is not in conflict with his justice. When his people see his justice, they will know that they have been chosen and spared.

Disputation 2: "How Have We Despised Your Name?"

■ READ MALACHI 1:6–2:9 ■

In the second unit, God asks why the people have not honored him (1:6). When the people defensively ask how they have failed to honor him, he responds that they have offered polluted sacrifices (1:7). We all know that the value of a gift is increased when it costs more time or money. Imagine how a wife would feel if her husband gave her weeds instead of roses, or how a guest would feel if his host served leftover soup from last week. When we cut corners and offer what is cheap, we dishonor the recipient. 📖

In the original covenant stipulations, God commanded that the people offer sacrifices that represent the first and best of what they own, not animals that are "blind or disabled or mutilated" (Lev. 22:22). Yet that's exactly what they were doing in Malachi's time. God says, "When you offer blind animals in sacrifice, is that not evil? And when you offer those that are lame or sick, is that not evil?" (Mal. 1:8). These animals were damaged goods—of little worth to the farmer. They would never dare to offer them to the governor, so why did they think that God would accept them? In 2:1–9 we learn that one of the reasons the people do not honor God is that the *priests* do not honor God (2:1–2). They have taught the people to do wrong (2:8).

Disputation 3: Why Will You Not Accept Our Offerings?

■ READ MALACHI 2:10–16 ■

This concerns two similar issues. First, Malachi announces that the people have broken the covenant with God by marrying women who worship other gods (2:10–12). Second, God will not accept their offerings because they have broken another covenant: their marriages (2:14). God is deeply offended by divorce because it demonstrates faithlessness, does violence by forcing women into a vulnerable socioeconomic position, and undermines the raising of godly offspring (2:15–16). 📜

"A Son Honors His Father"

Malachi is making an argument from the lesser to the greater.[a] One of the primary commandments in the covenant is that children are to honor their father and mother (Exod. 20:12). A few chapters later, Moses prohibits cursing a ruler of the people (22:28). Therefore, if parents and rulers (who were given their authority by God) were to be honored, how much more should the people honor God himself!

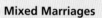

CANONICAL CONNECTIONS

Mixed Marriages

From the beginning of the nation, Israelites were prohibited from marrying outside the faith (Deut. 7:1–4). The issue was not that outsiders were of a different ethnicity but that they worshiped foreign gods and would tempt Israelites to do the same. (Note that in the book of Ruth there was no problem with Boaz marrying Ruth—a Moabite woman—because she committed herself to YHWH.) Ezra and Nehemiah dealt with mixed marriages as a part of their efforts to revitalize the faith of the returned exiles (cf. Ezra 9:1–2; Neh. 13:23–27). The prohibition against marrying nonbelievers is repeated in the New Testament as well (2 Cor. 6:14).

Disputation 4: How Have We Wearied YHWH?

■ READ MALACHI 2:17–3:5 ■

In the fourth disputation, the prophet states that the people have wearied God with their words. "How have we wearied him?" they ask (2:17). The answer is that they claim that God delights in evil and fails to do justice. In response to this accusation, God announces the coming of a messenger who will prepare the way for him (3:1). When YHWH comes, he will sort the people and distinguish those who belong to him from those who are destined for destruction (3:2–5). God *is* a God of justice. Perhaps the wicked seem to get away with their evil now, but in the eschatological future, a messenger will prepare the way for God himself to make things right. 📜

Disputation 5: "How Have We Robbed You?"

■ READ MALACHI 3:6–12 ■

In the fifth disputation, God accuses Israel of robbing him. Israel asks, incredulously, "How have we robbed you?" (3:8). The answer is that they have failed to give God adequate tithes and contributions. A "tithe" refers to giving a tenth of one's wealth or income back to God (Lev. 27:30–32). The tithe provided income for the Levites and priests, who served God full time (Num. 18:24, 26). These contributions also were intended to support the poor and needy in society, such as the widow and the orphan (Deut. 26:12). The tithe was not optional—it belonged to God. Therefore, by failing to contribute it or by failing to pay the full amount, the people were robbing God. However, God assures them that if they give what he requires, they should expect him to provide for them abundantly (Mal. 3:10–12). God *wants* to bless his people, but he will not do so if they fail to honor him with what he has given them.

> **CANONICAL CONNECTIONS**
>
> **"I Send My Messenger"**
>
> In the Gospels, Jesus quotes Malachi 3:1 and explicitly identifies John the Baptist as the messenger whom God would send to prepare the way for YHWH. Jesus says, "What then did you go out to see? A prophet? Yes, I tell you, and more than a prophet. This is he of whom it is written, 'Behold, I send my messenger before your face, who will prepare your way before you'" (Matt. 11:9–10; Luke 7:26–27). The Gospel of Mark begins with a combined quotation of Malachi 3:1 and Isaiah 40:3, which predicts a messenger crying out in the wilderness. Mark then identifies John the Baptist as the fulfillment of those predictions.

Disputation 6: "How Have We Spoken against You?"

■ READ MALACHI 3:13–4:3 ■

The final disputation involves an accusation by the people that "it is vain [or futile] to serve God" (3:14). They have analyzed the costs and benefits of serving God and decided that it is not worth it. Malachi's response is telling. He does not say that a person is saved from judgment by *earning* God's favor.

He says that a person belongs to God by fearing YHWH and honoring his name (3:16). It is faith that saves, and obedience is a result of that faith. God adds that a day is coming when he will certainly judge the wicked and spare his own people (3:17). Perhaps now it appears that the wicked flourish and the righteous suffer—so that faith in God seems useless—but someday the distinction between the two groups will be obvious (3:18). The wicked will be judged as though they were burned in an oven (4:1), but God's own people who fear his name will rejoice and enjoy victory over their enemies (4:2–3).

Conclusion

■ READ MALACHI 4:4–6 ■

The prophet Malachi, speaking for God, concludes the book with three crucial verses that guide God's people as they wait for victory and vindication. They (and we) must do two things. First, remember and obey the covenant. In other words, remain faithful to God and trust in him.

Second, look for a new Elijah that God will send before the great day of YHWH (4:5). This is the same messenger that we saw above in 3:1. The original Elijah confronted false prophets and those who had turned from God. This new, coming Elijah will do the same, preparing the way for God to reveal himself.[4] He will turn the hearts of the fathers and children back to each other (4:6a), a statement that readers and scholars have wrestled to understand. Most likely, it refers to the restoration of the family and the end of the cycle of covenant unfaithfulness.[5] If this does *not* happen, God will strike the land with a curse (4:6b). In other words, Israel's fate depends on their response to this Elijah when he comes.[6] If they accept him, they will accept the Lord—the Messiah—who comes after him. If they do not accept him—and the Lord—then they will suffer judgment.

Implementation

Malachi is short, but it offers a clear perspective on Israel's (broken) relationship with God. And it is relevant for us—the people of God—as well. Let us consider three important points in the book.

CANONICAL CONNECTIONS

"I Will Send You Elijah the Prophet"

We saw previously that the New Testament identifies the messenger in Malachi 3:1 as John the Baptist. Jesus also directly identifies John the Baptist as the new Elijah prophesied in Malachi 4:5, saying, "For all the Prophets and the Law prophesied until John, and if you are willing to accept it, he is Elijah who is to come" (Matt. 11:13–14). In the Gospel of Mark, Jesus's disciples ask him about Malachi 4:5–6, "Why do the scribes say that first Elijah must come?" (9:11). Jesus agrees that Elijah must come first, before the Messiah "should suffer many things and be treated with contempt" (9:12). He then adds, speaking about John the Baptist, "Elijah has come, and they did to him whatever they pleased" (9:13). The most explicit allusion to Malachi 4:5–6 occurs at the beginning of Luke, when an angel tells John the Baptist's father that John will go before the Lord "in the spirit and power of Elijah, to turn the hearts of the fathers to the children" (1:17).

First, Malachi warns against lackluster or *cheap* worship. It is God who has given us everything we have (James 1:17), and when we give back to him, we worship him and acknowledge that he is the giver of all things. By contrast, when we withhold our resources from him, or when we offer him our leftovers or things we do not want anyway, we dishonor him. In Malachi 1:6–2:9, the prophet warns against giving inferior gifts to God. Time can also be included in that category. Do we attend church only when we do not have something "more important" going on, like our child's soccer game or a sporting event on TV? In Malachi 3:6–12, God declares that if we fail to give financially to his work, we are *robbing* him. This makes it clear that our contributions are not optional. Throughout church history, the baseline of Christian giving has been 10 percent of one's income or wealth, on the basis of the Old Testament, although the New Testament suggests that we should give more than that to God's work. Paul says that we should not give "reluctantly or under compulsion, for God loves a cheerful giver" and that we should be "generous in every way" (2 Cor. 9:7, 11). However small or great our wealth, it has been entrusted to us by God. The appropriate response to his gifts is to give generously to his work. For most of us who are employed, dropping ten dollars in the offering plate at church constitutes theft because it is much less than God expects and deserves.

Second, Malachi makes a strong argument against divorce. Divorce is so common in the West today that it may no longer seem like a great problem. But Malachi shows that it is deeply offensive to God and destroys the ideal environment for passing on the faith to our children—something that God values highly (2:15). In God's view, divorce is not simply ending a relationship that is not working. He calls it "faithless" three times (2:14, 15, 16). It is the betrayal of a companion (2:14), a division of what God has joined by his Spirit (2:15), and an act of violence (2:16). Divorce is so repugnant to God that he will not accept their offerings because of it (2:13; cf. 1 Pet. 3:7). In the New Testament, Jesus acknowledges that Moses instituted the mechanism of divorce in Deuteronomy 24:1. And yet he says, "I say to you that everyone who divorces his wife, except on the ground of sexual immorality, makes her commit adultery, and whoever marries a divorced woman commits adultery" (Matt. 5:32). Many of us have been raised in families affected by divorce, and we know the pain it causes. Be assured: God hates it as well.

Third, we have seen throughout the Prophets that God's people were awaiting the "day of the Lord," in which he will come to forgive their sin, transform their hearts, defeat their enemies, and usher in his kingdom. It is fitting, therefore, that, as the last of the prophetic books, Malachi clearly identifies how we will know that the day of YHWH has begun: when the messenger, a new Elijah, appears and prepares the way. The New Testament unmistakably announces that this messenger is John the Baptist. When he appears, he indicates that the day of YHWH has finally arrived. It began with the incarnation of Jesus Christ, his payment for sin on the cross, and his resurrection from the dead in victory. It will be fully completed when Jesus comes a second time, spares his people from judgment, and rules over them in peace forever. Therefore, we are currently *in* the day of YHWH, or the "last days." That day is much longer than the prophets knew—thus far it has been more than two thousand years! But our hope that it will be completed is certain because John the Baptist has come and Jesus has already fulfilled the first part of God's promises. No matter how long we must wait, we know that Jesus will come again to fulfill the rest of his glorious salvation. For now, whether we prosper or suffer, whether we enjoy happiness or struggle with pain, we are at the end of history, and God promises that he will never leave us as we await his final victory.

Christian Reading Questions

1. Give some more thought to the "disputations" in the book of Malachi. How does the prophet characterize the people through their questions to God? Why do you think God sometimes does not directly answer their questions?

2. Malachi complains that the people dishonored God by offering blind or disabled animals on the altar (1:6–2:9). How might we give disrespectful offerings to God today? How do we recontextualize the point of this passage to our New Testament situation?

3. Reread Malachi 2:14–16 on the topic of divorce. What are some key words in this text that indicate God's perspective on divorce? How can the text serve as a corrective for the common perception of divorce in the church today?

4. Trace the themes of honor/respect for God and honor/respect for others in the book of Malachi. Where do these two themes appear? How are they related to each other, and how will they be resolved in the future?

Notes

The endnotes for each chapter appear first, followed by the notes to the sidebars for that chapter.

Chapter 1 Introduction

1. Gerhard von Rad, *Old Testament Theology*, vol. 2, *The Theology of Israel's Prophetic Traditions*, trans. D. M. G. Stalker (Edinburgh: Oliver & Boyd, 1965), 33.

2. John Bright, *Jeremiah: A New Translation with Introduction and Commentary*, Anchor Bible (New York: Doubleday, 1965), lvi.

3. Zachary Parush, "Legalese: Definition & Meaning," Termly, January 11, 2021, https://termly.io/resources/articles/legalese/#legalese-examples.

Chapter 2 The Theological Context of the Prophets

1. Italics in Scripture quotations have been added for emphasis.

2. Daniel C. Lane, "The Meaning and Use of *Berith* in the Old Testament" (PhD diss., Trinity International University, 2000), 314.

3. Some scholars hold that the first major theological covenant in the Old Testament is a "covenant with creation" in Gen. 1–3. They argue that even though there is no mention of the word "covenant" (Hebrew: *berit*), other language and literary features indicate that God is forming a divine-human covenant. On a more technical note, the typical Hebrew verb for establishing a covenant is *karat* (to make), whereas in Gen. 6:18 (the covenant with Noah), God says that he will "uphold" (*qum*) the covenant. The argument would then be that the covenant with Noah in Gen. 6 is actually upholding a previous covenant initiated by God and humans in the garden of Eden. For a clear articulation of this view, see Peter J. Gentry and Stephen J. Wellum, *Kingdom through Covenant: A Biblical-Theological Understanding of the Covenants*, 2nd ed. (Wheaton: Crossway, 2018), 187–201.

4. Stephen G. Dempster, *Dominion and Dynasty: A Theology of the Hebrew Bible* (Downers Grove, IL: IVP Academic, 2003), 23.

5. Bruce K. Waltke and Charles Yu, *An Old Testament Theology: An Exegetical, Canonical, and Thematic Approach* (Grand Rapids: Zondervan, 2007), 298.

6. Jacob Milgrom, *Leviticus: A Book of Ritual and Ethics,* Continental Commentaries (Minneapolis: Fortress, 2004), 46, 49, 58.

7. See the massive and comprehensive examination of forms and comparisons of biblical and ancient Near Eastern covenants in Kenneth A. Kitchen and Paul J. N. Lawrence, *Treaty, Law and Covenant in the Ancient Near East*, 3 vols. (Wiesbaden: Harrassowitz Verlag, 2012).

8. Gentry and Wellum, *Kingdom through Covenant*, 479.

9. For example, Heb. 8:13 says, "In speaking of a new covenant, he makes the first one obsolete. And what is becoming obsolete and growing old is ready to vanish away." This means that elements of the previous covenant with Israel, such as the priesthood, the temple, and the ritual elements and sacrifices, are no longer necessary once Christ's perfect sacrifice has met their demands and permanently removed the barrier between God and his people. However, the relational intent of the covenant and the revelation of God's character in his law remain valid and important.

Chapter 3 The Historical Context of the Prophets

1. The first occurrence of the word "prophet" in the Old Testament is in Gen. 20:7, when God calls Abraham a prophet because he is under God's protection. The second occurrence is when Aaron functions as Moses's prophet, or spokesman, and helps him talk to Pharaoh in Egypt (Exod. 7:1). The third occurrence refers to Miriam as a prophetess because she leads the community in singing a victory song after God delivers Israel from the Egyptians. See the full list of prophets in chapter 4.

2. Willem A. VanGemeren, *Interpreting the Prophetic Word: An Introduction to the Prophetic Literature of the Old Testament* (Grand Rapids: Zondervan, 1996), 28.

3. VanGemeren, *Interpreting the Prophetic Word*, 34.

4. VanGemeren, *Interpreting the Prophetic Word*, 36.

5. It actually fell to the Medes, who were allies of the Babylonians. However, the Medes were not interested in occupying the city, and the Babylonians were the beneficiaries.

Chapter 4 The Role of the Old Testament Prophet

1. Abraham Joshua Heschel, *The Prophets* (New York: Jewish Publication Society of America, 1962), 489, 495.

2. Mark E. Biddle, *Polyphony and Symphony in Prophetic Literature: Rereading Jeremiah 7–20*, Studies in Old Testament Interpretation 2 (Macon, GA: Mercer University Press, 1996).

Chapter 5 False Prophets and the Prophets of the Nations

1. Victor Harold Matthews, *The Hebrew Prophets and Their Social World* (Grand Rapids: Baker Academic, 2012), 17.

2. Nils P. Heeßel, "The Hermeneutics of Mesopotamian Extispicy: Theory vs. Practice," in *Mediating between Heaven and Earth: Communication with the Divine in the Ancient Near East*, ed. C. L. Crouch, Jonathan Stökl, and Anna Elise Zernecke (New York: T&T Clark, 2012), 17–18.

3. Ann Jeffers, *Magic and Divination in Ancient Palestine and Syria* (Leiden: Brill, 1996), 158.

4. Jeffers, *Magic and Divination*, 182.

5. See the brief discussion in John W. Hilber, "Prophecy, Divination, and Magic in the Ancient Near East," in *Behind the Scenes of the Old Testament: Cultural, Social, and Historical Contexts*, ed. Jonathan S. Greer, John W. Hilber, and John H. Walton (Grand Rapids: Baker Academic, 2018), 368–69.

6. Abraham Joshua Heschel, *The Prophets* (New York: Jewish Publication Society of America, 1962), 586.

7. Heschel, *Prophets*, 587.

8. This is a complex narrative because of Jonah's aversion to delivering YHWH's message. Therefore, there are two additional variables possible. First, Jonah may not be giving the full oracle that God has intended, or the narrator may not be *presenting* the full oracle for literary effect. Second, the word "overthrown" in Hebrew can have two senses: it can mean that a city is conquered, and it can also refer to repentance. Therefore, there may be a play on words here in which Jonah does not even grasp the full import of what he is saying. While Jonah

delightfully announces that Nineveh will be "overthrown," he does not realize that God intends for them to repent and be delivered from the coming destruction.

9. Georg Fohrer, *Introduction to the Old Testament* (Nashville: Abingdon, 1968), 352. Fohrer writes,

> It is inaccurate, if not misleading, to call the prophetical saying "prophecy" in the sense of "prediction.". . . The essential point is not the miraculous prediction of events soon to come; in fact, the prophets frequently erred in this matter. What is crucial is that what is announced is already on the point of coming to pass; the prophet has just enough time to point out what is happening and summon men to draw the proper conclusions for the present. The prophet speaks of the future in order to determine and structure the present in which he lives, which it is his task and goal to influence.

Note that Fohrer admits that the prophets attempted to predict the future, for he says they "frequently erred."

10. R. E. Clements, *Old Testament Prophecy: From Oracles to Canon* (Louisville: Westminster John Knox, 1996), 33.

11. Thomas Schneider, "A Land without Prophets? Examining the Presumed Lack of Prophecy in Ancient Egypt," in *Enemies and Friends of the State: Ancient Prophecy in Context*, ed. Chris A. Rollston (University Park, PA: Eisenbrauns, 2018), 59–86.

12. Nili Shupak, "Egyptian 'Prophecy' and Biblical Prophecy: Did the Phenomenon of Prophecy, in the Biblical Sense, Exist in Ancient Egypt?," *Jaarbericht van het Vooraziatisch-Egyptisch Genootschap Ex oriente lux* 31 (1989–90): 34. See also Hilber, "Prophecy, Divination, and Magic," 372.

13. Quoted with slight adjustments for style from James B. Pritchard, ed., *Ancient Near Eastern Texts: Relating to the Old Testament*, 3rd ed. (Princeton: Princeton University Press, 1969), 26.

14. ARM 26 200 (= M.6188), in *Prophets and Prophecy in the Ancient Near East*, by Martti Nissinen, ed. Peter Machinist, Writings from the Ancient World 12 (Atlanta: Society of Biblical Literature, 2003), 33.

15. ARM 26 219 (M.13496 + M. 15299), in Nissinen, *Prophets and Prophecy*, 54.

16. Herbert B. Huffmon, "A Company of Prophets: Mari, Assyria, Israel," in *Prophecy in Its Ancient Near Eastern Context: Mesopotamian, Biblical, and Arabian Perspectives*, ed. Martti Nissinen, SBL Symposium Series 13 (Atlanta: Society of Biblical Literature, 2000), 50.

17. SAA 9 1.4, quoted with slight adjustments for style from Nissinen, *Prophets and Prophecy*, 105.

18. SAA 9 1.6, quoted with slight adjustments for style from Nissinen, *Prophets and Prophecy*, 106–7.

19. Jonathan Stökl, "A Royal Advisory Service: Prophecy and the State in Mesopotamia," in Rollston, *Enemies and Friends of the State*, 104.

Chapter 5 Sidebar Notes

a. See the discussion in Cornelis Van Dam, "אורים [*'vrym*]," in *The New International Dictionary of Old Testament Theology and Exegesis*, ed. Willem VanGemeren (Grand Rapids: Zondervan, 1997), 324–26.

b. C. S. Lewis, *The Silver Chair* (New York: HarperCollins, 1981), 25–26.

c. William Blake, *The Marriage of Heaven and Hell* (Boston: John W. Luce, 1906; Project Gutenberg, 2014), https://www.gutenberg.org/files/45315/45315-h/45315-h.htm.

Chapter 6 The Message of the Prophets

1. For this general discussion, see O. Palmer Robertson, *The Christ of the Prophets* (Phillipsburg, NJ: P&R, 2004), 166–67.

2. Abraham Joshua Heschel, *The Prophets* (New York: Jewish Publication Society of America, 1962), 282.

3. Heschel, *Prophets*, 296.

Chapter 7 The Persuasive Strategies of the Prophets

1. Kelvin G. Friebel, *Jeremiah's and Ezekiel's Sign-Acts*, Journal for the Study of the Old Testament Supplement Series 283 (Sheffield: Sheffield Academic, 1999), 411–14.

2. Friebel, *Jeremiah's and Ezekiel's Sign-Acts*, 414.

3. Friebel, *Jeremiah's and Ezekiel's Sign-Acts*, 456.

4. Lakoff and Turner argue that all language is metaphorical in some sense. We use metaphors so frequently in all language that we often do not even realize it. George Lakoff and Mark Turner, *More Than Cool Reason: A Field Guide to Poetic Metaphor* (Chicago: University of Chicago Press, 1989), xi.

5. On this passage, see the helpful discussion by Iain M. Duguid, *Ezekiel*, NIV Application Commentary (Grand Rapids: Zondervan, 1999), 259–64.

6. Michael V. Fox, "The Rhetoric of Ezekiel's Vision of the Valley of the Bones," *Hebrew Union College Annual* 51 (1980): 9.

7. Fox, "Rhetoric of Ezekiel's Vision," 9.

8. David Noel Freedman, "Pottery, Poetry, and Prophecy: An Essay on Biblical Poetry," *Journal of Biblical Literature* 96, no. 1 (March 1977): 15.

9. J. P. Fokkelman, *Reading Biblical Poetry: An Introductory Guide* (Louisville: Westminster John Knox, 2001), 1.

10. Robert Alter, *The Art of Biblical Poetry*, 2nd ed. (New York: Basic Books, 2011), 176.

11. Alter, *Art of Biblical Poetry*, 11.

12. Fokkelman, *Reading Biblical Poetry*, 75.

13. Fokkelman, *Reading Biblical Poetry*, 78.

14. Some suggestions for further reading include Mark D. Futato, *Interpreting the Psalms: An Exegetical Handbook* (Grand Rapids: Kregel, 2007), 23–55; and Alter, *Art of Biblical Poetry*.

15. Mark J. Boda, *The Book of Zechariah*, New International Commentary on the Old Testament (Grand Rapids: Eerdmans, 2016), 118.

16. Boda, *Book of Zechariah*, 99.

17. Alan S. Bandy and Benjamin L. Merkle, *Understanding Prophecy: A Biblical-Theological Approach* (Grand Rapids: Kregel, 2015), 215.

Chapter 8 From Prophetic Word to Biblical Book

1. Rolf Rendtorff, *The Canonical Hebrew Bible: A Theology of the Old Testament* (Leiden: Deo, 2005), 7.

2. The seven stages come from Daniel I. Block, "Binding Up the Testimony: Concluding Reflections on the Origins of the Book of Isaiah," in *Bind Up the Testimony: Explorations in the Genesis of the Book of Isaiah*, ed. Daniel I. Block and Richard L. Schultz (Peabody, MA: Hendrickson, 2015), 293–303.

3. John Calvin, *Commentaries on the Book of the Prophet Isaiah*, trans. John Owen (repr., Grand Rapids: Baker Books, 2003), 199.

4. John N. Oswalt, *The Book of Isaiah: Chapters 1–39*, New International Commentary on the Old Testament (Grand Rapids: Eerdmans, 1986), 55.

5. Block, for example, suggests that Jeremiah probably did not participate in transcription, whereas Isaiah may have written some of his own oracles, and Ezekiel *probably* did so. See Block, "Binding Up the Testimony," 302.

6. Aaron Schart, "The Fifth Vision of Amos in Context," in *Thematic Threads in the Book of the Twelve*, ed. Paul L. Redditt and Aaron Schart, Beihefte Zur Zeitschrift Für Die Alttestamentliche Wissenschaft 325 (Berlin: Walter de Gruyter, 2003), 46–71.

a. Stephen G. Dempster, *Dominion and Dynasty: A Theology of the Hebrew Bible* (Downers Grove, IL: IVP Academic, 2003), 22.

b. Dempster, *Dominion and Dynasty*, 159.

Chapter 9 Isaiah

1. William Sanford LaSor, David Allan Hubbard, and Frederic William Bush, *Old Testament Survey: The Message, Form, and Background of the Old Testament*, 2nd ed. (Grand Rapids: Eerdmans, 1996), 276.

2. See John F. A. Sawyer, *The Fifth Gospel* (New York: Cambridge University Press, 1996).

3. J. C. Döderlein (1775) was one of the first to propose that another prophet wrote chapters 40–66. J. G. Eichhorn, *Einleitung in Das Alte Testament*, 3rd ed., vol. 3 (Leipzig, 1803), argued that some oracles in the book came from the historical prophet Isaiah, while chapters 40–66 come from a later period. Christopher R. Seitz, "Isaiah, Book Of," in *Anchor Bible Dictionary*, ed. David Noel Freedman (New York: Doubleday, 1992), 3:472.

4. Bernhard Duhm, *Das Buch Jesaja übersetzt und erklärt* (Göttingen: Vandenhoeck & Ruprecht, 1892).

5. John W. Miller, *Meet the Prophets: A Beginner's Guide to the Books of the Biblical Prophets—Their Meaning Then and Now* (New York: Paulist Press, 1987), 94.

6. H. G. M. Williamson, *The Book Called Isaiah: Deutero-Isaiah's Role in Composition and Redaction* (Oxford: Clarendon, 1994).

7. H. G. M. Williamson, "Isaiah, Book Of," in *Dictionary of the Old Testament: Prophets*, ed. Mark J. Boda and J. Gordon McConville, IVP Bible Dictionary 4 (Downers Grove, IL: IVP Academic, 2012), 370.

8. Jacob Stromberg, *Isaiah after Exile: The Author of Third Isaiah as a Reader and Redactor of the Book* (Oxford: Oxford University Press, 2011), 248. Stromberg writes that chapters 56–66 were written with dependence on earlier Isaianic material, but chapters 1–55 were also edited with an eye toward chapters 56–66. Thus the book has stages of authorship and revision. Stromberg, *An Introduction to the Study of Isaiah*, T&T Clark Approaches to Biblical Studies (London: T&T Clark, 2011), 49.

9. See the discussion in J. A. Motyer, *The Prophecy of Isaiah: An Introduction & Commentary* (Downers Grove, IL: InterVarsity, 1993), 26–28.

10. O. Palmer Robertson writes,

> [Some evangelical scholars] may be correct in saying that "the question of the authorship of Isaiah probably should not be made a theological *shibboleth*." For the issue is far more significant than a matter of alternative pronunciations of the same word by different communities. Their plea that this question not be made a test for orthodoxy must be considered with great care. It is not a light thing to recite the testimony of the Lord and his gospel writers and then to brush their uniform witness aside as though it were irrelevant to issues of faith and life today. (*The Christ of the Prophets* [Phillipsburg, NJ: P&R, 2004], 235)

11. The occurrences are 1:4; 5:19, 24; 10:20; 12:6; 17:7; 29:19; 30:11, 12, 15; 31:1; 37:23; 41:14, 16, 20; 43:3, 14; 45:11; 47:4; 48:17; 49:7; 54:5; 55:5; 60:9, 14.

12. See 2 Kings 19:22; Pss. 71:22; 78:41; 89:18; Jer. 50:29; 51:5.

13. On the structure of Isaiah, I have been heavily influenced by the work of John N. Oswalt: *The Book of Isaiah: Chapters 1–39*, New International Commentary on the Old Testament (Grand Rapids: Eerdmans, 1986); *The Book of Isaiah: Chapters 40–66*, New International Commentary on the Old Testament (Grand Rapids: Eerdmans, 1998); and *Isaiah*, NIV Application Commentary (Grand Rapids: Zondervan, 2003). I have also found help with the structure of Isaiah in Motyer, *Prophecy of Isaiah*.

14. Oswalt, *Book of Isaiah: Chapters 1–39*, 55.

15. Oswalt, *Book of Isaiah: Chapters 1–39*, 299.

16. These four songs (42:1–9; 49:1–6; 50:4–9; 52:13–53:12) were originally identified by Bernhard Duhm, the same scholar who argued for multiple authors of the book. He notes that these poems are distinct because the language is more exalted and sweeping, the servant is unidentified, the descriptions become graphic and more detailed, and there is a unique emphasis on what the servant will accomplish for the world. See Oswalt, *Book of Isaiah: Chapters 40–66*, 108.

17. See Motyer, *Prophecy of Isaiah*, 386.

18. Note that while critical scholars usually locate chapters 56–66 in the postexilic period, this condemnation is much more at home in the preexilic period during Isaiah's own time. Hezekiah's son Manasseh was infamous for burning his own son in the fire as an act of worship to idols (see 2 Kings 21:6).

19. Motyer, *Prophecy of Isaiah*, 544. John Oswalt also has a great quote on this verse: "The certainty of hope must never make us think that we can persist in our rebellion. . . . Hope is real, even for those who have lost all hope, but judgment is real as well, and the glories of heaven must not lull us into complacency over our rebellion." *Book of Isaiah: Chapters 40–66*, 691.

Chapter 9 Sidebar Notes

a. Thomas H. Troeger, *Borrowed Light: Hymn Texts, Prayers, and Poems* (New York: Oxford University Press, 1994), 171.

b. William W. Hallo and K. Lawson Younger Jr., eds., *The Context of Scripture: Canonical Compositions from the Biblical World*, 2nd ed. (Leiden: Brill, 1997), 264.

c. Hallo and Younger, *Context of Scripture*, 265.

Chapter 10 Jeremiah

1. Hetty Lalleman, *Jeremiah and Lamentations: An Introduction and Commentary*, Tyndale Old Testament Commentaries 21 (Nottingham: Inter-Varsity, 2013), 35–36.

2. For an introduction to the discipline of Old Testament textual criticism (the study of texts and versions of the Old Testament and how we establish the best reading), see Ellis R. Brotzman and Eric J. Tully, *Old Testament Textual Criticism: A Practical Introduction*, 2nd ed. (Grand Rapids: Baker Academic, 2016). For a discussion of complex cases like the book of Jeremiah, see appendix B on pp. 219–26.

3. On the structure of Jeremiah, I am heavily indebted to Peter Lee, "Jeremiah," in *A Biblical-Theological Introduction to the Old Testament: The Gospel Promised*, ed. Miles V. Van Pelt (Wheaton: Crossway, 2016), 277–303; see especially p. 283.

4. Note that 51:64 concludes with "Thus far are the words of Jeremiah." This suggests that chapter 52 stands outside the book as a postscript. Perhaps it was added later by Baruch or whoever finished editing the book together.

5. See Jeremiah Unterman, *From Repentance to Redemption: Jeremiah's Thought in Transition*, Journal for the Study of the Old Testament Supplement Series 54 (Sheffield: JSOT Press, 1987).

6. The purpose of this law was likely (a) to protect the wife by deterring the husband from divorcing her without good reason and (b) to prevent her from being passed back and forth between husbands. Divorce is a serious sin that God hates (Mal. 2:16).

7. Jeremiah uses the Hebrew word *shub* (return, repent) 115 times, the most of any book in the Old Testament. By contrast, Isaiah uses it 51 times, and Ezekiel uses it 64 times.

8. J. Daniel Hays, *Jeremiah and Lamentations*, Teach the Text Commentary Series (Grand Rapids: Baker Books, 2016), 218.

9. Damascus is the capital of the ancient nation of Aram. Today it is the capital of Syria.

10. "Hazor" is also the name of a well-known city in northern Israel. This "Hazor," however, refers to a country in Arabia to the south.

11. See the helpful discussion in Lalleman, *Jeremiah and Lamentations*, 36–37.

a. J. A. Thompson, *The Book of Jeremiah* (Grand Rapids: Eerdmans, 1980), 184.

b. Thompson, *Book of Jeremiah*, 281.

c. J. Daniel Hays, *Jeremiah and Lamentations* (Grand Rapids: Baker Books, 2016), 212. See also Shira J. Golani, "New Light and Some Reflections on the List of False Prophets (4Q339)," *Revue de Qumran* 28, no. 2 (2016): 257–65.

d. Craig Blomberg, "Matthew," in *Commentary on the New Testament Use of the Old Testament*, ed. G. K. Beale and D. A. Carson (Grand Rapids: Baker Academic, 2007), 9–10.

Chapter 11 Ezekiel

1. Tom Jacobs, "Conservatives and Liberals Have Differing Mental Images of God," *Pacific Standard*, June 13, 2018, https://psmag.com/news/conservatives-and-liberals-have-differing-mental-images-of-god. For the academic article reporting on the study, see Joshua Conrad Jackson, Neil Hester, and Kurt Gray, "The Faces of God in America: Revealing Religious Diversity across People and Politics," *PLoS ONE* 13, no. 6 (2018), https://doi.org/10.1371/journal.pone.0198745.

2. In some prophetic books, it is difficult to know whether the prophet is responsible for the message alone or whether he also wrote the book. Though scholars hold a variety of opinions, most (Christian and secular) agree that the book (or at least the vast majority of it) comes from Ezekiel himself. See Daniel I. Block, *The Book of Ezekiel: Chapters 1–24*, New International Commentary on the Old Testament (Grand Rapids: Eerdmans, 1997), 20–21.

3. Deirdre Fulton, "The Exile and Exilic Communities," in *Behind the Scenes of the Old Testament: Cultural, Social, and Historical Contexts*, ed. Jonathan S. Greer, John W. Hilber, and John H. Walton (Grand Rapids: Baker Academic, 2018), 233.

4. Fulton, "Exile and Exilic Communities," 232.

5. Iain M. Duguid, *Ezekiel*, NIV Application Commentary (Grand Rapids: Zondervan, 1999), 117.

6. For further reading on Ezekiel's use of Leviticus, see Michael A. Lyons, "Transformation of Law: Ezekiel's Use of the Holiness Code (Leviticus 17–26)," in *Transforming Visions: Transformations of Text, Tradition, and Theology in Ezekiel*, ed. William A. Tooman and Michael A. Lyons, Princeton Theological Monograph Series 169 (Eugene, OR: Wipf & Stock, 2010), 1–32.

7. Daniel I. Block, *The Book of Ezekiel: Chapters 25–48*, New International Commentary on the Old Testament (Grand Rapids: Eerdmans, 1998), viii.

8. O. Palmer Robertson, *The Christ of the Prophets* (Phillipsburg, NJ: P&R, 2004), 306.

9. Block, *Book of Ezekiel: Chapters 25–48*, 412.

10. Duguid, *Ezekiel*, 456.

11. Robertson, *Christ of the Prophets*, 313.

12. Duguid, *Ezekiel*, 547.

a. Peter Schäfer, *The Origins of Jewish Mysticism* (Princeton: Princeton University Press, 2009), 185.

b. Erich von Däniken, *Chariots of the Gods? Unsolved Mysteries of the Past* (New York: Bantam Books, 1969).

c. Josef F. Blumrich, *The Spaceships of Ezekiel* (New York: Bantam Books, 1974).

d. The translation "evil" likely comes from an older use in English that does not have a moral connotation but refers to something terrible. For example, in *The Two Towers*, the film in the Lord of the Rings trilogy, King Theoden says, "Alas, that these *evil* days should be mine." He is referring to war and the premature death of his son.

e. Gary T. Manning, *Echoes of a Prophet: The Use of Ezekiel in the Gospel of John and in Literature of the Second Temple Period* (London: T&T Clark, 2004), 145.

f. Lena-Sofia Tiemeyer, "Ezekiel: Book Of," in *Dictionary of the Old Testament: Prophets*, ed. Mark J. Boda and J. Gordon McConville, IVP Bible Dictionary 4 (Downers Grove, IL: InterVarsity, 2012), 223.

Chapter 12 Daniel

1. The identity of "Darius the Mede" (Dan. 6, 9, 11) has been much debated by scholars. Evangelicals and conservative scholars have identified this "Darius" as either Gubaru, the governor of Babylon appointed by Cyrus II, or, more likely, as Cyrus himself. Both of these views fit the chronological data and explain the name "Darius" as a secondary title. Those who hold to a late date of Daniel generally consider Darius the Mede to be fictional, claiming that the author of Daniel was incorrect about Babylonian and Persian historical facts. See Stephen R. Miller, *Daniel*, New American Commentary 18 (Nashville: Broadman & Holman, 1994), 171–77.

2. Josephus, *Antiquities* 10.11.7, §267.

3. For a more extended definition of the apocalyptic genre, see Miller, *Daniel*, 46. John Collins defines "apocalypse" as "a genre of revelatory literature with a narrative framework, in which a revelation is mediated by an otherworldly being to a human recipient, disclosing a transcendent reality which is both temporal, insofar as it envisages eschatological salvation, and spatial insofar as it involves another, supernatural world." Also, it normally serves to "interpret present, earthly circumstances in light of the supernatural world and of the future, and to influence both the understanding and the behavior of the audience by means of divine authority." John J. Collins, *Apocalypse: The Morphology of a Genre* (Missoula, MT: Society of Biblical Literature, 1979), 9.

4. Collins writes, "According to the consensus of modern critical scholarship, the stories about Daniel and his friends are legendary in character, and the hero himself most probably never existed." John J. Collins, *Daniel: A Commentary on the Book of Daniel*, Hermeneia (Minneapolis: Fortress, 1993), 1.

5. One scholar writes, "It will be noted that pseudepigraphy is said to fulfill functions that are mutually exclusive. On the one hand we are asked to believe that this was an accepted literary convention that deceived no-one, and on the other that the adoption of a pseudonym, which presumably went undetected, increased the acceptability and authority of a work. [One] cannot have it both ways." Joyce G. Baldwin, "Is There Pseudonymity in the Old Testament?" *Themelios* 4 (1978): 11. See also James M. Hamilton Jr., *With the Clouds of Heaven: The Book of Daniel in Biblical Theology* (Downers Grove, IL: IVP Academic, 2014), 37.

6. For further arguments for the traditional date of Daniel, see Miller, *Daniel*, 22–43; and Andrew E. Steinmann, *Daniel* (St. Louis: Concordia, 2008), 1–19.

7. Hamilton, *With the Clouds of Heaven*, 32.

8. See the helpful discussion on this in Christopher J. H. Wright, *Hearing the Message of Daniel: Sustaining Faith in Today's World* (Grand Rapids: Zondervan, 2017), 29–41.

9. Hamilton, *With the Clouds of Heaven*, 89.

10. Wright, *Hearing the Message of Daniel*, 86. Wright continues, "For of course, for every Shadrach, Meshach, and Abednego who enjoyed the truth of verse 17 in experiencing miraculous deliverance from danger or death, there have been many, many more who have had to live with the experience of verse 18 and yet have gone on affirming their faith even unto martyrdom" (86).

11. Note that the lion's wings are torn off (7:4). This may recall the humbling of Nebuchadnezzar in chap. 4 when his hair was like eagles' feathers (4:33).

12. James A. Montgomery, *A Critical and Exegetical Commentary on the Book of Daniel* (New York: Charles Scribner's Sons, 1927), 400.

13. For the view that the seventy weeks are 490 literal years, see Harold W. Hoehner, "Chronological Aspects of the Life of Christ, Part VI: Daniel's Seventy Weeks and New Testament Chronology," *Bibliotheca Sacra* 132, no. 525 (1975): 47–65. For views that the seventy

weeks are symbolic stretches of time, see Thomas E. McComiskey, "The Seventy 'Weeks' of Daniel against the Background of Ancient Near Eastern Literature," *Westminster Theological Journal* 47 (1985): 18–45; and Sidney Greidanus, *Preaching Christ from Daniel: Foundations for Expository Sermons* (Grand Rapids: Eerdmans, 2012), 285–340.

14. Adapted from Greidanus, *Preaching Christ from Daniel*, 314.

15. Hamilton, *With the Clouds of Heaven*, 99.

16. "This World Is Not My Home," Hymnary.org, accessed June 4, 2021, https://hymnary.org/hymn/AF1947/page/132.

Chapter 12 Sidebar Notes

a. James M. Hamilton Jr., *With the Clouds of Heaven: The Book of Daniel in Biblical Theology* (Downers Grove, IL: IVP Academic, 2014), 189.

Chapter 13 Hosea

1. See William G. Dever, *Did God Have a Wife? Archaeology and Folk Religion in Ancient Israel* (Grand Rapids: Eerdmans, 2008).

2. Hosea 2:8, 13, 16, 17; 9:10 (actually the name of a place); 11:2; 13:1.

3. W. Herrmann, "Baal," in *Dictionary of Deities and Demons in the Bible*, ed. Karel van der Toorn, Bob Becking, and Pieter Willem van der Horst (Leiden: Brill, 1999), 133.

4. John Day, "Hosea and the Baal Cult," in *Prophets and Prophecy in the Ancient Near East: Proceedings of the Oxford Old Testament Seminar*, ed. John Day (New York: T&T Clark, 2010), 205.

5. Eric J. Tully, "Israel's Relationship with Nature and with YHWH in the Book of Hosea," in *For Us, But Not to Us: Essays on Creation, Covenant, and Context in Honor of John H. Walton*, ed. Adam Miglio, Caryn Reeder, Joshua Walton, and Kenneth Way (Eugene, OR: Pickwick, 2020), 162.

6. See Eric J. Tully, "Hosea 1–3 as the Key to the Literary Structure and Message of the Book," in *An Excellent Fortress for His Armies*, ed. Richard E. Averbeck and K. Lawson Younger (University Park: Pennsylvania State University Press, 2020).

7. Eric J. Tully, *Hosea: A Handbook on the Hebrew Text* (Waco: Baylor University Press, 2018), 337.

8. George M. Schwab, "Hosea," in *ESV Expository Commentary*, vol. 7, *Daniel–Malachi*, ed. Iain M. Duguid, James M. Hamilton, and Jay Sklar (Wheaton: Crossway, 2018), 219.

Chapter 13 Sidebar Notes

a. D. A. Carson, "1 Peter," in *Commentary on the New Testament Use of the Old Testament*, ed. G. K. Beale and D. A. Carson (Grand Rapids: Baker Academic, 2007), 1032.

b. Douglas J. Moo, *The Epistle to the Romans* (Grand Rapids: Eerdmans, 1996), 613.

c. Mark A. Seifried, "Romans," in Beale and Carson, *Commentary on the New Testament Use of the Old Testament*, 646.

d. Carson, "1 Peter," 1032.

e. Duane A. Garrett, *Hosea, Joel* (Nashville: Broadman & Holman, 1997), 39. See also a midrashic tradition cited by Rashi and other rabbinic Jewish commentators: Hayyim Angel, "Rebuke Your Mother: But Who Is She? The Identity of the 'Mother' and 'Children' in Hosea 2:4–7," *Jewish Bible Quarterly* 44, no. 1 (2016): 13–20.

f. Siegfried Herrmann, "Ephraim in the Bible," in *Anchor Bible Dictionary*, ed. David Noel Freedman (New York: Doubleday, 1992), 2:551.

g. Eric J. Tully, *Hosea: A Handbook on the Hebrew Text* (Waco: Baylor University Press, 2018), 107.

h. Craig Blomberg, "Matthew," in Beale and Carson, *Commentary on the New Testament Use of the Old Testament*, 34.

   i. Craig Blomberg, "Matthew," 34.

   j. For further discussion of the use of Hosea 10:8 in the New Testament, see David Pao and Eckhard J. Schnabel, "Luke," in Beale and Carson, *Commentary on the New Testament Use of the Old Testament*, 396.

   k. Roy E. Ciampa and Brian S. Rosner, "1 Corinthians," in Beale and Carson, *Commentary on the New Testament Use of the Old Testament*, 748.

Chapter 14 Joel

   1. Steven L. McKenzie, "Joel (Person)," in *Anchor Bible Dictionary*, ed. David Noel Freedman (New York: Doubleday, 1992), 3:872–73.

   2. Paul R. House, *The Unity of the Twelve*, Journal for the Study of the Old Testament Supplement Series 97 (Sheffield: Almond, 1990), 78.

   3. James Nogalski mentions the apocalyptic imagery and the lack of hope for military liberation. See *Redactional Processes in the Book of the Twelve*, Beihefte zur Zeitschrift für die alttestamentliche Wissenschaft 218 (Berlin: de Gruyter, 1993), 55. Nogalski also notes that Joel shares wording with other prophets and that Joel 3:1–3 presupposes a devastated Judah and Jerusalem (49).

   4. Jason T. LeCureux, *The Thematic Unity of the Book of the Twelve* (Sheffield: Sheffield Phoenix, 2012), 132.

   5. My understanding of the structure of Joel has been influenced by Hans Walter Wolff, *Joel and Amos: A Commentary on the Books of the Prophets Joel and Amos*, Hermeneia (Philadelphia: Fortress, 1977).

   6. Quoted in S. R. Driver, *The Books of Joel and Amos* (Cambridge: Cambridge University Press, 1942), 85.

   7. Tom Embury-Dennis, "Locust Plague up to 20 Times Larger than Last Wave Could Devastate Parts of East Africa," *Independent*, April 11, 2020, https://www.independent.co.uk/news/world/africa/locust-plague-africa-somalia-kenya-ethiopia-east-africa-a9460816.html.

   8. Raymond B. Dillard, "Joel," in *The Minor Prophets: An Exegetical and Expository Commentary*, vol. 1, ed. Thomas E. McComiskey (Grand Rapids: Baker Academic, 2009), 295.

Chapter 14 Sidebar Notes

   a. George R. Beasley-Murray, "Revelation," in *New Bible Commentary*, ed. D. A. Carson, R. T. France, J. A. Motyer, and G. J. Wenham, 21st century ed. (Downers Grove, IL: InterVarsity, 1994), 1437.

   b. I. Howard Marshall, "Acts," in *Commentary on the New Testament Use of the Old Testament*, ed. G. K. Beale and D. A. Carson (Grand Rapids: Baker Academic, 2007), 533.

Chapter 15 Amos

   1. Bruce C. Birch, *Hosea, Joel, and Amos*, Westminster Bible Companion (Louisville: Westminster John Knox, 1997), 215.

   2. Michael G. McKelvey, "Amos," in *ESV Expository Commentary*, vol. 7, *Daniel–Malachi*, ed. Iain M. Duguid, James M. Hamilton, and Jay Sklar (Wheaton: Crossway, 2018), 304.

   3. R. B. Coote, *Amos among the Prophets: Composition and Theology* (Philadelphia: Fortress, 1981), 1.

   4. Harold P. Barker, *Christ in the Minor Prophets* (New York: Loizeaux Brothers, 1900), 30.

   5. Abraham Joshua Heschel, *The Prophets* (New York: Jewish Publication Society of America, 1962), 38.

   6. Robert R. Ellis, "Amos Economics," *Review & Expositor* 107, no. 4 (2010): 465.

7. Keshia McEntire, "The Church Should Be at the Forefront of the Fight for Social Justice: A Response to John MacArthur's Anti-Social Justice Manifesto," September 2018, https://relevantmagazine.com/current/the-church-should-be-at-the-forefront-of-the-fight-for-social-justice/.

Chapter 15 Sidebar Notes

a. *The Accordance Bible Lands PhotoGuide*, s.v. "Samaria," paragraph 2065 (OakTree Software, 2016).

b. Martin Luther King Jr., "I Have a Dream," speech delivered August 28, 1963, Lincoln Memorial, Washington, DC, https://kinginstitute.stanford.edu/king-papers/documents/i-have-dream-address-delivered-march-washington-jobs-and-freedom.

c. Michael B. Shepherd, *The Twelve Prophets in the New Testament* (New York: Peter Lang, 2011), 39.

d. I. Howard Marshall, "Acts," in *Commentary on the New Testament Use of the Old Testament*, ed. G. K. Beale and D. A. Carson (Grand Rapids: Baker Academic, 2007), 565.

e. Samantha Field, "The Prophecy of Amos, Revised" (blog), May 8, 2015, http://samanthapfield.com/2015/05/08/the-prophecy-of-amos-revised/.

f. Marshall, "Acts," 589–93.

Chapter 16 Obadiah

1. Siegfried Sassoon, "Finished with the War: A Soldier's Declaration (1917)," Wikisource, last edited January 2, 2021, https://en.wikisource.org/wiki/Finished_with_the_War:_A_Soldier%E2%80%99s_Declaration.

2. Anson F. Rainey and R. Steven Notley, *The Sacred Bridge: Carta's Atlas of the Biblical World* (Jerusalem: Carta, 2014), 266.

3. Eugene H. Merrill, *Kingdom of Priests: A History of Old Testament Israel* (Grand Rapids: Baker, 1987), 382. Merrill suggests that several historical events might qualify. For example, during the reign of Jehoram, the Philistines and Arabs attacked Jerusalem, sacked it, and carried off most of the royal family (see 2 Chron. 21:16–17).

4. Ehud Ben Zvi, *A Historical-Critical Study of the Book of Obadiah* (New York: de Gruyter, 1996), 260–61. Ben Zvi suggests that perhaps Obadiah is not historical, with Edom as *only* a symbol of Israel's enemies.

5. Daniel I. Block, *Obadiah: The Kingship Belongs to YHWH*, Hearing the Message of Scripture (Grand Rapids: Zondervan Academic, 2014), 22–25.

6. Paul R. Raabe, *Obadiah: A New Translation with Introduction and Commentary*, Anchor Bible (New York: Doubleday, 1996), 177–78.

7. Hans Walter Wolff, *Obadiah and Jonah: A Commentary*, Hermeneia (Minneapolis: Augsburg, 1986), 56.

8. Max Roglund, "Obadiah," in *ESV Expository Commentary*, vol. 7, *Daniel–Malachi*, ed. Iain M. Duguid, James M. Hamilton, and Jay Sklar (Wheaton: Crossway, 2018), 381.

9. Douglas K. Stuart, *Hosea–Jonah*, Word Biblical Commentary (Waco: Nelson, 1987), 422.

Chapter 16 Sidebar Notes

a. Jeffrey J. Niehaus, "Obadiah," in *The Minor Prophets: An Exegetical and Expository Commentary*, ed. Thomas E. McComiskey (Grand Rapids: Baker Academic, 2009), 500.

b. Max Roglund, "Obadiah," in *ESV Expository Commentary*, vol. 7, *Daniel–Malachi*, ed. Iain M. Duguid, James M. Hamilton, and Jay Sklar (Wheaton: Crossway, 2018), 376.

Chapter 17 Jonah

1. "Watts Family Murders," Wikipedia, last edited May 12, 2021, https://en.wikipedia.org/wiki/Watts_family_murders.

2. Michael Gryboski, "Colorado Man Who Murdered Wife, 2 Daughters Says He's Found God," *Christian Post*, March 28, 2019, https://www.christianpost.com/news/colorado-man-who-murdered-wife-2-daughters-says-hes-found-god.html.

3. Albert Kirk Grayson, *Assyrian Royal Inscriptions, Part 2: From Tiglath-Pileser I to Ashur-Nasir-Apli II* (Wiesbaden: Otto Harrassowitz, 1976), 124.

4. Grayson, *Assyrian Royal Inscriptions*, 124.

5. Personal conversation with Dennis R. Magary at Trinity Evangelical Divinity School, 2014.

6. Craig Blomberg, "Matthew," in *Commentary on the New Testament Use of the Old Testament*, ed. G. K. Beale and D. A. Carson (Grand Rapids: Baker Academic, 2007), 45.

Chapter 17 Sidebar Notes

a. Pieter Lastman, *Jonah and the Whale*, 1621, https://artsandculture.google.com/asset/IAFT8IfCTfplRQ.

Chapter 18 Micah

1. Stephen G. Dempster, "Micah," in *ESV Expository Commentary*, vol. 7, *Daniel–Malachi*, ed. Iain M. Duguid, James M. Hamilton, and Jay Sklar (Wheaton: Crossway, 2018), 425.

2. Kenneth H. Cuffey, *The Literary Coherence of the Book of Micah: Remnant, Restoration, and Promise* (New York: Bloomsbury T&T Clark, 2019), 227.

3. Dempster, "Micah," 428.

Chapter 18 Sidebar Notes

a. Delbert R. Hillers, *Micah: A Commentary on the Book of the Prophet Micah* (Minneapolis: Fortress, 1984), 9.

b. Craig Blomberg, "Matthew," in *Commentary on the New Testament Use of the Old Testament*, ed. G. K. Beale and D. A. Carson (Grand Rapids: Baker Academic, 2007), 6.

c. Hubrecht van Eyck and Jan van Eyck, *The Adoration of the Mystic Lamb*, 1432, Saint Bavo's Cathedral, Ghent, Belgium, https://www.artbible.info/art/lamb-of-god.html.

Chapter 19 Nahum

1. O. Palmer Robertson, *The Books of Nahum, Habakkuk, and Zephaniah*, New International Commentary on the Old Testament (Grand Rapids: Eerdmans, 1990), 7.

2. Daniel C. Timmer, "Nahum," in *ESV Expository Commentary*, vol. 7, *Daniel–Malachi*, ed. Iain M. Duguid, James M. Hamilton, and Jay Sklar (Wheaton: Crossway, 2018), 505.

3. Robertson, *Books of Nahum, Habakkuk, and Zephaniah*, 93.

4. Robertson, *Books of Nahum, Habakkuk, and Zephaniah*, 111.

Chapter 19 Sidebar Notes

a. Martin Luther, *Luther's Works*, ed. Hilton C. Oswald, vol. 18, *Lectures on the Minor Prophets I* (St. Louis: Concordia, 1975), 281.

b. John Calvin, *Commentaries on the Twelve Minor Prophets: Jonah, Micah, Nahum*, trans. John Owen (repr., Grand Rapids: Baker Books, 2003), 32:414.

c. Walter A. Maier, "Recent Archaeological Light on Nahum," *Concordia Theological Monthly* 7 (1936): 694.

d. Walter A. Maier, *The Book of Nahum: A Commentary* (Minneapolis: Concordia, 1977), 253.

e. Daniel C. Timmer, "Nahum," in *ESV Expository Commentary*, vol. 7, *Daniel–Malachi*, ed. Iain M. Duguid, James M. Hamilton, and Jay Sklar (Wheaton: Crossway, 2018), 521.

f. John Martin, *The Fall of Nineveh*, 1829, mezzotint with etching, Art Gallery of New South Wales, https://www.artgallery.nsw.gov.au/collection/works/DB4.1960/?tab=about.

g. Sarah C. Melville, Brent A. Strawn, Brian B. Schmidt, and Scott Noegel, "Neo-Assyrian and Syro-Palestinian Texts I," in *The Ancient Near East: Historical Sources in Translation*, ed. Mark W. Chavalas (Malden, MA: Blackwell, 2006), 282.

h. Brent A. Strawn, Sarah C. Melville, Kyle Greenwood, and Scott Noegel, "Neo-Assyrian and Syro-Palestinian Texts II," in Chavalas, *Ancient Near East*, 340.

i. But see Mordechai Cogan, "The Lions of Nineveh (Nahum 2:12–14): A Check on Nahum's Familiarity with Assyria," in *Birkat Shalom: Studies in the Bible, Ancient Near Eastern Literature, and Postbiblical Judaism Presented to Shalom M. Paul on the Occasion of His Seventieth Birthday*, ed. Chaim Cohen et al. (Winona Lake, IN: Eisenbrauns, 2008), 1:433–39. Cogan argues that there is nothing distinctively Assyrian about Nahum's mention of lions. Lions were common predators in Palestine and may have simply been a fitting image of ferocity and danger.

Chapter 20 Habakkuk

1. F. F. Bruce, "Habakkuk," in *The Minor Prophets: An Exegetical and Expository Commentary*, vol. 2, ed. Thomas E. McComiskey (Grand Rapids: Baker Academic, 2009), 831.

2. Bruce, "Habakkuk," 832.

3. Moisés Silva, "Galatians," in *Commentary on the New Testament Use of the Old Testament*, ed. G. K. Beale and D. A. Carson (Grand Rapids: Baker Academic, 2007), 802.

Chapter 20 Sidebar Notes

a. Richard Coggins and Jin H. Han, *Six Minor Prophets: Through the Centuries*, Blackwell Bible Commentaries (Chichester, West Sussex: John Wiley & Sons, 2011), 44.

b. Harriet Beecher Stowe, *Uncle Tom's Cabin*, Bantam Classic (New York: Bantam Books, 1981), 334.

c. Coggins and Han, *Six Minor Prophets*, 39.

d. Mark A. Seifried, "Romans," in *Commentary on the New Testament Use of the Old Testament*, ed. G. K. Beale and D. A. Carson (Grand Rapids: Baker Academic, 2007), 611.

e. George H. Guthrie, "Hebrews," in Beale and Carson, *Commentary on the New Testament Use of the Old Testament*, 984.

f. Edwin C. Hostetter, "כוס [kws]," in *New International Dictionary of Old Testament Theology and Exegesis*, ed. Willem VanGemeren (Grand Rapids: Zondervan, 1997), 2:609.

g. Craig A. Evans, "Dead Sea Scrolls," in *Dictionary of the Old Testament: Prophets*, ed. Mark J. Boda and J. Gordon McConville, IVP Bible Dictionary 4 (Downers Grove, IL: InterVarsity, 2012), 143.

h. F. F. Bruce, "Habakkuk," in *The Minor Prophets: An Exegetical and Expository Commentary*, ed. Thomas E. McComiskey (Grand Rapids: Baker Academic, 2009), 836.

i. Evans, "Dead Sea Scrolls," 149.

Chapter 21 Zephaniah

1. "D-Day," History.com, last updated June 5, 2019, https://www.history.com/topics/world-war-ii/d-day.

2. J. Alec Motyer, "Zephaniah," in *The Minor Prophets: An Exegetical and Expository Commentary*, vol. 3, ed. Thomas E. McComiskey (Grand Rapids: Baker Academic, 2009), 898.

3. O. Palmer Robertson, *The Books of Nahum, Habakkuk, and Zephaniah* (Grand Rapids: Eerdmans, 1990), 254–55.

4. Robertson, *Books of Nahum, Habakkuk, and Zephaniah*, 33.

5. Motyer, "Zephaniah," 898.

6. Robertson, *Books of Nahum, Habakkuk, and Zephaniah*, 256.

7. Motyer, "Zephaniah," 897.

Chapter 21 Sidebar Notes

a. Michael De Roche, "Zephaniah 1:2–3: The 'Sweeping' of Creation," *Vetus Testamentum* 30, no. 1 (1980): 106.

b. O. Palmer Robertson, *The Books of Nahum, Habakkuk, and Zephaniah*, New International Commentary on the Old Testament (Grand Rapids: Eerdmans, 1990), 284.

c. Richard Coggins and Jin H. Han, *Six Minor Prophets: Through the Centuries*, Blackwell Bible Commentaries (Chichester, West Sussex: John Wiley & Sons, 2011), 96.

d. "Dies Irae / Day of Wrath," Thesaurus Precum Latinarum, accessed June 9, 2021, https://www.preces-latinae.org/thesaurus/Hymni/DiesIrae.html.

Chapter 22 Haggai

1. Jeremiah had predicted that the exile would be for a period of seventy years (25:11–12). This may have been counted from 605 BC (the date of Jeremiah's prophecy and the first exile) to 539 BC (the edict of Cyrus announcing that the exiles could return home). Alternatively, it may be counted from 586 BC (the destruction of the temple) to 515 BC (the rebuilt temple's completion).

2. Ezra 2:64–65 says that there were just over forty-two thousand people, plus about seventy-three hundred servants.

3. Harmonizing the relevant biblical passages on the history and chronology of rebuilding the temple has been a persistent problem for scholars. Ezra 3:8–10 states that Zerubbabel and Joshua (the Aramaic spelling is "Jeshua," see ESV) took the lead in laying the foundations, but Ezra 5:14–17 attributes the foundations to Sheshbazzar. Some scholars have resolved the tension by suggesting that Sheshbazzar and Zerubbabel were the same person with two different names—e.g., F. Charles Fensham, *The Books of Ezra and Nehemiah*, New International Commentary on the Old Testament (Grand Rapids: Eerdmans, 1982), 63. This view has been largely discredited by scholars. One possible solution is that Sheshbazzar and Zerubbabel *both* worked on the temple foundations, perhaps in different ways or at different times; see Tamara C. Eskenazi, "Sheshbazzar (Person)," in *Anchor Bible Dictionary*, ed. David Noel Freedman (New York: Doubleday, 1992), 5:208.

Chapter 22 Sidebar Notes

a. Joyce G. Baldwin, *Haggai, Zechariah, Malachi: An Introduction and Commentary*, Tyndale Old Testament Commentaries (Downers Grove, IL: InterVarsity, 1972), 28.

b. Brian Beyer, "Zerubbabel (Person)," in *Anchor Bible Dictionary*, ed. David Noel Freedman (New York: Doubleday, 1992), 6:1085–86.

c. Beyer, "Zerubbabel," 1086.

d. George H. Guthrie, "Hebrews," in *Commentary on the New Testament Use of the Old Testament*, ed. G. K. Beale and D. A. Carson (Grand Rapids: Baker Academic, 2007), 990.

Chapter 23 Zechariah

1. Joyce G. Baldwin, *Haggai, Zechariah, Malachi: An Introduction and Commentary*, Tyndale Old Testament Commentaries (Downers Grove, IL: InterVarsity, 1972), 59.

2. Richard Coggins and Jin H. Han, *Six Minor Prophets: Through the Centuries*, Blackwell Bible Commentaries (Chichester, West Sussex: John Wiley & Sons, 2011), 151.

3. Baldwin, *Haggai, Zechariah, Malachi*, 69.

4. Anthony R. Petterson, "Zechariah," in *ESV Expository Commentary*, vol. 7, *Daniel–Malachi*, ed. Iain M. Duguid, James M. Hamilton, and Jay Sklar (Wheaton: Crossway, 2018), 637.

5. Mark J. Boda, *Haggai, Zechariah*, NIV Application Commentary (Grand Rapids: Zondervan, 2009), 216, EPUB.

6. Baldwin, *Haggai, Zechariah, Malachi*, 124.

7. Baldwin, *Haggai, Zechariah, Malachi*, 127.

8. Petterson, "Zechariah," 671.

9. See Mark J. Boda, *The Book of Zechariah*, New International Commentary on the Old Testament (Grand Rapids: Eerdmans, 2016), 376.

10. A. Wolters, "Zechariah, Book Of," in *Dictionary of the Old Testament: Prophets*, ed. Mark J. Boda and J. Gordon McConville, IVP Bible Dictionary 4 (Downers Grove, IL: InterVarsity, 2012), 894.

11. Mike Butterworth, "Zechariah," in *New Bible Commentary*, ed. D. A. Carson, R. T. France, J. A. Motyer, and G. J. Wenham, 21st century ed. (Downers Grove, IL: InterVarsity, 1994), 876.

12. Boda, *Book of Zechariah*, 768.

Chapter 23 Sidebar Notes

a. A. Wolters, "Zechariah, Book Of," in *Dictionary of the Old Testament: Prophets*, ed. Mark J. Boda and J. Gordon McConville, IVP Bible Dictionary 4 (Downers Grove, IL: InterVarsity, 2012), 891.

b. Joyce G. Baldwin, *Haggai, Zechariah, Malachi: An Introduction and Commentary*, Tyndale Old Testament Commentaries (Downers Grove, IL: InterVarsity, 1972), 164.

c. Hinckley G. Mitchell, John Merlin Powis Smith, and Julius A. Bewer, *A Critical and Exegetical Commentary on Haggai, Zechariah, Malachi, and Jonah*, International Critical Commentary (Edinburgh: T&T Clark, 1951), 306.

d. Paul L. Redditt, "Redactional Connectors in Zechariah 9–14," in *Perspectives on the Formation of the Book of the Twelve: Methodological Foundations, Redactional Processes, Historical Insights*, ed. Rainer Albertz, James Nogalski, and Jakob Wöhrle, Beihefte zur Zeitschrift für die alttestamentliche Wissenschaft 433 (Boston: de Gruyter, 2012), 214.

e. Baldwin, *Haggai, Zechariah, Malachi*, 183.

f. Craig Blomberg, "Matthew," in *Commentary on the New Testament Use of the Old Testament*, ed. G. K. Beale and D. A. Carson (Grand Rapids: Baker Academic, 2007), 95–96.

g. William Cowper, "There Is a Fountain Filled with Blood," in *The Handbook to the Lutheran Hymnal* (St. Louis: Concordia, 1942), 123, available in the Christian Classics Ethereal Library, https://ccel.org/a/anonymous/luth_hymnal/tlh157.htm.

Chapter 24 Malachi

1. Eric Ortlund, "Malachi," in *ESV Expository Commentary*, vol. 7, *Daniel–Malachi*, ed. Iain M. Duguid, James M. Hamilton, and Jay Sklar (Wheaton: Crossway, 2018), 731.

2. Joyce G. Baldwin, *Haggai, Zechariah, Malachi: An Introduction and Commentary*, Tyndale Old Testament Commentaries (Downers Grove, IL: InterVarsity, 1972), 211.

3. O. Palmer Robertson, *The Christ of the Prophets* (Phillipsburg, NJ: P&R, 2004), 392.

4. Robertson, *Christ of the Prophets*, 405.

5. Jonathan Gibson, *Covenant Continuity and Fidelity: A Study of Inner-Biblical Allusion and Exegesis in Malachi*, T&T Clark Library of Biblical Studies (London: Bloomsbury T&T Clark, 2016), 255–56.

6. Rikk E. Watts, "Mark," in *Commentary on the New Testament Use of the Old Testament*, ed. G. K. Beale and D. A. Carson (Grand Rapids: Baker Academic, 2007), 189.

Chapter 24 Sidebar Notes

a. Eric Ortlund, "Malachi," in *ESV Expository Commentary*, vol. 7, *Daniel–Malachi*, ed. Iain M. Duguid, James M. Hamilton, and Jay Sklar (Wheaton: Crossway, 2018), 741.

Index

Christ. *See* Jesus Christ
circumcision, 18, 20
   of heart, 27, 31, 183
commandment, 24–25, 27, 93–94, 192, 253,
      313, 383
compilation event, 136–37
contract, 13, 37, 307
covenant
   with Abraham, 14, 17–22, 27, 98, 165, 193
   as agreement, 12–13, 307
   ancient Near Eastern, 24, 307, 316
   ark of, 24–25, 84, 204
   blessings and curses, 21, 24–26
   with David, 14, 28–30, 91, 106, 167, 193
   with Israel, 14, 20–32, 34, 43, 45, 76, 91, 97,
      110, 168, 214, 248, 252, 274
   lawsuit, 307–8, 310, 316
   as marriage, 13, 245, 250, 261, 264
   new, 14, 30–34, 36, 46, 106, 166–67, 169, 171,
      173, 175, 178, 191–93, 197–98, 213–14, 216,
      273, 283, 390n9
   with Noah, 14, 15–18, 20, 34–35, 389n3
      (chap. 2)
   obligations of, 13, 21, 25, 30, 33, 91–93, 95,
      97, 253, 274–75, 307
   old, 198, 359
   of peace, 31, 34, 213, 216
   promise of, 14–16, 18–21, 24, 29–34, 36, 41,
      192–93, 198
   sign of, 14–16, 18, 20–21, 27, 29–31, 37, 167,
      187, 220, 245
   as treaty, 12–13, 74
   witnesses to, 24–25, 316
   See also contract; Sinai: covenant at
Cowper, William, 375
cows of Bashan, 279–80
creation, 15, 18, 91, 132, 134, 193, 204, 219, 338
   all, 14, 16, 159, 345
   of Israel, 14
   undoing of, 345
   of the world, 2, 14, 17
critical approaches, 140–44
cup in YHWH's right hand, 337
Cyrus, 48–49, 101, 150, 164, 237, 353
   Cylinder, 49

Daniel, book of, 82, 141, 223–44
Daniel, the prophet, 46, 52, 67, 223–24
Darius the Mede, 225–26, 234, 396n1
David. *See* covenant: with David
day of the Lord, 103–4, 107, 125–27, 264, 267,
      269, 271, 291–93, 344–45, 349, 386

day of YHWH, 103, 108, 126, 264, 266–67, 269,
      271–73, 280, 290, 292–93, 342, 344–50, 381,
      385–87
days of Gibeah, 257
Dead Sea Scrolls, 178, 190, 337
death, 14, 16–17, 27, 105, 171, 186, 210, 329
   of death, 106
   deliverance from, 300–305, 396n10
   eternal, 173, 262
   of God's people, 232, 241–42
   penalty, 16, 73, 81, 83–84
   swallowing up, 160–61, 241, 259
   victory over, 259
   of the wicked, 100
   See also Jesus Christ: suffering and death
den of lions, 234–35
Dies Irae, 346
divination, 73–76, 84–88, 108–9. *See also*
   prophecy: and divination
dream, 40, 64, 81, 104, 135, 159, 226, 230–32,
      235
dry bones, 122, 215–16
Duhm, Bernhard, 150, 152

editorial event, 137–39
Edom, 47, 96, 123, 125–26
   judgment on, 287–93
   as a symbol for all enemies of God, 213–14,
      294
Elijah, 43, 62, 67, 68–69, 79, 111, 133, 223, 364
   new, 381, 385, 387
Elisha, 62–63, 67, 69, 114, 133
Ephraim, 42, 94, 160, 254
Esau, 19, 47, 125, 259, 287, 382. *See also* Edom;
   Mount Esau
eschatological
   future, 102–5, 107, 126, 240
   judgment, 91, 104, 107, 126, 178, 266, 292,
      359, 365
eschaton. *See* eschatological: future
exile
   return from, 48–51, 101–2, 127, 134, 144, 150,
      156, 164, 190–91, 352–54
   seventy years, 46, 101, 353, 366, 402n1 (chap.
      22)
extispicy, 75. *See also* divination
Ezekiel, book of, 141, 200–222
   sexual violence in, 209
Ezekiel, the prophet, 47, 52, 67, 115–16, 176,
   200–201
Ezra and Nehemiah, 353, 380, 383

figurative language. *See* metaphor
First Enoch, 227